PONDICHERRY, TAMIL NADU AND SOUTH INDIA UNDER FRENCH RULE

This is a study of the colonization of Pondicherry, Tamil Nadu and south India by the French during the eighteenth century, and their interactions with the Indian rulers and populations in the political, economic, social and religious spheres. French Governors based in Pondicherry since François Martin up to Dupleix never acquired any territory for France through outright conquest. They or their masters in France never had any grand plan to establish a French empire in India. Some Indian rulers were friendly with the French and the English as it served their interests. The study demonstrates that the French colonizers and missionaries would not have survived in India without the collaboration of the Indian dubashes, merchants, certain Indian rulers and military men.

This collaboration was not on an equal footing, as the sepoys, merchants and dubashes were always subordinate and submissive to the Europeans. Even Ananda Ranga Poullé, the most famous of the Indian dubashes had to resort to the art of flattery to be in the good books of his 'master'. European arrival and presence in India heralded the beginning of a cultural clash between the Europeans and Indians, in which the former had the upper hand. There was never any partnership or 'master-bania' relationship between the French and the Indians. Instead, the relationship had all the trappings of a 'master-subordinate' relationship, where the subordinate even though he might be a dubash was always at the mercy of the colonizers. The element of force, aggressivity and violence was omnipresent in European presence and expansion in India, in the political, economic and religious fields.

J.B.P. More, also known as Prashant More obtained his doctorate in history from the Ecole des Hautes Etudes en Sciences Sociales, Paris. He currently teaches at Inseec, Paris. He specializes on history, sociology and politics of southern and colonial India. He has authored more than 22 books and 50 articles in English, French and Tamil.

Pondicherry, Tamil Nadu and South India under French Rule

FROM FRANÇOIS MARTIN TO DUPLEIX

1674-1754

J. B. P. MORE

LONDON AND NEW YORK

MANOHAR

First published 2021
by Routledge
2 Park Square, Milton Park, Abingdon, Oxon OX14 4RN

and by Routledge
52 Vanderbilt Avenue, New York, NY 10017

Routledge is an imprint of the Taylor & Francis Group, an informa business

© 2021 J.B.P More and Manohar Publishers & Distributors

The right of J.B.P More to be identified as author of this work has been asserted by her in accordance with sections 77 and 78 of the Copyright, Designs and Patents Act 1988.

All rights reserved. No part of this book may be reprinted or reproduced or utilised in any form or by any electronic, mechanical, or other means, now known or hereafter invented, including photocopying and recording, or in any information storage or retrieval system, without permission in writing from the publishers.

Trademark notice: Product or corporate names may be trademarks or registered trademarks, and are used only for identification and explanation without intent to infringe.

Print edition not for sale in South Asia (India, Sri Lanka, Nepal, Bangladesh, Pakistan or Bhutan)

British Library Cataloguing-in-Publication Data
A catalogue record for this book is available from the British Library

Library of Congress Cataloging-in-Publication Data
A catalog record for this book has been requested

ISBN: 978-0-367-64079-8 (hbk)
ISBN: 978-1-003-12206-7 (ebk)

Typeset in Adobe Garamond Pro 11/13
by Manohar, Delhi 110 002

MANOHAR

Contents

List of Illustrations	7
Preface	9
Abbreviations	13
Introduction	15
1. The French in Pondicherry: Early Phase	33
2. French Intolerance, 1706-1721	74
3. Pondicherry Develops and Expands	96
4. Expansion under Governor Benoist Dumas, 1735-1741	115
5. Governorship of Joseph François Dupleix: Early Phase	138
6. Rivalries in the Carnatic and the Capture of Madras	153
7. Siege of Pondicherry, 1748 and its Aftermath	167
8. Vedapuriswaran (Shiva) Temple Destruction and Related Events	180
9. Carnatic Wars, Promotion of Christianity and Senji Temple Destructions	194
10. Further Carnatic/Deccani Conflicts and Related Affairs	213
11. Decline of Dupleix	228
12. Conclusion	251
Bibliography	263
Index	285

Illustrations

(between pp. 144-5)
1. Drawing of Dupleix of the 19th century
2. Dupleix, Governor of Pondicherry, 1742
3. Dupleix statue at Landrecies, France
4. Robert Clive
5. Mahé de La Bourdonnai
6. Dupleix statue in Pondicherry
7. Bussy Castelnau
8. Ananda Ranga Poullé, Diwan of Governor Dupleix
9. Nasir Jung, son of Nizam-ul-mulk
10. Pratap Singh of Tanjore
11. Mohammad Ali Khan Walajah, Nawab of Arcot, 1749-95
12. Plan of Pondicherry
13. Plan of Pondicherry, 1691
14. German Plan of Pondicherry of Prévost d'Exilés
15. Dutch Plan of Pondicherry
16. Carte des Indes Orientales
17. Engraving depicting the death of the Nawab of Carnatic, Anwaruddin Khan at Ambur
18. Image of Fort St. George, Madras, 1754
19. Raghoji Bhonsle, the Maratha General
20. Anwaruddin Khan, Nawab of Arcot, 1744-9
21. Nizam-ul-mulk, Asaf Jah I, Nizam of Hyderabad
22. Nasir Jung, son of Nizam-ul-mulk created in 1745
23. Nizam Nasir Jung being shot dead by a carabine on top of his elephant
24. Muzaffar Jung, successor of Nasir Jung as Soubab of Deccan created in the 18th century

25. Meeting of Dupleix with Muzaffar Jung, the Soubab of Deccan in Pondicherry
26. Portrait of Madame and Monsieur Dupleix, according to a miniature belonging to Madame la Marquise de Nazelle
27. Salabat Jung, Soubab of Deccan, successor of Muzaffar Jung created in 18th century

Preface

IN 2014, I wrote a book called *From Arikamedu to the Foundation of Modern Pondicherry*, the present work is a continuation of that volume. It is a study of French rule and the foundations of colonialism in Pondicherry and the parts of India that came under their control from the time François Martin established a French colony there up to the Governorship of Joseph François Dupleix, the flamboyant French Governor of Pondicherry. The latter was promoted to the rank of *mansabdar* or local lord by the Mughal Emperor and to the rank of Marquis by the French king. The governorship of Dupleix lasted for about thirteen years, from 1742 to 1754.

In the year 2000, when I was working on my second book *Freedom Movement in French India: The Mahé Revolt of 1948*, I had met and talked several times with Professor M.P. Sridharan at his residence in Kozhikode (Kerala), not only about the history of Mahé but also about the history of Pondicherry and French rule in India in general. It was he who asked me to take up the writing of the history of Pondicherry and French rule there, during the seventeenth and eighteenth centuries. He gave me some guidelines about how to proceed with the research, especially with regard to the sources. He was an inspiration for me not only to write my first book on Pondicherry, but also the present one. I am greatly indebted to him for that and it is really a privilege for me to dedicate this book to his memory. It is noteworthy that Professor M.P. Sridharan hailed originally from Mahé, a former French colony on the Malabar coast.

Unfortunately I did not receive any help or advice for my research from any other scholar who has worked on the subject or some related subject, in spite of me approaching several of them quite earnestly. However, this has been largely compensated by the help rendered to me by the librarians and staff of the Bibliothèque Nationale of France, Paris, Institut des Langues et Civilisations Orientales, Paris, Archives Nationales, Paris, Archives d'Outre-mer, Aix en Provence, Ecole Française d'Extrême Orient Library and the Centre d'Etudes de l'Inde

Library, Paris, Institut Français Library, Pondicherry, National Archives, Pondicherry and the Archives of Versailles, Versailles. I am particularly thankful to Ramanujam, librarian of Institut Français of Pondicherry and Sundari Gobalakichenane, librarian at Bulac, Paris for their cooperation. My thanks are also due to Nalini Persad of British Library, London and Nagendra Prasad of Pondicherry Museum, Pondicherry.

In the course of my research I had the privilege to talk to some well informed citizens about the history of Pondicherry. The most prominent among them were Justice David Annoussamy of Pondicherry, Mannar Mannan, son of the late poet Barathidasan, Cyril Antony, the author of the *Gazetteer of Pondicherry*, Dr. V. Nallam, physician of Pondicherry, hailing from Yanam, the late Yves Perrier, former administrator of Mahé and Pondicherry during French rule, the late Saraswathi Subbiah, wife of the late Communist leader of Pondicherry, V. Subbiah, Veera Mathurakavy, a retired Tamil teacher of Pondicherry, Kulasegaran, social activist of Pondicherry, Prof. Aranga Murugaiyan, Community College, Pondicherry, G.S.M. Mubeen of Pondicherry, Roland Bouchet and Dr. Jacqueline Bouchet, French scholars interested in the history of Pondicherry. I am deeply indebted to them for the knowledge that they were willing to share with me about Pondicherry under the French. My special thanks are also due to Dr. Ezhil Vasanthan for his unfailing cooperation, and to my wife, Dr. Leena More for her enduring interest in my work.

The reader must realize that many of the histories that were written related to the period and subject under study were mostly by Western scholars, including the French. These scholars were or are generally conditioned by their past history and culture. I propose in this study of mine to come out of the trappings of the past, whether racial, cultural, nationalistic, ideological or religious and look at history as an outsider with fresh unprejudiced and unbiased eyes.

In other words, I am an 'uncommitted' historian, i.e. I am not tied up to any school of thought or identity while writing history and I do not look at history from a particular angle. I rely solely on facts to reconstruct history, whatever those might be. If in spite of all my attention, the reader comes across any errors of omission or commission, I request him to kindly point that out to me so that I can get them corrected after due verification and cross-checking in the next edition. Last of all, I would like to request the reader to take note of certain revisions that I have made in this book about certain historical points and personalities narrated in my earlier works on Pondicherry in the light of new findings

J.B.P. MORE

Abbreviations

AMAE	Archives du Ministère des Affaires Etrangères, Paris
AME	Archives des Missions Etrangères, Paris
AN	Archives Nationales, Paris
AOM	Archives d'Outre-mer, Aix en Provence, France
ARP	Ananda Ranga Pillai Diary (12 volumes)
AV	Archives de Versailles, Versailles, France
BNF	Bibliothèque Nationale de France, Paris
CS	Conseil Supérieur
Fr.	Français
IOL	India Office Library and Records, England
LEC	Lettres Edifiantes et Curieuses
NAF	Nouvelles Acquisitions Françaises
RHEP	Revue Historique de l'Etat de Pondichéry
RHIF	Revue Historique de l'Inde Française

Introduction

THERE IS A belief in scholarly circles that European traders and Indian merchants were in partnership with one another and were interdependent to carry on their trade profitably during the early phase of colonization.[1] P.J. Marshall thinks that the partnership was based on 'master and bania' relationship. On the other hand, Holden Furber thinks that the relationship between Europeans and Asians was marked by mutual respect and cooperation. However, scholars like Irfan Habib and following him Sanjay Subrahmanyam, think that European trade was dependent on the systematic use of armed force, gun powder and bullets. Scholars like K.M. Pannikar imbued with a greater Indian nationalist spirit denounced European writings and historiography on India as blatantly Eurocentric.[2]

In the course of this study, we will try to find out how far the assertions of scholars like P.J. Marshall, Holden Furber, K.M. Pannikar, Irfan Habib and Sanjay Subrahmanyam are true. This will be done on the basis of actual facts, backed by solid evidence.

We must not forget that the period under study did not still witness the emergence of industrial capitalists. It was still largely a world dominated by merchants, who indulged in buying and selling of products and accumulating profit thereby. The arrival of the Europeans on the Indian coast in search of products for the European market increased the demand for those products and the Indian merchants played a significant role in procuring those products for the Europeans and in supplying European products to the local market. The merchants were still not the producers of those goods. Neither did they control the production or the means of production. Instead they were mainly buyers and sellers. It was under these economic conditions that the Europeans and the European East Indian Companies established colonies all over the Indian coast, with the singular purpose of trading and creating profit. The French East India Company was no exception to this rule.

Unlike pre-European traders with India, like the Chinese and the

Arabs, who indulged in straight-forward trading without the need or thought of establishing colonies on the Indian coasts for that purpose, the Europeans right from the time they penetrated into India for trading sought to establish colonies called factories, where they were generally not bound by the jurisdiction of the Indian rulers and princes in various matters. Very quickly after establishing factories, they went about constructing forts, most of the time with the permission of the Indian rulers, who were more intent upon trading and making profits and finding an outlet for their products or procuring foreign products than about the loss of sovereignty in some parts of the country, however paltry that might have appeared to be.

Conceding some small outposts for trading purposes to Europeans was alright. But allowing the Europeans to construct forts on the lands thus ceded was a strategic error on the part of most Indian rulers, as forts could be used as vantage points for attacking and for defensive purposes. Thus the English built their fort in Madras, once the territory was conceded to them by the Raja of Venkatagiri, the Danes built their fort at Tranquebar, the Dutch had their fort at Nagapattinam and the French following them sought permission to construct their fort in Pondicherry. Once the forts were constructed, it was almost impossible for the Indian rulers to dislodge the Europeans from the territories ceded to them.

Thus the Europeans, right from the beginning, i.e. since the sixteenth century when the Portugeuse reached the Malabar coast, were not just traders, but also colonizers, who were always answerable to their respective political and commercial authorities back home, about the happenings in India. They never severed their ties with their homelands and generally received orders and directions on what they should do in India and how they should proceed in order to trade and make profits and control the territories under their rule. In the course of their colonization, they never gave up their religious and cultural identities or their political or ethnic idenitites in favour of a purely Indian one.

The Europeans in general, right from the Portuguese had one huge advantage over the Indians and others. They had in their possession sophisticated arms, canons and guns, ocean going vessels and warships. They had also developed their navigation and warfare skills accordingly.

Their ships were not sewn with coir as the Indian ships. Besides the latter had no artillery, unlike the European ships, which were made of iron bolts and nails and mounted with bronze canons. Indian and other ships were no match to these European ships. Very quickly they imposed their domination over the oceans. They maintained this advantage all throughout the colonial period and even later.

So the Indians in general and the merchants and rulers in particular had to deal with a new breed of traders of European origin who sought settlements all over the Indian coasts, not just to trade, but also to manage their own affairs, according to their own ideas and values, culture and religion, which meant that there was always a political, cultural, military and territorial dimension to their settlements. The Indian rulers generally were not quite aware of all these implications related to European presence in India or were willing to tolerate for their own economic reasons especially. Right from the beginning of their settlements in India, the Europeans never accepted or adopted Indian values and ideas, in any field of importance. Instead they sought to impose their own ideas and values, which they were accustomed to in their homelands, in the territories that came under their control.

There was no precedent for such a situation in Indian history. All the foreigners who entered India since more than two thousand years including the so-called Aryans, Dravidians and Mughals made India their home by severing their connections with the lands of their origin. But the Europeans were made of a different mould. They would never melt away into India. Instead they always maintained their connections with their homelands. That is why we can term them as 'colonizers' and their rule as 'colonialism'.

During the period of European penetration into India, India was not a united country. The Mughal Empire was crumbling fast and there were a multitude of rulers all over India. There was no sense or feeling that all Indians, irrespective of their linguistic, religious, racial and cultural differences belonged to one nation. In short, the idea of nationalism had not struck root in India, until the eighteenth century at least, unlike in Europe, where nations had emerged on the basis of territory, religion, language and ethnicity since the fifteenth century at least.

Nationalism as such is an imagined idea put together by man's thought. It does not have a factual existence like the law of gravity. The feeling of nationalism is a feeling of oneness felt by a particular people to the exclusion of others. The fire of nationalism is generally stoked by politicians in their quest for power in the name of their idea of nation. When Europeans came to India, they were already imbued by a sense of nationalism, on the basis of language, race, religion and culture. The Indians in general and the Indian rulers in particular did not possess any unified nationalist feeling.

In south India especially and in Tamil Nadu in particular, there was no sense of any nationalism or sub-nationalism, on the basis of religion, culture, race and language. Instead, rulers were fighting and quarrelling with one another in their quest for power and domination. It was under these highly favourable conditions that Europeans set foot in India and acquired territories in the Indian soil, since the sixteenth century.

Indian rulers as a rule had two main functions. The first one was the collection of taxes from the villages and the countryside, where more than 90 per cent of the population lived on agriculture. The second was the maintenance of an army, not only to ward off enemies but also to enforce the collection of taxes. They seem to have hoped generally that the arrival and establishment of Europeans in their territories would contribute to the augmentation of their revenues and the prosperity of their traders and producers, not realizing fully that allowing the Europeans to establish settlements or factories, protected by forts and soldiers and sailors with sophisticated weapons and warships, was like sowing the seeds for their own subjugation and colonization by the Europeans in the course of time.

The French, being the last European power to come to India, established their first colony and settlement in Pondicherry on the Coromandel Coast, with the permission of Sher Khan Lodi, the Pathan vassal of the Bijapur Sultan. In 1701, Pondicherry became the capital of all French settlements in India. Its governors were nominated directly from France, with a Council of five members under him. This confirmed the political dimension of French colonies where the French authorities had jurisdiction over the people, both European and Indian inhabiting their colonies.

In the course of the first half of the eighteenth century, the French expanded their territorial acquisitions, especially in southern India. As rulers, they had to interact with various segments of the Indian population at various levels: economic, social, religious, cultural and political. In the course of this study, we will go into such interactions right from 1674 up to 1754 when Governor Dupleix was called back to France, after a series of devastating wars, reverses and mismanagement. We have to determine the nature and type of relationship that the colonizers had with the Indians in every way. We have to determine also the special characteristics of every governor in their dealings with Indians.

Of all the governors of Pondicherry during this period, Dupleix alone seems to have captivated the attention of scholars and historians, especially in France and India, much more than the actual founder of modern Pondicherry, François Martin. So we have to conduct a special study of Dupleix and the state of south India, the Tamil country and Pondicherry during his period as Governor.

After Dupleix's recall to France in 1754, there were continuous struggles of the French against the rising English power in India. Besides, there was continuous Anglo-French rivalry in Europe, which led to the Napoleonic wars and the defeat of the French. Pondicherry and the other French territories in India were conquered thrice by the English since 1761. Finally through the Treaty of Versailles in the year 1814-15, Pondicherry and the other early outposts of the French in India namely Kariakal, Mahé, Yanam and Chandernagore were handed over to the French, on condition that they would no more raise an army in these territories. It was a humiliating end to French colonial aspirations in India, which seems to have been unwittingly inaugurated by Dupleix.

Just a few years after the conclusion of peace with the English, French historians and writers began to take a renewed interest in Dupleix's exploits and his legacy. Most French writers and historians began to consider Dupleix as one of the great figures of modern France. Already in 1744, Abbé Guyon had showered encomiums on Dupleix in his work on the history of East India. In 1757, a book on Dupleix's wars appeared under the name of *Abbé Jean Baptiste Le Mascrier*. In 1768, the renowned historian Jean Baptiste Targe started singing the glory of Dupleix. Abbé Raynal in his *Histoire Politique Et Philosophique* qualified Dupleix as one of the most skilful merchants of Europe, while Voltaire wrote that Dupleix had the qualities of a prince. For the scholar Anquetil Duperron, Dupleix was great in every way. He thought that praising Dupleix for India and Colbert for Europe would contribute to French national prosperity.[3]

Actually Dupleix was partly forgotten by the French historians during the second half of the eighteenth century due to the accusation by the French East India Company that 'this great man lacked in courage' when he was Governor of Pondicherry, in his fight against the English. But such a perception of Dupleix was gradually changing in the beginning of the nineteenth century. In the year 1818, the Frenchman Le Fèvre Claude-Noël published a short book glorifying the achievements of Dupleix in India.

In 1846, Armand Gallois Montbrun stumbled upon the diaries written on a day to day basis by Ananda Ranga Poullé (Pillai), of the various events, both important and trivial that took place in Pondicherry and elsewhere between 1736 and 1761. Poullé followed no order in the writing of his diary. Side by side important political events, he also noted in the diary the town gossip, family disputes and stories, horoscopes, and social and religious events. Montbrun published a notice of this diary along with a short life history of Ananda Ranga Poullé in the year 1849. Actually the diary went a long way to rehabilitate Dupleix in the eyes of the French.

At the same time British historians starting from Robert Orme to Macaulay, and later from G.B. Malleson and Colonel Wilks to Virginia MacLean Thompson, portrayed Dupleix in glowing terms. Robert Orme was in northern India when Dupleix was Governor of Pondicherry. In 1748, he was just 20 years old. Orme returned to England in the same ship as Robert Clive, the English rival of Dupleix, who was returning home. Ten years later Orme started writing his *History of Indostan*, at a time when the English had gained a stronger foothold in south India and Bengal at the expense of Dupleix and the French. It seems that whenever Orme wanted to gather information on Dupleix and his exploits, he drew inspiration from the work of Le Mascrier on the history of the last revolution in east India, published in France in 1757, when Dupleix himself was in France. It is believed that Le Mascrier was the pseudonym under which Dupleix wrote this book.

The anti-imperialist historian from Mahé, M.P. Sridharan thinks that Robert Orme's great enthusiasm for Dupleix arose from the realization that Dupleix having been recalled to France in 1754 was no more a threat to English fortunes in India. The trend established by Orme in lauding Dupleix and his achievements in India remained unabated for more than a century, as later is proven by G.B. Malleson's work on Dupleix, published in 1865. M.P. Sridharan wrote: 'Orme and Malleson could afford to lavish praise on Dupleix because the greatness of English victory could be flaunted once the vanquished could be recognized as a genius among empire builders.'

For Malleson, Dupleix worked for the glory of France and wanted to found an empire for France in south India. He thought that the English emulated Dupleix in founding their empire in India. The English went to the extent of erecting a statue for him in the Governor-General's palace in Calcutta. Following this, the Minister of State for Arts in France through a decree dated 29 April 1861, erected a second statue for Dupleix in the Versailles gallery.

Dupleix's majestic larger than life-size statue was installed in Pondicherry in the year 1870 by the French in the middle of the open ground, popularly called Place Dupleix, in front of the pier, mounted on equally majestic pillars with Hindu sculpted religious motifs. These pillars seem to have been brought over from Senji after the destruction of the temples there. The statue was designed and erected to portray the subjugation of India by Dupleix. For Virginia Mclean Thompson, Dupleix was an avowed nationalist. She wrote: 'Dupleix claimed to do anything for the nation in his letters'.[4]

It is significant to note that Pondicherrians including the Tamils and Telugus contributed Rs. 1615.5.17 towards the erection of Dupleix's statue in his native village of Landrecies, in the north of France. This statue was unveiled on 30 September 1888 in midst of great pomp and splendour. It was declared then that Dupleix was the greatest Frenchman of the eighteenth century. Actually the French Third Republic consecrated Dupleix as a front-ranking national figure.

Generally he was considered as a genius who wasted his youth and his wealth in the service of France and its ungrateful king, who repudiated him in the end.

However, there were no statues for him in Paris where he died a pauper's death in 1763. But a Paris metro station is named after him. After the integration of Pondicherry with the Indian Union in 1954 when nationalist opposition grew to Dupleix's statue standing atop Hindu religious pillars, the statue was removed discreetly to the French Consulate premises in Pondicherry. After a few years, the statue once again was re-erected at the southern corner of the Pondicherry beach, most certainly with the permission of the Pondicherry government, just besides the public toilet and a guest house belonging to the Sri Aurobindo Ashram which blocks the Pondicherry beach from being extended further southwards for the benefit of the local people.[5]

In the year 1870, the Frenchman, F.N. Laude brought out a translation of some extracts of *Ananda Ranga Poullé's Diary* during the inauguration of the statue of Dupleix in Pondicherry. He claimed that Ananda Ranga Poullé had done justice to him, contrary to the French East India Company.[6] Dupleix became a cult figure for the French henceforward.

In 1859, Charles Darwin propounded his theory on the origin of species. Many French thinkers, scholars and historians like Ernest Renan, Arthur de Gobineau and Jules Ferry thenceforth started to justify colonialism and the conquest of the non-white world by the white Europeans as something natural and not shocking at all, as it was in conformity to the Darwinian principle of evolution and the selection of the fittest in the struggle for survival. Thus Dupleix, one of the foremost of European conquerors was rehabilitated in their eyes as a torch-bearer of modern Western civilization and progress.

For Tibulle Hamont, Dupleix was one of the greatest geniuses of the eighteenth century. He believed that the stagnant Oriental societies have to be destroyed or absorbed by the progressive societies of Europe. This was in line with the general Western thinking. For Hamont, Dupleix seems to be a sort of precursor for the destruction and absorption of the archaic Oriental and Indian societies.[7]

French scholar, Julien Vinson brought out his own translation of some extracts of Ananda Ranga Pillai's diary in 1894. Thenceforth many French historians and writers starting from Prosper Cultru in 1901 up to Jouveau Dubreuil and Jacques Weber, with some rare exceptions, began to sing the praise and glory of Dupleix. They hold almost unanimously that Dupleix had contributed to the greatness of France. For Lionel Moreel, he was a magnificent almost unique model of France's national history. Chevalier de la Farelle described Dupleix as: 'the most gallant of men and the most polite in the world'.

In the year 1881, Tibulle Hamont wrote: 'Dupleix invented and put in place a vast and sound political system, which the English copied in a servile manner which permitted them to subjugate India'.

For Donneaud du Plan, it was Dupleix who conceived the idea of founding an empire for France in India.[8]

Julien Vinson thinks that India would have progressed better under 'the lovable and generous French' rather than under the business-minded monarchical English, if Dupleix had won his wars. He was of the view that the English copied the designs of Dupleix and conquered India. He further opined the following: 'The civilising role that Dupleix dreamt for France has fallen upon England; it is through her that India has been initiated to the progress of ideas, to the modern life, which would bring about its national unification'.[9]

For Castonnet des Fosses, Dupleix wanted to subject India to French domination and also desired to become a feudatory of the Mughal Emperor. He portrayed him as a patriot who only thought of France. For Cultru, Dupleix, in spite of everything, was a great man who had demonstrated for the first time the weaknesses of the Hindus. He asserted that Dupleix just after arriving in Pondicherry was already thinking about the conquest of India. He described Dupleix as follows: 'The historian sees in him one of the greatest geniuses of the eighteenth century'.

In 1908, Guérin produced a work of unadulterated adulation of Dupleix. Later in 1931, Guenin wrote: 'The English who wanted to destroy him (Dupleix), value him more than the French. The English saw him as the most capable among Frenchmen who could undermine their Company, by promoting that of his nation.'

Alfred Martineau, the former Governor of Pondicherry, with his four volume work on Dupleix created nostalgia for Dupleix in the French official circles which persists even today. For him, Dupleix was a precursor who inspired Europe to dominate the world. For Henry Bionne, Dupleix showed the way for the English to conquer India. He wrote: 'Dupleix founded in India a grand colonial empire… Here is the man that ungrateful France had forgotten for a long time. One century had to go by before France could remember the genius of the Governor, by erecting a sorrowful statue in Pondicherry. … Before the English Dupleix and Jeanne Begum possessed the Indian Empire, conquered by Dupleix'.[10]

For a staunch colonialist like Jouveau-Dubreuil, Dupleix was the one who invented the concept of *Nabob*, which was copied by Clive and Hastings later. He goes to the extent of claiming extravagantly that he was the founder of the modern Indian (European) empire and an icon of world stature and history. More recently, Jacques Weber had written that Dupleix was called back to France when he was at the peak of his glory.[11] In short, no Frenchman who served in India has received more praise and fame than Dupleix, Governor of Pondicherry, from 1742 to 1754.

Along with Dupleix, his wife Jeanne too became an object of glorification for the later day French historians and writers. She was almost unanimously lauded for her glorious role in Pondicherry by the side of Dupleix, in spite of the fact that Ananda Ranga Poullé, Dupleix's *dubash*, had a visceral hatred for her, arising probably out of the traditional misogynistic dislike for women involving themselves in public and political matters or out of a personal animosity and hatred that he might have developed due to the mixed ethnic origin of Jeanne and her religious leanings.

It was first Louis Guet who wrote an article about Jeanne Begum in 1892 in the *Revue Maritime et Coloniale*. However, it was left to Yvonne Robert Gaebelé who put Jeanne on a high pedestal, more than any other French or European woman in India, through her two works entitled *Créole et Grande Dame, Johanna Begum, Marquise Dupleix* (1934) and *Marquise Dupleix, 1706-1756* (1956). They were most certainly a belated attempt to paint a somewhat rosy picture of the life of the 'Great Lady' of Créole origin, who was consecrated as 'Begum Johanna' and as the 'Marquise of Dupleix'. Her reputation had taken a beating due to the coming to light of the Diary of Ananda Ranga Poullé in the second half of the nineteenth century and the publication of an English translation of it in 1912. Ananda Ranga Poullé had copiously run down Madame Dupleix in this Diary written between 1738 and 1761. It was left to Yvonne Robert Gaebelé to rehabilitate the tarnished image of Jeanne Dupleix. It is also noteworthy that it was Yvonne Gaebelé who attempted first to write a systematic biography of Ananda Ranga Poullé in French. She was most certainly conscious of the fact that it was Poulé's diary which contributed largely to the rehabilitation of Dupleix. Before her a Tamil biography of Ananda Ranga Poullé was authored by Tecika Pillai in the year 1941.

However, the French East India Company had run Dupleix down more than anybody else, for their own reasons, which finally cost Dupleix his life, before he could be shut in the Bastille. For the Directors of the Company, Dupleix who was their prime employee in India was a failure as he had mismanaged the affairs of India during his tenure as Governor, incurring heavy losses. Voltaire changed his opinion about Dupleix. For him, Dupleix was just an adventurer who sought to make fortune and had spoilt the name of France in India. Legoux de Flaix in his *Essai sur l'Indostan* dismissed Dupleix's territorial acquisitions as a 'political monstruosity'. He painted Dupleix as a frustrated person, ignorant of political realities with very little knowledge of the art of war.

However, generally historians of European origin were largely Euro-centric in their attitude and portrayal of colonized societies. They floated ideas like the 'White Man's Burden'. The French literally thought that they had a civilizing mission in the world of the uncivilized and less civilized people and that colonization itself was a sort of service to humanity. Even Indology developed by the Europeans, was made subservient to European interests. There were many Indian nationalist historians like K.M. Pannikar who were highly critical of Dupleix and his policies and actions in India and of the Eurocentric nature of most Western historians of India.[12]

It is therefore necessary for a neutral historian, to find out the truth about the preceding assertions, glorifications or derisions of Dupleix, in the light of actual facts and evidence. This is what we propose to do in this work not only of Dupleix, but also of every governor of Pondicherry since François Martin, within the limited pages of this book. We would have to see also if the French trading company representatives in India were in partnership with the Indian merchants and bankers in enslaving Indians or not. But before that, it would be useful to peep a little into the historical background prior to the establishment of the French in Pondicherry.

It has been established historically that the Cheras, Cholas and Pandyas were the three politically independent royal dynasties that ruled *Tamizhakam* (present Tamil Nadu and Kerala states together) since the ancient times. They were Tamil-speaking dynasties. For reasons into which we will not go into presently the Cheras and the Cholas disappeared from the Indian political horizon during the twelfth or the thirteenth centuries. The Pandyas with their capital in Madurai lingered on as a political power in Tamil Nadu during the fourteenth century. They were dealt a body blow by the Delhi Sultan's army under the command of Malik Kafur, a convert to Islam. This resulted in the establishment of a Turkish sultanate in Madurai, which heralded the extinction of the last major Tamil dynasty ruling over large parts of Tamil Nadu. Tamils were for the first time in their long history being ruled by foreigners or outsiders.

The Sultanate lasted for about fifty years. To make matters worse, Tamil Nadu was then overrun by the Telugu speaking Vijayanagar kings and their troops and Nayaks (generals) from the north. There was no more any Tamil dynasty to resist them. Since then Tamil Nadu became part of what came to be known as the Vijayanagar Empire. So it could be said that since the fourteenth century, Tamilians lost their political independence and became subject to Telugu rule or the *Vadugar* or northerner's rule as the Tamilians would have it.

Along with the invaders came a whole lot of Telugus – administrators, soldiers, farmers, musicians and priests. The Tamil country was divided into three divisions by the Vijayanagar king. They were Thanjavur, Madurai and Senji. All the three were put under the control of three different Telugu Nayakars or Nayaks. Thus started the rule of the Nayaks in Tamil Nadu.[13]

It seems that for some time the Vijayanagar Empire acted as a bulwark against the further expansion of the West and Central Asian Muslim rule into southern India. But the Vijayanagar troops were defeated by the combined troops of the Bahmani Sultanates of the Deccan in the year 1565 in the famous battle of Talikota. The

Vijayanagar Empire was considerably enfeebled by this defeat. Its hold on its vassals in the Tamil country too slackened considerably. Even the throne of Vijayanagar was transferred to Penugonda. However, the Nayaks of the Tamil country continued to send tributes to Penugonda until the close of the sixteenth century or the first decade of the seventeenth century.[14] The most prominent of the Bahmani sultanates were Bijapur and Golconda.

This was the time when Muthu Krishnappa Nayakar was ruling from Senji. It seems that it was during the Nayakar period which started more than one century earlier that the hill-fortress of Senji was constructed. The Nayakars also constructed many temples and temple structures which included the Senji Nayak temples.[15] The Pondicherry region was part of Nayakar territory.

At the turn of the fifteenth century, the great Arab navigator, Sulaiman al-Mahri had referred to Pondicherry as Bandikari in his accounts. He has also mentioned Cuddalore and Chidambaram alongside Pondicherry. Thus it is certain that Pondicherry had existed as a small port-town or village in the fifteenth century itself. We do not have evidence for its existence before this period. Arikamedu was not Podouké or Pondicherry, as claimed by Jouveau-Dubreuil, a high school teacher and following him many others, like Jean Deloche.

It has been demonstrated in my last book on Pondicherry that Arikamedu was at the most a seasonal port located at about 4 km to the south of Pondicherry at the mouth of the Ariyankuppam River. I have also demonstrated in that book how Bandikari would have evolved from *Vandichery* and *Pandichery*. *Pandichery* of the Tamils was corrupted as Pondichéry by the French and Pondicherry by the English. However, the name itself is of pure Tamil origin.[16]

Later, by the middle of the sixteenth century, Pandichery seems to have acquired a new name called Puducheira as noted by the Portuguese. Puducheira was obviously the Puduchery of the Tamils, which simply meant 'new town'. It was an appropriate name as the town would have come into existence recently. In any case, the names Pandichery and Puduchery seem to have co-existed among the people of the area since this period. It is noteworthy at this juncture that several maritime towns of India came into existence after the arrival of Arabs in India. Bandikari or Pandichery was one of them.[17]

Before we proceed further, it is interesting to note that Jouveau-Dubreuil was not without his critics while he was in Pondicherry, with regard to almost everything that he wrote on Pondicherry especially. Gabriel Monod Herzen, the manager of the Government distillery, who knew him in Pondicherry had written that nobody was actually interested in his works in Pondicherry and that he had to leave his findings with regard to Arikamedu and Pondicherry to the Madras Museum. French administrators like Mr. Josselin, Chief of the Education Department simply dismissed his works as 'whimsical'.

At the turn of the sixteenth century, Muthu Krishnappa Nayakar was the ruler at Senji. During his rule, he seems to have allowed the Portuguese to have a settlement or rather a godown (*pandasalai* or *pandikasalai*) in Pondicherry, in order to develop trade in the region and find an outlet for local products. The Portuguese were followed by the Danes and the Dutch. The Portuguese, having withdrawn from Pondicherry, the Danes established a settlement there in 1624, with the permission of the Senji Nayakar. Pondicherry was ideally situated at the cross-section of two routes. One route ran from Cuddalore through Pondicherry towards the north, while the other one ran from Pondicherry towards Senji. It was accessible by sea and was defended by the fort of Vazhudavur, on the road towards Senji.[18]

By the middle of the seventeenth century, the Nayakar rule in Senji and Pondicherry was drawing to a close due to the invasion by the troops of the Bijapur Sultans. The troops of the Sultan were made up also of a good number of Marathas. Thus Senji territory came under Bijapur rule. It was first put under the control of Shahji, the father of the famous Shivaji. He was a general in the Bijapur army. Shivaji broke away from his father's *jagir* in 1656. He defeated and conquered the More family lands in Maharashtra, by eliminating Chandra Rao More and the More brothers, who were vassals of the Bijapur Sultan. The More clan were *Kshatriyas*.[19]

Later Nasir Mohammad Khan, a Deccani, ruled from Senji as a vassal of the Bijapur Sultan.[20] It was thus that Senji fort and treasury fell into Bijapur hands. Senji was renamed as 'Badshabad'. Sher Khan Lodi, related to a Pathan general in the Bijapur army was nominated as Governor of Valgondapuram which included Tiruchirappalli in

Tamil Nadu. Pondicherry too was under his jurisdiction. The Dutch had retreated from there. So Sher Khan Lodi decided to invite the French to fill up the vacuum and promote trade in the region.

NOTES

1. P.J. Marshall, *East India Fortunes: The British in Bengal in the Eighteenth Century*, Oxford, 1976, pp. 44-5; Holden Furber, *Rival Empires of Trade in the Orient, 1600-1800*, 1976, pp. 315-16.
2. Holden Furber, 'Asia and the West as Partners before Empire and After', pp. 711-21; P.J. Marshall, 'Masters and Banians in the Eighteenth Century Calcutta', 1979, pp. 191-215; Marshall, *East India Fortunes: The British in Bengal in the Eighteenth Century*, Oxford, 1976; S. Subrahmanyam, *The Political Economy of Commerce, Southern India*, 1990, Ch. 5; Habib, 'Merchant Communities in Pre-colonial India', 1991, p. 399; K.M. Pannikar, *Asia and Western Dominance*, 1959.
3. Duperron, *L'Inde en rapport avec l'Europe*, II, Paris, 1798, p. 360; Abbé Guyon, *Histoire des Indes Orientales*, Paris, 1744; Le Mascrier, *Histoire de la Dernière Révolution des Indes Orientales*, Paris, 1757; Abbé Raynal, *Histoire Philosophique et Politique des Etablissements et du Commerce des Européens dans les deux Indes*, 1770; Voltaire, *Précis du Siècle de Louis XV et Fragments sur l'Inde, Œuvres Complètes*, Tomes xxvii et xxxvi, Paris, 1826-8.
4. *Annuaire des Etablissements Français dans l'Inde*, Pondichéry, 1939, p. 124; G.B. Malleson, *Dupleix*, 2001 (re-edition), pp. 89, 92, 119, 159-60, 165; M.P. Sridharan, *Papers on French Colonial Rule in India*, 1997, pp. 35-7; Cyril Antony, *Gazetteer of Pondicherry*, II, Pondicherry, 1982, p. 1196; Robert Orme, *History of Indostan*, 2 vols., Madras, 1913; Le Mascrier, op. cit., V. Mclean Thompson, *Dupleix and His Letters, 1742-1754*, New York, 1933, p. 898.
5. Sridharan, ibid., pp. 35, 37; *Annuaire des Etablissements Français dans l'Inde*, Pondichéry, ibid.; Marc Vigiè, *Dupleix*, 1993, pp. 10, 526, 530-41, 547.
6. F.N. Laude, *Dupleix. Le Siège de Pondichéry en 1748*, Pondichéry, 1870, p. 6.
7. Vigie, op. cit., 1993, pp. 542-6; Sridharan, op. cit., 1997, pp. 38-9; Charles Darwin, *On the Origin of Species*, Cambridge, 1966.
8. La Farelle, *Mémoire et Correspondances du Chevalier et du Général de la Farelle*, Paris, 1896, p. 45; L. Moreel, *Dupleix, Marquis de Fortune et Conquérant de l'Inde*, 1963, p. 150; T. Hamont, *Un Essai d'Empire français dans l'Inde aux XVIIIème siècles*, 1881, pp. i, ii, 15; Donneaud du Plan, *Histoire de la Compagnie Française de l'Inde*, 1889, p. 536.
9. J. Vinson, *Les Français dans l'Inde, Dupleix et Labourdonnais*, 1894, p. 9;

Julien Vinson, 'Pondichéry Sauvé', *RHIF*, 1920, p. 66; J. Weber, 'La Vie Quotienne dans les Comptoirs', 1995, p. 90.
10. Marc Vigie, op. cit., 1993 p. 555; M.P. Sridharan, op. cit., 1997 p. 38; E. Guérin, *Dupleix*, d'après les documents inédits..., Paris, 1908; Castonnet des Fosses, *L'Inde Française avant Dupleix*, Paris, 1887; Castonnet des Fosses. *L'Inde Française au XVIIIème siècle*, Paris, s.d.; Alfred Martineau, *Dupleix et l'Inde Française*, I, II; P. Cultru, *Dupleix, ses plans politiques, sa disgrâce*, Paris, 1901, pp. viii, 584f; H. Bionne, *Dupleix*, 1881, pp. 12, 165, 308-12; Thompson (ed.), *Dupleix from his Letters*, London, 1933, p. 901; G. Guénin, *L'Epopée Coloniale de la France racontée par les Contemporains*, Paris, 1931, p. 158.
11. Jouveau-Dubreuil, *Dupleix ou l'Inde Conquise*, Pondichéry, 1941, pp. 125, 131, 187; J. Weber, *Les Etablissements Français en Inde au XIXéme siècle*, I, Paris, 1988, p. 2.
12. Marc Vigie, op. cit., 1993 pp. 528, 557; Legoux de Flaix, *Essai sur l'Indoustan avec le tableau de son Commerce*, Paris, 1807, 2 vols.; Castonnet des Fosses, op. cit., s.d. p. 451; Sridharan, op. cit., pp. 38-9; Edward Said, *Culture Imperialism*, London, 1994; Cf. J.B.P. More, *Freedom Movement in French India: The Mahé Revolt of 1948*, Tellicherry, 2001; K.M. Pannikar, *Asia and Western Dominance: A Survey of the Vasco Da Gama Epoch in Asian History, 1498-1948*, London, 1959; Yvonne Robert Gaebelé, 'Enfance et Adolescence d'Anandarangapoullé', *Revue Historique de l'Etat de Pondichéry*, 9ᵉ volume, 1955, pp. 1-134; Louis Guet. Les Origines de l'Inde Française. Jeanne Begum (Madame Dupleix), Revue Maritime et Coloniale, Numéros d'Aôut, Septembre et Octobre, 1892.
13. J.B.P. More (ed.), *La Civilisation Indienne et Les Fables Hindoues du Panchatantra de Maridas Poullé*. Pondichéry, 2004, p. 59; K.P. Aravanan, *Tamizh Makkal Varalaru. Nayakar Kaalam*, Chennai, 2013; J.B.P. More, *Rise and Fall of the 'Dravidian' Justice Party 1916-1946*, Tellicherry, 2009, pp. 18-19.
14. M.A. Nayeem, *External Relations of the Bijapur Kingdom (1489-1686 A.D.)*, Hyderabad, 1974, pp. 23, 118-26, 142; K.P. Aravanan, ibid.; Narayana Poullé, *Histoire Détaillée des Rois du Carnatic*, Pondichéry, 1939, pp. 36-8; C.S. Srinivasachari, *A History of Gingee and its Rulers*, Annamalainagar, 1943, p. 11.
15. Sridharan, op. cit., 1997, p. 35; Narayana Poullé, ibid., pp. 20, 23, 30, 32, 34; Srinivasachari, ibid. pp. 9, 40; Jean Deloche, *Senji (Gingee) A Fortified City in the Tamil Country*, Pondicherry, 2000, p. 54; W. Foster, *History of the East India Company*, London, vol. 12, 1925, p. 90; N. Karashima, *South Indian History and Society: Studies from Inscriptions AD 850-1800*, Delhi, 1984, pp. 104-5.

INTRODUCTION 31

16. More, *From Arikamedu to the Foundation of Modern Pondicherry*, 2014, Ch.VII; G.R. Tibetts, *Arab Navigation in the Indian Ocean before the Coming of the Portuguese*, 1981, p. 467.
17. Paulin de Saint-Barthélemy, *Voyage aux Indes Orientales*, I, Paris, 1808, p. 25; De Barros, *Asia. Primeira Decada*, Lisboa, MCMXLX, pp. 360-1.
18. More, op. cit., 2014. pp. 72-4; Price & Dodwell, *The Private Diary of Ananda Ranga Pillai*, II, Madras, p. 369 (henceforth *ARP Diary*); Robert Sewell, *List of Antiquarian Remains in the Presidency of Madras*, I, p. 211; Letter from Gabriel Monod Herzen to a friend, dated 9 March 1941, Pondichéry, in volume 372, pp. 67-9, AMAE; vol. 374, Inde Française, p. 7
19. S. Gordon, *The Marathas,* 1993, pp. 53, 62, 84; my father Panjab Rao More, Maratha bhakti poet and early disciple of Sri Aurobindo, belonged to the More clan.
20. Srinivasachari, op. cit., 1943, pp. 11, 169, 171, 173, 184; Nayeem, op. cit., 1974, pp. 42, 118-26, 142; K.P. Aravanan, *Islamiyar Kalat Tamizh Makkal Varalaru*, Chennai, 2012.

CHAPTER 1

The French in Pondicherry: Early Phase

FRANÇOIS MARTIN AND HIS CHRISTIAN *DUBASHES*

AS POINTED OUT BY Sulaiman al-Mahri, Pondicherry seems to have come into existence as Pandichery in the fifteenth century itself. It was first, the Telugu vassal of the Vijayanagar king, Muthu Krishnappa Nayakar who developed it as a port-town. It seems to have waxed and waned until it came into the hands of the French, thanks to Sher Khan Lodi, the Pathan vassal of the Bijapur Sultan. He issued a *firman* for the French to establish a trading station there.[1] Lodi allowed the French to establish themselves in Pondicherry, on the express condition that they would not interfere in the religious affairs of the Indians and respect their customs and traditions. This showed that the Muslim rulers prior to arrival of the French were quite tolerant towards all Indians including the Hindus, as far as religious matters were concerned. Bellanger de Lespinay was the first Frenchman to set foot in Pondicherry.

During Muslim rule in India, generally there was no such thing as private property. All lands were held by the sovereign. Some like Anquetil Duperron and William Jones think that private property did exist in ancient India before Muslim rule. However, in Pondicherry Sher Khan Lodi transferred the land to the French without any opposition or hesitancy as there were no such thing as landowners in the area, other than the sovereign of the land.[2]

He finally reached Pondicherry by sea on 4 January 1674. It was the year when Shivaji crowned himself as an independent Indian monarch in western India, in defiance of the Mughal emperor, Aurangzeb as well as the Bijapur Sultan. François Martin was accompanied to Pondicherry by ten sailors and about 100 others, men, women and children, mostly Indians. Some interpreters, writers, middlemen or merchants seem to have accompanied or followed François Martin to Pondicherry from San Thomé. As ships could not reach the Pondicherry coast, as Pondicherry had no natural harbour, they all came by boats. These boats were called *chelingue* in local parlance.

One of them was Antoine Cattel, a native Portuguese of San Thomé who served as interpreter to the Company. François Martin had also a writer called Lazarou with him. He did not specify anything about the origin or background of this Lazarou in his *Memoirs*. The French were dependent on such middlemen or *dubashes* (interpreters) to establish contacts with the local Tamils or Telugus. They in their turn received commissions from the buyers of imported French Company goods as well as commissions from the merchants who provided goods for exportation. It was a lucrative job indeed. They were also considered as the principal chief of the Malabars, i.e. the Tamils from at least 1690.

Such middlemen or chiefs were known as *Mudaliar* to the Tamils.[3] So the term *Mudaliar* need not signify always a distinct caste group in the Tamil caste system. It could also be a title borne by these middlemen. The Mudaliars also dispensed indigenous justice and they enjoyed certain honours and privileges like the right to enter Fort Louis, seated in a palanquin, preceded by a large white umbrella.[4]

The Mudaliars or *dubashes* were part and parcel of the rising merchant class in Pondicherry. Their interests coincided with those of the French East India Company. Their existence and prosperity depended entirely on the French traders or factors and the demand in Europe for their goods, produced locally.

Antoine Cattel died very soon, on 5 December 1678. We do not know who took his place as interpreter after that. François Martin has not told us anything about it.[5] Martin himself left Pondicherry for Surat about two years later. Pondicherry was under the charge of Captain Pierre Deltor from 1681 to 1686, in the absence of François Martin. When Martin returned to Pondicherry in 1686, there was still no official *dubash* for the Company.

In the year 1688, Cozhandaiappa, François Martin's trusted Tamil Christian broker was an intermediary. He seems to have hailed from

San Thomé (Mylapore, Madras). On 15 July 1688, he obtained for the French from the king of Tanjore the *paravana* or decree that ceded Caveripatnam, situated to the north of Tranquebar, at the mouth of the Cauvery River. It seems that some Brahmins were against Cozhandaiappa and wanted his removal as an intermediary of the French company. But François Martin had full confidence in him and protected him against the 'ploys' of the Brahmins. Unfortunately, Cozhandaiappa died suddenly on 6 May 1691.[6] Otherwise he would have probably been nominated as the new *dubash* by François Martin.

It is quite surprising to note that François Martin from the time he stepped into Pondicherry for trade reasons, never failed to show his profound regard for Christianity. There is no indication that he ever appreciated the local traditions and customs, rituals and ceremonies. He was never favourably disposed especially towards the Brahmins, probably because they were the leaders of the indigenous Hindu religion. He laid the responsibility squarely on the Brahmins for the degeneration of south India. He accused them of extorting money from the foreign traders as well as from the Tamils for their own selfish reasons.

However, following the order of Sher Khan Lodi, François Martin hardly interferend in the religious affairs of the Indians in the early stages of his tenure as the Director of the French Company in Pondicherry. However he seems to have been exasperated once when a Brahmin lady was determined to commit *Sati* in Pondicherry. He tried to dissuade the Brahmin lady from burning herself to death along with her dead husband. But it was of no avail and François Martin could do nothing but witness the Brahmin lady commit *Sati* in Pondicherry.

As Martin began to organize the French settlement in Pondicherry, he naturally felt the need to have Christian priests to cater to the spiritual needs of the French Christians. As a result, he invited the Capuchin missionaries from Madras to settle in Pondicherry. The Capuchin Father Louis built a chapel within the premises of the fortress on the seashore. This fortress was first built by François Martin with the permission of the Indian vassal. The chapel built by Father Louis was called Saint Pierre. Saint Pierre chapel was replaced by the church of Saint Louis later in 1722.[7]

The Capuchins built their first Notre Dame Des Anges Church in 1707 near the seashore. It was also François Martin who preferred employing indigenous and Portuguese Christians like Antoine Cattel, Cozhandaiappa, André Mouliapa and Lazarou as brokers and writers of the French Company, in spite of the fact that most of the merchants, traders and producers were Hindus. Probably he thought that being Christians like the French, they would be more trustworthy and reliable than non-Chrsitian (Hindu) brokers. As long as he lived, François Martin never swerved from the policy of nominating only Christians as brokers. His principal broker or *dubash* was always a Christian.

There are records dated 28 May 1676 that attest that a certain Lazaro da Mota donated some land for the construction of a church on the seashore, near the French *loge*, to the Capuchin missionaries, in order to cater to the religious needs of the local Tamil converts. The land that he donated was most probably given to him previously by François Martin, as all land on which the factory came up belonged to the Company. François Martin had mentioned in his *Memoirs* the name of Lazarou, who was writer of the Company. It is quite possible that this Lazarou was the same as Lazaro da Mota. But it is not a certainty, as François Martin has not told us anything about it.[8]

The small 'Malabar' church, known as Saint Lazare church came up by 1684 due to the generosity of Lazaro da Mota. The French usually called the local Tamil people as 'Malabars' during this period. The church was located on a plot just outside the fort on the southeast. A document in Portuguese signed by Lazaro da Mota himself at Madras in October 1686, confirmed the donation on the express condition that the Capuchins prayed for the salvation of his soul and worked for the conversion of 'Hindus' to Christianity.

The Capuchin missionary Norbert had mentioned in his *Memoirs* a certain Lazare Mudaliar, along with other Tamils like Mottou (Muthu), the catechist of the St. Paul church of the Jesuits. Norbert had also mentioned a certain Lazaro Marta, belonging to the Gambadi (probably Agambadia) caste. We do not know if Lazare Mudaliar and Lazaro Marta were one and the same person or if they had anything to do with Lazarou or Lazaro da Mota, the future *dubash* of François Martin.

It however appears that in 1703 the total population of Indians in Pondicherry stood at around 30,000, while in 1706 the total number of Christians in Pondicherry was 1122. Many of them including several members of the depressed castes (parayas) attended mass at the St. Lazare Church together. Neither the Capuchins nor Lazaro da Mota as far as I know raised any objection to the *parayas* attending mass along with the other castes in the same church without any form of discrimination or separation.[9] This was indeed an achievement in those days when in the big 'Hindu' temples, only the higher castes were permitted entry.

The St. Lazare Church was in usage until 1709. It was perpendicular to the sea. On 15 August 1709, the Capuchins took possession of a new church built a little away on the coast. This church was parallel to the sea. In 1728, it was decided to destroy the St. Lazare Church and transfer the cemetery, located on the northern side of the church. All the huts of the fishermen and the depressed castes around the church and the cemetery too were demolished. But this new church was quite near the Fort. It collapsed partially in 1734 due to torrential rains. In 1739, the Capuchins demolished this church with the approval of the Superior Council.

On 15 August 1739, they shifted to a new church called Notre Dame des Anges, situated just behind the old one. It was perpendicular to the sea like the first one. The Company bore the expenses to the tune of 3,000 pagodas for the construction of this new church. It also paid for the upkeep of the Capuchin fathers, who officiated at this church as well as in the chapel inside the fort. Both these churches were reserved for the white Europeans in principle. The original Notre Dame des Anges was destroyed by the English in 1761. A new church was rebuilt on the ruins of the old one and consecrated on 2 August 1765.[10]

It must be noted further that Lazarou functioned as a writer of the French company in the beginning. He was not appointed as the official *dubash*, interpreter or intermediary of the French Company during the early period. There were few others such as Cozhandaiappa and André Mouliapa or André Moutiapa, employed by the Company. It was only when François Martin re-assumed charge of Pondicherry in 1686, that the necessity for an official intermediary between the

French and the Tamils was felt. As a result in 1690, André Mouliapa was appointed as *dubash* by François Martin to succeed Antoine Cattel. Even then, François Martin had preferred André Mouliapa to be the Company's first courtier or intermediary, and not Lazaro da Mota. André Mouliapa's ancestors seem to have been early converts to Christianity and were at the service of the French. They had been buried in the St. Pierre chapel of the Fort.

But unfortunately for Mouliapa, the Dutch conquered Pondicherry in 1693. It was during Dutch rule in Pondicherry that the Maratha king of Senji, Ram Raja sold the villages of Ariyankuppam and Virampatnam as well as Ozhukarai which eventually became part of Pondicherry. When Pondicherry was given back to the French in 1699, François Martin appointed Lazaro da Mota as courtier very soon.[11] We do not know if André Mouliapa (also known as André Velevendra) was related to Lazaro da Mota or not. There is no indication in the records that I have consulted that they were related.

Family histories maintained by Cojandé Dairianadin (Cozhandai Dairianathan) (1906-85) who claims to be a descendant of Mouliapa assert that Mouliapa was revoked from his position as Mudaliar of the French Company. It seems that the revocation plunged Mouliapa in sorrow and caused his death. But unfortunately this piece of information is not backed by first-hand evidence. Cozhandai Dairianathan was the son of the renowned Pondicherry jurist, Gnanou Diagou (1877-1959). There is also no credible evidence forthcoming to attest the claim that André Mouliapa and Lazaro de Mota were the ancestors of Diagou Mudaliar (d. 1849), who was a landlord, and Gnanou Diagou (1877-1959), the jurist.[12] However, in 1765 according to Henri de Closets d'Errey and E. Gaudart, a certain Saverimuthu or Saveri Mudaliar, a grand-nephew of Pedro Canagarayen was the *diwan* of the Company in Pondicherry. We do not know if Diagou Mudaliar was related to Saverimuthu in any way.[13]

On the other hand, the *Almanach of Pondicherry* of 1839 reveals that a certain Cojandé Dairianada Mudaliar (Cozhandai Dairiyanatha Mudaliar) was a member of the Consultative Committee of Indian Jurisprudence.[14] It is quite possible that this person was a descendant of Cozhandaiappa. Much earlier in 1717, a certain Cojandé Savarirayen (Cozhandai Savarirayen), son of Savériacoutty Mudaliar had donated some land to Cojandéammalle (Cozahandaiammal).[15] From the name one can infer with some certainty that Cozhandai Savarirayen of the first quarter of the eighteenth century, was related to Cozhandaiappa of the seventeenth century as well as Cozhandai Dairianatha Mudaliar, also known as Dairianathan, of the first half of nineteenth century or even Cozhandai Dairiyanathan of the twentieth century. Cozhandai Dairyanatha Mudaliar of the nineteenth century was the nephew of Diagou Mudaliar. On the other hand, there is no evidence to attest that the preceding persons were related to Lazaro da Mota or Pedro Cangarayen in any way.

However in the year 1701, André Mouliapa passed away. His family as well as François Martin wanted him to be buried in the chapel of the Fort, in honour of the services that he had rendered to the Company. As André Mouliapa belonged to the Malabar (St. Lazare) church, this was considered not possible. But François Martin used his power and influence and forced the burial to take place in the Fort chapel. If François Martin had really revoked Mouliapa from his position as Mudaliar and was against him, he would not have thrown around his weight to get Mouliapa buried in the chapel of the Fort.[16]

As for Lazaro da Mota, his name is more intriguing. In the Cathedral of San Thomé, there is a burial inscription dated 1603 in the name of Luis da Mota, hailing from Santaren in Portugal. It is quite possible that Lazaro da Mota or Lazaro de Mota was a descendant of Luis da Mota. There is also another burial inscription dated 1691 in the St. Mary's Church of Fort St. George, bearing the name Lazarus Timothy. This name has been identified with a certain Thaniappa Mudaliar of the Agambadi caste, who died in 1691 according to the inscription. It must be borne in mind that Lazarus Timothy was an English name and has nothing to do with Lazaro da Mota or even Thaniappa Mudaliar. There is no reason or evidence to equate Lazarus Timothy with Lazaro da Mota as the latter lived even beyond 1691 and was *dubash* of François Martin since 1700-1.

But the French historian of the nineteenth century, Henri de Closets d'Errey had relied on this inscription to equate Lazaro da Mota with Thaniappa or Tanappa Mudaliar. This equation has been repeated by many scholars including the jurist Cojandé Dairianadin (Cozhandai

Dairianathan) who claims to have descended from Lazaro da Mota and Pedro Canagarayen. He of course did not provide any proper evidence. This may be a historical aberration which needs further clarification.[17]

Lazaro da Mota knew Portuguese and was also most certainly conversant in Tamil. He seems to have been introduced to François Martin by the French Capuchin missionaries established in Madras. In some records of the late seventeenth century that I have consulted, his name is given as Lazaro Motta. But in the birth register edited by Alfred Martineau, he bears the pompous name Lazaro de Molta. He was shown in the register to have married a certain Hieronimo. It is quite strange to note that even his wife bore a purely Portuguese name, and not a Tamil name as is usual among converted Christian women of the higher castes. It is not mentioned in the registers that Lazaro de Molta was a Malabar, i.e. Tamil. *Malabar* was a derogatory term used by the French to identify Indians or Tamils during their colonial rule.[18] It is quite obvious from the preceding that this Lazaro de Molta or Lazaro da Mota had nothing to do with Lazare Mudaliar mentioned earlier by Rev. Norbert.

If Lazaro da Mota and his wife were of pure Indian descent, it would have been mentioned in the civil register as was the case with several others. There was also no mention of his caste name in the civil register or in the records of the seventeenth century. This seems to lend credence to the belief in some quarters that he was of partial Portuguese descent or of mixed Indo-Portuguese descent at least. His identification as Mudaliar was something that might have been suffixed to his name when he was actually appointed as Mudaliar or *dubash* in 1700-1. Until then he was only a writer or interpreter of the Company as mentioned in the civil register as well as in François Martin's memoirs.[19]

Lazaro de Mota and Hieronimo had a son by the name of Anthonio de Molta, born on 20 March 1677 and a daughter called Françoise de Molta, born on 5 February 1681. François Martin himself was the godfather of Françoise de Molta. These are typical European names and they have not been identified in any other way in the birth registers of the period concerned to indicate that they were pure Tamils, belonging to the Mudaliar caste. We do not have any further records of either the parents or their children in the birth, marriage or death registers of the eighteenth century related to Pondicherry. This raises the possibility of them having left Pondicherry at some point of time. This seems to be the only plausible explanation for their names not figuring any further in the civil registers of Pondicherry of the eighteenth century, apart from the fact that there were many missing links in the parish registers.[20]

It is also claimed that Anthonio de Molta, the son of Lazaro de Molta was none other than André Moutiapa. There is no factual evidence for this too. Besides, there is no chance of Anthonio de Molta becoming *diwan* in the year 1690 when he was just thirteen years old. As a matter of fact, Lazaro da Mota had succeeded André Moutiapa in the year 1700-1. It is clear from the evidence and records that I have consulted that Lazaro da Mota and André Moutiapa were not related to one another and the latter was surely not the son of the former. Since 1700 François Martin was dependent on Lazaro da Mota alone for his business operations as well as for his dealings with the local people, as the latter was also the chief of the Tamils, in spite of him being a Christian.[21]

All these Christian brokers were in very good terms with the French Christian missionaries and even helped them in their proselytizing activities. We have seen Lazaro da Mota donating land and constructing a church for the Capuchins. After Cozhandaiappa's death, his widow Maria Diaz, also known as Marie May or Maria de Monte donated a big garden known as the Garden of Cozhandaiappa, along with a well, through an Act dated 21 September 1691, to the French missionaries of the *Société des Missions Etrangères*. These missionaries had reached Pondicherry after 1689. The garden was situated to the south of the public square or *bazaar*. A chapel was built in the terrain and an inscription about the donation was placed upon it according to Maria Diaz's desire, on condition that the missionaries prayed for the salvation of Cozhandaiappa's soul. Besides, the Company built hundred small shops near the garden on land donated by Cozhandaiappa's mother, which practically laid the foundations for the *peria kadai* or grand *bazaar*. The chapel was adjacent to it and was therefore known as the *kadaikovil* or *bazaar* temple.

In 1700, Maria Diaz, the widow of Cozhandaiappa donated to the missionaries of the *Mission Etrangères*, land to construct a seminary, in the western part of what is today the big bazaar. It was none other than the *dubash* of the French Company, André Moutiapa, also called André Velavendra, who was witness to this donation in the year 1700. The site of the big clock tower in the bazaar which is a landmark of Pondicherry today was actually donated to the Fathers of the *Missions Etrangères* by Maria Diaz. Upon this site was built the residence of the Fathers.

In the year 1720, a certain Pouchiammal, probably related to Cozhandaiappa, gifted the land situated in the Grand Bazar premises to the Fathers of *Missions Etrangères* for the construction of a seminary. This site stood adjacent to the land given by Maria Diaz. A church was built there with money from Coja Saffar, the Armenian merchant, and was dedicated to the *Presentation of the Blessed Virgin* on 13 October 1745. This *bazaar* church as well as the church of the Jesuits and Capuchins was destroyed by the English in 1761. Right in front of the *bazaar* church was located Ananda Ranga Poullé's house who became *diwan* of the French.[22]

The origin of the name Maria Diaz is quite intriguing. The name indicates that she was of Portuguese origin like Hieronimo, the wife of Lazaro da Mota. As generally the high caste Hindu female converts retain their Tamil name, it is possible that Maria did not belong to the Mudaliar caste to which Cozhandaiappa seems to have belonged. Besides, the other name for Maria Diaz, i.e. Marie May or rather Marimayi indicates the Tamil caste goddess, Mariyamman, who was the goddess of the lower castes. Marimayi literally means 'Mother of Small-pox'. This seems to suggest that Maria Diaz was a convert or of mixed Tamil-Portuguese descent, married to Cozhandaiappa. However, in the missionary records it has also been recorded that a certain Tamchem Mudali was Maria Diaz's father.

Julien Vinson has reported that in 1685, the Jesuits started building a church on the plot given to them in 1675 by a certain Tanappa Mudaliar. In this connection, Tanappa Mudaliar's name has also been reported by the missionary, Adrien Launay in 1898 without citing the source of his information. This was simply taken over by many other later French historians without verification. Actually it seems that in 1691, when the Jesuits were given the right by King Louis XIV to indulge in evangelization in the French territories in India, the French Company under François Martin gave land to the Jesuits, on the southern and western sides of the Vedapuriswaran temple, which was situated then at the site where we find today the Mission Press of the church. François Martin himself laid the foundation stone for this church. By September 1692, the Jesuits built on this land hurriedly a church dedicated to the Virgin Mary under the title 'Notre Dame de la Conception' or 'Our Lady of Conception'. But this church built well beyond the fortress towards the west, facing the Uppar River was made of mud and bricks. It was quite small and uncomfortable.[23]

On 28 May 1728, the Superior Council of Pondicherry granted permission to the Jesuits to reconstruct a new church towards the north of the old one, provided it was not an obstacle to the defence of Pondicherry. In 1740, the Jesuits were also allowed to reconstruct their residence adjacent to the church. In 1761, the Jesuit church was razed to the ground by the English. On 20 June 1792, the Fathers of the *Missions Etrangères* rebuilt the Jesuit church on the old foundations. This church stands till today and is known as Samba Kovil. *Samba* may be a corrupt Tamilized form of Saint Paul, as the previous Jesuit church was known as St. Paul.[24]

The Jesuits functioned always independently of the Capuchins in Pondicherry under the Bishop of Mylapore, in the name of the Carnatic Mission since 1691. Father Tachard was the Superior of the Jesuits in Pondicherry. His residence was located at the northern extremity of what is today the Manakula Vinayakar Street.[25]

According to some, Tanappa Mudaliar was none other than Lazaro da Mota who was the first *dubash*, while André Moutiappa was his son. In fact, to my knowledge, there are no first-hand French records related to the last quarter of the seventeenth century which states that Tanappa Mudaliar was none other than Lazaro da Mota, as seen above. Ananda Ranga Poullé had never mentioned in his diary accounts that this Tanappa Mudaliar was the same person as Lazaro da Mota of François Martin's period or his descendant. Instead it has been mentioned that a certain Lazar Mudaliar was the brother of Pedro

Canagaraya Mudaliar who became *diwan* after Guruvappa's death. Another name for this Lazar was Tanappa Mudaliar and his wife's name was Gnanamouthammal. He was also known as Chinnadu Mudali. I did not find any evidence connecting Lazar Mudaliar, the brother of Pedro Canagarayen, with Lazaro de Mota and his wife Hieronimo of François Martin's period. There was no evidence either to the claim that Pedro's grandfather was Lazaro da Mota and André Moutiappa was the son of Lazaro da Mota. All these claims were actually unfounded.[26]

Besides, in the light of the above, it seems problematic to claim that Lazaro da Mota and Pedro Cangarayen were the ancestors of Diagou Mudaliar or even Gnanou Diagou. As a matter of fact, it was Cozhandai Dairianatha Mudaliar or Dairiyanathan, a nephew of Diagou Mudaliar who built and erected the clock tower in July 1852 at his own expense on the land donated earlier by Maria Diaz, which eventually became the Big Bazaar. Cozhandaiappa and Pouchiammal had also donated land on which stands the Big Bazaar today. This bazaar formally came up on 25 November 1826, at the site were the church of the *Mission Étrangères* stood.

So it is highly probable, given that Dairianatha Mudaliar had decided to erect his clock tower in the middle of the big bazaar, in the name of his uncle Diagou Mudaliar, that the latter was a descendant of Cozhandaiappa's and Maria Diaz's families and not a descendant of Lazaro da Mota and Pedro Canagarayen, as claimed by Cojandé Dairiyanathan of the twentieth century. We do not know at the present state of our knowledge if Lazaro da Mota or Pedro Canagarayen were related to Cozhandaiappa in any way or not. But towards the end of the nineteenth century, there was a notary in Pondicherry by the name of Appavou Belevendirassamy Diagou Mudaliar, who might well be a grandson or descendant of Diagou Mudaliar, the landlord.

About the year 1690, a chapel was built at the village of Ariyankuppam, by a Syrian Catholic Bishop. That was at a time when Ariyankuppam area was still not under French control. This church was ceded to the French Jesuits later. On 31 August 1714, the Jesuits obtained from the Company a large plot of land where they constructed a new church. This church was also destroyed by the English in 1761.[27]

Developments in Pondicherry

François Martin had to face Dutch invasion of Pondicherry in 1693. The Dutch had paid the Maratha king of Senji, Ram Raja 20,000 livres to obtain permission from him to besiege Pondicherry. In that year, François Martin seems to have pulled down an old Hindu temple consisting of galleries and *mandapas*, with flat roofs and vaulted structures that lay towards the west, in close proximity to the fort, probably for defensive purposes. It was not unusual during the formative stage of modern Pondicherry to witness old temples disappearing or being displaced and new temples springing up. Some temples might have simply gone unnoticed in the plans. This becomes quite obvious when we scrutinize closely the early Dutch and French plans of Pondicherry.

Pondicherry was actually besieged by the Dutch during August-September 1693. Very soon François Martin surrendered to the Dutch with 36 Europeans and 300 to 400 drilled Indian *sepoys*. One must not fail to note that François Martin had already under him trained Tamil *sepoys* for the defense of Pondicherry. It was he who conceived first the idea of using Tamils as soldiers to compensate the lack of European soldiers in Pondicherry. Thus François Martin appears to be the first Frenchman to realize the importance of associating Tamils/Indians as soldiers in the governance and protection of his territory. These sepoys along with the brokers, intermediaries and *dubashes* were the early Indian collaborators in the French colonial enterprise.

After the recovery of Pondicherry from the Dutch in 1699, François Martin was appointed as the Governor of all French possessions in India by the French king. This appointment came about in 1701. Besides a Sovereign Council of five members was created of which François Martin was the President. He had under his command 200 Europeans then and several engineers and a large supply of arms and ammunitions. There was no Indian/Tamil member in the Sovereign Council. Pondicherry became the headquarters of all French factories in India. Those factories included a small plot of land of about 6 acres at Masulipatnam, a decaying establishment of about 8 acres at Surat, which was abandoned in 1714, a settlement at Chandernagore on the right bank of the Hugly and six small plots of land of about 46 acres at Calicut, Balasor, Dacca, Patna, Kasimbazar and Jougdia.[28]

François Martin was literally the 'little king' of Pondicherry thenceforth, with almost absolute power and jurisdiction over the inhabitants both European and Indian of the territories under him.

Almost immediately François Martin concentrated his efforts to develop Pondicherry into a trade centre on a firmer footing. For this he needed a stronger fort, in the place of the older one. The fort was needed not just to ward off his European enemies, but also the Indian powers from the north that were encroaching upon the Tamil country.

It appears that when the Dutch conquered Pondicherry in 1693, the White town had already come into existence towards the east of the Ariyankuppam River which joined the Uppar River flowing from the west. Beyond the Ariyankuppam River towards the west as well as towards the north of Uppar River was the Black town of the Tamils and Telugus. The Ariyankuppam River was extended later northwards by a canal parallel to the sea. The areas situated to the east of the canal on both sides of the fort became the White town, where the French predominantly stayed, while the areas beyond the canal became the Black town of the Tamils and Telugus, which spread northwards and westwards and only later southwards during the governorship of Le Noir. Every caste grouping had its own locality in the Black town during Frnaçois Martin's period itself.

In the present state of our knowledge we are not aware if it was François Martin or Pierre Deltor, who had allocated particular areas or localities to particular castes. We think nevertheless that it was the French who arranged Pondicherry town on the basis of castes. In any case, there was no question of mixing up castes in the Hindu social system. The Dutch when they took over Pondicherry simply formalized this caste arrangement in a more regular manner as could be seen from the Dutch plans of Pondicherry drawn immediately after their occupation of Pondicherry in 1693 and a little later in 1694. These plans were identified in the Dutch archives by G.S.M. Mubeen of Pondicherry.

In the plan of 1693, drawn immedialtely after the occupation of Pondicherry by the Dutch, we could see that the White town, located towards the east of the Ariyankuppam River was already set in rectangular blocks, with roads almost running straight and cutting at right angles. When the Dutch occupied Pondicherry, they extended the rectangular block arrangement plan of the White town to the Black town, where roads ran parallel to one another and cut at right angles. This is quite visible in their plan of Pondicherry drawn in 1694.

Obviously if we take into consideration the Dutch plan of 1694, the entire Black town, including the area beyond the Uppar River towards the south, was planned in rectangular blocks. But we also know that this plan was never implemented in the southern part of the town, south of Uppar, until the governorship of Le Noir. Whether the plan was actually implemented by the Dutch in the northern part of the Black town is also not very sure.

When the French recovered Pondicherry in 1699, they seem to have maintained the town planning that existed earlier and formalized by the Dutch. This planning of Pondicherry town is more or less in vogue even today. Some French scholars like Jean Deloche tend to attribute the planning of Pondicherry town to the Dutch alone, neglecting completely the role of Frenchmen like François Martin, Father Louis, engineer Denyon and Pierre Deltor in designing the town. But it is certain from the Dutch plans that the organization of the town by rectangular blocks was a French invention, though imperfectly implemented first in the White town by the French and then extended to the Black town. Besides, there is nothing forthcoming from the Dutch records as far as I know which established that it was the Dutch who planned Pondicherry with straight roads, cutting at right angles.

It is true that before the Dutch occupation, if we are to believe the accounts of François Martin, the layout of Pondicherry town was quite irregular and the scattered houses or rather huts of the Tamils were made of earth mixed with wooden pieces. It also seems that during Dutch period a fence was built around Pondicherry, which later became the famous *Boulevards* of Pondicherry.[29] But neither François Martin nor the French architects and engineers like Denyon or Father Louis as far as I know had left us any account or even a hint that they were inspired by Dutch town-planners in planning and constructing Pondicherry after 1699.

François Martin started to build the new fort in 1700-1, following the model of the fort at Tournay in France. The workers who built the fort were Tamilians. The Capuchin Father Louis directed the construction, along with the French engineer Denyon. While the old fort was dug up, some idols and copper vessels used in the Hindu ceremonies were unearthed. François Martin handed over the idols to the Hindus. It is quite possible that there was a temple in the site of the old fort which was levelled to the ground to construct the fort.[30]

The wood to construct the fort and the houses was procured from the Kalapet forests. Kalapet was given to François Martin in the year 1702 by Daoud Khan Panni, the Mughal chief in the Carnatic.

François Martin needed money to construct the new fort. He borrowed money from merchants like the Armenian Safar Zachary. Besides, he resorted to goods seized from Indian or other ships to not only replenish the French ships bound for France, but also to refurbish somewhat the finances of the Company, as the funds from France were never adequate. There was frequent import-export activity in Pondicherry until about 1704. But after François Martin's death, there was a downturn in commercial activity.[31]

The fort was completed in the year 1706. The benediction of the new fort took place on 25 August 1706. It was built on the space which is occupied presently by the Puduchery Government Park called Bharati Poonga and the adjacent areas, especially on the southern side. The fort was protected by five big bastions. The western bastion of the fort extended beyond the drain (canal) which separated the White town from the Black town. Actually in those days this canal or rather the Ariyankuppam River, did not extend beyond the southern side. When the fort was completed a canal was dug further northwards as a prolongation of the river. Beyond the canal on the west and towards the north resided the Tamils. The roads and the areas today between the Cathedral Street (formerly rue des Missions Etrangères) and the canal was just marshy land covered with water bodies. It was the same on the southern side beyond the Jesuit church up to the small river called Uppar (Salt River) which formed the southern limits of the town. This river actually flowed into the Ariyankuppam River further south. The Uppar which is known as the Petit Canal even today constituted the southern limits of the town. It was a low lying marshy land. Beyond that there was nothing but fields and marshes.

The *Sainte Thérèse* street and quarters had not come into existence then. Just beyond the Uppar was located the cemetery of the depressed caste Christian converts.[32]

It was also in the year 1706, that the village cluster of Ozhukarai or Oulgaret was acquired by the French in a definitive manner, through gifts to the tune of Rs. 12,000 to Nawab Daoud Khan, the Carnatic representative of the Mughal Emperor Aurangzeb, who always considered Pondicherry as part of his domains, though the Dutch had bought it earlier from Ram Raja, the Maratha king of Senji. It procured annual revenue of about 1,000 pagodas. Subsequently other villages like Olandai, Pakkamudianpet, Karuvadikuppam and Murungapakkam were also given to the French.[33]

It was these same Jesuits under the impulse given by Father Tachard who seem to have laid the foundations for modern education in India. It appears that a school was started by them as early as 1703 in Pondicherry. In 1711, Father Tachard wrote that nothing was more important for the Indian nation than to open public schools for educating young Indians. Father Tachard was of course thinking in terms of educating the Indians on European lines, long before Lord Macaulay would think about it in British India.[34]

During the last two decades of the seventeenth century, the French were running short of money to trade profitably in India. They were also at loggerheads with the sultan of Golconda, the rival of the Bijapur sultan. This obliged the French to take to piracy. François Martin himself posted in Masulipatnam before he reached Pondicherry seems to have indulged in piracy. He was therefore a pirate before he came to Pondicherry as a colonizer. In 1702, Emperor Aurangzeb reacted to the depredations caused by European pirates by interdicting all trade with the French, Dutch and the English in his empire. It also appears that during this period when the Dutch domination of the Indian Ocean was almost complete, mostly all goods that arrived in France from India were pirated goods.[35]

Besides, as Louis XIV was embroiled in the Spanish succession wars, the French Company in Pondicherry received inadequate funds from France. François Martin had to borrow from moneylenders like the Armenians to carry on with the trade. Actually the import-export activity seems to have picked up somewhat during François Martin's rule since 1690 upto at least 1704. There were 40,000 Tamils in the town and their prosperity was dependent on the trade with France.[36] The interests of trade more than anything else seems to have prevented François Martin from toeing the intolerant line of the Jesuits as it would have been detrimental to French Company commerce.

By the time of François Martin's death, Pondicherry had taken shape. The houses were still lowly built and roads were badly paved or not paved at all. During rainy season, they were inundated and from the stagnant water in the pits around the town emanated a nauseating odour. The sea was quite at a distance at that time. Thorny bushes around the town was the only defence.[37]

HINDU-CHRISTIAN INTER-ACTION

Since the period of François Martin, the Jesuits under Father Tachard swung back into action. In order to attract more converts from the higher Tamil castes as well as the lower castes, the Jesuits, following the example set by the Italian Jesuit Robert de Nobili in Madurai, began to tolerate certain Hindu customs and ceremonies which were in practice among converted Christians, in a slightly modified form like adding a small cross on the 'pagan' *thali* tied around the neck of the bride during marriage.[38]

The Capuchins and the missionaries of the *Société des Missions Etrangères* were opposed to this stand of the Jesuits. Many Hindu idolatrous habits and ceremonies were actually modified or forbidden by Cardinal Maillard de Tournon through the decree of 23 August 1704. Among the customs and ceremonies prohibited were: the use of Hindu names, infant marriages, the use of Hindu *thali*, exclusion of women from churches during certain periods, ceremony on the girl's attainment of puberty, the making of distinction between *parayas* and others by a small wall within the church, separate entrances for the parayas and others into the church, the assistance of Christian musicians at Hindu ceremonies, the use of ceremonial washings and bathings, the drinking of a beverage made of milk, butter, cow-dung and urine, use of cow-dung ashes and the reading and use of Hindu books.[39]

However, the Capuchins and the missionaries of *Missions Etrangères* continued to accuse the Jesuits of mixing 'idolatrous' customs with Christian sacraments, as the Jesuits never accepted the jurisdiction of Cardinal Tournon over Pondicherry. Even the Public Prosecutor of Pondicherry, Jean Jacques de Querelay in his work on the Hindu religion entitled 'Traité de la religion des Malabars' had pointed out the ways in which the Jesuits have adopted Hindu customs and habits. Following them they did not even admit Christian converts from the lower castes into their churches and they kept the parayas separate from the higher castes in their churches. They would not even enter the houses of the Parayas to administer the Sacraments. They would distribute cow-dung ashes to the Christians and allow them to cover their faces with sandalwood and cow-dung ashes. Father Tachard and Father Bouchet who succeeded Tachard at his death in 1712 as the chief of the Jesuits in Pondicherry, were very much convinced of such cultural and religious mix up, in order to attract more converts to Christianity.[40]

Besides, in order to strike a relationship with the Indians, the Jesuits learnt Tamil, Telugu and Sanskrit so that they could read Hindu sacred books and challenge Hindu beliefs and traditions. The Jesuits also needed Tamil interpreters, preachers and catechists. They had to recruit them and train them.[41]

On the other hand, François Martin also needed to attract more merchants to settle in Pondicherry. It was thus that Nainiappa Poullé who had a flourishing business in Madras came and settled in Pondicherry. He belonged to the Idayar caste, which was placed lower in the Hindu social hierarchy. Besides, he was a Telugu. On 24 September 1704, he obtained tobacco and betel farms on a lease from the Superior Council of Pondicherry for two years at a yearly rent of 2400 pagodas. François Martin also built a palace for the Governor outside the fort on the northern side (presently Villa Aroumé, No. 4, Rangapillai street).[42]

We have already noted that Tamilians had lost their independence and Tamil kingdoms had ceased to exist since the fourteenth century. After the Turks and the Telugus, came the incursions of the troops of the Persian-speaking Bijapur Sultans, made up of Muslims and Maratha Hindus. The French had actually obtained Pondicherry from Sher Khan Lodi, the Pathan invader and vassal of the Bijapur Sultan.

But in their turn the Bijapur sultans lost power to the invading Mughals in the 1680s. This brought the Mughals into the Tamil country. Emperor Auragnzeb was the Mughal Emperor at that time. Along with the Mughals came the Marathas who had risen suddenly as a power under Shivaji in western India. Very soon the Marathas spread their wings into the Tamil country and for a time the French had to deal with them in order to retain their hold on Pondicherry. Shivaji's half-brother Ekoji established a Maratha kingdom at Tanjore in 1674. After the conquest of the Bijapur sultanate by the Mughals, Tamil Nadu saw the beginning of the rule of the Nawabs of Arcot subject to the Nizam of Hyderabad. Both the invading Hindu Marathas as well as the Mughals or the Nawabs of Arcot who were of foreign origin, became the new rulers of the Tamilians. The French in Pondicherry had to deal with these new rulers. Using diplomacy rather than force, François Martin managed to retain Pondicherry for the French. He even obtained permission from the Nawab to build a veritable fort in Pondicherry.

When the preceding political changes were taking place in south India and the Tamil country, the Jesuits were intent upon spreading Christianity in Pondicherry. They continuously mounted pressure on François Martin to do away with or restrict all pagan or Hindu ceremonies, processions and festivities in the town, to eradicate all temples and mosques, to ban trumpets and dancing girls on the streets which were contrary to Christian values and to demolish the Vedapuriswaran temple, the principal temple of the Hindus of Pondicherry. The Jesuits were fanatical. They considered the Hindu gods as demons and devils and the phallus (*lingam*) symbol in the temples as obscene and disgusting. Some described the Hindu saintly men called yogis or gurus as vulgar gang leaders, who had clandestine promiscuous relationships with women. One missionary from the French factory of Chandernagore in Bengal opined that Banaras would be destroyed by God like Sodom.

When in 1710, the prince of the Maravas of the southern Tamil country died, 47 of his wives mounted the pyre of their husband and were consumed by the flames. The Jesuits were flabbergasted by such atrocious practices. Their voice became increasingly strident, calling for the abolition of idol worship and other Hindu ceremonies in

Pondicherry.[43] The Jesuits in particular and the French in general were always convinced about the superiority of their religion, culture and civilization. They thought that the Hindus were only fit to be civilized through conversion and the imposition of their values and ideas over them.

In 1701, the Jesuits under Father Tachard wanted the destruction of the Vedapuriswaran temple as well as other temples and mosques in the town and abolish 'paganism' altogether, following the example set by the great French king who abolished all heresy in France. François Martin being a fervent Catholic acceded to this request and gave orders for the demolition of the Vedapuriswaran temple on 10 August 1701. He prohibited the gathering of Hindus in their temples. He also prohibited temple processions accompanied by the beating of drums and the blowing of trumpets during the Easter days and Sundays.

On 15 August, François Martin asked for the keys of the temples. The Tamil and Telugu inhabitants of Pondicherry decided to leave Pondicherry. More than 10,000 among them made their way out of Pondicherry during this period. Tamil masons and coolies who were constructing the fort stopped their work. Five to six thousand weavers and others assembled at the Vazhudavur gate with their tools, asking permission to leave. All shops were closed and houses abandoned.

On 16 August François Martin himself rode on horseback and visited the Madras gate where he saw 12,000 to 15,000 inhabitants, ready to leave. Martin panicked as he needed the inhabitants. He also ran the risk of losing the workers who were building the fort. Besides, he needed the Hindu merchants and weavers, etc., so that he can carry on trade profitably. So he asked the caste headmen to come and meet him in the fort. After discussion, Martin cancelled his orders and prevented the Hindus from migrating.[44]

But again on 30 August 1702, under pressure from the Jesuits, François Martin prohibited Hindu processions in the streets. But he had to retract once again due to Hindu opposition. Though François Martin too was religiously inclined, yet for the sake of commerce, he withstood the pressure of the Jesuits and allowed the Hindus to follow their customs and traditions in Pondicherry.

Father Tachard, the chief of the Jesuits had a very poor opinion of the Hindu 'idolatrous' priests and priestesses. He wrote to Father de la Chaise in 1702, the following: 'She (priestess) imagines the devil (pronounces) mysterious words accompanied by terrible cries and a frightful quivering of the body'.

In the year 1704, the Hindus once again were dissatisfied with François Martin for not allowing them to go on procession during Pongal festival. François Martin, in spite of the assurance given earlier to Sher Khan Lodi that he will not interfere in the religious affairs of Indians, almost succumbed to the pressure exerted by the Jesuits and passed orders once again in 1705 prohibiting the Hindus from gathering in the Vedapuriswaran temple, adjacent to the Jesuit Church. In the night of 5 September 1705, the Jesuits of Pondicherry entered the temple by forcing in the doors. At the time a festival was being celebrated. Several of the Brahmins were beaten with shoes and their hair was pulled. The other men present were treated in the same way. They defiled the idols by urinating upon them and then broke them into pieces.[45]

As a result, there was a general revolt. The coolies and carpenters abandoned their work in the fort, the weavers stopped weaving, the fishermen took to flight, the officials disappeared and the shops were closed. Of these, 2,000 Hindu families left the town. The others numbering about 40,000 were prevented from leaving by the sentries. Many Hindus who had means to live comfortably elsewhere left Pondicherry. The Jesuits even spat at the Hindus and insulted them and their idols at that time. The rising lasted for 12 days. When the Tamils were ready to quit Pondicherry, Father Tachard, the chief of the Jesuits went to the fort and asked François Martin to fire canon balls at the people assembled. The Father suggested that it was a good opportunity to kill them all. The Italian traveller Manucci who was in Pondicherry at that time has recorded all these events in his accounts.

In the face of the passive opposition of the Hindus and their intention to leave the town en masse, if they were not allowed religious freedom, François Martin had no other alternative but to back down from executing his orders to restrict Hindu ceremonies and festivities. Otherwise he ran the risk of losing all the Hindu merchants, weavers and workers, who were essential not just for the commerce of the

French Company, but also for the settlement to prosper on the whole. The weavers alone constituted one-third of the population. Some French missionaries too supported François Martin in this respect and did not want to convert the Hindus forcibly to Christianity.[46]

Besides, in the same year 1705 Father Tachard, the Superior of the Jesuits, along with two other Jesuits, entered another temple (probably the present Manakula Vinayakar temple), which was located near his residence in the White town. They overturned the lamps and removed the ornaments of the idols in the temple. There is no indication that François Martin, the Governor of Pondicherry objected to such indecent and inappropriate behaviour, which would have hurt the feelings of Hindus. There was a sacred temple tank called the 'Mankulam tank' adjoining the temple. This tank had somehow disappeared during the eighteenth century, when the site was occupied by the French. The sacred tank seems to have stood at the site of the building and/or the open space now occupied by the Sri Aurobindo Ashram, adjacent to the Pillaiyar temple. This Pillaiyar tank still existed in 1748.[47]

The Christian brokers, chiefs and *dubashes* of François Martin like Lazaro da Mota or André Mouliapa, in spite of them being designated as the chief of the local people, never seem to have intervened on behalf of the Hindu population of Pondicherry to put an end to the vexations to which the Hindus were subject due to the high-handedness of the French Jesuits especially. Neither did the local Muslim and Maratha rulers who had ceded Pondicherry to the French care to intervene to protect the religious interests of the Indians, both Hindus and Muslims. They were instead the early Indian collaborators, in the political, trade and cultural fronts, which helped the French to consolidate their position in a predominantly Tamil Hindu society.

Besides, religious conversions were taking place in Pondicherry right from the time François Martin set foot there. Already when the State-controlled French East India Company was founded in 1664, it was thought fit that the Company, apart from its commercial ventures, should strive also to propagate the Christian faith among the Gentiles.[48] As a result when the Company's political power was being consolidated by François Martin and his successors in

Pondicherry, the French missionaries, especially the Jesuits, naturally thought it fit to use French political power and influence to bring about conversions to Christianity.

It appears that from the time of the establishment of French power in Pondicherry, preferences were shown especially in the employment and economic fields to those who were Christians or who had embraced Christianity. It was thus that François Martin appointed only Christians and that too mostly higher caste Chrsitians as *Diwans*. The Jesuits actually proposed open preference to Indian Christians in matters of employment and farming to encourage the expansion of Christianity. The French government since François Martin's time generally agreed to implement the proposals of the Jesuits.

But there were obstacles since François Martin's time itself for the spread of Christianity. The first was the caste obstacle. It was the tradition of the Hindus not to allow the lower castes into their temples since olden times. So when Lazaro da Mota built the first church for the Malabars (Tamils), one would naturally expect some form of discrimination or separation between the higher and lower caste converts to Christianity. But in the present state of our knowledge, we do not have any information regarding this phenomenon. In any case, the Capuchin fathers, who were in charge of the first church, did not accept or tolerate any Hindu custom in their churches, as we have seen, unlike the Jesuits. So it is quite possible that there was no separation in this early church between the higher and lower caste converts. Generally speaking the missionaries dismissed the Hindu forms of worship as idolatrous and obscene pagan worship.[49]

There was another major obstacle for the conversion of Hindus to Christianity. Actually the missionaries held the European Christian colonizers responsible for that. India of the eighteenth century was an extremely conservative society and Pondicherry was no exception, as Ananda Ranga Poullé's diary proves amply. Not only the frontiers between the castes and religions were strictly maintained, but the conventions governing sexual relationships were particularly severe and lapses hardly tolerated.

The Portuguese were the first Europeans to come to India. A French Jesuit missionary in a letter dated 1 June 1700, attributed the difficulty of converting the Hindus to the conduct of the Portuguese:

The Portuguese never understood in the beginning the differences between the castes...; they never troubled themselves to differentiate between the high and low castes; they employed freely the paraiahs and fishermen and made use of them to satisfy their various needs. This conduct of the Portuguese shocked the Indians and became very prejudicial to our religion; for they (Hindus) considered thereafterwards the people of Europe as a despicable and miserable lot with whom one cannot deal without dishonouring oneself. If we had taken wise precautions from those very days, as in the Madura for more than a century, it would have been easy to win all these people ... for Jesus Christ.[50]

In another letter dated 30 January 1699, Reverend Martin wrote:

... They (Hindus) have no relationship with the Europeans of whom some by their debauchery and bad examples have spoilt and corrupted the entire Christianity of India. The horror of the Indians for the Europeans has more than one cause. We have often indulged in great violence in their country. They have seen terrible kinds of debauchery and vice of all kinds; but what shakes them particularly is that the Firangis ... drink (alcohol) and eat flesh, regarded by them as horrible and treat those who eat (flesh) and drink as vile.[51]

Even the French Jesuit priest Bouchet, based in Pondicherry, cautioned the missionaries not to identify themselves with the European colonizers, in the following terms: '... All our attention should tend to hide from these people (Indians) that we are what they call 'Firangis'; the smallest doubt that they have in this regard, will be an insurmountable obstacle for the propagation of the (Christian) faith.'

He further held: 'The idolators reasonably perceive the missionaries as persons who want to destroy the religion of the country.... Generally speaking, the Indians, except the Untouchables, hate drunkenness. They never drink liquor that will render them drunken. They actually express against this vice more strongly than our zealous missionaries and this inspires in them partly a great disdain for Europeans.'[52]

Many other missionaries had held that the Hindus of south India were very slow in taking to Christianity because of the extreme aversion and contempt that they had for all foreigners in general, due to the scandals and bad conduct of the Europeans which affected even the small number of conversions obtained during the early period of European colonization of India. It appears then that the early missionaries like Saint Francis Xavier and Robert de Nobili obtained more success in converting some of the local populations, than the missionaries from the time of François Martin.[53]

Thus the missionaries held the European colonizers responsible for the paucity of conversions in southern India. Anyhow, there is certainly a large element of truth in the missionaries' contention that the conduct of the European colonizers made conversions extremely difficult, given the conservative nature of Indian society, though the effect cannot be exactly quantified. Martin or his successors never seems to have worried very much about the conduct of the Europeans. They wanted to spread Christianity by all means, though not at the expense of their commercial interests. On the whole, it could be said that though there were pressures, persuasions and preferences operating on one side to induce conversions, there were on the other side certain cultural and moral aspects like vegetarianism which made conversions difficult.

It is also noteworthy that among the Christian converts during the period of François Martin, the most numerous were the Parayas and not the high caste Hindus. In 1709, there were just 1,100 Chrsitian converts in Pondicherry. These conversions were brought about due to the efforts of both the Capuchin and Jesuit missionaries.

In a letter dated 15 February 1710 by the Governor of Pondicherry, Hébert, who had succeeded Martin, to the Secretary of State (Marine), Pontchartrain, we read: 'Of all the Gentiles (Hindus) who had embraced the Christian faith, the most numerous are Paraiahs, who are more licentious than the others. They get drunk easily; they rob when they can and are very much addicted to lubricity. They imagine still that being Christians – as necessity had pushed many of them to convert – as we are charitable towards them, they do not want to work.'

Thus it is clear from the statements above that the fact of Europeans mixing freely with the parayas who intoxicated themselves became in itself an obstacle for the conversion of the higher castes to the Christian faith. Besides, conversion to Christianity of the Parayas was out of material necessity and not because of some illumination. In fact, the converted Parayas thought that as the French missionaries provided them with the basic necessities charitably, they need not work to eke out a living, as it was the case when they were Hindus. In fact, they seem to have found a sort of freedom through the conversions.

The missionaries also considered the priests or gurus of the Hindus as a major obstacle for the spread of Christianity. In a missionary letter, we read the following:

One of the greatest obstacles in the propagation of the Gospel comes from the gurus – They are venerated like the spiritual Fathers in Europe, the difference being that these gurus have no other work other than amassing money.

Some of them appear to be celibates in public, but they indulge in the greatest licentiousness in secrecy. The others are married. . . .

The Jesuit priest Bouchet, operating in Pondicherry wrote:

. . . the chiefs of the various castes who view the Gospel that we preach to them as the destruction of their laws and customs; the priests of the idols tremble with rage to see their false divinities held in contempt . . . finally the penitents among the Gentiles witness the decrease in alms wherever the faith has struck root; these people get together against us. . . .

The idolators perceive with reason the missionaries as people who want to destroy the religion of the country. The most unworthy tricks and the darkest calumnies are used by the priests of the idols to excite the people and to make them revolt against the missionaries.

Another missionary wrote: 'Nothing here is more contrary to Religion than the caste of the Brahmins. They are the ones who seduce India and who inspires in all these people a hatred for the Christians.'

Thus the European missionaries perceived the gurus, priests and the Brahmins, who were the custodians of the Hindu religion as a major obstacle for the expansion of Christianity in south India since François Martin's governorship of Pondicherry. They accused them of extorting money from the people. Besides, the system of caste itself was an obstacle to the conversions to Christianity as there were not enough Christians for the potential convert to marry and establish a family. Those who converted in spite of this were subjected to ostracism by their very 'idolatrous' parents and driven away from the family without the possibility of communicating with them.[54]

CASTE AND RELIGION IN PONDICHERRY

At François Martin's death in December 1706, the total population of Pondicherry was just about 50,000 persons. Various endogamous castes ranging from the Brahmins, Vellalas (mainly agriculturists, many of them migrants to Pondicherry), Komutti Chettys (Telugu traders, migrants from Andhra), Chettys (Tamil traders, migrants from the south), Kaikollars (ordinary weavers), the Sedars (weavers of fine tissues), Seniyars (silk tissue weavers), Vanniyars (Nayagar, Nayanar, Padayatchi), Pallis (Kavundar) and Parayas (dalits) had their streets or quarters starting from the Vedapuriswaran temple street or Brahmin quarters in the south to the northernmost depressed caste quarters.

Besides, it is claimed that the more intelligent, more wealthy and the more educated among the Pallis became Vanniyars. They were agriculturists and manual labourers. They seem to take pleasure in considering themselves as belonging to high castes, though they have been classified traditionally among the eighteen lower castes. In Pondicherry their numbers were quite considerable even in the eighteenth century. Many of them were *sepoys* during French rule. They assume prestigious titles like Nayagar or Nayakkar (lord), Nayanar (great) or Padayatchi (army chief). There were other castes too like the Telugu Reddis (agriculturists, migrants to the area), the Telugu Cavareys or Balijas, the Idayars (milkmen), Sembadavas (river fishermen), Pattinavas (mukkuwas), Kareyas (fishermen, boatmen) the cotton beaters, the potters, the washermen, the Kammalars (artisan castes) and the Valangamougattars (soldiers of the right-hand castes).

It is strange to note that for the famous diarist Ananda Ranga Poullé, only the Brahmins and the higher castes among the Shudras were 'Tamizhar' or Tamils while the rest were just low castes starting from Palli (presently known as Vanniyars) downwards to the Parayas. He seems to have considered the Telugu caste members, settled in Pondicherry, including the Telugu-speaking Idayar caste to which he belonged as 'Tamizhar', though he did not explicitly state it. Thus the word 'Tamizhar' denoted only the higher castes including the Brahmins till the eighteenth century at least. It was later that it was generalized to include all Tamils of all castes.

It is significant to note that in his voluminous diary, Ananda Ranga Poullé had never used the word 'Hindu' to denote the Tamils or Telugus. Even his contemporary, Maridas Poullé, the pioneer Indologst, hailing from Pondicherry, who preceded even William Jones, had never used the term 'Hindu' in his monumental translation and other works, written in French. Neither did they use the term 'Aryan' and 'Dravidian'. In fact, they were unaware of these words or notions which came into vogue only much later in the nineteenth century due to European scholars and missionaries like Max Müller and Rev. Robert Caldwell, at a time when India was fully colonized and made subservient to the Europeans.

All these castes were hierarchically ranked with the Brahmins at the top and the parayas at the bottom. They were at the same time endogamous. Each caste was functioning in a world of its own. Things have been like that since a very long time. The ideology and belief in the hereditary caste system was not a natural fact. It is a product of man's thought and therefore fundamentally divisive, irrational and viral. The arrival of the Europeans did not change the fundamental characteristics of the caste system. Neither did the Europeans attempt to change it in the territories under their control, though they considered their own culture and religion to be superior. Instead, the Jesuits tolerated it even after the Hindus converted to Christianity, a religion that claimed that all men were equal before God and fraternal, unlike in Hinduism.

Most of these Hindu castes were divided between the right hand and left hand castes. We do not know exactly when such divisions came into existence. But what we know is that they disappeared by the early part of the twentieth century. We know that generally the castes involved in agriculture were the right hand castes while the rest were left hand castes. We also know that the right hand castes were more numerous than the left hand castes.

Those belonging to the left hand were the Chettis, Kamalans and Pallis, while the Valangamugattars, Sembadars, Pattanavas, Cavareys, Vellalas, Agamudaiyas and Idayans belonged to the right hand castes. Valangamugattars or Valangas of the Paraya castes were the warriors of the right hand castes. These Hindus were again divided between worshippers of Shiva and worshippers of Vishnu. Besides the right hand castes had their own temples like the Varadaraja Perumal temple and the Vedapuriswaran temple, while the left hand castes had their temples like the Kalatisparin temple and the Camatchiamman temple within the town.[55]

Thus the Hindus on the whole were a house divided among themselves on the basis of their caste and sectarian beliefs, customs and traditions. They constituted what may be termed as a 'split' civilization. The Brahmins were particularly responsible for such a situation, as they were officiating in the temples and were the traditional religious leaders, gurus and astrologers of the Hindus of the non-polluting 'high' castes, who generally did not take to menial physical work. There was no chance for a common feeling of oneness to emerge in such conditions, in spite of the fact that Hindus were being dominated by Muslim rulers, almost all over India.

Obviously the above multi-layered caste system has nothing to do with the four-fold caste system enunciated in some ancient Hindu scriptures like the *Bhagavad Gita*. The traditional Kshatriya and Vaishya castes of probable Vedic origin, that we find in northern India were completely absent in Pondicherry as well as in the rest of Tamil Nadu. Instead, there were just the Brahmins at the top, the Shudras in the middle and the polluting 'low' castes at the bottom. This in itself shows the late and incomplete penetration of the four-fold Hindu caste system into south India.

Even before the French established themselves in Pondicherry, there were at least four temples in what became Pondicherry town. They were the *Ellaiamman* Kovil or Border Goddess temple, near the present Muslim quarters in the south of Pondicherry town, and the Vedapuriswaran Kovil, lying towards the west of the fort, adjacent to the Jesuit site and the old temple. The old temple was also towards the west of the fort, on the bank of river Uppar which was destroyed in August 1693 by François Martin for reasons that we do not know. All these three were located in the Black town. There was at least one more temple in the White town. It was the Manakula Vinayagar temple, near the then Governor's House (the site of Villa Aroumé and Villa Selvom presently). Manakula is nothing but 'mankulam' which meant 'mud pond'. This mud pond or tank had disappeared, but the temple had survived to this day. To these temples may be added the Draupadiamman Kovil on the northern boulevard. It seems that there was also a temple near the Madras gate.[56]

To the south, almost adjacent to the fort and stretching south-westwards, beyond the Ariyankuppam River or canal, was the Muslim quarter which was called later as Mirapalli. Originally the Muslims seems to have inhabited in the southern part of the town a little away from the seaside. But later in the eighteenth century, they were relocated beyond the canal that separated the White town from the Black town, always towards the south. The Muslims who inhabited there were the Tamil-speaking Sonagars. We do not know if they were descendants of migrants to the area or the descendants of local converts or the descendants of Arab traders and local women. We do not also know their previous caste origins, though some like M. Husain, the late Qazi of Pondicherry, claim that they originally belonged to the Lebbai group of Muslims of the Tamil country. But, there is no factual evidence to attest that. In any case, they were not Rawthers or Marakkayars as they never bore these titles along with their names. Besides, they were Hanafis. At least three mosques and a Muslim grave have been identified in early plans of Pondicherry by the French and the Dutch, towards the south and south-west of the fort.

The name of one of the mosques might have been Mirapalli, which literally meant Mira mosque. This mosque was also known as the Nawab mosque, as it was believed to have been constructed by a Muslim ruler. This mosque might have been removed to the present site of the Mirapalli mosque in the Muslim quarters, during the second half of the eighteenth century, after the destruction of the White town by the English in 1761. Another mosque called the Kutbapalli or the Juma Masjid, which seems to have been originally located in the site towards the south of the fort, seems to have been relocated to the Muslim quarters beyond the canal after 1761. Some stones bearing Persian or Arabic inscriptions that we find even today in the mosque precincts of Mirapalli seem to bear testimony to the fact that the original mosque was built by a Muslim ruler. The Muslim graveyard was originally located towards the south of the site of the present General Hospital, where there was another mosque as shown in the Dutch plans of the 1690s.

There was a small bazaar in Mirapalli, which I think became at least partially the site of bazaar St. Laurent, known later as *Kitchi Kadai* to the Tamils. This *kadai* or bazaar does not exist anymore. Fishermen inhabited areas towards the north and south of the fort, while we find settlements of the depressed castes (Parayas) near the seashore towards the south and north of the fort as well as in an area situated towards the south-west where we find today the General Hospital.[57] These people including the Muslims were the early inhabitants of the sea-side areas, even before the arrival of the French.

Now the question naturally arises about how did one of the mosques acquire the name of Mirapalli. It appears that during the second decade of the eighteenth century, a Tamil Muslim merchant called Chera Mudali Marecan was given land near the old hospital site. This land was allotted subsequently to a mullah of Congimer or Kunimedu around 1738. His name was Sheikh Mira. He seems to have had a hand either in the construction of the mosque in the site allotted to him or he was the mullah in the mosque. Therefore the mosque in which he officiated and the area where he lined became known to the people as Mirapalli. Within the precincts of the Mirapalli mosque today, there is an old tomb. It is quite possible that Sheikh Mira was buried there.[58]

THE LEGACY OF FRANÇOIS MARTIN

From the foregoing it is clear that the French had never come to Pondicherry to melt away into the Indian population and become one of them like the Mughals did earlier. They always maintained their racial, cultural, religious and political identity, in their dealings with the Indians. They never sundered their ties with their homelands. Christianity was the basis of their cultural values. Missionaries were brought into Pondicherry by François Martin to serve first the religious needs of the French colonizers and settlers. In the course of time, the missionaries took to their chosen mission of converting the local Tamil populations to the Christian faith.

François Martin had an inborn penchant for Christianity due to his upbringing and past conditioning. This is quite obvious from the fact that he always appointed Christians as his *dubashes* and interpreters in spite of the fact that the overwhelming majority of the population was Hindu and most of the traders were Hindus. Besides, he was a trader, representing the French Company in India as well as the Governor of Pondicherry, having jurisdiction over its inhabitants, both Indian and European.

During his governorship, the French Jesuit missionaries deployed their zeal to convert the Hindus of the various castes to Christianity, which alone was the true religion for them. François Martin himself was a devout Catholic Chrisitian. Following Colbert's directive, he would have wanted to do his bit for the spread of Christianity in Pondicherry. He employed only Christians as his interpreters or *dubashes*. He allowed the French Capuchin and Jesuit priests to operate freely in Pondicherry and wished to eradicate 'pagan' worship from Pondicherry altogether. Under the influence of the Jesuits François Martin passed several orders to restrict Hinduism in all its forms. He did not stop with that. He even wanted to do away with Islam or at least restrict it in Pondicherry. He was also asked by the Jesuits to destroy the Vedapuriswaran temple, the principal temple of the Hindu higher castes.

François Martin acquiesced to their demands off and on, but very quickly he realized that the Hindus of all categories from the merchants to the weavers and workers would leave the town en masse and boycott the French, if they continued with their intolerant attitude towards the Hindus and their religious customs and ceremonies. François Martin needed them in order to develop the commercial interests of the Company. So due to the threat of mass migration of Hindus to neighbouring territories, François Martin did not carry out his orders to its logical conclusion. He rescinded them to the great dismay of the Jesuits. The passive resistance put up by the Hindus against the highhandedness of the French in Pondicherry during this period, is an early example of the age-old Indian principles of non-cooperation and non-violence in operation.

The Hindus of Pondicherry never took to violence to resist the French. Instead they preferred to boycott them and force them to allow them religious freedom. If the Hindus had remained quiet without reacting non-violently to François Martin's orders, the Jesuits would have probably wiped out Hinduism from Pondicherry, with the helping hand of François Martin. But as the French were dependent on the Hindus to trade profitably, Martin refrained from taking stern measures against the Hindus. He would not employ force or violence to convert the Hindus to Christianity. Instead, he allowed the Jesuits to continue with their proselytizing missions, in which of course they were successful to some extent, in spite of the caste obstacle.

The Christian *dubashes* of François Martin, though they were theoretically the chiefs of all the Tamils, never interceded with François Martin, in order to solve the religious problems created for the Hindus by the Jesuits. Instead, they were mute spectators of such problematic events. This shows that they did not have much influence either with the Hindus or with the French in this matter. It is hardly possible to say that they represented all Indians. Their relationship with the French seems to have been restricted to trade. They were not in any sort of partnership with the French on the basis of equality. They were rather at the service of the French. Besides, they owed their position most certainly to the fact that they were Christians. If they indulged in any anti-Christian activities they ran the risk of losing their jobs. Otherwise, there was obviously certain interdependence between the French and the Indian merchants, artisans and weavers, which was mutually profitable in the trade and economic domain.

It is also noteworthy that during François Martin's rule in Pondicherry, he and the territory under his control did not face any threat to its existence from the Mughal or Maratha rulers, who rarely interfered in the local affairs of Pondicherry. He managed to steer clear of all conflicts with them and trade profitably and even expand his territory through gifts and acquisitions from the nawabs and kings, in spite of the fact that he was at logger-heads with the Hindus on the question of religious practices in Pondicherry. The Muslim Nawabs hardly interfered in the religious problems faced by the Hindus in Pondicherry.

François Martin fell sick when he was 73 years old. He was treated by the famous Italian Niccolao Manucci and the French Company doctors, Maqari and Albert. Though cured, he succumbed a few months later on 31 December 1706. He was buried in the old chapel premises of the fort, which stood at the intersection of Rue de la Monnaie (presently Rue Victor Simonel) and Rue St. Ange. Even François Martin's wife was buried at the same place. Martin's funeral oration was recited by Father Laurent of Angouleme, a Capuchin missionary of Pondicherry, who glorified him for the first time as the founder of Pondicherry. Angouleme wrote in the church register the following: 'Today the 31st Xbre 1706, I have buried in the fortress of Fort St. Louis of Pondicherry, Mr. François Martin, Knight and Governor of Pondicherry after receiving all the sacraments of the church. Pondicherry owes to him what it is today.'[59]

Thus the myth was created thenceforth that François Martin was the founder of Pondicherry. François Martin himself had never laid claim to such status. As a matter of fact, Pondicherry had existed at least since fifteenth century as pointed out by Sulaiman al Mahri. It is pure fantasy to assume like some twentieth century French scholars like Julien Vinson and Jouveau-Dubreuil that the Pondicherry town of today was the Poduké, mentioned by Ptolemy some two thousand years ago and equate the seasonal mart of Arikamedu with Pondicherry town.

It was Muthu Krsihnappa Nayakar of Senji who allowed the Portuguese to establish their godown in Pondicherry town in the sixteenth century. François Martin was not even the first Frenchman to set foot in Pondicherry. It was Bellanger de Lespinay. However, François Martin can be deemed to be the founder and developer of 'modern' Pondicherry. In this he was ably assisted by certain Frenchmen like Pierre Deltor, engineers like Denyon and Father Louis as well as his Tamil *dubashes*. The Dutch too had contributed their bit to develop modern Pondicherry.

When François Martin died, it seems that he left a beautified town. But the houses were still very low and the roads were badly paved or not paved at all. The town was prone to inundation during the rainy season. The moat around the wall encircling the town retained foul water, whose stench was all pervading. The sea was quite far away at that time.

Fort St. Louis had ceased to exist after 1761, when the English methodically razed to the ground, the entire White town. With this destruction, the tomb of François Martin too was destroyed. No French Governor tried to restore the tomb later. As a result, nobody knows the exact location where he was buried. However, François Martin was buried within Fort St. Louis, at the intersection of Rue de la Monnaie and Rue St. Ange most certainly in front of the General Hospital of Pondicherry. There is no monument erected to commemorate the memory of François Martin or to indicate to the curious passerby that the builder of modern Pondicherry was buried there during the winter day of 31 December 1706. This site today is a garden called Bharati *Poonga* or Bharati Park. Subramania Bharati was a Tamil and Indian nationalist and poet, who had spent ten years in Pondicherry from 1908 to 1918.[60] This nomenclature overrides a historical fact, intimately related to the very foundation of modern Pondicherry.

When François Martin was in charge of Pondicherry from 1674 to 1706, there was turmoil and upheavals all around Pondicherry and in south India. The Mughal Emperor Aurangzeb's troops had marched up to Senji after conquering Bijapur and Golconda, where they confronted the Marathas. François Martin prudently steered clear off the internecine quarrels between the Indian princes and concentrated on expanding and organizing Pondicherry to augment his trade prospects. He did not take the side of one prince against another. His prime concern was not to conquer territories, but to trade peacefully and profitably. It is quite noteworthy that the Pondicherry region became a French colony not through conquest or use of force, but through outright purchase of territories by Captain Deltor and François Martin. Actually the territory belonged to the French East India Company. Even Chandernagore and other small outposts were acquired peacefully through purchases and cessions. But François Martin was prepared to defend Pondicherry, from any external encroachment. That is why he built Fort St. Louis. He did not wage any war in the Indian soil. But he prepared for future wars to be waged by his successors.

Today in Pondicherry François Martin's name is almost forgotten. There is still a road in his name that had come into existence during French rule. Formerly this road was known as Rue des Gouverneurs. Later it was renamed after François Martin as Rue François Martin. But nobody is aware of the history behind that name. Nobody is also aware that François Martin was one of the principal builders of 'modern' Pondicherry.

NOTES

1. More, *From Arikamedu to the Foundation of Modern Pondicherry*, 2014, pp. 81, 88-9; *ARP Diary*, I, pp. 6, 119; IV, 44, 140; N. Poullé, *Histoire Détaillée des Rois du Carnatic*, 1939, pp. 39-44.
2. Esquer. *Essai sur les Castes dans l'Inde*, Pondichéry, 1870; Anquetil Duperron, *Législation Orientale*, 1778.
3. Fr. 6231, f. 8, BNF; Martineau, *Dupleix et l'Inde Française*, 1923, p. 7; Launay, *Histoire des Missions de l'Inde*, I, lxxiiif; Love, *Vestiges of Old Madras*, I, pp. 330, 336; Vinson, *Les Français dans l'Inde, Dupleix et Labourdonnais*, 1894, p. lxxxiii; Henri Carré. *François Martin, Fondateur de l'Inde française, 1665-1706*, p. 79; Oubagarasamy, *Un Livre de Compte de Ananda Ranga Poullé*, pp. xiv, xv; Boudriot, *Compagnie des Indes, 1720-1770*, Paris, 1983, pp. 83, 248; Anquetil Duperron, *Recherche Historique et Géographique sur l'Inde*, 1783, p. 234; *Mémoire de François Martin, fondateur de Pondichéry (1665-1694)*, I, pp. 482, 555-7.
4. Oubagarasamy, ibid., p. xv.
5. *Mémoire de François Martin*, ibid. II, p. 154.
6. Ibid. II, p. 547, 554; III, pp. 68-71; Martineau, Dupleix et l'Inde Française, 1923, p. 7; Martineau, *Résumé des actes de l'état-civil de Pondichéry*, II, p. 21.
7. Launay, op. cit., I, xxx; Norbert, *Mémoires Utiiles et Nécessaire...*, 1742, p. 104; Sebastian, *Puduchery Mudal Governor François Martin Vazhkai Varalaru*, 2000, pp. 118, 193-6, 231; Jacques Weber, Review of Hallet, Anne-Sophie's 'Les Malabars Chrétiens dans La Mission du Carnate au XVIIIème siècle', 1995, p. 8; Cf. also Hallet, 'Les Malabars Chrétiens dans La Mission du Carnate au XVIIIème Siècle'.
8. Fr. 25286. BNF – Relation Historique de l'Eglise de Pondichéry par le Père d'Epernay, Capucin, p. 6; Launay, ibid., I, pp. xxx, xxxi; Love, op. cit., I, p. 336; Vinson, op. cit., 1894, p. xv; *Mémoires de François Martin*, I, p. 600; More, op. cit., pp. 102, 122, 124; Jouveau Dubreuil, 'Plan de Pondichéry en 1699', *RHEP*, 9ème volume, p. 262.
9. Launay, ibid. p. xxx; Cf. map of R.P. Faucheux; Norbert, op. cit., 1742, pp. xix, 104, 171, 225, 226, 278; Vinson, ibid. p. 12.
10. Vinson, ibid. pp. 20, 21; Correspondence du Conseil Supérieur de Pondichéry et de la Compagnie, I, p. 56; II, p. 11; III, pp. xvii, xviii; Launay, ibid., p. xvii; De Closets d'Errey, *Précis Chronologique de l'Histoire de l'Inde Française*, 1934, p. 22.
11. Launay, ibid., p. lxxiiif; Fr. 6231, f. 20, BNF.
12. Vinson, op. cit., see Introduction; De Closets d'Errey, *Histoire de l'Inde Française, 1664-1814*, 1940, p. 64; Lernie-Bouchet, 'Les Modeliars de la

Region de Saint-Thome, Caste: Savalla Velaja: Un Essai de Généalogie', pp. 99-102.
13. De Closets d'Errey, ibid. 1940, p. 65; Lernie-Bouchet, ibid., pp. 100-1; Gaudart, *Catalogue*. . ., 1931, p. 169; *Annuaire des Etablissements Français dans l'Inde*, 1938-9, p. 107
14. *Almanach de Pondichéry*, 1839, p. 52; Lernie-Bouchet, ibid. pp. 99-102.
15. Gaudart, ibid. 1931, p. 169.
16. Norbert, op. cit., 1742, pp. 278, 281; Annuaire des Etabliseements Français dans l'Inde, 1938-9, p. 110.
17. De Closets d'Errey, op. cit., 1940, pp. 61-3; Cultru, *Dupleix, ses plans politiques, sa disgrâce*, 1901, pp. 6, 212; De Closets d'Errey, *Revue Historique de Pondichéry*, XIV, 1981-6.
18. Martineau, *Résumé des actes de l'état-civil de Pondichéry de 1676 à 1735*, I, pp. 2, 4; *Procés-Verbaux des délibérations du Conseil Supérieur de Pondichéry*, I, p. 5.
19. Martineau, ibid., pp. 2, 4.
20. Ibid., pp. 2, 4.
21. More, op. cit., 2014, p. 193; Martineau, ibid., I, p. 21; Fr. 6231, f. 8, BNF; Launay, op. cit., I, lxxiiif; Procés-Verbaux des délibérations du Conseil Supérieur de Pondichéry, II, 1914, Ier Septembre 1738; *Mémoires de François Martin*, II, pp. 547, 554.
22. More, ibid., 2014, p. 124; Vinson, op. cit., pp. xviii, 21; Launay, ibid., I, pp. xviii, xli, 7-8, 117; Fr. 6231, f. 25, etc. BNF; Lernie-Bouchet, op. cit., Cf. also Map of Faucheux; Donation par Maria Diaz, 8 Fév. 1700, vol. 990, Pondichéry, p. 479, AME; Donation par une Indienne d'un emplacement pour la Procure, 3 Mars 1700, Pondichéry, p. 270, vol. 963. AME; *ARP Diary*, IX, pp. 81-2.
23. Vinson, ibid., p. 21; Launay, ibid. I, pp. xvii, xxiv, xxxi, xlviii; Map of R.P. Faucheux, 1690; *Mémoires de François Martin*, III, pp. 149, 233; Valentino, *Notes sur l'Inde,* Paris, 1906, pp. 202-6.
24. Vinson, ibid., p. 21; Correspondance du Conseil Supérieur de Pondichéry et de la Compagnie, I, p. 56; Launay, ibid., xxxvi.
25. Map of Faucheux, 1690 in Labernadie, *Le Vieux Pondichéry (1753-1815); Missions Catholiques Françaises dans l'Inde*, 1943, p. 4; Launay, ibid., I, p. xxxii; Mémoires de François Martin, III, pp. 149; 238; Kaeppelin, *Les Origines de l'Inde Française*, 1908, p. 554; Weber, Review of Hallet, Anne-Sophie's 'Les Malabars Chrétiens dans La Mission du Carnate au XVIIIème siècle', 1995, p. 7.
26. Gnanou Diagou, *Arrêts du Conseil Supérieur de Pondichéry*, II, p. 141; III, p. 365; IV, p. 161; Lernier-Bouchet, op. cit.; Alalasundaram, *The Colonial World of Ananda Ranga Pillai, 1736-1761*, 1998, p. 34.
27. Launay, ibid. I, pp. xlii, xliii, 161; Gaebelé, 'Ariancoupam, Terre d'Histoire

et de Prière'. *Revue Historique de l'Inde Française.* 8ème volume, 1952, p. 6; *Annuaire des Etablissements Français dans l'Inde, 1938-39*, pp. 107, 110; Inde Française – Notariat, Inde 237, 1893-5; Inde 256, 1910, AOM, Aix en Provence.

28. Malleson, *Dupleix*, 2001, pp. 19-22; *Mémoires de François Martin*, III, pp. 3, 6, 27, 125, 310, 341, 344, 356, 360, 533, 549; *Annuaire des Etablissements Français dans l'Inde*, 1938-9, p. 50; Vinson, op. cit., p. 11; Deloche, *Origins of the Urban Development of Pondicherry*, 2004, p. 26; Cultru, *Dupleix, ses plans politiques, sa disgrâce*, 1901, p. 90.
29. Deloche, ibid. pp. 31, 36-44; *Mémoires de François Martin*, III, p. 10; Sebastian, op. cit., 2000, p. 145; cf. Dutch plan of Pondicherry in 1693.
30. Fr. 6231, f. 25, BNF.
31. Lettre du 20 Septembre 1717, Pondichéry, p. 581, vol. 991, AME; C² 67, f. 143-5, 10 Fév 1704, A.N.; Kaeppelin, op. cit., Ch. 11, pp. 507, 653; Lettre du 2 Octobre 1704, C² 67, f. 130, A.N.; Fr. 6231, f. 25, 29, 30, BNF; Cf. also, C² 67, f. 137-8, A.N.; Haudrère, 'The Compagnie des Indes Orientales', 1990, p. 32.
32. Launay, op. cit., I, xxxi; Cf. also map of R.P. Faucheux, 1690; Castonnet des Fosses, op. cit., pp. 112-13; Vinson, op. cit., p. 12; Naf, 9354, f. 76, BNF.
33. Haudrère, op. cit., p. 32; Antony, *Gazetteer of India*, I, p. 2; De Closets d'Errey, *Précis Chronologique de l'Histoire de l'Inde Française*, 1934, pp. 14-16; *Procès-Verbaux des délibérations du Conseil Supérieur de Pondichéry, I, 1911*, pp. 14, 30, 78-9, 146.
34. Lettre de Rév. Tachard au Père Trévou, Chandernagore, 18 Janvier 1711, LEC, vol. 12, p. 7.
35. Mémoires de François Martin, I, pp. 359-63, 419, 448, 451, 467, 503; II, p. 231; Sottas, *Histoire de la Compagnie Royale des Indes Orientales*, 1905, p. 396; Richards, *The New Cambridge History of India – The Mughal Empire*, 1993, p. 241.
36. Malleson, op. cit., p. 22; Kaeppelin, op. cit., pp. 507, 653.
37. Gaebelé, *Créole et Grande Dame, Johanna Begum, Marquise Dupleix*, 1934, p. 4; Haudrère, *La Compagnie Française des Indes au XVIIIe siècle*, I, p. 305.
38. Hallet, 'Les Malabars Chrétiens dans La Mission du Carnate au XVIIIème Siècle', pp. 66-76, 77, 78; Fr. 25286, ff. 18-46, BNF; Norbert, *Mémoires Historiques...*, 1744, pp. 411, 565.
39. Weber, op. cit., p. 8; K.S. Mathew, 'French Missionaries, Tamil Catholics and Social Changes in Pondicherry (1674-1793)', 2006, pp. 290-4, 297-301; Yule, Burnell, Hobson-*Jobson*, 1994, p. 542.
40. Francis Richard, 'Les Missions Catholiques', 1995, pp. 70-1; Castonnet des Fosses, *L'Inde Française avant Dupleix*, Paris, 1887, pp. 147-8; Norbert, op. cit., 1749, I, pp. 48-9, 50, 52, 53, 65, 156-7, 257.

41. Naf. 6557, Lettre de M. Signard, Procureur du Roi à Pondichéry à l'Abbé Defourment, 1 Octobre 1778, LEC, vol. 10 Paris, MDCCLXXXI, pp. xiij, xvi, xiv, xvij-xviij; Hallet, op. cit., pp. 8-12; Remarques présentées au Pape Clément XI, pp. 665-6, vol. 990, AME; Kaeppelin, op. cit., pp. 556-7; Naf, 8871, Père Coeurdoux sur la religion et la langue hindoue, BNF; Naf 9114, Grammaire de la langue Malabare, BNF.
42. Oubagarasamy, op. cit., p. xvi; Castonnet des Fosses, *L'Inde Française au XVIIIème siècle*, Paris, s.d., p. 108.
43. LEC, 2000, pp. 53-4, 63, 64, 69, 129-31.
44. Vinson, op. cit., p. 55.
45. Manucci, *Storia Do Mogor*, IV, p. 214; Fr. 6231, f. 32, BNF; Isabelle & Jean Louis Vissière (eds.), *Lettres Edifiantes et Curieuses. . .*, S-Seine, 2000, p. 64.
46. Fr. 6231, f. 27, 29, 30, 35-7, 41; Naf, 9225, f. 292-5, BNF; More, op. cit., 2014, pp. 130-4; Vinson, op. cit., pp. 31-2; Deputation du Père Cima, 8 Septembre 1705, vol. 970, AME; Manucci, ibid., IV, p. 215.
47. Fr. 6231, f. 41, BNF; *ARP Diary*, V, p. 38; VIII, pp. 182-3.
48. Mss. Fr. 8972, Déclaration du Roy, 1664, LEC, tom 10, Paris, 1781, p. ix.
49. Mss. Fr. 6231, Mémoires des Jésuites, fl. 46-7, BNF: Launay, I, op. cit., 1898, xxxii, xxxiii; Relation d'un Voyage que le Père Maudui a fait à l'ouest de Carnate en 1701, *Lettre Edifiantes et Curieuses des Jésuites de l'Inde au dix-huitième siècle*, ed. Isabelle & Jean-Louis Vissière, S-Seine, 2000, p. 69.
50. Lettre de Père Martin, Missionaire de la Compagnie de Jésus au Père de Gobien de la même Compagnie, Royaume de Madura, 1 June 1700, *LEC*, tome 10, Paris, Mérigot, 1781, pp. 66-71.
51. Lettre de Père Martin, Missionaire de la Compagnie de Jésus au Père de Vilette de la m^me Compagnie, Balasore, 30 January 1699, *LEC*, tome 10, Paris, Mérigot, 1781, pp. 44-6.
52. Lettre du Père de Bourges, Jésuite à Madame La Comtesse de Sondé, Mission de Maduré, 21 Septembre 1713, LEC, tome 12, Paris, Mériogt, 1781, p. 777; See also LEC, tome 10, Paris, Mérigot, 1781, Preface; Lettre du Père Bouchet au Père de la même Compagnie Jésuite, LEC, tome 13, MDLCLXXXI, pp. 45, 50.
53. Origine, Progrès et Etat Actuel de la Mission Française du Carnate dans les Indes Orientales, 26 May 1802, vol. 996, AME; Lettre de l'Evêque de Tabraca du 14 Octobre 1777, Pondichéry à M. Alari, prêtre et Directeur du Séminaire des Missions Etrangères à Paris, vol. 995, AME; Lettre de M. Dubois, Missionaire à M. Boiret, 26 May 1802, Pondichéry, vol. 996, AME; Lettre du Père Saignes à Sainte Hyacinthe, 3 July 1736, Attipakkam, *LEC*, tome 14, Paris, Mérigot, 1781, p. 41.
54. Paul Olagnier, Les Jésuites à Pondichéry et l'Affaire Naniapa (1705 à 1720), Paris, 1932, p. 16; Mss. NAF 9364, Lettre de M. Hébert, Pondichéry,

12 Février 1709, BNF; Isabelle and Jean Louis Vissière, eds., *Lettres Edifiantes et Curieuses*..., S-Seine, 2000, p. 64; Lettre du Père Bouchet, Jésuite au Père de la même Compagnie, *LEC*, tome 13, Paris, Merigot, MDCC LXXI, pp. 22-4, 45, 50; Lettre du Père Le Caron, Jésuite à Mme. Les Sœurs Religieuses Ursulines, de la Mission de Carnate, 20 Novembre 1720, *LEC*, tome 13, Paris, MDCC LI, pp. 201-11; Lettre du Père Calmette, Jésuite à M. Le marquis de Coetlogoen, Vice Amiral de France, Ballapuram, Carnatic, 28 September 1930, *LEC*, tome 13, Paris, Merigot, MDCCLI, S-Seine, 2000, pp. 342-62; Lettre du Père Lle Gac à M. le Chevalier Hébert, Gouverneur de Pondichéry, Krishnapuram, 10 Décembre 1718, *LEC*, vol. VIII, Toulouse, 1810, pp. 113-14.

55. Castonnet des Fosses, op. cit., 1887, p. 144; Vinson, *Les Castes au Sud de l'Inde*, 1868, pp. 12-35; Esquer, *Essai sur les Castes dans l'Inde*, Pondichéry, 1870, pp. 116-19, 127, 128; *Almanach de Pondichéry*, 1834, pp. 34, 35, 36; 1838, pp. 31, 32: Sebastian, op. cit., 2000, p. 202; Vinson, op. cit., 1894, pp. 71f, 290f, 292f; Alalasundaram, op. cit., 1998, p. 10; *ARP Diary*, I, p. 153; Arjun Appadorai, 'Right and Left Hand Castes in South India', *Indian Economic and Social History Review*, 1974; cf. also J.A. Dubois, J.A. *Hindu Manners, Customs and Traditions*, Oxford, 1906; J.B.P. More (ed.), *La Civilisation Indienne et les Fables Hindoues du Panchatantra de Maridas Poullé*, Pondichéry, 2004; J.B.P. More, *Maridas Poullé of Pondicherry, 1725-1796: A Pioneer of Modern Indological Studies and the First Modern exponent of Indian philosophy, Religion and Literature*, Pondicherry, 2004.

56. Launay, op. cit., I, pp. xxviii-xxix; Vinson, op. cit., 1894, pp. 11, 29, 30; *ARP Diary*, IX, p. 62.

57. Gaudart, *La Criminalité dans les Etablissements Français de l'Inde*, pp. 69, 172; Deloche, op. cit., 2004, p. 19; See map of Pondicherry, 1693; *ARP Diary*, IX, pp. 359-60; Launay, op. cit., I, p. xxviii; Antony, op. cit., I, p. 532; Bourdat, *Les Grandes Pages du "Journal" d'Ananda Ranga Pillai*, p. 141; cf. also Dutch plan of Pondicherry as well as French plans before 1715; J.B.P. More, 'Hindu-Christian Interaction during French rule in Pondicherry', in J.B.P. More, *Religion and Society in South India*, Tellicherry, 2006, pp. 71-105.

58. Interview with Mr. M. Mubeen of Pondicherry; *Procés-Verbaux des délibérations du Conseil Supérieur de Pondichéry*, III, 3 Juin 1738, ed. Gaudart.

59. Mss. NAF, 9352, fl. 286, 287, BNF; J.B.P. More, *From Arikamedu to the Foundaion of Modern Pondicherry*, Chennai, 2014, pp. 108-9.

60. Cf. J.B.P. More, *L'inde Face à Bharati: Le Poète Rebelle*, Tellicherry, 2003; Yvonne Robert Gaebelé, Créole et Grande Dame, Johanna Begum, Marquise Dupleix, Paris, 1934, p. 4.

CHAPTER 2

French Intolerance, 1706-1721

EVENTS LEADING TO THE MARTYRDOM OF *DUBASH* NAINIAPPA

FRENCH HISTORIANS GENERALLY think that the death of François Martin was a great misfortune to the development of Pondicherry. Martin was succeeded by a certain Dulivier who functioned as Interim Governor until the arrival of Chevalier Hébert from France who took over as Governor. Under Dulivier and Hébert, revenue from trade took a downturn. Besides, Dulivier failed to cultivate the agricultural land under French control, which was a source of revenue since François Martin's time.[1] It seems that this situation was not entirely of Dulivier's making, though he had been viewed by some as incapable.

Even after François Martin's death, Lazaro da Mota continued to be the Company's *dubash*. The Jesuits supported Lazaro da Mota to stay in that position as he was a Christian. The Jesuits were not just missionaries. They were also businessmen. It was suspected that they wanted to take over the commerce of the French Company through Lazaro da Mota. The latter's position as *Mudaliar* was a powerful one as he was the sole intermediary between the merchants, weavers and artisans. He was the interpreter, the drafter of contracts and guarantor of Tamil farming, besides being chief of the Indians.[2]

But during that period Lazaro da Mota was becoming known for his incompetence, probably due to old age. His relationship with the predominantly Hindu merchants and weavers as well as with the Indian powers seems to have been inadequate, probably due to his Portuguese origin. This was not very conducive to the interests of the Company. Besides, he reported all his commercial dealings faithfully to the Jesuits and their head, Father Tachard, which he was not supposed to do. He seems to have known, however, that with the Jesuits help he could continue to be the *Mudaliar*.[3] Dulivier did nothing to remedy this.

But Chevalier Hébert, who succeeded Dulivier in 1708, was not of the same type as Dulivier. Right from the beginning, he was for freedom for everyone to follow his own customs and manners. Nawab Daoud Khan was reminding the French at that time to respect the religion of the Hindus in Pondicherry. Hébert fired Lazaro da Mota and replaced him with Nainiappa Poullé, the Telugu Hindu merchant from Madras, settled in Pondicherry since some time. His house stood just opposite to the Vedapuriswaran temple.

Nainiappa belonged to the Idayar caste, which was placed lower in the then caste hierarchy, in which the Brahmins and Vellalas were placed at the top. But Nainiappa was considered to be highly competent as he had established a smooth relationship with the Indian merchants, weavers and others as well as with the Indian powers. In the year 1708, the corporation of Company merchants wanted to increase the price of cotton goods to Europe by 12 per cent. Nainiappa Pillai came to the rescue of the French Company in Pondicherry. He obtained the goods at a lower price and allowed the Company to defeat the collusive designs of its distributors. Another time, the Company was unable to sell its coral merchandise, Lazaro da Mota too was unable to help the Company. It was Nainiappa who stepped in, and using his relations and influence, sold the corals at a good price. It was also due to the help of Nainiappa that the lands were farmed out, which procured considerable revenue. It was due to such services rendered by Nainiappa to the Company, that the new Governor Chevalier Hébert nominated him as the *Mudaliar* or *dubash*, though he was a Hindu, in place of Lazaro da Mota who had the unflinching support of the Jesuits and Father Tachard. This choice was necessitated by the development of trade and the augmentation of the population who were mainly Hindu. Nainiappa was better placed than Lazaro da Mota to strike advantageous commercial relationships for the Company due to his caste and probity. They also needed him to administer the town as chief of the Malabars. The Jesuits had no influence on Nainiappa.[4]

In spite of opposition from the French Jesuits, Governor Hébert backed Nainiappa with all his authority, for the sake of commerce. He declared the freedom to trade on the payment of the customary duties and the freedom to follow one's own customs and beliefs. The

Jesuits led by Father Tachard, accused Nainiappa of being an idolator, unfit to be a *Mudaliar*. But Hébert was determined to undermine the power of the Jesuits too. He accused them of interfering in the affairs of the Company needlessly. He also accused them of tolerating certain Hindu practices of the converted Christians, which the Jesuits had resorted to since 1703 at least in order to attract converts to Christianity.[5]

Around that time in 1708, Governor Hébert seems to have got reconfirmed the cession of Ariyankuppam and also obtained the cession of Murungapakkam village from Nawab Daoud Khan. Murungapakkam was located between Pondicherry and Ariyankuppam.[6] Nainiappa seems to have played a role in such territorial procurements using his influence with the nawab and preventing him from demanding more money. Governor Hébert also reminded the charitable dispositions of Nainiappa who even gave free oil to the missionaries and also helped the miserable Tamil Christians. He genuinely feared that if Nainiappa was removed from his post as *dubash*, the Muslim nawabs would attack Pondicherry while the farmers and others would leave Pondicherry.

In the year 1709, the French Governor intervened favourably in the matter concerning the construction of a small hall within the precincts of the temple on Madras road. In the same year, the Jesuits blocked the road leading to the small Pillaiyar (Ganesh) temple in the White town. They held that the Hindus assembled in this temple every night to perform the rituals in honour of the elephant-headed God Pilliayar and complained that this disturbed their tranquility very much and therefore they had to block the road. Governor Hébert intervened and got the small temple which stood in the middle of the road destroyed by the Hindus themselves in the year 1710 and then opened up the road blocked by the Jesuits. This temple seems to have been rebuilt later on the side of the road where it stands even today. Apparently the Jesuits were not happy with the actions of Governor Hébert.[7]

Besides, Governor Hébert solved the conflict between the right hand and left hand castes, with regard to caste rights and ownership of the Vedapuriswaran temple. He allowed the left hand castes who were Telugu Komutti Chettys to construct a new temple called the Kalatiswaran temple, a little towards the north of Mission Street.

Devadasis (temple dancing girls) were attached to this temple. It was also during Hébert's governorship that permission was given to the Hindus to construct the Varadaraja Perumal temple in Madras Street, as a sort of compensation for the temple that was destroyed in 1693 during François Martin's time.[8]

Unable to get Governor Hébert to toe their lines, the Jesuits complained to the King's Council in France. The French king and his Council through a decision dated 14 February 1711 expected the Governor of Pondicherry to reserve the post of *Mudaliar* in Pondicherry always for a Christian and to remove Nainiappa from that post at once; to demolish the Vedapuriswaran temple; to give six months to Nainiappa to convert to the Christian faith or else to replace him with a Christian; to prevent the Hindus from taking out their temple processions which would be detrimental to Christianity, to leave the Hindus with just two temples, the Vedapuriswaran temple and the Varadaraja Perumal temple at the intersection of the weaver's street and the Grand bazaar or Madras road; to drive the Temple *devadasis* who were 'prostitutes' out of Pondicherry, to give preference in employment and farming to the Christians in order to attract the Hindus to Christianity; to give equal status to the Christian merchants with the Hindu merchants; to exhort the Company employees to employ Christian valets; to punish any Hindu who would prevent the conversion of Hindus to Christianity; to permit the Jesuits to construct a new chapel in Ariyankuppam; to prevent the sale of Christian slaves to heretics; Muslims and Hindus; to prevent the Untouchables whether Christians or Hindus to wear European dresses as it was an insult to Christianity and the French nation.

But the order with regard to Nainiappa was never executed by Governor Hébert as he was dependent upon Nainiappa for whatever little trade that occurred in Pondicherry during that period when the Company was in dire financial straits.[9] Though Hébert was against the Jesuits as far as the appointment of Nainiappa was concerned, he did not turn his back on the Jesuits completely. On 31 August 1714, he gave them land on behalf of the Company, according to the wishes of the French king, in the Ariyankuppam village near the old church where they built a fairly big church. This naturally seems to have contributed to more conversions in the area in the course of time.

When Chevalier Hébert arrived in Pondicherry as Governor, there were about 1,000 or 1,100 converts to Christianity in Pondicherry. But Hébert expressed his doubts about the progress of Christianity there due mainly to the caste obstacle. Hereditary caste usages and customs were deeply embedded in the Hindu psyche. Even the king had no power over the castes, which functioned autonomously on the basis of occupations generally. The Hindus, especially the 'noble' Brahmins always looked upon the 'white people' with suspicion and dismissed them as the horrible 'Firangis' due mainly to their moral depravity, violence, debauchery, licentious behaviour, their excessive consumption of alcohol, and other vices contrary to their religion. They would not tolerate the Europeans mixing with the Parayas, the lowest in the caste hierarchy, as well as with the other castes on an equal footing. Most of the higher castes equated the Europeans with the Parayas. Unlike the Hindus, the Muslims generally held the Christian religion in high respect. However there was hardly any instance when a Muslim converted to Christianity either in François Martin's time and even much later.[10]

Chevalier Hébert was the first person to envisage the education of girls in Pondicherry in the year 1710. Of course he was concerned only about European girls. But the idea of a girl's education seems to have sprouted in his mind first. Even before him, since 1703 the Jesuits under Father Tachard had taken to educate young Indians. Tachard especially wanted the government to open schools for young Indians. It is significant to note that it was in the Jesuit school, established by Père Tachard and his likes that the pioneer Indologist, Maridas Poullé of Pondicherry was educated and trained.[11] But Governor Hébert consistently sought to reduce the power of the Jesuits. He wanted to remove education from the hands of the Jesuits too.

Rev. Tachard, the Superior of the Jesuits had died in the year 1712 in Bengal. But the students studying under the Jesuits caused trouble to the Hindus by breaking their jars and cooking ustensils, and throwing stones on their temples. The caste headmen complained several times about such acts to the Governor.[12] It must not be forgotten that the Jesuits were continuously deploying their efforts to convert the Tamils to Christianity at that time. Famines, drought and the cholera epidemic which continued to prevail in Pondicherry and its neighbourhood during that period seems to have contributed to some extent to the spike in conversions.[13]

On 14 February 1711, the king of France decided to prohibit the Hindu caste headmen from indulging in ceremonies in their temples during Easter, the day of the Holy Sacrament, Ascension, the feast of Saint Louis, Sundays, All Souls Day and Christmas. Ceremonies were also prohibited on New Moon day if it fell on a Sunday. Music was also prohibited on Sundays if it was a burial day.[14]

Meanwhile Governor Hébert was called back to France due to the debts that he had incurred in Pondicherry. Dulivier reached Pondicherry on 7 October 1712 to replace Hébert. Following Hébert, Dulivier too refused to replace Nainiappa. But he was aware of the desires of the French king and the Company. However he would not precipitate the destruction of the temples and mosques which would irritate the Tamils and Muslims. Instead he preferred to adopt a gradual method like not allowing any repairs to be done in them. As a result, Dulivier summoned the chief of the Moors and the Tamil Chulias (Muslims) and reproached them for having white-washed their mosques without permission and prohibited them not to undertake any repairs in their mosques in future without his permission.[15]

Meanwhile the Jesuits were insistant on the reinstatement of their favourite, Lazaro da Mota, as *dubash*. Dulivier finally found a compromise solution by nominating a Tamil Christian called Saveri as co-*mudaliar* to assist Nainiappa, with the same powers, prerogatives and honours as Nainiappa. Dulivier continued to hold that Nainiappa was indispensable for business as he had wide contacts with Indian merchants and the local rulers, unlike Lazaro da Mota who was old and incapable. The French Jesuits were not happy with Dulivier's position and were waiting for an occasion to execute their plans to make Pondicherry free of Hinduism.[16]

On 9 March 1714, the Superior Council of Pondicherry, following the directives of the French king in 1711 and due to the pressure from the Jesuits, decided to implement those preceding measures ordered by the king. They especially wanted to maintain the Vedapuriswaran temple and the Perumal temple, with the freedom to perform sacrifices there two or three times a week, except during Easter, Sundays, the Ascension Day, the Holy Sacrament day,

Assumption, All Saints day and Christmas. They wanted to prohibit the construction of new temples. Above all they wanted the replacement of Nainiappa with a Christian *Mudaliar*, if he did not convert within six months.[17]

On 16 September 1714, the Superior Council of Pondicherry resolved to promulgate the decisions of the king of France of 14 February 1711. The caste headmen asked for eight days to respond to it. Given the impending danger to their way of life, the Hindus on their part seem to have taken some steps towards the intolerant attitude of the Jesuits. In the early days of November 1714, some caste chiefs met at the house of one Tenavaraya Pillai, on the same day when one Kumarappa Chetty was driven out of Pondicherry. They arrived at a decision that in case the French made any attempt to destroy the Vedapuriswaran temple, they would rather give up their lives rather than allowing that to happen. Another meeting was held in the house of one Kalavai Tandaven. It was decided then that every one of them would quit Pondicherry if permission was denied to them to play their musical instruments on Sundays. Further meetings were held in the houses of other caste chiefs and the same resolution was adopted. They further met at the house of the weaver Chandan, near the Pillaiyar temple. All caste headmen including Tenavarayamudali, Chegapamudali, Kalavai Tandaven, Tiruvengadam Poullé and Moutchi Kandappan, signed the petition, which was a repetition of the previous resolutions. But the Chettys and Kammalars refused to sign it. This shows that the Hindus were not united. Tiruvengadam Poullé, brother-in-law of Nainiappa Poullé, seems to have reached Pondicherry in the year 1714 from Madras, with his little son, Ananda Ranga Poullé who was born in Perambur, Madras in 1709.[18] The French government was aware of their activities. All these Poullé's were Telugus by origin and caste and not Tamils in the then prevailing south Indian society, though they operated in the Tamil country.

On 16 November 1714, Dulivier summoned the caste chiefs to apprise them that they could continue with their ceremonies in their temples and elsewhere during Easter days, the feast days of Ascension, Assumption, Saint Louis, the Sacred Sacrament, All Saints Day, Christmas and Sundays as well as during the days of the full moon when they fell on a Sunday. It was also allowed for music to be played during their marriage and death ceremonies on Sundays.[19]

Thus Dulivier struck a conciliatory note with the Hindus, considering the prosperity of the colony on the whole. But unfortunately these decisions were put on hold on 21 November 1714, when the three leaders of the Tamils, Chegapa Mudali (tax-collector on buffalos loaded with rice), Kalavai Tandaven (recruiter of weavers) and a certain Vellaiambalam were arrested and driven away from Pondicherry. They were prohibited from entering Pondicherry. In case they did, the government warned that they would be subjected to corporal punishment and their houses would be razed to the ground. It was also resolved that if any Hindu induced any Christian to apostasise, he would be also subjected to corporal punishment. The Hindus were terribly upset with the turn of events.[20]

On 1 February 1715, seven or eight caste chiefs met Governor Dulivier and asked him to grant permission to celebrate the new moon day which fell on 3 February. The Governor refused. The very next day in the morning, half the Tamil population left the town, especially the shopkeepers, Chettis, bleachers, fishermen, artisans and labourers who were necessary to load the two ships bound for Saint Malo. Besides, all shops and stores were closed. It became truly impossible even to buy provisions to eat. There remained only about 2,500 Christians including women and children, out of a total population of about 60,000. The French were totally taken aback at the turn of the events.

Father Bouchet, the new chief of the Jesuits, since the death of Rev. Tachard opined that it was a good occasion to demolish the Vedapuriswaran temple, which was a disturbance to the Jesuits nearby. On 4 February 1715, Reverend Bouchet wrote to the French Governor, Dulivier the following: 'It is necessary to destroy the (Vedapuriswaran) temple now and that is the best means to make the Malabars (Tamils) come back to Pondicherry. . . . The root cause of all these disorders was Naniapa. . . . As long as Naniapa is maintained in the position [of *diwan*], we will face similar troubles and we could do nothing in favour of the (Christian) religion.'[21]

Unlike the Jesuits, the Capuchin priests as well as those of the *Société des Missions Etrangères de Paris* wanted the Governor to allow

Hindu ceremonies for the sake of the commerce of the Company. Finally on 6 February 1715, taking into consideration the commercial interests of the Company, the Superior Council of Pondicherry resolved to allow the Tamils celebrate their ceremonies.[22]

On 20 February 1715, Rev. Bouchet apprised the Governor that Nainiappa was charitable towards the Christian converts with the aim of reconverting them to Hinduism. The very day, the Superior Council decided to send Saveri, the Christian co-*Mudaliar* along with another Tamil Christian Pedro Canagaraya Mudaliar (b. 1695) in order to prevent Nainiappa from distributing alms to Christian converts.

'Pedro' was the name given by the French Jesuits to Canagaraya Mudaliar or Canagarayen. Vincent seems to think that Pedro was of Portuguese origin. But Canagarayen seems to have been none other than the son of André Moutiappa and the chief of the latter's family. It appears that Pedro's father or rather grandfather converted to Christianity.[23]

Meanwhile Hébert had patched up with the Jesuits in France. The Jesuits were quite powerful and influential in the king's court. This reconciliation between Jesuits and Hébert took place after the latter gave his consent to remove Nainiappa from the post of broker and nominate a Tamil Christian in his place. Hébert returned to Pondicherry as 'General of the French Nation' on 16 January 1716. His intention was to nominate the young Pedro Canagarayen as *Mudaliar* to succeed Nainiappa.

Nainiappa's Martyrdom

From the time of Hébert's return, Governor Dulivier was divested of many of his powers. Hébert, who earlier was sympathetic towards Nainiappa, changed his position drastically. He then accused Nainiappa of being a great obstacle to the conversion of Hindus to Christianity. He also accused Nainiappa of embezzlement and other crimes.[24]

Very soon on 19 February 1716, Nainiappa was arrested with two of his close colleagues, Tiruvengadam Poullé and Ramanatha. Amanachetty, Andiappa and Vengapapoullé were also accused by Hébert. Under Hébert's orders, Nainiappa was thrown into the dungeon in Fort Louis, without any enquiry. The dungeon was full of insects and completely humid as the dirty water of the pit around the citadel was seeping into the dungeon. Nainiappa had just a wooden plank on which he could lie down and he was not allowed to have any change of dress. Hébert also ordered Nainiappa's legs to be chained. Nainiappa underwent all such inhuman atrocities that finally he fell grievously sick. No doctor was allowed to visit him or attend to him. He was prevented from communicating with anyone. His family members were not allowed to visit him. Even the jailer of the fort dungeon was prevented from speaking with him.[25]

Nainiappa was put on trial on 29 February 1716. It was none other than Pedro Canagarayen who fabricated false witnesses. As a reward, Pedro was nominated as the new *Mudaliar*. Hébert accused Nainiappa of sedition too as according to him he was behind the exodus of the Tamil population from Pondicherry earlier, when the Superior Council prohibited Hindus from celebrating the new moon day on a Sunday. A certain tobacco merchant by the name of Tanapa Chetty accused Nainiappa of collecting the signatures of the caste chiefs by which all agreed to quit Pondicherry. Besides it was said that some Tamil Christian converts refused to sign the declaration and they were forcibly taken out of the town. Nainiappa rejected all the accusations.[26]

Nainiappa was condemned to three years imprisonment on 5 June 1716. He was taken to the Grand Bazaar located in the Black town where his naked shoulders were publicly whipped fifty times. He was asked to pay 8,888 pagodas to the Company. He was also fined another 4,000 pagodas and was ordered to be banished from Pondicherry after serving the prison sentence. All his furniture and shops were sold in auction. Pedro Canagarayen, who succeeded Nainiyappa as *dubash*, bought a good part of them – Persian carpets, China silk, gold and silver objects and jewels, palanquin, one gold *taly*, the horses of Nainiappa, houses of Nainiappa, shops built in bricks in the Grand Bazaar and godowns. Others bought Nainiappa's clothes and his gardens. On his part, Benoist Dumas, one of the young Council members bought two twelve year old girls as slaves, one for 12 pagodas and 13 *fanams* and the other for 12 pagodas. Hébert bought one woman slave for 7½ pagodas. Slavery had existed in Pondicherry since François Martin's times.[27]

Others who bought Nainiappa's belongings were Vedagirichetty, Mariannachetty, Muthubalchetty, Apoupachettay, Shankara, Nevenachetty, Chitrachetty, Lazarou, Papureddy, Tanappa Mudaliar and Tirnathapoullé. False accusations were foisted on Tiruvengadam Poullé for defying the Christians in the Jesuit church and for claiming the 1,022 pagodas that Hébert's son owed him. Governor Hébert condemned Tiruvengadam to pay a hefty fine of 1,000 pagodas, to be whipped fifty times in the Grand Bazaar and to be banished for life from the lands of the Company. But this sentence was not executed.[28]

Some of Nainiappa's friends were also arrested, sentenced, their properties confiscated and exiled. Such persistent persecution and injustice led to a lot of protests from some sections of the French society in Pondicherry as well as from the general Tamil population, against the cruel activities of Hébert, who was aided by none other than his own son. Many Tamils even chose to quit Pondicherry. The news about the protests against Hébert reached Paris very soon.

Finally Nainiappa's health deteriorated in the dungeon to the point of no return. No doctor was allowed to treat him, though he was bleeding profusely. He died in the dungeon of Fort Louis (presently Bharati *Poonga*) on the night of 8 August 1717. His three minor sons, Guruvappa, Moutappa and Venkatachelam, feeling unsafe in Pondicherry, preferred to leave the town, three days after the death of their father. Hébert sent some men to apprehend them in the territories of the nawab of Arcot. Nainiappa's brother, Tiruvengadam Poullé and his nephew, Ananda Ranga Poullé fled to Madras.[29] Before Nainiappa died, the ministerial authorities of France had formally ordered Governor Hébert by a letter dated 13 February 1717, not to destroy any of the Hindu temples of Pondicherry including the Vedapuriswaran temple. The Jesuits were demanding the demolition of the Vedapuriswaran temple since François Martin's time. Hébert seems to have abided by this order.[30]

Hébert himself was accused of embezzlement and falsification of the Company's accounts very soon. He was called back to France forcibly in the year 1718, but not before Nainiappa died. The dismissal of Hébert was a great relief to the Tamils of Pondicherry and also to a good number of the French in Pondicherry. Many Tamils who had left the town voluntarily and many others who had been banished by Hébert returned to the town. Even several caste leaders who had been dismissed by Pedro Canagarayen under orders from Hébert as well as the weavers and Brahmins who did not want to give false witness against Nainiappa under the instigation of Pedro Canagarayen, were allowed to return to Pondicherry. Even lands and licences for arrack, fishing, money changing, betel and tobacco were farmed out to Tiruvengadam Poullé on 26 October 1718 for a sum of 5,200 pagodas. This induced Tiruvengadam Poullé and his son Ananda Ranga Poullé to return to Pondicherry.[31]

However, the Company's finances were in doldrums when Hébert was in Pondicherry. There was no cash and no goods in the godowns of the fort and the revenues from farming had decreased considerably.[32] As a result, on 1 January 1718, a new Governor called De La Prévostière was appointed. Hébert was dismissed.

Though Nainiappa had died, a retrial was ordered by the new Governor de la Prévostière. The Governor also dismissed Pedro Canagarayen from his post as *Mudaliar*. Tanapa Chetty accepted that his declaration against Nainiappa was false. He was imprisoned. A certain Kalianatanda told that Hébert had imprisoned him in order to compel him to make false statements that Nainiappa was behind the exodus of the Tamils from Pondicherry in the year 1715. Finally the decree of the Superior Council of Pondicherry condemning Nainiappa was cancelled in Paris.[33]

CONVERSION OF DUBASH GURUVAPPA AND RELATED EVENTS

Nainiappa's death and Hébert's arrest along with his son on 15 December 1718 put the French Jesuits on the defensive. Nevertheless when Hébert and his son were taken to Paris they were released by the king's order. The other missionaries like those of the *Société des Missions Etrangères* and the Capuchins as well as the former Governor Dulivier and some merchants of Saint Malo actually took up the case of Nainiappa in Paris. They held that Nainiappa was always generous and charitable towards them. He even had lent them money without interest in times of need to carry on with their missionary work.

Guruvappa, the eldest son of Nainiappa went to Paris to be present at the case in an attempt to recover Nainiappa's properties in Pondicherry, claim damages and reinstate the memory and honour of his father. Tiruvengadam Poullé and Ramanada too submitted similar requests in Paris. It appears that Guruvappa in order to obtain redressal of his grievances was persuaded to convert to Christianity by the missionaries of the *Société des Missions Étrangères*. He was baptized by a priest of the Mission at the chapel of the Palais Royal (Royal Palace) at Versailles by Monseigneur Louis de la Verge de Tresson, Bishop of Nantes. His godfather was none other than the Regent Philippe d'Orléans. He was even naturalized as French and was awarded the title of *Chevalier de l'Ordre de Saint Michel*. Guruvappa was the first Tamil and Indian to obtain this honour from the French government. He was thenceforth known as *Chevalier* Charles Philippe Guruvappa.

The Directors of the French Company in Paris ordered the Superior Council of Pondicherry to nominate Guruvappa as the *diwan* or *Mudaliar* of the Company and allow him to have a palanquin to which the *diwans* were usually entitled. Guruvappa stayed in a mansion in Mission Street, with his family, his uncle and the latter's son. However the Jesuits claimed that since the destitution of Nainiappa there were about 1,200 to 1,500 conversions, which had never occurred since the beginning of the colony. They thus tried to justify their actions against Naniappa.[34]

On 10 September 1720, Hébert and his son were released by the French Marine Council and their properties were given back. No damages were paid by the Council to Ramanada. Contrary to the claims of Guruvappa, the old Company was ordered to give back to the children of Nainiappa 10,000 pagodas as compensation for the sale of Nainiappa's properties with a 10 per cent interest from the date of the sale. Hébert was ordered to pay Nainiappa's children 20,000 pounds as damages and 10,000 pounds as damages to Tiruvengadam Poullé. The old Company was ordered to give back 131 pagodas with 10 per cent interest to Ramanada.[35]

On his return to Pondicherry in 1722, in the same ship that brought Joseph François Dupleix to Pondicherry, Guruvappa was nominated as the new *Mudaliar*. He and his descendants were also nominated as 'Registrar' for life. Tiruvengadam Poullé assisted him as co-*Mudaliar*. He indulged in tobacco farming and business.

Guruvappa's wife, aged 14, was baptized on 18 January 1723 at the Capuchin church of 'Notre Dame des Anges'. Joseph Dupleix, Benoist Dumas, Le Noir, all future governors of Pondicherry, along with Pierre (Pedro) Canagarayen had attested the baptism with their signatures. Tiruvengadam and Ananda Ranga Poullé were also present on the occasion in the church, though they remained as Hindus. On the same day, remarriage was performed between Guruvappa and his wife, according to Christian rites.[36]

In 1723, there was a danger of the invasion of Pondicherry by the nawab of Arcot, Sadatullah Khan. Pondicherry was practically undefended with only a flimsy hedge surrounding it. It seems that Guruvappa along with Tiruvengadam Poullé were sent to Arcot with hefty presents to dissuade the nawab from coming to Pondicherry. It seems that Guruvappa Poullé had the habit of keeping records of the daily events in the form of a diary. Ananda Ranga Poullé was aware of it but had claimed that this diary was lost.[37]

Guruvappa died on 12 August 1724 while he was returning from Sadras, where he had gone to take rest. He was buried at the cemetery of the St. Lazare Church near the beach (presently this cemetery site is occupied by the French Consulate and the French Institute). Guruvappa never adhered strictly to Christian traditions. He however ate beef and lived like a European.[38] It was not Tiruvengadam Poullé of Telugu descent who succeeded Guruvappa, but the Tamilian Pedro Canagarayen (also known as Pedro Canagaraya Mudaliar), who obviously had the support of the Jesuits. Thus the post of *diwan* was vested once again on a Tamil Christian.

Tiruvengadam Poullé passed away in 1726. But by then his young son Ananda Ranga Poullé who had a small areca nut shop near the Grand Bazaar, had learnt the tricks of the trade. Tobacco, areca and betel farms were leased out to him in association with his cousin Muthiah Poullé. He also entered foreign trade and loaded his goods in ships along with Pedro Canagarayen, Le Noir and Jacques Vincens, the first husband of Jeanne de Castro, and Benoist Dumas. He had several godowns in the town.

Ananda Ranga Poullé owned lands around Pondicherry. He had a weaving factory at Lalpettai and a trade agency at Arcot and Porto Novo, apart from supervising the factory of the Company in Porto Novo. He also owned an arack distillery. His areca nut shop was situated in a portion of the site by the side of the Pillaiyar temple, near the Governor's residence, which later belonged to Gallois Montbrun. Gallois Montburn was none other than the person who discovered the diaries of Ananda Ranga Poullé in 1846.[39] Ananda Ranga Poullé spoke French, Tamil, Telugu (mother tongue), Hindustani and a little Persian. He later married the daughter of the *polygar* of Chinglepet, Mangathayi and had two sons and four daughters.

However, in the trade front, things were a bit shaky due to the fact that the monopoly of the French Company, established way back in 1664 was nearing its end in 1714. Even before this ending, when the Company was in dire financial straits, the monopoly of trade between India and France was transferred to a group of shipowners of Saint Malo in France, provided that they paid 10 per cent of the profits to the Directors of the Old Company. But their colleagues in other ports were not ready to cooperate with the Saint Malo shipowners. This caused trade between India and France to slacken and decline to a considerable extent and debts accumulated in all French factories in India.

Besides, during this period, i.e. from 1701 to 1713, the king of France Louis XIV was embroiled in the Spanish War of Succession. He was not very much interested in the colonies. At the death of Louis XIV in 1714, France was in deep financial difficulties. His successor Louis XV was still an infant. The Duke of Orleans became the Regent. Louis XV ascended the throne only in 1723. Due to financial difficulties in France, the French in India had to borrow money from moneylenders in order to carry on with their trade. They were unable to repay the debts as well as the accumulating interests. The Armenian merchant of Madras, Safar Zacary and Coja Safar were among those who had lent money to the French. The former had to approach the French king to get his debts reimbursed by the Company in Pondicherry.[40]

All such factors naturally had a negative impact on trade in Pondicherry. The Hindu merchants and weavers of Pondicherry and elsewhere were affected by them. Such a situation continued till about the year 1719, when the French royal government decided to reorganize trade with India by amalgamating the French East India Company with the French Occidental Company. The new Company was called 'Perpetual Company of India'.[41]

Pierre André De la Prévostière who succeeded Hébert as Governor had dismissed Pedro Canagarayen from his post as Mudaliar. But the economic situation of Pondicherry had never evolved since François Martin's death. The town was somewhat protected. The fort was surrounded by a 12 feet thick and 10 feet high hedge. There were about 60,000 Indians, who were indulging mostly in cotton manufacturing, 400 French, made up of Company servants, soldiers and inhabitants, and 200 persons of Indo-Portuguese breed were also present in Pondicherry during that period.[42]

By the year 1719, Pondicherry had expanded considerably. It was a fairly big town, with the roads cutting at right angles. European houses were built with bricks, while the Indian houses were built of mud, plastered with lime. This of course seems to have included the wealthy Indian merchants' houses. In some roads, lines of trees had been planted and the weavers worked their cotton cloth under its shade.[43]

SOME OBSERVATIONS

Nevertheless it is quite astonishing to note the increasing dominance of the French governors and officials since the death of François Martin. The new governors did not mind having a Hindu, Nainiappa Poullé as their *diwan*. This was a serious departure from the traditional policy of appointing only Christian *diwans*. The Jesuits were particularly infuriated by this appointment. Considerable pressure was brought upon the governors to dismiss Nainiappa and appoint a Christian in his place as *dubash*. Governor Hébert during his second term in Pondicherry finally succumbed to it, foisted false charges on Nainiappa and shut him up in the dingy dungeon of the fort where he died a martyr's death.

Nainiappa Poullé could have very well abandoned his religion and converted to Christianity and maintained himself as *diwan* without much difficulty. He had everything to gain economically if he converted. But Nainiappa, in spite of all odds, stuck to his religion and never would succumb to the pressure brought upon him by the Jesuits and the French Governor. He preferred to give up his life, his wealth and properties rather than cater to the desires of the French. An Indian merchant could rise and prosper in the colonial set up only if he was in the good books of the European colonizers which included the missionaries and helped them not only in their private trade, especially sea-borne-trade, but also in propagating the Christian faith. Nainiappa seems not to have realized this fact. He was not prosecuted for his economic role, but for having been an impediment to the propagation of Christianity.

Nainiappa's martyrdom clearly shows that economic reasons alone cannot determine the evolution of an individual or society. There were strong emotional ties to age-old customs, culture and traditions, which pushed Nainiappa to sacrifice his prosperity and well-being in order to uphold them and his way of life. Nainiappa probably did not know that the French could go to the extent of killing him, as there was no precedent. The French had begun by persuading him to toe their line. But as it did not work, they resorted to force and violence to impose their views on others. This was their modus operandi. Nevertheless, Nainiappa's martyrdom was an exceptional event.

Nainiappa's grisly end showed that though he was a powerful man, holding a powerful post, in the political and economic system put in place by the French colonizers in Pondicherry, he was still very much a subject to them. There was no question of equality between him and the French. The French would not tolerate any sort of opposition or rebellion or independence on his part, even in cultural and religious matters. It is simply absurd to say that Nainiappa and the French were in a sort of commercial partnership, where Nainiappa had complete freedom of thought and action. But during this early period of colonization, commerce and religion and culture were intertwined which finally cost Nainiappa his post and his life.

When Nawab Daoud Khan was alive, he did caution the French to be careful in their dealings with the Tamils. But the nawab of Arcot Sadatullah Khan had never come to the assistance of Nainiappa, as far as I know. Either he was unaware of it or he simply disregarded it, in spite of the fact that the French were allowed to settle in Pondicherry earlier by Sher Khan Lodi on the express condition that they would respect the customs and traditions of the Tamil people. The French increasingly behaved as if they were the absolute masters of the colony, whereas all Indians including Nainiappa, under their jurisdiction, had no other alternative but to obey and submit themselves to the desires and wishes of the French. In this situation, it is not right to claim like Holden Furber that there was mutual respect and cooperation between the colonizers and the colonized, though there was interdependence due to economic and commercial needs, where the Indian partner was always vulnerable.

The French had come to India to trade and not to adopt the customs and traditions of the Indian people in the territories under their control. On the contrary, they sought to impose their culture and traditions on the colonized people in the course of time or favoured their own religion and beliefs to the detriment of the Tamil religions and beliefs. Right from the beginning, they seem to have believed in a clash of values and civilizations. They considered their own culture, religion and traditions as superior to those of the Hindus and they sought to impose them on the natives, whenever the opportunity arose. They, especially the missionaries thought, probably that in this way they would be saving the souls of the Hindus.

However, the order for a retrial of Nainiappa and the arrest and prosecution of Governor Hébert put an end to this tragic episode. Many merchants including Tiruvengadam Poullé who had properties and commercial stakes returned to Pondicherry and resumed their activities. Guruvappa, the son of Nainiappa even went to France to get a redressal of the grievances of his family. He and his relatives and colleagues were compensated, but not before Guruvappa was persuaded to convert to Christianity in France, by the Capuchin missionaries and those of the *Société des Missions Etrangères*. It was in fact on this condition that he seems to have been re-nominated as *dubash* of the French government in Pondicherry.

Guruvappa had to give up his Hindu identity and submit himself to Christianity to be in the good books of the French, recover his properties and become the *dubash*. But unfortunately for him, he was *dubash* only for two years. At his death in 1724, Pedro Canagarayen, a staunch Christian, who was briefly *dubash* after the incarceration of Nainiappa was re-nominated as the *dubash*, most certainly under the influence of the Jesuits and in keeping with the tradition established by François Martin to have only dubashes of the Christian faith in Pondicherry.

No power, either of the nawabs of Arcot or the Marathas could do anything about this internal politics of Pondicherry. This demonstrated that Pondicherry was not just a trading outpost since 1673-4, but had also grown to become a political entity, with its own government, with its own rules and regulations, with its own army, fort and defensive constructions, with its own values and culture and with its own systems of justice. The Indian rulers had allowed such political entities to prosper in their own backyard, just in order to reap trade and commercial benefits. They always looked for short-term gains. But they never took into consideration their long term interests, especially with regard to the security of their domains.

NOTES

1. Castonnet des Fosses, *L'Inde Française au XVIIIème siècle*, Paris, s.d., pp. 113-14; Kaeppelin, *Les Origines de l'Inde Française. . .* , 1908, ch. 11, p. 607.
2. Olagnier, *Les Jésuites à Pondichéry et l'Affaire Naniapa*, 1932, p. 15.
3. Olagnier, ibid., 1932, p. 15; Norbert, *Mémoires Historiques. . .* , 1749, I, p. 190.
4. De Closets d'Errey, *Précis Chronologique de l'Histoire de l'Inde Française*, 1934, p. 16; *ARP Diary*, II, 57.
5. Olagnier, op. cit., 1932, pp. 16, 17; Deliberation du CS de Pondichéry, 28 Juillet 1708, fr. 8927, f. 141, BNF; Kaeppelin, op. cit., 1908, pp. 614, 615f; AME, vol. 964, Lettre de Père Tachard au Chevalier Hébert, 16 October 1708, Pondichéry, p. 45; Lettre de Hébert au Père Tachard, 20 October 1708, Pondichéry; Fond Ariel 8927, f. 141, BNF.
6. Fond Ariel, 8927, f. 141 et 143, BNF; Labernadie, *Le Vieux Pondichéry (1753-1815)*, 1936, p. 15.
7. Olagnier, op. cit., 1932, p. 18; Vinson, *Les Français dans l'Inde, Dupleix et Labourdonnais*, 1894, pp. 32-3, 34, 35; Délibérations du CS de Pondichéry, 29 Juillet et 10 Août 1708, fr. 8927, ff. 141-3, BNF: Fr. 6231, ff. 41-3, BNF: Kaeppelin, op. cit., 1908, pp. 615, 616; *Annuaire des Etablissements Français dans l'Inde*, 1938-9, p. 31.

8. Vinson, ibid. 1894, pp. 32-3; *ARP Diary*, ix, 62; xii, 204; Isabelle & Jean Louis Vissière. *Lettres Edifiantes et Curieuses*..., S-Seine, 2000, pp. 129-31.
9. Olagnier, op. cit., 1932, pp. 19, 20; Kaeppelin, op. cit., 1908, p. 608; Fr. 6231, ff. 46, 47, BNF.
10. Naf. 9364, Lettre de Hébert, 12 Fév 1709 and 15 Fév 1709, Pondichéry; Launay, *Histoire des Missions de l'Inde*, 1898, I, xlii, xliii, Lettre du Père de Bourges, Jésuite à Madame de la Comptesse de Soudé, de la Mission de Maduré, 21 September 1713, LEC, 12, Paris, MDCCLXXXI: LEC, nouvelle edition, 10, Paris, MDCCLXXXI, xiij, xiv, xvj, xvij, xviij, xix, xx, 36-46, 54-71, 141-9; Lettre du Père Tremblay, p. 203, LEC, vol. 14; LEC, vol. 15, Lettre d'un missionaire des Indes, p. 127.
11. Naf. 9364, Lettre de Hébert, 15 Février 1710, Pondicherry; LEC, tome 12, Paris, MDCCLXXXL, p. 7, Lettre du Père Tachard, Missionaire de la Compagnie de Jésus au Révérend Père de Tréven, de la même Compagnie, Chanderngore, 18 Janvier 1711); More, *Maridas Poullé of Pondicherry*..., 2004.
12. Fr. 6231, f. 51, BNF.
13. Castonnet des Fosses, *Le R.P. Charles de Montalembert*, 1886, p. 5; Castonnet des Fosses, *L'Inde Française avant Dupleix*, 1887, p. 155; Labernadie, op. cit., 1936, p. 113.
14. Vinson, op. cit., 1894, pp. 39-40.
15. Fr. 6231, f. 50, 51, BNF; Oubagarasamy, *Un Livre de Compte de Ananda Ranga Poullé*, pp. xvi, xvii
16. Olagnier, op. cit., 1932, pp. 22, 23-5.
17. Launay, op. cit., 1898, I, xxxiii; Vinson, op. cit., 1894, pp. 34, 37, 39, 40.
18. Vinson, *Catalogue des Manuscrits Tamouls*, 1867, p. 39; Fr. 6231, f. 54, BNF; Tecika Pillai, *Anantarankapillai*, Madras, 1955, pp. 1-2; Kalavai is a village in Tiruvallur taluk, Chingleput district (*ARP Diary*, IV, 292f.).
19. Olagnier, op. cit., 1932, pp. 25-6.
20. Launay, op. cit., 1898, I, lxxiii, xxxiii; Vinson, op. cit., 1894, pp. 34, 37, 39, 40-*Délibération du CS sous Dulivier*, Fort Louis, 16 September 1714, pp. 39, 40; Olagnier, op. cit., 1932, p. 25.
21. Launay, ibid., 1898, I, liii; Olagnier, ibid., 1932, 28; Fr. 6231, f. 55, BNF.
22. Délibérations du CS de Pondichéry, 6 février 1715, in Vinson, 1894, pp. 48-9; Fr. 6231, f. 55, BNF; Olagnier, ibid., 1932, pp. 26, 28-9; Launay, ibid., 1898, I, xxxiii; Deliberations du CS de Pondichéry, 14 Fev. 1715, in Vinson, 1894, pp. 41, 42-5.
23. Gaudart, *Catalogue*..., 1931, p. 36; *ARP Diary*, II, 150; XII, 87; Olagnier, Ibid. 1932, p. 55; Vincent, *L'Aventure des Français en Inde – XVIIe-XXe siècles*, 1995, pp. 67, 76; Vinson, 1894, pp. 50-1; *Procés-Verbaux des délibérations du Conseil Souverain de la Compagnie des Indes*, I, Pondichéry,

1911, p. 236; cf. also Alfred Martineau, *Résumé des actes de l'état-civil de Pondichéry de 1676 à 1735.*

24. Olagnier, ibid., 1932, pp. 33, 35, 36, 44, 45; Col. C² 70, f. 236, A.N.
25. Olagnier, ibid., 1932, p. 46; Olagnier, *Le Grand Colonial Inconnu. Le Gouverneur Benoist Dumas,* 1938, pp. 26, 28.
26. Olagnier, 1932, p. 48; Olagnier, ibid., 1938, p. 24.
27. Laberandie, op. cit., 1936, p. 89.
28. Gaebelé, 'Enfance et Adolescence d'Anandarangapoullé', RHEP, 1955, pp. 34, 39, 41.
29. Olagnier, op. cit., 1932, pp. 53-7, 64, 69, 71, 74; Olagnier, op. cit., 1938, p. 24; AME, vol. 992, Lettre de la veuve du Chevaiier Guruvappa au Supérieur et Directeurs du Séminaire, 17 Jan 1726; Arrêt contre Nainiappa, 5 Juin 1716, C² 70, A.N.; Vincent, op. cit., 1990, p. 39; Gaebelé, ibid., p. 46.
30. Vinson, op. cit., 1894, pp. 56-7; Gaebelé, ibid., pp. 35-8.
31. Gaebelé, ibid. p. 51.
32. Olagnier, op. cit., 1932, pp. 74-5; Délibérations du CS de Pondichéry, 9 Sept., 26 Oct., 16 Dec. 1718, Fr. 8929, f. 151, 152; Kaeppelin, op. cit., 1908, p. 631; Le Treguilly. 'La présence Française en Inde: aléas politiques et militaires', p. 36; De Closets d'Errey, op. cit., 1934, p. 18.
33. Olagnier, ibid., 1932, pp. 87-8, 95; Olagnier, op. cit., 1938, pp. 24, 32.
34. Fr. 6231, f. 58, BNF; Oubagarasamy, *Un Livre de Compte de Ananda Ranga Poullé...*, 1930, p. xxiv; Olagnier, ibid. 1932, pp. 102, 106; Olagnier, ibid. 1938, pp. 37, 38, 39; Launay, op. cit., 1898, I, xxxv, xxxvi; Lettre de M.de Querelay Tessier aux M. les Directeurs du Séminaire des Missions Etrangères, 18 Sept 1709, Pondichéry, vol. 955, p. 125, AME: Lettre de M. de Querelay aux Mons. Du Séminaire des M.E., 19 Fév., 1719, vol. 960, AME; Gaudart, *Catalogue...*, 1931, p. 37; Gaebelé, op. cit., 1955, pp. 67-8.
35. Olagnier, ibid., 1938, p. 28.
36. Gaebelé, op. cit., 1955, p. 63; Martineau, Résumé des actes de l'état-civil de Pondichéry..., I, pp. 247, 252; Launay, op. cit., 1898, I, lxxiii; Naf 9357, f. 14, BNF; De Closets d'Errey, *Histoire de l'Inde Française...*, 1940, p. 62; Vincent, 'Zenith in Pondicherry', 1990, p. 41.
37. *ARP Diary,* VII, 104; Gaebelé, ibid., 1955, p. 71.
38. Oubagarasamy, op. cit., 1930, p. xxv; Launay, op. cit., 1898, I, xxxvi.
39. Gaebelé, op. cit., 1955, 72, 76-80, 85; Bourdat, *Les Grandes Pages du "Journal" d'Ananda Ranga Pillai,* 2003, pp. 33, 34; Oubagarasamy, ibid., 1930, pp. xxvi, xxvii.
40. Vol. 991, Lettre du 20 Sept 1717, Pondichéry, AME; Lettre de M. de Querelay à M. Tremblay, 3 Fév 1720, vol. 991, p. 685, AME; Fr. 6231, F 50, BNF; Deveze, *Histoire de la Colonisation Française en Amérique et aux Indes au XVIIIème siècle,* 1948, pp. 7, 10; Malleson, *Dupleix,* 2001, p. 23.

41. Haudrere, 'The Compagnie des Indes Orientales', 1990, pp. 36-7; Longchampt, *Dupleix et la politique coloniale sous Louis XV*, 1886, p. 7; Malleson, ibid., 2001, p. 24; Sottas, *Histoire de la Compagnie Royale des Indes Orientales...*, 1905, chs. IV & V.
42. Col. C² 69, f. 235, A.N. Kaeppelin, op. cit., 1908, p. 634; Castonnet des Fosses, op. cit., 1887, p. 157.
43. Lettre du Père Bouchet, Missionaire de la Compagnie au Père de la même Compagnie, Pondichéry, 19 Avril 1719, LEC, xiii, 1810, pp. 72, 81.

CHAPTER 3

Pondicherry Develops and Expands

AT THE DEATH OF Pierre de la Prévostière, Pierre Christophe Le Noir was appointed as Governor of Pondicherry and the French outposts in India on 11 October 1721. At this time, Tiruvengadam Poullé was the assistant Mudaliar. Le Noir exercised his function until 6 October 1723, when he was replaced by Beauvollier de Courchant. Benoist Dumas was second-in-command then. Dumas naturally expected to become Governor. But the Company was not happy with his private trade. So Le Noir came back to Pondicherry as Governor on 21 August 1726. When Le Noir became Governor of Pondicherry, the French Company still enjoyed a trade monopoly. Le Noir like his predecessors had borrowed money from Armenian merchants which he was unable to repay. But from 1726 onwards, the agents of the French Company were allowed to indulge in intra-Asian private trade.[1]

MAHÉ AND THE MALABAR COAST

In March 1721, already before Le Noir's arrival, the French Company had given instructions to André Mollandin, the chief of the French factory at Calicut to settle a trading centre further north up the Malabar Coast, in order to procure pepper which was extremely costly in Europe. Accordingly Mollandin obtained the cession of a strip of land at the mouth of the Mahé River from the Vazhunavar, the chief of the country, on condition that he would sell the pepper of his country to the French alone. It was also stipulated that the Vazhunavar was entitled to customs duties on the pepper acquired by the French. A mud fort was built then in Mahé. It seems that at this time the French by their money and ships had raised their credit with the Malabar kings.

When the French settled in Mahé, the power of the ancient Kolatiri king of Malabar was restricted to the Chirakkal taluk, north of Mahé.

The Puranad kings ruled in the territory north-east of Mahé and the territory close to the river Mahé was under the Iruvalinad Nambiars and Kurangod Nayar. South of Mahé was the territory of the Vazhunavar of Badagara, from whom the French obtained Mahé. Mahé was inhabited mostly by Hindus. The Muslim Mappilas were in considerable numbers too, while the Christians were very few. The Saint Thérèse Church was built only in 1735-6. The area of the Mahé factory was just 50 or 60 hectares. However, pepper trade never really picked up in Mahé, apart from a few prosperous years, and the wars had cost the Company 3,75,955 livres.[2]

The English, who had a factory in neighbouring Tellicherry, about 6 km north of Mahé, were not happy with this rise of French power on the Malabar Coast. At their instigation, the Vazhunavar ordered the French to quit the country in the month of April 1724, leaving just three or four Frenchmen to carry on with the trade. Naturally the French had to dismantle their factory and retreat to Calicut. They were not very happy with this turn of events where they were practically evicted from Mahé. They could do nothing about it as they did not have the military power to resist.

But towards the end of the year, a French squadron consisting of 15 ships and commanded by Marquis de Pardaillan arrived on the Malabar Coast. Mahé de La Bourdonnais and Major de la Farelle accompanied the fleet. There was an open conflict between the French and the Malayali soldiers of the Vazhunavar. The French overpowered the Malayalis (including Muslim Mappilas) and re-occupied Mahé on 3 December 1725. Three hundred Malayalis were killed while 15 Frenchmen lost their lives in the conflict.

But in order to sign a peace treaty, they had to wait for reinforcements from Pondicherry. Finally a peace treaty was signed and a payment of 1,50,000 *fanams* was made by the French to the Vazhunavar. The treaty restored the rights of the French as before. The French engineer Deidier reconstructed the old fort, which was subsequently strengthened with the addition of some new bastions by 1732.[3] Thus the French re-acquired Mahé by the use of force. They established that Mahé was not just a trading post, but also a political entity under the control of the French, subject to the French Governor of Pondicherry. The English recognized the preceding treaty on 20 March 1728. It was also agreed that the two Companies would not fight each other or attack each other's ships on the Malabar Coast, though France and England might be at war elsewhere.[4]

The attack on Mahé, however, was the first time that the French utilized military force in order to safeguard their territorial and trade interests in India. This happened when Le Noir and Beauvollier de Courchant were Governors at Pondicherry. For the first time, French forces measured themselves against an Indian power on the Malabar Coast in a battle and they came out victorious because of their superior arms and ammunitions and more advanced techniques and skills of warfare. The intentions of the Governors during this period were not outright conquest of territories, but only an attempt to safeguard what they thought to be their legitimate territorial and political interests. However, as Malabar was away from the Mughal-controlled territories in India, the events there did not have much impact even in Pondicherry.

ON THE ANDHRA COAST

The French factory at Masulipatnam was re-established in the year 1720. A house was bought there in 1724. Masulipatnam was a flourishing textile centre surrounded by weaving villages and salt pans. Trade picked up a little there in the 1720s. In March 1729, under Governor Le Noir, two pieces of land bought at Rs. 300 and 30 pagodas respectively were added to the French factory. Five years later, on 1 February 1734, a large piece of land called Francepet was conceded by Nizam-ul-mulk to the French in Masulipatnam.[5]

In the year 1723, Haji Hussein, the *faujdar* of Rajamundry, Elluru and the adjoining areas allowed the French to set up a factory at Yanam, situated about 50 km north of Masulipatnam, between the rivers, Godaveri and Coringa. Trade picked up in the 1730s when Nawab Rustum Khan issued a *parvana* to the French to trade there.[6]

When Benoist Dumas succeeded Le Noir and became Governor of Pondicherry, he obtained the accord of Nizam-ul-mulk to acquire the lands in front of the factory of Yanam, which yielded revenue of Rs. 1,000. These lands were very much greater in size than the original factory, acquired during Le Noir's period. In August 1742, a *parvana* was issued by Nawab Mohammad Ali Khan with the seal of the Qazi of Golconda, confirming the concession of Nizam-ul-mulk. The population of Yanam around 1740, consisting of weavers, farmers, artisans, merchants, etc., seems to have been around four to five thousand.[7]

However, the French paid a rent for the lands in Yanam to the Muslim chieftain at Rajamundry until a *parvana* was issued in 1743, when Dupleix was Governor, suppressing it formally. In spite of the *parvana*, the Muslim chieftain extracted money from the French in the form of presents, etc., which hampered trade at Yanam to a great extent. Nevertheless the French held the lands like a *jagirdar* or *inamdar* who never paid taxes or rent for the lands to the *faujdar*.[8] Yanam and Masulipatnam factories were French possessions, always under the control of the Governor of Pondicherry, since the governorship of Le Noir.

Situation in Pondicherry under Le Noir's Governorship

Around 1700, there were just a few Christians in Pondicherry. But by 1725, there were 3,000 of them. Between 2 October 1724 and 12 October 1725, 601 baptisms were administered in Pondicherry through the efforts of Father Turpin and most of the converts were Shudras of the 'good' or rather 'soft' castes, i.e. those who did not take to menial work by tradition. By 1725, there were about 400 Christians in Ariyankuppam alone. Chances for more conversions, especially from the higher castes were also bright. Some 12 or 13 years back, there was just one Christian in the area.[9]

It is quite possible that the conversion of Guruvappa Poullé to Christianity might have led many Hindus of the 'soft' castes to convert to Christianity. Otherwise we don't see any valid reason with regard to why there were so many baptisms administered during that period in Pondicherry and its neighbourhood.

The preceding evidence suggests that high caste conversions to Christianity during the early decades of French colonization of Pondicherry were also quite numerous. This was because the French at that time were mainly concerned with trade, which naturally brought them into contact with high caste men, who were traditionally dominant in these fields. During this time, the French were among the buyers of cotton and other goods produced in and around Pondicherry for the European market. This provided many non-Pariah men the opportunity to involve themselves in trade and in the production of goods for the French that could be exported to Europe.

Besides, the French as a colonial power needed Indian subordinates to run the administration. Here too, the non-Pariah higher caste men were better placed to occupy the subordinate posts provided by the French administration, rather than the lower castes for obvious historical reasons. Undoubtedly the French preference for Christians in the employment and economic fields provided a strong reason for many higher caste men and their families to convert to Christianity, for them alone and not the others were in a position during those early decades of colonization to avail of the trade and employment opportunities provided by the French. Even today, many elderly caste Hindus of Pondicherry with whom I had talked to, criticize the caste Christians in the following Tamil terms: *moonu kaasukku odiponavanga*, meaning 'those who ran away to Christianity for three paisa'.

Though Guruvappa's conversion might have led to other conversions, yet Guruvappa himself who was *dubash* then, never adhered strictly to the Christian traditions. As he had obtained the award of *Chevalier de l'Ordre du Saint-Michel*, he belonged to the Parish of the Capuchins. He was highly Europeanized and even ate calf meat without any hesitation. However he passed away very soon and was buried at the beach cemetery enclosure of the St. Lazare Church on 13 August 1724. The Capuchin father, Esprit de Tour presided over the burial. After his death, Guruvappa's widow expressed in no uncertain terms the injustices meted out to her husband by the Jesuits and Governor Hébert.[10] Nevertheless, another Christian of the 'soft' caste, Pedro Cangarayen had succeeded Guruvappa as *dubash*. Le Noir retained him as *dubash* all throughout his tenure as Governor of Pondicherry.

Trade seems to have somewhat picked up since 1722. The situation in Pondichery was quite comfortable until 1727. Generally, during this period, the French Company earned their revenues by farming out lands for tobacco and betel cultivation and through money exchange. They also earned through imposition of a 3 per cent tax ad valorem on all goods entering Pondicherry and a tax of 1 per cent on all goods exiting Pondicherry. The Indian princes, both Hindu and Muslim earned their revenues mainly by collecting taxes from the cultivators, which they needed for the upkeep of their armies and power. Troops or rather force was employed by the princes as well as the French Governors in order to collect these taxes.[11]

Governor Le Noir seems to have been the first top Company official to take interest in Oriental studies and knowledge. Of course, the Jesuits were into that job for their own purposes since they came to Pondicherry. They produced dictionaries and grammar books. But it was Le Noir who allocated funds for the purchase of Hindu holy books, grammar books in Tamil, Sanskrit and Telugu, dictionaries, books on astronomy, etc. The Jesuit missionaries, established in south India and Chandernagore took full advantage of this and transferred many of their purchases and collections to the Royal library in Paris.[12]

In 1721, Le Noir ordered to dig up and extend the crucial Madras Road as well as the Vazhudavur Road. Three other parallel roads for the weavers were constructed too. The French cemetery was transferred to the Capuchin enclosure, near the church and in 1845 a new European cemetery was constructed outside the town in Uppalam. Later on 15 November 1726, another cemetery for the *topas* and the other Christians was created towards the north of the fort, in what is today the site of the Calvé College. This was transferred outside the town in 1827.[13]

In 1723, the nawab of Arcot, in the name of the Mughal emperor prohibited any construction of walls fortifying Pondicherry. If he had wanted he could have retaken Pondicherry. But Beauvollier de Courchant, the then governor of Pondicherry pacified him with costly gifts. In June 1724, it was decided to build a high protective wall around Pondicherry town, and some advanced outposts, disregarding completely the order of the nawab of Arcot. The inhabitants both French and Tamil were expected to pay a special tax every month according to their ability to build the wall, in the place of the hedge that existed since François Martin's time. Eighteen caste headmen of Pondicherry under Guruvappa, had signed a treaty with the Company for this purpose.[14]

On 8 May 1725, the Company decided to spend 12,000 pagodas in three years for the construction of the wall. Father Louis was the architect of the wall. In Februrary 1726, this tax was cancelled for the French. In the year 1727, the nawab of Arcot again objected to the construction of the wall. The French gave him a present worth 960 pagodas to buy his silence. Pedro Canagarayen seems to have played a crucial role in pacifying the nawab of Arcot. On 27 July 1728, the tax was cancelled for the Indians too. But it was re-imposed very quickly. The wall was completed only in 1735 and in 1747 during Duplexi's governorship, the wall on the seaside was complete.[15]

In the year 1728, a special tribunal for Tamils/Indians called 'tribunal de chaudrie' was established in Pondicherry. This tribunal was made up of a consultative committee with eight principal caste and religious leaders. They were expected to give their opinion on the administration of justice. The *dubash* presided over the tribunal.[16]

In 1728, there was drought and famine in Pondicherry which continued until 1729. It was during this period that the Muslim chief of Villianur attempted to construct a canal to connect the Senji River with the Big Usteri Lake from where water flowed through sub-canals to irrigate lands around Villianur and Ozhukarai. The French were expected to pay a part of the expenditure. Revenue through farming out lands for cultivation by the Superior Council diminished during this period.

However the lease-holders like Ananda Ranga Poullé deployed their efforts to repair the tanks and canals. New tanks and canals were off and on constructed by the Superior Council. It also undertook repairs of existing ponds, tanks and canals. Lands were also freely distributed to the poor peasants to expand cultivation. Besides, Ananda Ranga Poullé was appointed as the chief supervisor of the Company's factory at Porto Novo by Le Noir.[17]

Due to the high price of the grains, the tax imposed on the inhabitants in 1724 for the construction of the walls around Pondicherry was annulled temporarily. Rice was brought into Pondicherry from as far as Orissa, Bimlipatnam and Masulipatnam. The scarcity of water put the weavers and bleachers in great difficulty. The Government dug the lakes and wells in order to provide water for the bleachers without which no cotton cloth could be obtained for trade.[18]

Favouritism Towards 'Higher Caste' Hindus and Muslims

During Le Noir's tenure, the Tamil Hindus wanted to construct an enclosing wall around the Varadaraja Perumal temple on the Madras Street (presently Mahatma Gandhi Road) which was open on all sides. Several times they approached the Governor to grant them permission to build this wall in order to prevent European sailors and soldiers from entering the temple in a drunken state, especially at night when the womenfolk were assembled there. They argued that as permission was given to them to practice their religion freely, they should be given the right to have temples and keep it in good condition. On 3 July 1733, the Superior Council finally decided to grant this permission, just in order to retain the few merchants in Pondicherry, who were necessary for the commerce of the Company.[19]

Caste disputes between right-hand and left-hand castes continued during Le Noir's tenure as Governor. They had their respective temples too. Kalatiswaran belonged to the left-hand while the Vedapuriswaran was right-hand. The depressed castes had their temples of Mariamman too in their localities. Brahmins and the higher caste Shudras looked down upon these low caste or outcaste temples.

The arterial roads of Pondicherry were thrown open to all castes by Le Noir, at a time when the right hand castes prohibited left hand castes from crossing their roads on horseback or on a palanquin. During this period, an agreement was signed between the left-hand and right-hand caste chiefs regarding the ceremonies at the Akilandacody Swamiyar temple in Pondicherry.[20] During Le Noir's tenure, attempts seem to have been made to get rid of the small Pillaiyar temple in the White town. This temple belonged to the *mainas* or washermen of the town. The Jesuits even offered considerable money to the authorities of the temple for them to dismantle it. But the *mainas* withstood Jesuit pressure. The Jesuits had also rebuilt their church during Le Noir's period by 1728.[21]

In the year 1732, some reparations were carried out at the Vedapuriswaran temple, near the Jesuit Church, without the permission of the French government. It was sponsored by two Vellala caste headmen who were grain merchants. Six workers worked on the reparations. The chief of the police was dispatched to visit the temple.

As a result the six workers and the two merchants were arrested and put in prison. But no damage was done to the temple by the French as they feared a backlash from the Hindu population. After sometime, the merchants and the workers were released. But the merchants were blamed publicly for having contravened the law by sponsoring reparations without government permission.[22]

In 1733, there was an instance of favouritism towards the high castes. A Vellala caste man was caught attempting to rob the house of the French merchant in Pondicherry by the name of Nicolas Le Faucheur, near the St. Laurent market. This area located near the coast beyond the Capuchin Church also included a Paraya quarter where missionaries like Tachard had deployed their efforts to convert Parayas to Christianity.

The Vellala man was sentenced to death. But taking into consideration the fact that the man belonged to a higher caste and as the incident would discredit the higher caste men in Pondicherry, the Superior Council decided to set him free. It seems that a Muslim by the name of Imam Sahib, an influential Nawayat merchant, intervened with the Superior Council members in order to secure his release. [23]

Earlier in 1729, a Brahmin called Vinayagan had forged several notes worth about 1,300 pagodas. But the caste chiefs met the Governor and the Superior Council members and asked them to deliver Vinayagan to them, rather than condemning him to death according to the French law. It was finally decided to deliver Vinayagan to the caste headmen so that punishment might be meted out to him according to their customary laws. As a result he was banished from Pondicherry and his properties confiscated. He was also thrown out of his caste.

Governor Le Noir accepted this punishment, on condition that the confiscation of Vinayagan's property would benefit the poor of Pondicherry and not the Company. A similar leniency was shown to a certain Perumal of the Vellala caste, accused of stealing in the year 1733. Muslims too were singled out and shown leniency, so as to not offend the Muslim noble women and horsemen. As a result, the death sentence of Mahmoud Ahmed Sheikh which was to be carried out in the Mirapalli area was reduced to perpetual imprisonment in the year 1740 by Governor Dumas. But such lenient treatment was not shown to the Parayas and Pallis of lower castes. However there were a few exceptions to the leniency shown towards the higher castes. On 17 November 1735, a certain Muthu of the Chetty caste was accused of theft and was condemned to death and hung at the Big Bazaar square.[24]

Punishments were very severe during French rule. It consisted of whipping and cutting of the ears. Sometimes the hands and legs of the criminals and deserters were broken in public on a scaffold in the fort and their kidneys detached to teach a lesson. Others were deported to the French islands to work as slaves. Many Tamils found their way to Mauritius and Réunion Island in this way. One Ponnan who robbed Pedro Canagarayen of his shawl and cap was exiled to the Bourbon Island as a slave of the Company. Others were simply carried away clandestinely and sold in the islands as slaves, as it happened in Bimblipatnam in 1742.

When Benoist Dumas was Governor of the islands, Tamil slaves were exported in greater numbers. Benoist Dumas actually visited Pondicherry during this period to buy 100 slaves, boys and girls between the ages of 8 and 25. They were boarded on the 'Sirène' bound for the islands of Bourbon and Mauritius. Almost all the slaves belonged to the lower castes like the Pallis and Parayas.[25]

Besides, Le Noir, unlike Hébert, gave freedom to Hindus to practice their religion. He also refrained from destroying the Vedapuriswaran temple, though the French king wanted it. The Jesuit priests persisted in their attempts to destroy the small Pillaiyar (Ganesh), located in the White town. But Le Noir never supported them. Le Noir also took part evey year in the grand chariot ceremony organized at the temple in Villianur. Villianur was not still part of French Pondicherry. But still Le Noir was invited to take part in the ceremonies by the temple authorities. The temple itself seems to have been built in the eleventh century or a little before during Chola rule. It is one of the oldest and biggest temples built in the Pondicherry region. It is a quadrilateral temple set in a vast area, facing east. There are towers on the eastern and southern sides. The eastern tower which is the *Rajagopuram* is 67 feet tall. The southern tower is 97 feet tall. There is a big and beautiful square-shaped tank called 'teppakulam' spread over 1.8 acre, with a beautiful pavillon at the centre, used for ablution purposes. The entire area is hemmed by a granite wall, which gives it the appearance of a fortress. There was no mention of Pondicherry town in the numerous inscriptions found on the temple walls dating from the eleventh century.

Shiva is the chief deity of this temple. The form of Shiva is that of Kameesan, i.e. the half female form of Shiva. The chief goddess of the temple is Kokilambigai. Villiyanur temple has always been a pilgrimage centre for the Tamils of the region. That was why the temple festival was a very grand affair. The French Governor being a power in the region was naturally invited to attend the ceremonies related to the temple chariot festival every year.

Governor Le Noir and the French officials and visitors who went with him witnessed all along the road leading to the temple, numerous penitents performing the most arduous and troublesome things like standing with one hand or with both the hands lifted above the head the whole day, others rolling continuously on the road towards the temple as an act of devotion and some others with faces painted in varied colours.

The most 'atrocious' act during the festival which they witnessed was the historical fact that some people sacrificed their lives in full view of the assembled crowd, by lying down on the road when the temple chariot, carrying the idol of Lord Kameeswarar rolled over them crushing them to death. After the procession Lord Kameeswarar was taken to the pavilion in the middle of the sacred pond within the temple for further ceremonies and ablutions, surrounded by Brahmins, *devadasis* and musicians. Governor Le Noir seems to have witnessed such events without interfering with them or trying to stop them.

On 11 February 1733, the Company adopted a set of rules concerning the Catholic religion in Pondicherry. Accordingly, the presence of Hindus in Pondicherry was accepted and authorization was given for the celebration of their ceremonies. Instructions were also given to the French missionaries not to interfere unnecessarily with the ceremonies of the Hindus, for the sake of commerce. They were told that it was absolutely necessary to have rich Hindu merchants as well as workers and artisans in the town and attract more of them from the neighbouring territories than to interfere in their rituals which would force the Hindus to flee Pondicherry to the territories under the English and the Dutch.

On the contrary, the presence of more and more Hindus in Pondicherry would only serve the proselytizing interests of the missionaries. The missionaries were asked to be prudent in their dealings with the Hindus. Rather than resorting to force, they were asked to persuade the Hindus to restrict their ceremonies within their temples and to abandon their idolatrous 'indecent' processions or restrict them around their temples.[26]

However, in spite of the lenient attitude towards the Hindus during Le Noir's period, it must not mean that the French Jesuit priests had stopped all their proselytizing missions. The policy of preference for Christians in the employment field was well in place during Le Noir's tenure. Guruvappa had converted to Christianity and had become *diwan*. After his death, the higher caste Christian, Pedro Canagaraya Mudaliar took his place. In any case, Le Noir never preferred a Hindu for the post, probably because he did not want to antagonize the Jesuits who were still quite influential.

By the time Le Noir became Governor of Pondicherry, it became quite obvious that famine and epidemics had become major causes leading to the conversion of many Hindus, especially Parayas to Christianity. Though we do not always have the exact caste-wise figures of the conversions, the Parayas who were economically poor and at the most oppressed end of the Hindu social hierarchy, seem to have been the most vulnerable during periods of famine and epidemics. During such periods, it was the French missionaries who were often zealous in coming to the aid of the afflicted and not the higher castes for obvious traditional reasons. At that time, some Telugu-speaking Reddiars seem to have converted to Christianity.

The French Jesuit priest Barbier wrote in 1723: 'More than 200 adults were baptized . . . such an enduring famine had provided the Fathers a new occasion to exercise their zeal. . . . Several Gentiles (Hindus) have found along with the preservation of their physical life, an assurance of the eternal life of the soul, through the baptisms that they received.'

When there was famine in Pondicherry in the 1730s, there were a good number of converts to Christianity. On the western Malabar

Coast, during the same period, Mahé was stricken by smallpox. M.P. Sridharan, the noted historian from Mahé, maintains that abandoning the infected patients in the forests and hilltops was the practice that had been adopted in Mahé and its environs in those days by the Indians. But the Christian Carmelite missionaries who came to the area brought nursing and medical treatment in place of the quarantine and abandonment procedures. They set up a large hospital and brought many missionaries from Verapoly to Mahé to care for the diseased. Clement, Innocent, Roque, Paulinus and Germanian were the missionaries who toiled for eighteen months at great risk to their own health and life to control the epidemic. They used locally available herbs and medicines like margosa, *chenthamarai* and turmeric for the treatment of their patients. The result was a mass conversion of the locals to Christianity. Fr. Ignatius called it 'Conversion in crowds'.

Later the French priest Fourcade noted the following: 'Famine was the most terrible and most heeded of the predications. God knows well the Indians. He knows hunger is the best way to bring them into his beautiful heaven. . . . There were no high castes who converted, but only low castes.'[27]

Generally it seems that conversions diminished considerably after the famine and epidemics were over. The preceding details, however, illustrate the role of the missionaries during periods of famine and epidemics, in bringing about conversions in a peaceful and persuasive manner by offering voluntary material and psychological help to the needy and helpless Hindus, especially of the lower castes, who in all probability would not have converted otherwise. Neither Governor Le Noir nor any of the French colonial authorities objected to such type of conversions.

OTHER DEVELOPMENTS AND EVENTS

Le Noir seems to have been responsible for the extension of the town beyond the Uppar River towards the south. This extension seems to have been planned by the Dutch since 1694. It was during Le Noir's time that Pondicherry which was almost a jungle became a town. Double storeyed houses in bricks, covered with tiles were built in the White town, whereas the Tamil houses in the Black town were made of mud and wood. Actually Le Noir promulgated a law to construct only in bricks and tiles in the White town. Le Noir also was responsible for the planting of more number of trees on both sides of the straight roads.

The town was surrounded by a 30 feet high wall, with four beautiful gates and seven bastions of which two, mounted with artillery and mortars were placed in front of the sea to protect the ships that anchor off Pondicherry. At the entrance of the town, near the principal Madras gate, two big pools were created on either side of the gate, for the benefit of the washermen. All these works were executed by the Capuchin Father Louis. He was honoured for his role in the building and beautification of Pondicherry, with the right to be carried in a palanquin by Le Noir. Outside the town, the countryside was beautiful, with hardly any roads, but with bushes off and on in the passages.

During Le Noir's time the population of Pondicherry was 50,000. 5,000 houses were built. Poverty decreased. Merchants like Ananda Ranga Poullé prospered and people migrated to Pondicherry in large numbers in search of employment. Besides, Le Noir had adopted the policy of religious tolerance. All such measures attracted people to Pondicherry.

However all was not well with Pondicherry town from the hygienic point of view. Stench emanated from the fort area which was terribly unpleasant. So in February 1724, the Governor ordered the cleaning up of the whole fort area. If this was the case in the White town, one could guess that it would have been still worse in the Indian part of the town, where the roads were muddy and marshy and the Tamils lived in actual slums and huts, into which one could not enter or leave without bending low on their knees. There were also infectious pools of water gathered here and there. The canals stank during the dry season when the rain-waters receded and in the rainy season, it was impossible to walk on the roads due to heavy slush.[28]

Le Noir seems to have functioned from the Governor's House, just outside the fort towards the north. But there are indications that this House was constructed during the time of François Martin itself and all his successors until Dupleix lived in it. Actually both the Company office and residence of the Governors were located in the same building. This building stood at the site now numbered No. 4, Rangapillai Street (Ville Aroumé) and No. 5, Nehru Street (Villa Selvom). It was surrounded by a garden that Le Noir decorated with beautiful statues. It was initially rented out and then bought from a certain Février. It was most probably destroyed by the English in 1761 and rebuilt later in the same style.[29]

It was during Le Noir's period in 1734 that the foundation for a hospital was laid towards the south of Pondicherry town, in the Mirapalli area, which extended from the south of the fort towards the west in front of the present Railway station. Father Louis was the architect of this hospital. Some Europeans, Muslims and Christians lived in Mirapalli.[30]

In the year 1732 Sadatullah Khan, the nawab of Arcot since 1710, died without an issue. He was of Nawayat descent, unlike Daoud Khan, the representative of the Mughal emperor earlier. The Nawayats were of Arabic origin, unlike the Mughals. Sadatullah had earlier adopted two sons of his brother. The elder Dost Ali Khan succeeded to the throne of Arcot, while the younger Boker Ali, was appointed governor of Vellore. One of Dost Ali Khan's daughters was given in marriage to Murtuza Ali, son of Boker Ali, while another daughter was married to a distant relation, Chanda Sahib.

It was then that Le Noir sought permission from the nawab to mint rupee coins in Pondicherry through Mir Ghulam Husain, whom the French affectionately called Imam Sahib. Imam Sahib was the *dubash* of the nawab. But before Imam Sahib could obtain the licence, Le Noir had left Pondicherry.[31]

When Le Noir quit Pondicherry, it seems that he took with him just 2,00,000 pounds of which the major part was made up of his Company salary. This must not mean that he did not make any money during his governorship of Pondicherry. He had acquired a plantation in Isle de France along with Vincens, worth 3,200 livres. He is also known to have possessed diamonds worth 17,000 livres. Le Noir also indulged in Asian trade with La Bourdonnais and Dupleix.[32] This shows that Le Noir did enrich himself through private trade or some other means while he was Governor of Pondicherry.

However, the French Company made a profit of 4,90,01,519 livres during the period from 1725 to 1736, through sale of goods brought from India. Le Noir was no doubt the man who had largely contributed to this. He had also improved upon the foundations laid by François Martin for the development of Pondicherry. But Le Noir exercised power in his own way. During his period, Company employees as well as others rose in their positions, not because of their capacities or status, but because they were in the good books of Le Noir. Ananda Ranga Poullé was no doubt in his good books, which allowed him to prosper during Le Noir's governorship.[33]

It is necessary to point out that it was during Le Noir's rule that the French expanded their territories away from Pondicherry. They acquired territories in Yanam and Mahé, which were subjected to Pondicherry. These territories were obtained not through conquests but through legitimate acquisitions. They belonged to France. That is why when the Vazhunavar of Malabar threw the French out of Mahé, the French retaliated with the military might at their disposal and reconquered Mahé. This was the first time when the French were embroiled in an open conflict with an Indian power. This once again demonstrated that the French were not just a peaceful trading company, but they were also a political entity in south India, prepared to defend the territories ceded to them by the Indian powers and even enter into treaties of peace with them on an equal footing.

It would not be an exaggeration to conclude that the colonization of India began right from the time when the Europeans acquired territories from the Indian powers. The territories acquired by the French in India literally belonged to France and the French East Indian Company, right from the time when they were ceded and the French were determined to protect and defend those territories by all means, as they considered them as their colonial or national possessions. This they did to the best of their ability, as long as they were in India.

NOTES

1. Law de Lauriston, *Mémoire sur quelques affaires de l'Empire Moghole...*, 1913, p. xxv; Lettre de M. Guéty au Supérieur et Directeurs du Séminaire, 17 Fév. 1720, Pondichéry, vol. 960, AME; Vinson, 1932, p. 62; M.P. Sridharan. Papers on French Colonial Rule in India, Calicut, 1997, p. 27.
2. Morellet, *Mémoire sur la situation actuelle de la Compagnie des Indes*, 1869, p. 38; Martineau, 1 *Les Origines de Mahé de Malabar*, 1917, p. 198; Deloche,

Old Mahé (1721-1817) According to the Eighteenth Century French Plans, 2013, p. 19.
3. Deloche, ibid., 2013, pp. 5-7, 19; I/1/1, French In India, 1664-1810, Pt. 1 – Letters relating to the French on the Malabar coast, pp. 84, 92-100, IOL; Naf 9354, Concession de Mahé par le Bayanor, 1720-5, BNF; Castonnet des Fosses, *L'Inde Française au XVIIIème siècle*, Paris, s.d., p. 139; *Exposition coloniale*, 1931, pp. 13-14.
4. *Exposition Coloniale*, 1931, pp. 13-14; Naf, 9354, Concession de Mahé par le Bayanor, 1720-5; Martineau, op. cit., 1917, pp. v, viii, 198, 199.
5. Arasaratnam and Ray, *Masulipatnam and Cambay*, 1994, pp. 23-4, 85-9; *Annuaire des Etablissements Français dans l'Inde*, 1853, p. 117; 1934, p. 53; 1938-9, 23, 24, 25; Gaudart, *Catalogue des Manuscrits. . .* , VI, p. 31.
6. Note de Courton du 23 Janvier 1723, Naf 9354, pp. 98-9, BNF; *Annuaire des Etablissements Français dans l'Inde*, 1884, pp. 5, 17, 21; 1938-9, p. 56; Arasaratnam and Ray, 1994, p. 89: Mémoire sur Mazulipatnam, Naf 9359, BNF: Gaudart, ibid., VI, p. 2; Pitoef, 'Yanaon, un Etablisssement de l'Inde Française entre 1817 et 1870', p. 30: Martineau, *Dupleix et l'Inde Française*, vol. I, pp. 6, 7, 39.
7. Gaudart, ibid., VI, p. 2; Naf 9359, Mémoire sur Mazulipatam, p. 281, BNF; *Annuaire des Etablissements Français dans l'Inde*, 1884, p. 9; Martineau, *Dupleix et l'Inde Française*, vol. II, p. 141.
8. Gaudart, ibid. VI, p. 2; Martineau, ibid., pp. 143-4; Manning, *Fortunes à Faire. . .*, 1996, p. 52; *Annuaire des Etablissements Français dans l'Inde*, 1884, p. 25.
9. Launay, *Histoire des Missions de l'Inde*, I, xliii; Lettre du Père Ducros à M. l'Abbé Ragnet, Directeur de la Compagnie des Indes, Ariancoupam, 17 October 1725, pp. 335, 336, LEC, vol. 13, Paris, 1781.
10. La veuve du Chevalier Gourouvappa au Supérieur et Directeur du Séminaire des M.E., 17 Jan. 1926, Pondichéry, vol. 991, AME; Launay, ibid., 1898, I, xxxvifn; Martineau, *Resumé des Actes de l'Etat Civil de Pondichéry*, I, p. 269.
11. Cultru, *Dupleix, ses plans politiques, sa disgrâce*, 1901, pp. 39, 103; *Correspondance du Conseil Supérieur de Pondichéry et de la Compagnie 1726-67*, I, 1920, p. 31.
12. Filliozat, *Catalogue du Fonds Sanscrit*, 1941, I-VI.
13. Vinson, *Les Français dans l'Inde, Dupleix et Labourdonnais*, 1932, p. 15; Favier, *Les Européens et les Indes Orientales au XVIIIe siècle*, 1997, p. 87.
14. *Procés-Verbaux des délibérations du Conseil Supérieur de la Compagnie des Indes*, II, 29-30; Gaebelé, 'Enfance et Adolescence d'Anandarangapoullé', RHEP, 1955, p. 72; Col. C² 73, ff. 37-8, A.N.
15. Favier, op. cit., 1997, p. 87; Vincent, 'Zenith in Pondicherry', 1990, p. 44; *Procés-Verbaux des délibérations du Conseil Supérieur de la Compagnie des*

Indes, II, p. 30; *Correspondance du Conseil Supérieur de Pondichéry et de la Compagnie 1726-67*, I, pp. 54-5, 79-80; Vinson, op. cit., 1932, 16.
16. De Closets d'Errey, *Histoire de l'Inde Française, 1664-1814*, 1940, p. 8.
17. Ibid., 1940, p. 64; *Correspondance du Conseil Supérieur de Pondichéry et de la Compagnie*, I, pp. 31-2, 224; De Closets d'Errey, *Précis Chronologique de l'Histoire de l'Inde Française (1664-1816)*, 1934, p. 22; Manickam, *Trade and Commerce in Pondicherry (1701-1793)*, 2001, pp. 34, 35; *ARP Diary*, I, pp. v, 427; IV, p. 38.
18. *Correspondance du Conseil Supérieur de Pondichéry et de la Compagnie*, I, pp. 31-2.
19. Conseil Supérieur, Pondichéry, 3 Jan. 1733, Pondichéry, in Vinson, op. cit., 1932, p. 52; *Procés-Verbaux des délibérations du Conseil Supérieur de la Compagnie des Indes*, II, pp. 370-1.
20. Gaudart, *Catalogue des Manuscrits . . .* , I, p. 3; Géringer et Chabrelie, *L'Inde Française . . .* , II, 20ème livre; I, 11ème livre; Abbé Guyon, *Histoire des Indes Orientales*, 1744, III, p. 248.
21. La Farelle, *Mémoire et Correspondances du Chevalier et du Général de la Farelle*, 1896, p. 71; Weber, 'La Vie Quotienne dans les Comptoirs', 1995, p. 89.
22. Vinson, op. cit., 1932, pp. 51, 52.
23. Gaudart, *La Criminalité dans les Etablissements Français de l'Inde*, 1938, pp. xiv, 6.
24. Gaudart, ibid., 1938, pp. 56-7, 67, 69, 84-5, 105, 146, 147.
25. *Correspondance du Conseil Supérieur de Pondichéry et de la Compagnie*, I, pp. 249, 254; Sridharan, *Papers on French Colonial Rule in India*, 1997, pp. 27-8; Gaudart, ibid. 1938, pp. xvi, xvii, xxiii, 40, 136, 144, 145, 147.
26. Launay, op. cit., 1898, I, xxxiv, xxxv; Favier, op. cit., 1997, p. 88; *ARP Diary*, I, p. 326; IX, p. 6; X, p. 6, XI, p. 24; XII, pp. 260-1; Y.R. Gaebelé. *Créole et Grande Dame . . .* , Paris, 1934, pp. 34-9; J.B.P. More, *From Arikamedu to the Foundation of Modern Pondicherry*, Chennai, 2014, pp. 34-6.
27. Lettre du Père Barbier, Jésuite au Père de la même Compagnie, Pinneipundi, Mission de Carnate, 15 January 1723, *LEC*, tome 13, Paris, Mérigot, 1781, pp. 296-7; Extrait d'une lettre de Père Calmette au Père de Tournemine, Vencataguiry, 16 Septembre 1737, *LEC*, tome 14, Paris, Mérigot, 1781, p. 10; Sridharan, op. cit., p. 19; Launay, op. cit., III, p. 31; Lettre du Père Le Gac Missionaire de la Compagnie de Jésus à M. le Chevalier hébert, Gouverneur de Pondichéry, Krishnapuram, 10 Décembre 1718, LEC, VIII, 1810, Toulouse, pp. 113-14.
28. Col.c^2 80, ff. 70-1, A.N.; Vinson, op. cit., 1932, p. 15; Cultru, op. cit., 1901, pp. 180-2; Favier, ibid., 1997, p. 88; *ARP Diary*, I, 326; IX, p. 6; X, p. 6; XI, p. 24; XII, 260-1; Y.R. Gaebelé, *Créole et Grande Dame, Johanna*

Begum, Marquise Dupleix, Pondichéry, 1934, pp. 30-4; cf. also, La Farelle, *Mémoire et Correspondances du Chevalier et du Général de la Farelle,* Paris, 1896.
29. Gaudart, op. cit., 1938, pp. viii, 379; Deloche, *Le Papier Terrier de la Ville Blanche de Pondichéry,* 2002, map 1741; Gaebelé, *Créole et Grande Dame, Johanna Begum, Marquise Dupleix,* 1934, p. 88; Vigie, *Dupleix,* 1993, p. 103; *ARP Diary,* IV, 96f; i:379; XII, p. 164.
30. La Farelle, op. cit., 1896, p. 83; *Correspondance du Conseil Supérieur de Pondichéry et de la Compagnie,* III, p. 339; see Map 1741 in Deloche, 2002; *ARP Diary,* II, 253; V, 159; XII, 116, 119, 338.
31. *ARP Diary,* I, pp. 42-4; Vinson, op. cit., 1932, 194f; Orme, *History of the Military Transactions of the British Nation in Indostan,* 1803, p. 38; Wilks, *Historical Sketches of South India,* 1869, I, p. 150.
32. Vigie, op. cit., 1993, pp.103-4; La Farelle, op. cit., 1896, p. 89.
33. Haudrère, ed., *Les Français dans l'Océan Indien au XVIIIe siècle . . . ,* 2004, pp. 49-51; Morellet, op. cit., 1769, p. 123.

CHAPTER 4

Expansion under Governor Benoist Dumas, 1735-1741

PIERRE BENOIST DUMAS succeeded Le Noir in 1735. He came with his wife, Marie Gertrude Venzil, whom he had married earlier in Pondicherry. She was a Dutch Protestant, while Dumas was a Catholic. Dumas' private trade with the Dutch Ostend Company seems to have made this marriage possible.

Since 1728 Dumas was Governor of the French islands of Bourbon and France in the Indian Ocean. He then needed slaves to work in his plantations of coffee, tea, indigo, jute and cotton. He paid a visit to Pondicherry for that purpose when Le Noir was still Governor. Dumas bought 100 slaves, boys and girls between the ages of 8 and 25 and took them to his islands by ship in the most abominable conditions. Besides, the treatment meted out to them in the plantations was cruel and inhuman. It was thus that Benoist Dumas had enriched himself. Dumas was already a slave-owner when he came back to Pondicherry as Governor. He continued to indulge in private trade even after he became Governor.

La Bourdonnais succeeded Dumas as Governor in the islands of the Indian Ocean. Benoist Dumas is believed to be the 'bastard' son of the previous Governor of Pondicherry, Dulivier. He was more interested in fostering the commerce of the Company and his own private trade since he took over power from Le Noir. He continued to be an adept of private trade and recommended it to the Company Directors as a means for the Councillors and their families to be free of want and live in relative ease and comfort, as their salaries were not high enough. Both Dupleix and La Bourdonnais were partners in his private trade.

Dumas had earlier, as member of the Superior Council of Pondicherry been against the prosecution of Nainiappa Poullé. He even assisted his son Guruvappa Poullé in his attempts to rehabilitate the name of his father and recover his properties.[1]

DEVELOPMENTS IN PONDICHERRY

Pondicherry had a population of 80,000 when Benoist Dumas took over power. Of them, 8,000 were Christians.[2] Christianity was making steady progress in Pondicherry due to the zeal of the missionaries and official patronage.

The White town, where Europeans mostly lined, consisted of houses built of wood and *chunam* (lime). Some were double-storeyed. But the Black town beyond the Ariyankuppam River, which was prolonged later northward by a canal, consisted of huts and small dwellings. The Tamils who were mostly weavers worked on the roads during daytime, under the shade of trees and slept in the verandahs or on the terraces of their houses by night. They earned very little. But they managed their families with the meagre income. They mostly ate rice cooked in water.

It has been noted generally that the Hindus were hard working, while the Muslims lived often in utter idleness. The surroundings of Pondicherry were well cultivated, with wells to water the fields. Rice, coconuts and all sorts of fruits and vegetables like cucumber, orange, lemon, pumpkins and pineapples were grown. Toddy was fermented. The surroundings also contained forests and woods, filled with deers and wild pigs, hares and partridges. The Europeans loved to hunt them.[3]

Marriages between the French and Tamils were rare. But it was the policy of the French to encourage it later in order to create a race of mixed blood, who would contribute to the consolidation of the French colonies in the south. The Portuguese were the pioneers as far as the policy of miscegenation were concerned. The French simply followed them.[4]

It seems that the fortifications of Pondicherry started way back in 1724, was completed in 1736. On 22 July of that year the tax imposed on the people for the fortification was cancelled. But the parapets still remained to be completed. The rampart was surrounded by a moat. Thousands of trees were planted inside and outside Pondicherry.

Dumas also went on a cleanliness drive in Pondicherry through a proclamation on 11 June 1739. He ordered people against committing nuisance within the limits of Pondicherry town, on the beach, the banks of the Uppar, running south of St. Paul's Church or in public roads. Offenders were liable to a fine of 6 *fanams*, two of which to be paid to the person who seized the delinquent in act and four to the court. This decree was strictly enforced though the people thought that it was very stringent and harsh.

During Dumas' govenorship, the right-hand castes objected to the Chetties and other left-hand castes to enter the town by the Madras Road. Dumas did not sit idle. He intervened in this caste affair and was instrumental in throwing the Madras Road open to all public, irrespective of caste or creed.[5]

Besides the hospital whose construction had started in 1734 near the old Cuddalore gate, south of the Fort and at the East of Uppar was not yet completed in 1738. A bridge was constructed to connect the White town with the Black town, near the old Cuddalore Gate.[6]

Until the arrival of Dumas, the education of the children and young Europeans and the converted Hindus was completely in the hands of the Jesuits. They taught them to read and write French and some arithmetic. Besides, the increase in the number of Europeans in Pondicherry led to the construction of a school for European children. Dumas thought of changing this pattern. He disliked the domination of the Jesuits in education to some extent.

On 8 September 1738, three Ursuline sisters of France, under the Mother Superior Marquez de Sainte Gertrude, came to Pondicherry to take charge of education. They started a school for girls. They were actually dispatched by the Bishop of Vanves. But a smooth relationship was not established between the Ursuline sisters and Dumas, as the former would not take orders from the latter. Besides, the sisters began to talk openly about the illegal commercial activities of the Company officials, including Dumas. This situation continued when Dupleix became Governor of Pondicherry in 1742, which pushed the Ursuline sisters to quit Pondicherry altogether in 1744.[7]

In 1728, Nawab Sadatullah Khan built a fort at Alamparai, located at about 50 km to the north of Pondicherry on the coast. He appointed Imam Sahib as the Governor of the area and set up a mint there to manufacture Arcot rupees. Since 1715, the French had been trying to get permission from the nawab to mint rupees in Pondicherry.

On 6 July 1736, Dumas sent as gift 900 pagodas to the nawab, 290 pagodas to his brother Sadat Ali Khan, 345 pagodas to his minister Imam Sahib and 296 pagodas to his treasurer Citisjorkan. Finally in the year 1736, Governor Dumas, following Le Noir obtained licence to mint rupees in Pondicherry itself instead of using the Arcot money minted at Alamparai, by further gifting Rs. 80,000 to the nawab of Arcot, Dost Ali Khan, 25,000 to the *durbar*, and 15,000 to Imam Sahib, who was *dubash* and intermediary of the nawab in this affair. Besides, for every ship coming from France, 80,000 pagodas of silver was agreed to be delivered to the nawab's treasury. A payment of one rupee for every thousand rupees minted in Pondicherry was to be also made over to the prime minister of the nawab, i.e. Imam Sahib and his descendants. However the licence to mint was profitable both to the nawab and the Company.[8]

Pedro Canagarayen himself went to Alamparai to collect the charter delivered by Dost Ali Khan, the successor of Sadatullah Khan. On 17 August 1736, Dumas was confirmed of the right to mint money in Pondicherry by the Mughal Emperor Muhammad Shah and the nizam through Imam Sahib. The emperor also conferred the title of nawab and mansabdar on Dumas. Besides, Dumas was knighted by the French government for this achievement and admitted to the Order of St. Michel. Pedro Cangarayen, who had also worked for this licence, was awarded a medal by the French government.[9]

The *parachery*, near the old Cuddalore gate, which was located right in the middle of the then town, was cleared. In its place, Dumas started constructing the Hôtel de Monnaie, i.e. the mint in 1736. It was completed in 1738 at the cost of 5,520 pagodas. It was actually located at the site of the present Public Works Department. Here the silver that came from France was minted into Arcot or Alamparai rupees by merchants like Sukurama, Trivedy, Balachetty, Guntur Vingen Chetty and Pedro Canagarayen. In 1741, Canagarayen and his children were accorded half a rupee for every thousand rupees minted. Imam Sahib assured Canagarayen and Dumas that the Pondicherry money would be valid everywhere.[10]

At the same time on 10 January 1738, Dupleix, who was Director of the French Company at Chandernagore, unilaterally obtained permission from Nawab Shuja Khan to mint rupees in gold, silver and copper at Murshidabad in Bengal by gifting him Rs. 50,000 rupee. Dumas was unhappy with this move as he wanted to offload a part of the rupees minted in Pondicherry to Bengal. Thus the relationship between Dumas and Dupleix was never smooth during this period. But Godeheu, one of the Directors of the French Company at this time, favoured Dupleix.[11]

At that time, Canagarayen was also given the contract for dyeing the Company's cloth blue and payment was made after delivery. He also benefitted from commissions given by the buyers of the Company's products and the furnishers of the products needed for exportation by the Company.[12]

In February-March 1737, Pedro Cangarayen was suffering from acute diabetes and was completely bed-ridden. Ananda Ranga Poullé never got along well with Pedro, as he knew that the latter had played a role earlier in prosecuting his uncle Nainiappa. He then thought that his time had come to become *dubash*. But Pedro survived and Dumas preferred to continue with him as *dubash*. Ananda Ranga Poullé was second only to Pedro until 1746.[13]

On 10 November 1739 the Company bought from Dupleix a garden, with magnificent trees, situated to the west of the Governor's house/fort for an amount of 1,200 pagodas. In the midst of the garden was a magnificent and furnished palace, constructed by Dupleix. It was used to lodge the Muslim princes, dignitaries and ambassadors. The garden was open to the public. Presently the site is located between the canal and Cathedral Street (Mission Street).[14]

In the same year, Benoist Dumas started the work on the construction of a new Government House within the fort. But he continued to live in the old Governor's residence, located presently at 4, Ananda Ranga Poullé Street (Villa Aroumé). He also allotted 3,000 pagodas for the reconstruction of the Capuchin Church.[15]

By 1740 the construction of the hospital begun in 1734 was completed. Father Louis was succeeded by the engineer, Charpentier de Cossigny. They planned the fortification of Pondicherry too. In October 1740, Pondicherry town was protected on all sides, except the side facing the sea. In October 1741, de Cossigny left for France.

He was succeeded by Paradis who came to India in 1737. He was first posted in Mahé and then in Karaikal. By 1741, Pondicherry seems to have emerged as one of the most beautiful and strongest on the whole of the Cholamandalam coast.[16]

In 1737, there was a terrible famine in Pondicherry which continued until the end of 1738. The weavers and bleachers almost died of hunger. The local Indian princes, lords and ministers laid their hands on the rice kept in reserve in the towns and villages, leaving the people in total distress. The merchants sold the grains at such a high price that only the rich could buy them. As a result, the French government distributed rice to the poor at a low price, brought in from as far as Bengal.[17]

Dumas traded not only in goods, but also continued to trade in human beings. Though the nawab of Arcot did not approve slavery, Dumas exported slaves to the Bourbon and France Islands for work, especially when there was famine in Tamil Nadu, where Tamil-speaking and other slaves were more easily available, than in other parts of India.[18]

The farming out of Company lands, especially for tobacco and betel cultivation, every three or five years was a steady income for the Company government to meet all the local expenses especially those incurred due to the various constructions.[19] Besides Europeans were favoured for Company jobs. Indians and persons of mixed origin were incapable of obtaining a grade superior to the clerk grade in the Company administration, with a salary of 800 pounds annually, during Dumas' governorship.[20]

DEVELOPMENTS IN MAHÉ

In 1739, Mahé entered a period of prosperity which lasted for about two decades until 1761 when the English conquered it. Pepper trade accounted for its prosperity. The English at Tellicherry provided munitions to the Malabaris. But through the treaty of 22 December 1739, the French obtained the mountains of Paitara and Chembra and the safe passage of pepper to Mahé. The French then asked the Regent-Queen of Badagara to give them two other mountains overlooking Mahé. They were duly ceded on 1 January 1740. Thus the French acquired an additional 400 to 500 hectares of territory to its initial 50 hectares. They started some defensive works to protect their territory. Louis Paradis de la Roche, a Swiss free-booter was sent to Mahé from Bourbon Island to supervise the fortifications.

But that was not enough to make Mahé politically important in the region. In fact, there was no indication that the Company or its agents including Governor Dumas at Pondicherry had any desire to establish a French political empire on the Malabar Coast, which was outside the sphere of Mughal influence. This in spite of the fact that they were conscious of their superior military power and organizational skills and of the turmoil that existed in the surrounding Malayali kingdoms. Whatever territories Dumas obtained in Mahé were through treaty and largely peaceful means.[21] Nevertheless, Mahé grew as a political and trading entity on the Malabar Coast, subject to Pondicherry.

The English at Tellicherry were alarmed by the growing influence of the French and their pepper trade on the Malabar Coast. The chief of Tellicherry, Mr. Wake brought the Regent, the Nambiar chiefs of the region and the Kolattiri Raja together and committed some minor aggressions against the French. The French had to defend themselves.[22]

As Dumas feared a Maratha invasion of Pondicherry, La Bourdonnais came to Pondicherry from *Isle de France* in the Indian Ocean with seven warships on 30 September 1741. But by then the Marathas had retreated. Instead, La Bourdonnais was instructed to go to Mahé with his squadron to protect it from the Nair militiamen who were blockading it. La Bourdonnais reached Mahé on 24 November 1741. On 3 December La Bourdonnais' troops attacked the Nairs and Mappilas (Malabar Muslims). By 5 December the French defeated them and made them flee. La Bourdonnais lost 56 Frenchmen in the attack, while the Nairs lost 500. It seems that Dumas employed sepoys of Mahé in that conflict with the local princes.[23]

The Mahé operation cost the Company 4 or 5 million livres nevertheless. This was a drain in the Company's finances. Subsequently three peace treaties were concluded, two with the Nambiar chiefs and one with the English. Pepper trade and navigation security was assured for the French. But this peace was nevertheless obtained by the payment of 1,25,000 *fanams*, in spite of the fact that La Bourdonnais had won the war.[24]

It needs to be noted nevertheless that even on the Malabar Coast

Dumas did not indulge in any forcible conquest of territory by military means. Mahé was made up of about 200 to 300 hectares only. Five hundred French soldiers were needed to protect it, apart from 200 locally recruited sepoys. In a similar fashion, Dumas expanded Yanam factory by obtaining some lands from the Nizam through peaceful means.[25] However, whenever there was threat to the existence of these miniscule territories, the French Governors reacted and employed military power to safeguard them as they considered them as France's possessions in the East.

Acquisition of Karaikal

Already in 1738, with an objective to increase Company's trade, Dumas sought for a coastal territory in the Tanjore region which was under Maratha rule since 1674. In 1688, François Martin did obtain Kaveripatnam through his interpreter Cozhandaiappa. But that fizzled out. But then Dumas was determined to have a foothold in Tanjore, a rice-producing area. It happened that Sahaji Maharaja, the king of Tanjore was acutely short of funds. This compelled him to enter into a treaty with Dumas on 10 July 1738 to sell Karaikal, the fort of Karakalancheri and five adjoining villages for a total sum of 40,000 *chakras* of gold. Dumas also advanced some money to the king of Tanjore to keep off a rival.[26]

Karaikal was situated at about 150 km south of Pondicherry in the Cauvery delta. It was a very old port town, mentioned in Sekkizhar's Periya Puranam.[27] It was a fertile rice-producing region.

However, Sahaji did not keep his promise. He complained that the Dutch in Nagapattinam were not happy with the French settlement at Karaikal.

By then Nawab Dost Ali Khan (1732-40) had sent an army of 30,000 men under his son-in-law and Diwan Hussein Dost Khan known popularly as Chanda Sahib and his brother Bada Sahib, in order to exact tributes from the Rajas of Tanjore and Trichinopoly. The raja of Trichinopoly Vijaya Ranga Soccappa Naiker seems to have been imprisoned in the magnificent Shiva temple of Tiruvannamalai, which was under Governor Abu Sahib. He died in 1736. The Regent was a woman, by the name of Meenakshi who ruled the country.

According to the French engineer, Charpentier de Cossigny, Chanda Sahib was a magnificent man, reputed to be brave, as white as a European, who admired the French very much.[28] It appears that Meenakshi was attracted by Chanda Sahib's magnificent personality.

Chanda Sahib captured Trichinopoly fort. Naturally Governor Dumas courted Chanda Sahib in order to safeguard his interests in Karaikal. Pedro Canagarayen on his part sent his men to Karaikal to tell that the town belonged to the French. Chanda Sahib, heeding to Dumas, promised to intervene with his troops on behalf of the French.

But Chanda Sahib was not a tender man. He ordered his troops to devastate the Tanjore-Trichinopoly region, plunder the villages, appropriate the corn in the fields and enslave the Tamil people. He occupied Karaikal town, the fort and the adjoining regions and handed them over to the French through a *parvana* dated 12 February 1739. The raja of Tanjore closeted himself in his fort. Frenchman Gratien Golard took possession of Karaikal along with some villages. Three companies of Mahé sepoys were also deployed by Dumas to defend Karaikal. Thus the French thenceforth drew closer to Chanda Sahib, a local potentate and a possible successor to the throne of Arcot.

But the Raja of Tanjore who stood out still, counted on the Marathas to defend him. He raised his price for the Karaikal town and fort to 50,000 *chakras*. He also demanded from the French a loan of 1,50,000 *chakras* without interest repayable in 3 years and an annual rent of 4,000 pagodas for five villages. Dumas agreed to all the terms, but managed to reduce the loan to 10,000 *chakras* and the annual rent for the villages to 2,000 *chakras*. Besides, the *parvana* of Chanda Sahib dated 1 July 1739 ceded two more villages including Neravi to Dumas. Dumas sent 1,400 pagodas to Chanda Sahib, 600 to his brother Bada Sahib and 200 pagodas to be distributed to his officers as gift.[29]

In the meantime, Sahaji lost his throne to Pratap Singh who renewed the demand for a loan of 1,00,000 *chakras*. As a first instalment the French gave him 40,000 *chakras* and obtained 8 more villages from Pratap Singh. On 12 Febraury 1740, Pratap Singh sold these villages to the French for 60,000 *chakras*. Some more villages like Tirunallar, Vanjour and Neravy were pledged to the French for 1,15,350 *chakras*.

In July 1741, a *parvana* was received from the Mughal emperor confirming Karaikal and the adjoining regions as French possessions. The French made a payment of Rs. 6,000 to Imam Sahib to obtain it. Thus it is clear that the French obtained Karaikal and the adjoining regions, not through conquest, but by paying for it.[30] Dumas did not resort to war for acquiring Karaikal. It is also significant that Chanda Sahib became a steadfast friend of the French thenceforth, as he had helped the French to recover Karaikal.

Karaikal contained 638 brick houses, covered with tiles and 240 huts, when the French occupied it. Its population was about 5,000. There were five mosques, five big temples and nine small ones. Tamil-speaking Muslims indulged in trade there. The surroundings of Karaikal were fertile, with a number of lakes and the Arsalar River. Rice, cotton, indigo was cultivated there.[31] Lands were farmed out for fixed periods to a Brahmin called Muthiah and also to Pedro Canagarayen, the *dubash*, for 4,600 pagodas. Tirumalairayanpattinam was rented out to Pedro Canagarayen, on condition that all fabrics manufactured for the Company were exempt from taxation. Later during the 1740s some lands were also leased out to Louis Pregachem Mudaliar, Labbai Tambi Marakkayar and others. The sale of arrack and betel and goods imported by sea as well as fishing was also leased out.

It seems that there were Christians in Karaikal even before this date. The Jesuits were given the right to occupy the chapel at the fort of Karaikal. They were also allowed to indulge in their proselytizing mission among the Hindus and Muslims of the town. During the 1750s when cholera struck Karaikal, more than 4,000 Hindus including children of all castes died, of whom some converted to Christianity at the time of death.[32]

The first *dubash* of the French Company in Karaikal was the squint-eyed Pondicherrian Prakasa Mudali, son of Arunasala Mudali. The latter was tax collector and agricultural administrator under the French. Prakasa Mudali seems to have converted to Christianity at this time. He was previously native ship captain.[33]

The acquisition of Karaikal had cost the French Company 55,247 pagodas, while its annual revenue was just about 12,283. Additional revenue was procured by farming out lands to Ananda Ranga Poullé in May 1741 for 3,500 pagodas. Besides Dumas had obtained from the Nizam, the lands in front of the factory at Yanam, which yielded a revenue of Rs. 1,000.[34]

MARATHAS, MUSLIM REFUGEES AND FURTHER ACQUSITIONS

In the meantime in 1740, the Maratha Hindus numbering 50,000 had gained entry into the Carnatic or rather northern Tamil Nadu due to the connivance of Nizam-ul-mulk himself or rather his son Nazir Jung, who detested Dost Ali Khan, and some Hindu chiefs or polygars who probably wanted to shake off Muslim domination. At the same time, the Hindu kings of Mysore and Tanjore asked the Marathas to attack Tamil Nadu and avenge the violations of their temples and sacred places by Chanda Sahib and his men. In May 1740 an army of 10,000 Maratha soldiers and 7,000 to 8,000 cavalry under General Raghoji Bhonsle entered the Carnatic.[35]

On 20 May 1740, Nawab Dost Ali Khan and his son Hassan Ali were killed in the battle of Damalcheri on the north of Pennaiyaru by Maratha invaders. The Marathas took over part of the treasury of Dost Ali, 40 elephants, several horses and the emperor's flag. Safdar Ali Khan, the other son of Dost Ali took refuge in Vellore. Arcot was ransacked and robbed by the Marathas under Fateh Singh for several days. Much of the town was burnt. They then raided Tiruvannamalai during the Kartigai festival in September 1740. The Marathas forced the people to pay taxes wherever they went and ruined the whole region. They obtained a good booty. Tamil Brahmins, Komuttis and Maratha Brahmins bearing the title Rao or Pandit, as well as others, altogether about 3,000 poured into Pondicherry with their valuables from places like Arcot, Vellore, Alamparai and Vandavasi.[36]

Raghoji Bhonsle, the Maratha chief proceeded to Trichinopoly where he imprisoned Chanda Sahib on 28 May 1741. Chanda Sahib had offered Rs. 7 lakh to the Marathas for his freedom, but the Mysore Hindu king wanted the Marathas to kill or imprison Chanda Sahib and restore Hindu Nayaka rule there. Chanda Sahib's brother, Bada Sahib was killed by the Marathas on 1 October 1741. It seems that Safdar Ali Khan, the new nawab, unable to pay the tribute demanded by the Marathas, had agreed to give them Trichinopoly.

On capturing Trichinopoly the Marathas sent back 40,000 of their horsemen to Mysore with Chanda Sahib. They left back about 20,000 cavalry under Morari Rao in Trichinopoly. The Marathas looted Trichinopoly and its people on their way back.[37]

Governor Dumas had fortified Pondicherry to such an extent that it was considered as a safe haven by the Muslim nobles fleeing the Marathas, as well as by other people, both Hindus and Muslims. He had about 1,200 Europeans to combat at his disposal. He also recruited Indians, mostly Muslims to form an Indian army of sepoys, consisting of 4,500 men. He also asked for the help of La Bourdonnais.[38]

Assured of safety in Pondicherry, the wife of Imam Sahib arrived in Pondicherry from Alamparai. She was received by Pedro Canagarayen and Muthiah Poullé. Dost Ali Khan's widow and family came in two palanquins to Pondicherry from the fort of Vandavasi, with 1,500 cavalry, 80 elephants, 300 camels and more than 200 carts pulled by buffalos, filled with treasure and people of the widow's entourage. Dumas received them at the Vazhudavur gate. The widow was lodged at the Governor's garden. Ten days later, the wife of Nawab Safdar Ali Khan and his three sisters, the sister of Dost Ali Khan and the two and a half year old son of Dost Ali Khan and some officials as well as the wife of Bada Sahib and many others came to Pondicherry fleeing the fort of Vellore. Some of them brought presents for Dumas and Pedro Canagarayen.[39]

The Marathas, who were Hindus by religion, and who were expected to avenge the destruction of temples by Chanda Sahib, did not spare the Tamil people. They looted many towns like Vellore, Tiruvannamalai and Kanchipuram, in spite of the fact that the Tamils were Hindus too. Parangipettai or Porto Novo was raided and pillaged by a Maratha free-booter and his men from 14 to 25 December 1740. Earlier in November he had ransacked Kanchipuram, which had many temples. It is estimated that they looted about 50,000 pagodas from Parangipettai. Ananda Ranga Poullé in charge of a factory at Parangipettai lost 1,00,000 pagodas. The French Company had lost 3,901 pagodas worth of goods in Porto Novo.[40] Sadraspatam, Malayanur, Senji, Peddapettai, Kalasapakkam, Tindivanam, Velliamedu, Karadi, Palakolai, Venkatammalpettai and places close to Pondicherry like

Tiruppapuliyur, Manjakuppam, Singirikovil and Azhizapakkam were all looted by the Marathas.

In Tiruvannamalai especially they laid their hands on a huge treasury. In fact, the people of the neighbourhood had confided their wealth to the temple authorities of Rudra at Tiruvannamalai, thinking that the Marathas would hold the temple in respect and would not dare to approach it. But they had miscalculated as the Maratha soldiers not only plundered and confiscated the wealth stored in the temple, but also took away the temple dancers as well as the girls of the temple, who were presumably Tamil Brahmins. It is noteworthy that in this temple *Sati* was practised and women were burnt alive along with their dead husband in considerable numbers, all in order to maintain the purity of the women.[41]

The Marathas were a real terror to the Tamils. A single Maratha horseman could put to flight 1,000 Tamils according to a French account of this period.[42]

However, in order to meet the extra expenses caused by the continuous influx of refugees into Pondicherry, Dumas, following the advice of Pedro Cangarayen, decided to tax the incomes of the merchants of Pondicherry and those traders like the Komuttis and Gujaratis and also the Muslim nobility who had sought refuge in Pondicherry. As a result, the Company's merchants were expected to pay 1,000 pagodas, Seshachela Chetty 500 pagodas, Ananda Ranga Poullé 400 pagodas, Muthiah Pillai 300 pagodas and so on.

Some merchants like the cloth shop owner Ambalavana Chetty refused to pay taxes. They were imprisoned until they paid the amount. Ananda Ranga Poullé found fault with Pedro Canagarayen for such a situation, who it seems had a hand in advising Dumas to impose such a tax. Poullé even held later that he did not know if the amount collected thus was remitted to the Company by Dumas or not. The old enmity and ill-will of Ananda Ranga Poullé against Pedro Canagarayen had still not died down.[43]

The Maratha generals, Raghoji Bhonsle and Fateh Singh, with the intention of capturing the treasury of the Muslim refugees in Pondicherry, threatened Governor Dumas with dire consequences, if they were not handed over to them and if he did not pay Rs. 5 lakh and the annual tribute due to the king of the Marathas since 50 years. They sent messengers to Pondicherry with this objective.

But Dumas was made of sterner stuff. He did not succumb to the Maratha threats. He told that the French had not paid any tribute to the Marathas since 40 years. He refused to hand over the widow and son of Dost Ali with the treasury. His men had actually repulsed Maratha incursions from the Fort at Ariyankuppam, but not before incurring a loss of 4,826 pagodas. Dumas sent Pedro Canagarayen, Ananda Ranga Poullé and about ten other merchants to talk to the messengers. Also Azhagappan, brother-in-law of Pedro Canagarayen was sent to Villianur to negotiate a settlement with the messengers. The Marathas detained Azhagappan. Thereupon Dumas boldly and promptly imprisoned the Marathas and freed Azhagappan. Naturally Dumas was expecting the Marathas to fall upon Pondicherry, but as a precaution he had already strengthened its defences.[44]

Meanwhile Safdar Ali Khan had entered into a treaty with the Marathas and agreed to pay them as tribute at stated periods a sum of Rs. 1 crore, equal to one year's revenue of the Carnatic, on condition that they went back to their country at once. That was why Raghoji Bhonsle decided to retreat from the Carnatic after the middle of May 1741 and not because they feared Dumas and his soldiers and the fortifications in Pondicherry. It was not also because Raghoji Bhonsle's wife was so infatuated by the ten bottles of French liquor offered by Dumas to Raghoji that the latter renounced his plans to invade Pondicherry. Thenceforth Safdar Ali Khan assumed the title of Nawab and Chanda Sahib himself came to Arcot subsequently to pay homage to him.[45]

Nevertheless, it is to the credit of Dumas that he did not succumb to the Maratha threats. His men had actually repulsed minor Maratha incursions into Pondicherry at Ariyankuppam. Due to Maratha incursions in and around Pondicherry, trade came to a stand-still. Besides the fabrication of cotton goods were interrupted, the villages were robbed and ruined and the weavers had left the town. To add to this terrible misery, famine reared its head in Pondicherry in the year 1740, costing the lives of several people and cattle. Dumas imported rice in ships from Bengal as well as from Yanam and Masulipatnam to alleviate the sufferings of the Pondicherry people.[46]

The new nawab of Arcot, Safdar Ali Khan as well as Chanda Sahib paid a visit to Pondicherry to thank Dumas for his timely help. Dumas received them at the Vazhudavur gate. Dumas received costly presents from Safdar Ali Khan. He got the armour of Anwaruddin, richly adorned with gold and precious stones, together with three elephants, several horses, many swords and jewelled weapons. The Khan left for Arcot with his family members while Chanda Sahib left the women of his family and one of his sons in Pondicherry while making his way to Trichinopoly.

The nawab gave Dumas in the month of September 1740, the villages of Archivak (Abhishekapakkam or Azhisapakkam), yielding a revenue of Rs. 10,000 and Teduvanatham in Vazhudavur area as well as Odiyampattu and Tirukanji, as a reward due to the help rendered by the French to the nawab's families. Dumas transferred them to the French Company, but he retained the right to collect revenues from these places as long as he lived, with the consent of the Company.[47]

This cession was confirmed later by the Mughal emperor, who also granted Dumas a *mansab* of 4,500 horse, with a standard. Thus Dumas was the first Frenchman to become a *mansabdar* of the Mughal. Thenceforth he was a vassal or local lord of the Great Mughal. He had to have under his order 4,500 horses for the title. *Mansabdar* was a highly prestigious title, which involved complex paraphernalia. But this title was not given to Dumas personally, but was given in his capacity as Governor of Pondicherry and was transferable to all future governors. It raised the prestige of the French, in the eyes of the Indian princes.

However, Dumas did not receive the title of Nawab. In the *parvana* conferring the title Dumas is qualified as *jamedar*, which literally meant Second Officer. Pondicherry always remained a concession given to the French Company of which Dumas was the Governor. Dumas never drew any personal revenue from the territory of Pondicherry, except from those small villages donated to him by Safdar Ali Khan, which served to affirm that he was a 'jagirdar' of Pondicherry.[48]

Archivak seems to have been leased out to Pedro Canagarayen, the *dubash*. At the latter's death, his brother Lazar inherited it. Besides, many of the Hindustani Muslim migrants who had sought refuge in Pondicherry during the Maratha incursions stayed back, which led to the increase in the Muslim population of Pondicherry. They spoke Urdu or Deccani and had a separate mosque for themselves in the Muslim quarters that grew on the south-western side of the Uppar River.[49]

Further Developments under Dumas

It seems probable that it was during Dumas' or Dupleix's governorship that the Tamil Muslim graveyard as well as the tomb of Moula Sahib which was located in between the site of the Public Works Department and the present government hospital, were shifted to the Muslim quarters, beyond the Ariyankuppam River towards the west. There we find today the majestic dargah of Moula Sahib. Though the Muslims were few in number, they had three mosques even in 1735 in the area towards the south of the fort which included the Mirapalli area.[50]

In 1739-40 Imam Sahib, deputy of the nawab of Arcot at Alamparai had lent 90,000 pagodas to the French Company on interest. He also traded with foreign countries through Pondicherry. He had married a daughter of Chanda Sahib. However in 1740 after the death of Dost Ali, Imam Sahib moved to Hyderabad. Nizam-ul-Mulk made him the *faujdar* of Masulipatnam, where the French had a factory.[51]

It is noteworthy that during Dumas' rule trade flourished. The town had a population of 80,000 in 1735. The Company borrowed money from Indian merchants like Imam Sahib, Narenachetty, Sittambala Sankararayen, Pedro Cangarayen and Ananda Ranga Poullé to carry on profitably with its trade and commerce. The Company exported to India silver, iron and lead, wine, *eau de vie* (alcohol), coral, manufactured objects, canons and guns, gun powder, glass and crystals. It imported cotton cloth, handkerchiefs, saltpetre, red wood, teak wood, pepper slaves, rice and beasts, etc.

The Company also derived revenues as usual by leasing out the lands. The French Company on the whole made a profit of 42,824,315 livres through the sale of goods from India. But this commerce was disturbed since 1739 due to the invasion of the Marathas and the conquest of Delhi by Nadir Shah.[52]

Besides, the Jesuits mounted pressure on Governor Dumas, as they had done always since François Martin's time, to prohibit all Hindu ceremonies and customs and idol worshipping in Pondicherry. Dumas, following Le Noir, did not succumb to the pressure of the Jesuits and allowed the Hindus complete freedom of religion. In 1738, the Jesuits, infuriated by the behaviour of Dumas petitioned the Company Directors in France requesting them to intervene so that Dumas adopted a severe attitude towards the pompous ceremonies of the Hindus and curtail the Hindu processions parading 'obscene idols'. But Dumas refused to budge. He was even present on the occasion of performance of *Sati* by a 24 year old young widow who burnt herself alive in the pyre of her dead husband. This non-intervention in the ceremonies of the Hindus had earned for him the respect of the Marathas and the Hindus who had invaded Tamil Nadu.[53]

Following Le Noir, Dumas too retained the Christian Pedro Canagarayen as *dubash*, in spite of his ill-health. Ananda Ranga Poullé was always aiming to become the *dubash*. But Dumas would not abandon Pedro. Obviously, Ranga Poullé could not put up with this. This reflects very well in his entries about Dumas in his diary. But it must be said that it was not Dumas who had appointed Pedro Canagarayen as *dubash*. Instead, it was his predecessor Le Noir, who chose to favour the Jesuit line of appointing a Christian to the post. Besides, it appears that Poullé and his father had prospered and enriched themselves immensely more under Le Noir's rule than under Dumas. Naturally Poullé credited Le Noir as being a better and strict manager of Company funds than Dumas.[54]

During Dumas' time the town was surrounded by a wall with five gateways and 17 outposts. All this area including the side open to the sea needed to be protected. He had at his disposal 350 white soldiers and 220 sepoys. Dumas actually following François Martin recruited Tamil and Indian sepoys for his troops. He also raised a battalion of 300 indigenous security guards called 'peons'.[55]

A pit was dug since March 1740 around the outer wall with the objective of fortifying the town, under the supervision of the French engineer, Charpentier de Cossigny. The mud that was taken from the pit was used to fill up the low marshy land that lay to the west of the fort, bordering the Jesuit quarters and the Vedapuriswaran temple. The land was marshy due to the fact that all the waters of the neighbourhood found their way there. Besides, when the sea entered during high tide through the opening at the south of the town and when it receded, it left behind a good amount of dirt and waste, which when heated by the sun emitted an awful smell. The government imposed a tax on the inhabitants for the digging of the pit. By 1741 a wall was being built at the seaside, starting from Fort Louis upto St. Laurent post towards the south.[56]

Safdar Ali Khan knowing that Dumas was about to leave Pondicherry, sent him costly presents, consisting of jewels, pearls, gold and diamonds, which added up to his already rich collection of the same. When Dumas was actually relieved from his office on 16 October 1741, he was a very wealthy person. He had always indulged in private trade, along with his younger brother Gabriel Dumas as well as with Dupleix. Nallatamby Chetty and Arunasala Chetty were the chief agents of Dumas in his private trade. Even when he left India, he entrusted his business dealings including the revenues that he got through the lands given to him by Nawab Safdar Ali to the care of a certain Du Laurens.

In France, he had bought an estate and the lordship of Stains for 3,75,000 livres including paintings, furniture, ornaments and glass. He bought a house in Paris at Rue Richelieu for 1,50,000 livres including paintings, glass and furniture and another small house at rue Sainte Apolline. He also had some properties in the country-side. This and the Paris properties brought him an annual rental of 24,000 livres.

Dumas had also invested in 438 slaves bought in Senegal with four others. He had also properties in Isle de France and Isle de Bourbon. He had regular revenues from these properties. Dumas died childless in October 1746. At the time of his death, he had invested 95,000 livres in various commercial ventures. His wife had a large quantity of jewels, pearls and diamonds, along with a necklace of four rows, each set with forty large pearls. Dumas thus became a self-made *Nabob*, i.e. a person who had enriched himself in India.[57]

It is quite clear from the above that Dumas did not swerve from the policies established by François Martin and amplified by Le Noir, with regard to French establishments in India. Whatever territories that the French acquired since 1673-4 through concessions or purchases became French territories belonging to France. Even Dumas did not acquire any territory by conquest. He only sought to assert his authority over territories like Karaikal that was ceded or bought by him, in the name of the Company.

However, he sought to re-assert his authority over Karaikal, not through diplomacy or by employing his own forces, but with the help of the forces of Chanda Sahib, the son-in-law and *diwan* of the nawab of Arcot, Dost Ali Khan. As a matter of fact, the interests of Chanda Sahib and Dumas coincided at this time. Chanda Sahib wanted to extract tributes from the Maratha Tanjore king as a sign of his subjugation to the nawab of Arcot, while Dumas wanted French control over Karaikal against the wishes of the same Tanjore king. On his part, the Tanjore king called upon the Marathas, who were a power to be reckoned with since the time of Shivaji, to help him out against the French and Chanda Sahib.

Thus Dumas, probably influenced by Pedro Canagarayen, waded unwittingly into the internal quarrels of the Indian powers and started taking the side of one Indian ruler or prince against another. This move was naturally fraught with danger in the fast evolving political scenario of southern India. As expected, the Marathas invaded Tamil Nadu. They plundered and devastated the Tamil country including many temples, without making any distinction between Hindus and Muslims. Tamilians suffered a lot due to their merciless raids. They killed Nawab Dost Ali Khan and imprisoned Chanda Sahib as earlier mentioned.

Governor Dumas, an ally of Chanda Sahib, were naturally one of their targets. To add to this, Dumas had given asylum to the Muslim nobles and their families in Pondicherry, who had fled Tamil Nadu with their treasures to escape the fury of the Marathas. But the Maratha general, as he had patched up with Nawab Safdar Ali Khan, spared Pondicherry and returned to his homelands with Chanda Sahib.

Nevertheless the policy of taking the side of one Indian power against another, inaugurated by Dumas, was naturally going to have its consequences. It was to find its fullest expression during the Governorship of Dupleix, who succeeded Dumas. Dumas also became a *mansabdar* or local lord of the Mughals. This was a reward given to him for the service that he rendered to the Muslm nobility during the Maratha invasion. It was a title without any tangible consequences. Dumas remained always the Governor of Pondicherry and a Company servant, who ruled the French territories under his control. But for the Mughals, he was their vassal or local lord or *jamedar*.

Further Dumas' intention to expand French possessions in India brought him into conflict with the raja of Tanjore and the Marathas. As a result, it would not be wrong to conclude that he contributed his bit to the subsequent invasion of Tamil Nadu by the Marathas, to the killing of Dost Ali Khan, to the devastation of the Tamil country by the Marathas and the imprisonment of Chanda Sahib by them.

Dumas or the French were probably never aware of the unfortunate consequences of their desire to expand, which caused the destablization of the Carnatic and Tamil Nadu. Dumas of course reaped benefits in the process by allying with the Muslim ruling class, in the form of gifts and territories. He also consolidated French hold over Karaikal. Thus Dumas set the French seriously on the road of expansion in India, which had the potential to bring them into conflict with the Indian princes and rulers as well as with other European powers.

NOTES

1. Castonnet des Fosses, *L'Inde Française au XVIIIème siècle*, Paris, s.d., p. 143; Olagnier, *Le Grand Colonial Inconnu. Le Gouverneur Benoist Dumas*, Paris, 1936, p. 18; M.P. Sridharan, *Papers on French Colonial Rule in India*, Calcicut, 1997, pp. 27-8, 30.
2. Castonnet des Fosses, ibid., Olagnier, ibid., p. 18.
3. Castonnet des Fosses, ibid., pp. 144-5.
4. More, *Portuguese Interactions with Malabar and its Muslims in the 16th Century*, Pondicherry, 2013; More, *Offerings to the Muslim Warriors of Malabar: Foundation Document of Colonialism and Clash of Civilisations*, Chennai, 2015, see Introduction by J.B.P. More; Castonnet des Fosses, ibid. p. 150.
5. *ARP Diary*, I, pp. 98-9, 177; Vinson, *Les Français dans l'Inde, Dupleix et Labourdonnais*, p. 17.
6. Correspondance du Conseil Supérieur de Pondichéry et de la Compagnie, II, p. 11; III, p. xxxiii; Vincent, 'Zenith in Pondicherry', 1990, p. 49; Castonnet des Fosses, op. cit., p. 142.

EXPANSION UNDER GOVERNOR BENOIST DUMAS   135

7. Correspondance du Conseil Supérieur de Pondichéry et de la Compagnie, II, p. 11; III, pp. iii, xxii; IV, p. xi; Olagnier, op. cit., pp. 166, 167; Sridharan, *Papers on French Colonial rule in India,* p. 31.
8. Olagnier, ibid. pp. 184-5, 186: *ARP Diary,* I, pp. 3, 4; Sridharan, ibid., pp. 29-30.
9. Olagnier, ibid., 1936, p. 198.
10. De Closets d'Errey, *Précis Chronologique de l'Histoire de l'Inde Française,* 1934, p. 23; Vinson, op. cit., p. 17; Correspondance du Conseil Supérieur de Pondichéry et de la Compagnie, II, pp. 10, 22-5, 128-30; Zay, *Histoire Monétaire des Colonies Françaises,* pp. 310, 311f, 315, 323; *ARP Diary,* I, pp. 42-5; Martineau, *Lettres et Conventions des Gouverneurs de Pondichéry...*, 1914, p. 41; Martineau, *Dupleix et l'Inde Française,* I, pp. 403-10; Gaudart, *Catalogue des Manuscrits...*, I, p. 5.
11. Zay, op. cit., p. 326; Sridharan, op. cit., p. 30.
12. *ARP Diary,* I, pp. 4, 61, 217; Bourdat, *Les Grandes Pages du "Journal" d'Ananda Ranga Pillai*, pp. 32, 58-60, 63.
13. *ARP Diary,* I, pp. 12, 13, 67-8; IX, 201.
14. Castonnet des Fosses, op. cit., p. 142; Gaudart, *Catalogue...*, 1931, p. 46.
15. Vinson, op. cit., p. 18; Correspondance du Conseil Supérieur de Pondichéry et de la Compagnie, II, p. 11; Olagnier, op. cit., p. 170.
16. Abbé Guyon, *Histoire des Indes Orientales,* III, pp. 148-9; Correspondance du Conseil Supérieur de Pondichéry et de la Compagnie, III, pp. xxvii, xxxiii; Zay, op. cit., pp. 310, 311, 315.
17. Correspondance du Conseil Supérieur de Pondichéry et de la Compagnie, II, pp. 10, 92-3; LEC, 14, Lettre du Père Tremblay, pp. 178-9.
18. Gaudart, *La Criminalité dans les Etablissements Français de l'Inde,* p. 17; Manning, *Fortunes à Faire...*, 1996, p. 173; Olagnier, op. cit., pp. 75-8.
19. Correspondance du Conseil Supérieur de Pondichéry et de la Compagnie, II, pp. 13, 209; III, xviii
20. Ibid. II, p. 21.
21. Olagnier, op. cit., pp. 252, 255, 257; Martineau, *Les Origines de Mahé de Malabar,* Paris, 1917, pp. ix, x; Correspondance du Conseil Supérieur de Pondichéry et de la Compagnie, III, p. xxii.
22. Olagnier, ibid., pp. 257-70; Sridharan, op. cit., p.32; Correspondance du Conseil Supérieur de Pondichéry et de la Compagnie, III, pp. xxii, xviii.
23. Vinson, op. cit., p. 80f; Mahé de La Bourdonnais, *Mémoire Historique de B.F. Mahé de la Bourdonnais,* 1890, pp. 50-2; Correspondance du Conseil Supérieur de Pondichéry et de la Compagnie, III, p. xviii; Castonnet des Fosses, op. cit., p. 181; Srinivasachari, op. cit., p. 174.
24. Correspondance du Conseil Supérieur de Pondichéry et de la Compagnie, III, p. xviii; *Exposition Coloniale Internationale de Paris,* 1931, p. 14; Cultru, 9 *Dupleix, ses plans politiques, sa disgrâce,* 1901, p. 5; Olagnier, op. cit., pp. 272-80.

25. Naf 9359, f. 281, BNF; Correspondance du Conseil Supérieur de Pondichéry et de la Compagnie, III, p. xxiv.
26. Correspondance du Conseil Supérieur de Pondichéry et de la Compagnie, II, pp. 12, 144-8; Naf, 9144, f. 241, BNF; Gaudart, Catalogue des Manuscrits..., 1933, IV, Paris, pp. vi, 1,2; Naf, 8925, f. 23, BNF.
27. Sundararajan, *Glimpses of the History of Karaikkal*, Madras, 1985, pp. 5, 7, 91-103.
28. Col. C²80, f. 70, A.N.: Lehuraux, *La Découverte de Dupleix-Fatheabad*, Pondichéry, 1944, pp. 39-40; Narayana Poullé, *Histoire Détaillée des Rois du Carnatic*, pp. 165-6; LEC, Lettre de Père Tremblay à Monsieurs, tome 14, p. 187.
29. *ARP Diary*, I, p. 64; Srinivasachari, *Ananda Ranga Pillai: The 'Pepys' of French India*, p. 174; Gaudart, op. cit., IV, Paris, 1933, pp. vii-viii, 4; Naf, 8925, f. 17, BNF; Olagnier, op. cit., p. 230.
30. Antony, *Gazetteer of Pondicherry*, I, pp. 5-6; Gaudart, ibid., pp. vii-ix; Olagnier, ibid., 236.
31. Castonnet des Fosses, op. cit., p. 164; Cf. also, More, 'The Marakkayar Muslims of Karikal, South India', *Journal of Islamic Studies*, Oxford, 1991; 'Muslim Evolution and Conversions in Karaikal, South India', 1995.
32. Launay, *Histoire des Missions de l'Inde*, 1898, I, pp. xliv, xlvi; LEC, VIII, 328, 334; Gaudart, op. cit., IV, Paris, 1933, pp. x, 6, 7, 8, 9, 10, 12; Olagnier, op. cit., p. 233; *ARP Diary*, I, p. 240.
33. *ARP Diary*, I, pp. 13, 59, 83; V, p. 131; Vinson, op. cit., pp. 71f, 78.
34. Naf, 9354, f. 281, BNF; Correspondance du Conseil Supérieur de Pondichéry et de la Compagnie, III, pp. xx; 100 *chacras* = 43 pagodas.
35. Olagnier, op. cit., p. 299.
36. *ARP Diary*, I, pp. 119-21, 122-3, 124, 126, 129; Orme, *History of Indostan*, I, pp. 37-9, 41, 42; col.c²80, f15-16, A.N.; Dodwell, *A Calendar of Madras Records, 1740-1744*, Madras, 1917, pp. v, 40; Olagnier, op. cit., p. 299.
37. Olagnier, ibid. pp. 312-14; Dodwell, ibid., pp. 117, 159.
38. Castonnet des Fosses, op. cit., p. 171; Olagnier, ibid., pp. 299-300.
39. *ARP Diary*, I, pp. 119, 120, 121-6, 145-6; Olagnier, ibid., p. 300; Correspondance du Conseil Supérieur de Pondichéry et de la Compagnie, III, pp. i, ii, 46-7, 51, 238.
40. Correspondance du Conseil Supérieur de Pondichéry et de la Compagnie, III, pp. 202-3.
41. Lettre du Père Saignes, Missionaire jésuite à Mme de Sainte Hyacinthe, Religieuse Ursuline à Toulouse, Pondichéry, 18 Janvier 1741, LEC, 14, pp. 94-8; Lettre de Père Claude-Antoine Barbier, Missionaire de la Compagnie de Jésus, au Père Petit, Provincial de la même Compagnie, ci-devant Missionaire des Indes, Pinneypundi, 1 déc 1711, LEC, vol 12, Paris, MDCC. LXXXL, p. 67, *ARP Diary*, I, pp. 139-44, 148f, 120, 134-6, 149-50: Dodwell, op. cit., 1917, pp. vii, 118-19.

EXPANSION UNDER GOVERNOR BENOIST DUMAS 137

42. Correspondance du Conseil Supérieur de Pondichéry et de la Compagnie, III, pp. 203-4.
43. *ARP Diary*, I, pp. 106, 138; IX, p. 116.
44. *ARP Diary*, I, pp. 166-71.
45. Orme, op. cit., I, pp. 42; De Closets d'Errey, *Précis Chronologique de l'Histoire de l'Inde Française*, 1934, p. 25; Castonnet des Fosses, op. cit., p. 177; Malleson, Dupleix, 2001, pp. 31-2.
46. Correspondance du Conseil Supérieur de Pondichéry et de la Compagnie, III, pp. i, ii, x.
47. Correspondance du Conseil Supérieur de Pondichéry et de la Compagnie, III, pp. ii, 61-6; Orme, op. cit., I, p. 43; Dodwell, *Clive and Dupleix*, 1989, p. 109; Naf, 9227, f. 214, BNF; Dernis. *Recueil des titres, édits, déclarations, arrêts, règlements* . . . , t. 4, pp. 656-660; Malleson, op. cit., 2001, p. 32; Olagnier, op. cit., pp. 302-3.
48. Abbé Guyon, 1744, III, p. 357; Col. C²80, f. 20, A.N.; Martineau, *Dupleix et l'Inde Française*, I, pp. 196-8; Vinson, op. cit., pp. 62, 319, 321; Cultru, op. cit., p. 182.
49. Weber, *Les Etablissements Français en Inde au XIXéme siècle (1816-1914)*, I, p. 554; Antony, I, p. 2; *Procès Verbaux des Délibérations du Conseil Souverain de la Compagnie*, I, 188-9; *ARP Diary*, I, pp. 129-34.
50. More, 'A Tamil Muslim Sufi' (in) *Islam and Christian-Muslim Relations*, 10, 1, 1999; Castonnet des Fosses, *L'Inde Française avant Dupleix*. Paris, 1887, p. 214.
51. *ARP Diary*, I, pp. 4, 87-8; IV, p. 346f; Manning, op. cit., 1996, pp. 208-9; Correspondance du Conseil Supérieur de Pondichéry et de la Compagnie, III, pp. 79, 205; Records of Fort St. George, Despatches to England 1743-6, Madras, 1931, p. 7; *ARP Diary*, IV, pp. 346f.
52. Morellet, *Mémoire sur la situation actuelle de la Compagnie des Indes*, p. 124; Castonnet des Fosses, op. cit., 1887, p. 213 (Correspondance du Conseil Supérieur de Pondichéry et de la Compagnie, III, pp. 33-5, 105, 146; Olagnier, op. cit., pp. 174, 177).
53. Olagnier, ibid., p. 172; Sridharan, op. cit., p. 31.
54. *ARP Diary*, I, pp. 7, 11, 57, 30-1.
55. Castonnet des Fosses, op. cit., 1887, pp. 216, 265.
56. Correspondance du Conseil Supérieur de Pondichéry et de la Compagnie, III, pp. 205, 397.
57. Olagnier, op. cit., pp. 331-5, 342-4, 349, 350, 354; Sridharan, op. cit., p. 33; *ARP Diary*, I, pp. 12, 34, 35, 104; III, 110-11; Manning, op. cit., 1996, pp. 99-104.

CHAPTER 5

Governorship of Joseph François Dupleix: Early Phase

THE MAN WHO succeeded Benoist Dumas as Governor of the French possessions in India was Joseph François Dupleix. He was born at Landrecies in France on New Year's Day in 1697. His father was a farmer's general, comfortably well off and quite influential in the then French East India Company circles. Dupleix was educated in a Jesuit school.[1]

Dupleix came to Pondicherry on the same ship as Guruvappa on 16 August 1722. He was nominated as a Councillor of the Superior Council of Pondicherry straightaway due to the unfair lobbying of his father at the royal court. This was a veritable scandal which created a lot of commotion in Pondicherry. From 9 September 1722, he was appointed as Councillor at Masulipatnam.[2]

In 1724, Dupleix went as subcargo in a merchant ship bound to China. He was dismissed from his functions as Councillor in Pondicherry on 28 December 1726. He was re-instated about two years later on 30 September 1728. In 1727, Dupleix wrote a memoir about French Company trade in India at that time. In it, there is not even the faintest indication that Dupleix was interested in founding an empire or even a kingdom in India.[3] Instead, all his attention was devoted to commerce and trade in India and how to develop it. The French had to face an ever increasing competition from the English in the trade domain. They were certainly on a collision course with the English who were increasing their trade volume with India.

DUPLEIX AT CHANDERNAGORE

As a compensation for the disgrace that he endured during 1726-8, Dupleix was nominated as Director of the French factory at Chandernagore. He arrived in Chandernagore on 28 August 1731.

He was 34 years old then and still unmarried. Indinaram or Indranarayan Chaudhuri was his *dubash* in Bengal. Dupleix obtained a small village called Gondalpara on behalf of the Company and farmed it out to his *dubash* Indinaram.[4]

Dupleix had private trade with Masulipatnam from Chandernagore. While in Chandernagore and even later, Dupleix had trade relations with Ananda Ranga Poullé in Pondicherry. Poullé loaded ships with goods on behalf of Dupleix to various destinations like Masulipatnam, Mahé, Surat, Maldives, Burma, Pegu, Malacca and China. Thus Ananda Ranga Poullé also seems to have played a role in the relative enrichment of Dupleix in Chandernagore. The enrichment was however mutual.

It seems that 72 ships owned by Dupleix and his partners sailed across the seas in Asia. Apart from the usual goods like textiles in which Dupleix traded, he also took to trading in slaves and opium. Indian slaves were exported by him to work in the French plantations in Mauritius, Bourbon and Madagascar. He exported opium to China and made immense profits. With such trade transactions, it was not long before Dupleix turned into a Nabob, i.e. an European who had enriched himself in India.[5]

It is quite surprising to note that even after the acquisition of Karaikal, Chandernagore remained the most flourishing of the French factories after Pondicherry. Dupleix loaded two or three or even four ships every year to Europe worth about 2 million livres and ten other ships for the country trade.

Short of funds, Dupleix borrowed money from the money-changer Fatechand Jagatseth of Patna, in order to carry on with his lucrative trade operations. He entered into commercial operations with the English merchants of Bengal as well as with the local merchants like Dayaram and Monohar Boral of Chandernagore. He also had trade connections with Armenian merchants like Coja Elias, as well as with Frenchmen like Vincens, Le Noir, Mahé de La Bourdonnais, Mahé de la Villebague, Benoist Dumas, Pilavoine and Tremisot who were established in the various French territories in India and the Indian Ocean.[6]

Some French historians hold that Dupleix single-handedly built Chandernagore. From 1731 to 1740 alone, it seems that 10,000 brick houses were built when he was Director in Chandernagore. Besides, 15 ships and 72 boats were also constructed for the purpose of trade. But this information is not backed by proper verifiable evidence.[7]

Dupleix also transferred his earnings, especially those gained through private trade back to France, through legitimate means and unauthorized channels. This he did as his intention at that juncture seems to have been to return to France after amassing a fortune. But unfortunatly for him, he incurred some losses especially after 1737, due to ships being lost in the sea and the harassment of the nawabs as well as his extravagant way of living.

Dupleix had least regard for the nawabs. He once wrote about the nawab of Murshidabad thus: 'An old drunkard, given to the worst vices . . . surrounded by a band of rogues who make him commit all sorts of stupidities'.

At one stage he was considering accepting the title of 'mansabdar' or local lord, from the Mughal emperor, in order to avoid harassment in Bengal. He is believed to have even refused *jagirs* and the title of *mansabdar* of 5,000 horses from the Mughal at that time. It is a bit of exaggeration on the part of the British scholar G.B. Malleson and others to call Dupleix as nawab at this juncture, just because some local Mughal lords and officers held him in high esteem for trade reasons.[8]

In Chandernagore Dupleix was still a bachelor. But he was in the company of Jacques Vincens and his wife, Jeanne Vincens. Jeanne's mother was Rosa Elisabeth De Castro. Her father was Portuguese while mother was of Tamil extraction, by the name of Jeanne. She probably hailed from the Palli or Paraya caste. Jacques Albert, the Company's surgeon at Pondicherry married Elisabeth de Castro. Jeanne was born in Pondicherry on 2 June 1706. She was the second of the three daughters of Jacques Albert. She spoke Portuguese, Tamil and French fluently. She grew up to be a charming young girl of Pondicherry of mixed Indo-French-Portuguese blood.

Jacques Vincens married Jeanne when she was just 13 years and six months old, at the *Notre Dame des Anges* church, siuated on the sea side. The marriage took place on 5 June 1719. She bore him eleven children of whom five died. In the year 1733, on the invitation of Dupleix, Jacques Vincens and his family left Pondicherry and settled in Chandernagore. Jacques Vincens was the subcargo in Chandernagore.

In September 1737, vincens drowned in sea along with his ship loaded by Dupleix. Earlier, he and Dupleix were also members of the Superior Council in Pondicherry. They were also partners in private trade in Chandernagore. Vincens died on 26 September 1737, leaving his wife and children in the care of his friend, Dupleix.

Dupleix was almost a member of the Vincens family even before the death of Vincens. It is almost quite certain that he had an affair with Madame Vincens, even before her husband died. As a result, it was not at all surprising that Dupleix remarried Jeanne on 17 April 1741. In his marriage contract, an illicit relationship between Dupleix and Jeanne Vincens was publicly confessed.

Dupleix declared a considerable fortune. He had made this fortune through trade in Chandernagore. It seems that Madame Dupleix ably assisted her second husband with her language skills in Urdu, Bengali and Tamil, and pidgin English, as Dupleix never knew English and never had any inclination to learn the Indian languages. Jeanne acted as interpreter for Dupleix and also served as his private secretary.[9]

In Chandernagore Dupleix was favourably disposed towards the French Jesuit missionaries. He was never submissive to the French governors of Pondicherry like Le Noir and even Benoist Dumas. In 1737, Dumas had obtained permission to mint rupees in Pondicherry from the nawabs of Arcot and the nizam. But on 10 January 1738, Dupleix obtained a similar permission from the nawab of Murshidabad Shuja Khan to mint rupees in gold, silver and copper. This was detrimental to Dumas' Pondicherry rupee, which he thought of using in Bengal too. Instead he had to send silver that he received from France to Chandernagore. Naturally, Dumas was not very happy about it. As a result an antagonistic relationship developed between Dumas and Dupleix, until the former's departure to France on 15 October 1741.[10] At this juncture, Dupleix is not known to have any political ambitions. All he wanted was to make enough money through trade.

DUPLEIX AS GOVERNOR

Even while Dupleix was Director of the factory in Chandernagore, he was appointed as Governor of Pondicherry. However, it was actually on 23 August 1742, that Dupleix assumed power in Pondicherry as

Governor of all the French possessions in India. He and his wife did not choose to reside in the fort. Instead they resided in a mansion on the northern side of the fort.

In the plan of Pondicherry town of 1741, the house of the Governor is shown exactly at the site of the present Villa Aroumé at No. 4, Ananda Rangapillai Street (presently Aurobindo Ashram Dining Hall) surrounded by a garden and other dependencies like the Villa Selvom, at 5, Nehru Street (formerly Vazhudavur or Dupleix Road). By the side of it towards the east was the *Hotel de la Compagnie* or the Company House, surrounded also by a garden. The later day *Hotel du Gouvernment* or the Government House and the the present day Governor's House or Raj Niwas is almost in the same place as the Company House during the first half of the eighteenth century.

Villa Aroumé and its dependencies were reconstructed almost identically after 1761. According to Yvonne Robert Gaebelé, this property was owned by Dupleix in the 1740s. Both the Company House and garden and the Villa Aroumé and its dependencies and garden formed parts of the same complex. Only later, they were divided into two by the creation of Rue François Martin (road) which exists even today.[11]

Dupleix's only son, who lived for just a day died on 2 October 1742 at Villa Aroumé. Dupleix and his family lived in the villa for at least ten years. Apu Mudali was Dupleix's servant, while Varlam Mudali was Madame Dupleix's servant. Dupleix was never inclined to learn Tamil or English, unlike his wife Jeanne who spoke fluent Tamil. Dupleix had at his disposal 250 Europeans, 130 *topas* and 250 local guards to defend Pondicherry and govern it. He moved about in a richly decorated palanquin carried by ten local men.[12] There was no chance of him having grandiose plans to found a French empire in India with such limited resources.

Pondicherry was very much the same since Le Noir's time. Revenues were generated through farming out of lands and the taxes imposed on incoming and outgoing goods. There was no industry worth the name apart from textiles. Even to buy good furniture one had to go to Madras.[13] Contrary to what one may think, in any case, he did not make any usage of that title. Dumas never had those 4,500 horses or cavalry that went along with the title of *mansabdar*. So Dupleix did not inherit any cavalry worth the name. This shows that the title *mansabdar* or local lord was purely honorific.

In 1742, Bussy who had come to India with La Bourdonnais was just a lieutenant. He along with Paradis, the free-booter from Switzerland, who started as land surveyor in the islands of Bourbon and France in the Indian Ocean and ended up as engineer in Pondicherry, became the most devoted collaborators of Dupleix in the course of time. By 1743, Dupleix had completed the construction of a large and comfortable country mansion for his vast family at Mortandi Chavadi in the western limits of Pondicherry. By 1744, he had at his disposal a Company of trained sepoys from Mahé.[14]

During Dupleix's tenure as Governor, slave trade was quite prevalent in Pondicherry. Dupleix tolerated it like his predecessors. Louis Judde, who was a Company servant then, earning just 600 livres per year, blatantly indulged in slave trade from Pondicherry to augment his revenues. A certain Tamil Christian, Arulanandam, who was the servant of Louis Judde, used to procure slaves from as far as Karaikal and Tarangapadi, Tanjore and Tirunelveli and kept them in Judde's godowns in Pondicherry, before shipping them to the French islands of Bourbon and France and even Madagascar.[15] Arulanandam used to catch naïve and gullible Tamilians and bring them to Pondicherry with false promises and then shipped them out. Actually Judde was in partnership with Mahé de La Bourdonnais and his brother in this human trade. Even Pedro Canagarayen and Ananda Ranga Poullé failed to intervene with Dupleix to stop this nefarious trade, as they were aware that certain influential Frenchmen were involved in the trade.

Most of these slaves were from the lower castes. Once, it happened that two men, 15 women and four children belonging to the higher castes were procured as slaves for Judde against their will by Arulanandam. An enquiry was ordered by Dupleix, on the complaint of Ananda Ranga Poullé and one Thiagappa Chetty and all the eighteen were set free. It is noteworthy that Ananda Ranga Poullé had intervened with Dupleix to save some 'soft' or 'good' caste men from being exported as slaves. But he is never known to have come to the defence of the 'low' castes, i.e. those who took to menial work. However Judde was never obstructed from indulging in slave trade by

Dupleix. He and Arulanandam never underwent even a semblance of punishment for indulging in human trafficking.

Later however, due to incessant complaints against Arulanandam, the Public Prosecutor, Mr. Guillard launched criminal proceedings against him. On 28 June 1743, the Prosecutor visited the godowns of Judde where the slaves were held for shipment. He interrogated 32 persons of whom, nine were men, twelve were women and the rest children. Twenty one of them were set free three days later because Judde could not produce valid documents for holding them as slaves. Nevertheless Arulanandam was never punished while his master Judde did not even figure among the accused.

Besides, whenever the slaves revolted against their masters, the cruelest and barbarous treatment was meted out to them. It happened that a slave had killed his master. He was tried by the Superior Council and sentenced to death. According to the ruling of this Council, he was dragged upto the Big Bazar from the White town, with his face to the ground and his legs chained to a chariot. He was then suspended by his legs until he died. This was how the slaves were terrorized if they misbehaved or revolted against their master. But if the white master murdered a slave, it was not considered as a grave offence. It is quite certain that Dupleix and his *dubashes* including his wife and Ananda Ranga Poullé were aware of all such atrocities. But they hardly seems to have intervened to put an end to it.[16]

Even during Dupleix's period as Governor, as earlier, certain members of the higher castes enjoyed certain privileges, even though they might indulge in theft and other criminal activities. For instance in the year 1743, a certain Subba, in charge of the accounts of the Company was accused of embezzlement by none other than Pedro Canagarayen, along with the writer of the washermen called Ganapathy. Subba had also swindled Arumbattai Poullé (who was 40 years old), the supplier of provisions to the troops. He was arrested and was condemned to be whipped in public at the Big Bazaar, marked with the Lys flower and banished from the territory of the Company.

Normally Subba should have been sentenced to death. But because he was a Brahmin, the sentence was reduced according to the customary laws. But the lower castes were at the receiving end for their crimes. They were either hung or deported as slaves to the French Islands. Certain other punishments like the cutting off of the ears of

PLATE 1: DRAWING OF DUPLEIX OF THE 19TH CENTURY [*SOURCE:* HTTPS://WWW.LOOKANDLEARN.COM/HISTORY-IMAGES/SEARCH.PHP?T=4&N=12995]

PLATE 2: DUPLEIX, GOVERNOR OF PONDICHERRY, 1742
[*SOURCE*: HTTP://IDATA.OVER-BLOG.COM/1/99/19/66/AJUIN09/DUPLEIX_2.JPG]

PLATE 3: DUPLEIX STATUE AT LANDRECIES, FRANCE
[*SOURCE*: HTTPS://STATUES.VANDERKROGT.NET/FOTO/FR/FRNP007-2.JPG]

PLATE 4: ROBERT CLIVE [*SOURCE:* HTTPS://CDN.BRITANNICA.COM/17/12817-004-0E6BDFED/ROBERT-CLIVE-REPLICA-OIL-PAINTING-N-DANCE.JPG]

PLATE 5: MAHÉ DE LA BOURDONNAI
[*SOURCE*: HTTPS://WWW.ALAMY.COM/STOCK-PHOTO/MAHE-DE-LA-BOURDONNAIS.HTML]

PLATE 6: DUPLEIX STATUE IN PONDICHERRY
[*SOURCE*: ARCHIVES D'OUTRE-MER, AIX EN PROVENCE, FRANCE]

PLATE 7: BUSSY CASTELNAU
[*SOURCE:* HTTPS://WIKIVISUALLY.COM/WIKI/JEANNE_DUPLEIX]

PLATE 8: ANANDA RANGA POULLÉ, DIWAN OF GOVERNOR DUPLEIX
[*SOURCE:* HTTPS://EN. WIKIPEDIA.ORG/WIKI/ANANDHA_RANGA_PILLAI]

PLATE 9: NASIR JUNG, SON OF NIZAM-UL-MULK
[*SOURCE:* HTTPS://COMMONS.WIKIMEDIA.ORG/WIKI/FILE:NASIR_JUNG.JPG]

PLATE 10: PRATAP SINGH OF TANJORE [*SOURCE:* HTTPS://EN.WIKIPEDIA.ORG/WIKI/FILE:PRATAP_SINGH_OF_THANJAVUR.JPG]

PLATE 11: MOHAMMAD ALI KHAN WALAJAH, NAWAB OF ARCOT, 1749-95
[SOURCE: HTTPS://UPLOAD.WIKIMEDIA.ORG/WIKIPEDIA/COMMONS/5/5D/MOHAMED_ALI_KHAN_WALAJAN.JPG]

PLATE 12: PLAN OF PONDICHERRY [SOURCE: BIBLIOTHÈQUE NATIONALE DE FRANCE LIBRARY, PARIS]

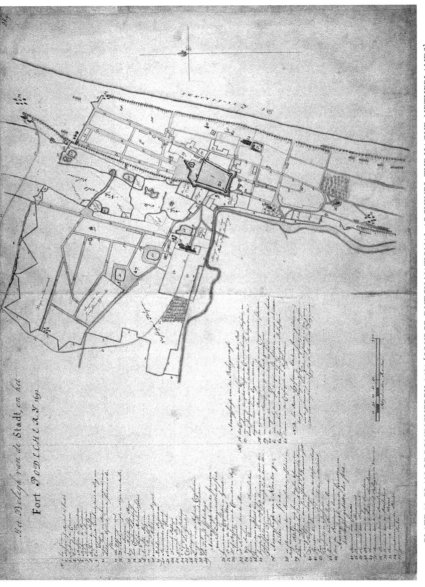

PLATE 13: PLAN OF PONDICHERRY, 1691 [SOURCE: DUTCH NATIONAL ARCHIVES, THE HAGUE, NETHERLANDS]

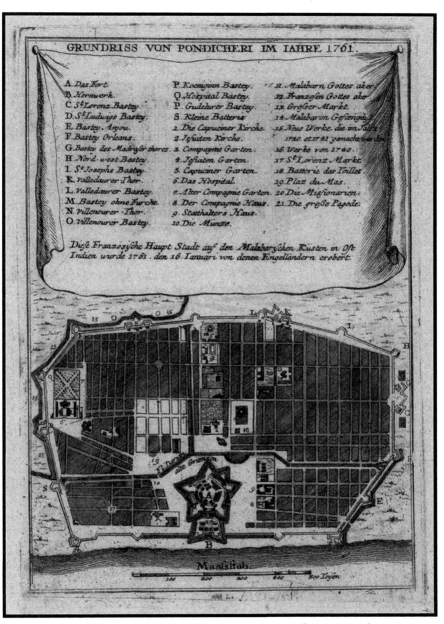

PLATE 14: GERMAN PLAN OF PONDICHERRY OF PRÉVOST D'EXILÉS
[SOURCE: HTTPS://WWW.RAREMAPS.COM/GALLERY/DETAIL/28079/GRUNDRISS-VON-PONDICHERI-IM-IAHRE-1761-PUDUCHERRY-BELLIN]

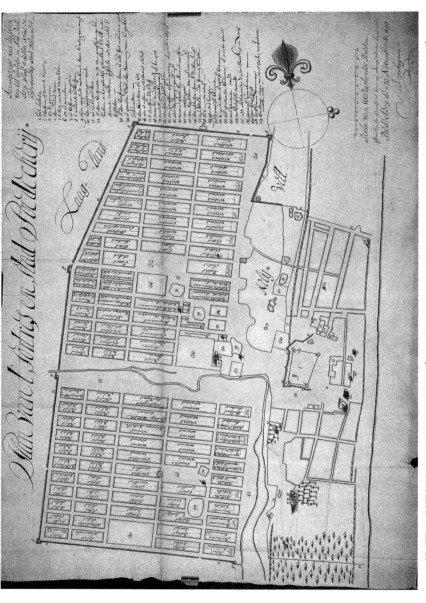

PLATE 15: DUTCH PLAN OF PONDICHERRY [SOURCE: DUTCH NATIONAL ARCHIVES, THE HAGUE, NETHERLANDS]

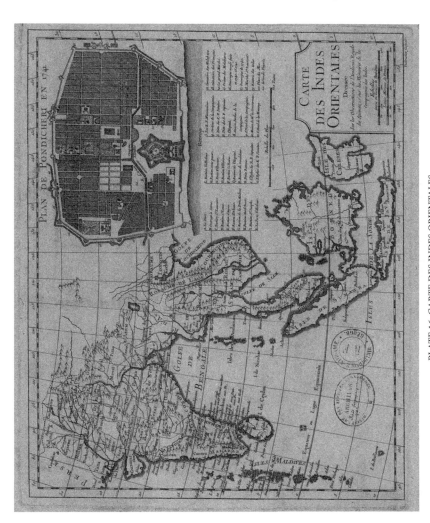

PLATE 16: CARTE DES INDES ORIENTALES
[SOURCE: BIBLIOTHÈQUE NATIONALE DE FRANCE LIBRARY, PARIS]

PLATE 17: ENGRAVING DEPICTING THE DEATH OF THE NAWAB OF CARNATIC, ANWARUDDIN KHAN AT AMBUR BY PAUL PHILIPPOTEAU CREATED BEFORE 1923 [*SOURCE:* HTTPS://EN.WIKIPEDIA.ORG/WIKI/ANWARUDDIN_KHAN]

PLATE 18: IMAGE OF FORT ST. GEORGE, MADRAS, 1754
[*SOURCE*: HTTPS://WIKIVISUALLY.COM/WIKI/NASIR_JUNG]

PLATE 19: RAGHOJI BHONSLE, THE MARATHA GENERAL
[*SOURCE*: HTTPS://EN.WIKIPEDIA.ORG/WIKI/FILE:RAGHUJI_BHONSLE.JPG]

PLATE 20: ANWARUDDIN KHAN, NAWAB OF ARCOT, 1744-9 [SOURCE: HTTPS://EN.WIKIPEDIA.ORG/WIKI/ANWARUDDIN_KHAN]

PLATE 21: NIZAM-UL-MULK, ASAF JAH I, NIZAM OF HYDERABAD [SOURCE: HTTPS://EN.WIKIPEDIA.ORG/WIKI/FILE:ASAF_JAH_1.JPG]

PLATE 22: NASIR JUNG, SON OF NIZAM-UL-MULK CREATED IN 1745
[*SOURCE*: HTTPS://EN.WIKIPEDIA.ORG/WIKI/NIZAM-UL-MULK,_ASAF_JAH_I]

PLATE 23: NIZAM NASIR JUNG BEING SHOT DEAD BY A CARABINE ON TOP OF HIS ELEPHANT [*SOURCE:* HTTPS://WIKIVISUALLY.COM/WIKI/NASIR_JUNG]

PLATE 24: MUZAFFAR JUNG, SUCCESSOR OF NASIR JUNG AS SOUBAB OF DECCAN CREATED IN THE 18TH CENTURY [*SOURCE*: HTTPS://FR.WIKIPEDIA.ORG/WIKI/MUHYI_AD-DIN_MUZAFFAR_JANG]

PLATE 25: MEETING OF DUPLEIX WITH MUZAFFAR JUNG, THE SOUBAB OF DECCAN IN PONDICHERRY [*SOURCE*: ALPHONSE DE NEUVILLE, *A POPULAR HISTORY OF FRANCE FROM EARLIEST TIMES*, VOL. VI, P. 174; WIKIPEDIA.ORG]

PLATE 26: PORTRAIT OF MADAME AND MONSIEUR DUPLEIX, ACCORDING TO A MINIATURE BELONGING TO MADAME LA MARQUISE DE NAZELLE [SOURCE: HTTPS://WWW.GOOGLE.COM/SEARCH?Q=MONSIEUR+ET+MADAME+ MARQUISE+DE+DUPLEIX+IMAGE&RLZ=1C1BLWB_ENFR522FR527&BIW= 1366&BIH=657&TBM=ISCH&SOURCE=IU&ICTX=1&FIR=60NS0TEK8_YAZM%253A %252CLUQQE_3GVLKWSM%252C_&VET=1&USG=AI4_-KT3XQJEK1EI2A21R2P WPAETFKGOMW&SA=X&VED=2AHUKEWIOWPAW59FKAHU463 MBHDYPAD0Q9QEWBXOECAUQFQ#IMGRC=60NS0TEK8_YAZM:]

PLATE 27: SALABAT JUNG, SOUBAB OF DECCAN, SUCCESSOR OF MUZAFFAR JUNG CREATED IN 18TH CENTURY [SOURCE: HTTPS://FR. WIKIPEDIA.ORG/WIKI/ASAF_AD-DAWLA_MIR_ALI_SALABAT_JANG]

the criminals in public, especially of the lower castes, were also in vogue during Dupleix's governorship too.[17] It is quite astonishing to note that Dupleix too favoured the 'soft' castes in matters of crime and reduced their punishments.

Besides, the problems between the left hand castes and the right hand castes continued during Dupleix's period. The latter considered themselves superior to the former. The right hand caste dancing girls frequented the left hand caste men only in secret. But the left hand caste dancing girls were at the service of the right hand castes. Once when these girls did not show respect to the right hand caste men by standing up when they passed by, they were imprisoned. This incident was brought to the notice of Dupleix. Dupleix asked for a loan from the left handers to settle the affair.[18] Thus Dupleix had made it into a habit to collect money as gifts or loans to settle disputes between the Tamils during his governorship of Pondicherry.

Dupleix seems to have earned the reputation for his miserly attitude very quickly in Pondicherry, if we are to believe the accounts of Ananda Ranga Poullé. When Le Noir gave 150 or 200 pagodas to the beggars and the Capuchin Church every year and Dumas gave 1,000 or 2,000, Dupleix would give every year only about Rs. 100 to the Christian Malabar beggars and another Rs. 100 to be distributed to the beggars through two Tamil choultries (local tribunals).

On her part, Madame Dupleix became the centre of attraction of a small coterie composed of French gentlemen. Many of them had married her sisters or her daughters, of whom the most prominent were Combault d'Auteuil, Arboulin, de Barneval, de Saint-Paul, d'Esprésmesnil, de Schonamille, Desnos de Kerjean (nephew of Dupleix), de Choisy and O'Friell. She had a *dubash* for herself. He was the pot-bellied Uravu Narayanan.[19]

Dupleix's *Dubashes*

Dupleix continued with Pedro Canagarayen of Tamil descent as his *dubash*. He did not want to displease the Jesuits by replacing him with a Hindu. His penchant as well as that of his wife towards Christianity was well known. So it is not surprising to note that he preferred to retain Pedro as his *dubash* until he died.

Pedro Canagarayen's house was in a narrow lane in Pondicherry town at this time. Opposite his house stood the house of Prakasa Mudali (the *dubash* of Karaikal), which the Governor used to accommodate his Muslim guests. On 21 July 1743, Pedro gave rich presents (*varisai* in Tamil) on the occasion of the marriage of one of the daughters of Madame Dupleix. On 1 January as it was the custom, the chariot festival and procession at the Vedapuriswaran temple took place in great pomp. Pedro Canagarayen seems to have been favourably disposed towards this festival.[20]

Pedro Canagarayen benefitted largely from the French. He was given five villages near Tiruvannamalai for five years. Pedro had even obtained the lease of Archivac and its dependencies for 2,600 pagodas annually. Dumas still enjoyed the revenues from these lands. But when Pedro Canagarayen died, his brother Lazar Mudaliar (also known as Tanappa or Chinnadu Mudali) refused to pay the annual amount on the pretext that the wars had prevented cultivation of lands and therefore he did not have adequate revenue to pay. But the Superior Council of Pondicherry ruled against Lazar's claims. When Pedro died he was worth 36,000 pagodas, with a further 20,000 pagodas concealed.[21]

Pedro Cangarayen was a trade partner of Dupleix as well as his rival Ananda Ranga Poullé. He lent money to Europeans. His brother Lazar inherited them too. The Company had leased out several villages to him, giving him the right to collect rent from them. Kommapakkam was in his possession. He had a share in almost all the official and private transactions of the French. With such money, he erected a spacious residence in Pondicherry. He also had a garden full of trees behind the Ariyankuppam Church.[22]

At the death of Pedro, his body was handsomely dressed, placed in a coffin and carried on the last journey in a stately fashion, with forty soldiers leading the procession, bearing arms, with the sound of the drum beat. Forty European boys studying in the Jesuit College marched along in two lines, on either side of the procession. The Capuchin and Jesuit priests recited prayers. Dupleix, his wife, the Councillors and other Europeans waited at the Kalatiswaran temple to bid farewell, holding candles in hand. A service was held at the Capuchin Church near the beach. Dupleix and other Company officials attended it.[23]

It seems that Pedro wanted his brother Chinnadu Mudali and his sister's son Asarappan and her other children to inherit his huge properties. But Pedro's wife Nakshattirammal opposed this plan and was supported by her brothers, Jaganivasa Mudali (previously supercargo) and Malayappa Mudali, whose father was Tambicha or Tambuswami Mudali. Therefore in his last days, Pedro had to live separately from his wife. Pedro was lying ill in another one of his houses. But it seems that Madame Dupleix intervened and patched up things between both of them. The wife wanted to seal Pedro's house and properties at his death. As a result, the properties were sealed.[24]

The dispute between Lazar and the wife of Pedro, Nakshattirammal and his daughter-in-law Chandramuthu with regard to the inheritance and partition of the properties of Pedro was becoming very problematic for Governor Dupleix. Lazar was prepared to give half of the inheritance to Dupleix and 10,000 pagodas to his sister-in-law, Nakshattirammal, if he was declared sole inheritor. Dupleix himself heard the claims and complaints of the two parties. He then assembled 20 Hindu caste headmen to ask their opinion about the matter. Among them were: Latchoumy Naiker, Subrayer, Ananda Ranga Poullé, Sunku Muthiramachetty, Saladu Venkatachalachetty, Virachetty, Ariapa Mudaliar, Chinnadu Mudaliar, Pattuchettiar, Nallatamby Mudaliar, Tillayappa Mudaliar, Caroutamby Naynar, Arunachalachetty, Calatychetty, Comdychetty, Bimanna Mudaliar and Peddachi Chettiar.

Madame Dupleix took the side of Nakshattirammal. It seems that Lazar pleaded with Ananda Ranga Poullé to undervalue the property. Thus many of Pedro's houses, garden, warehouses, stables, one of his villages and his commission from the mint were omitted by Poullé. Dupleix himself was aware of the under-estimation of the property by Ananda Ranga Poullé.[25]

The headmen decided that Lazar Mudaliar was the only heir of Pedro, while the entitlements of Nakshattirammal and Chandramuthu would be decided according to the customs of the land. On 28 March 1746, the 20 caste chiefs decided that Lazar should give 2,800 pagodas worth of silver and jewels to Nakshatirammal and 1,400 pagodas to Chandramuthu. Besides, two adjacent stone houses were to be given to them for them to reside, under certain conditions, in Vedapuriswaran

Street.[26] The two ladies were to deposit the money in the Company's treasury and live on the interest payable thereon. The preceding shows that though Pedro and Lazar and their families were Christians, yet Dupleix himself preferred to divide the property on the advice of Hindu castemen according to Hindu custom.

Lazar was not happy with the award. He turned against Ananda Ranga Poullé and used disgusting language against Nakshattirammal. Nevertheless, for having solved the dispute, he paid Dupleix a third part of the estate, amounting to 4,000 pagodas. He paid Dupleix another 6,000 pagodas, with a promise to pay another 1,000 in ten days. Madame Dupleix got 1,000 pagodas. Thus Dupleix and his wife gained enormously by mediating between Lazar and Pedro's widow. Further Dupleix expected Lazar to make a loan to the Company.[27]

Besides Lazar was acting chief *dubash* since the death of Pedro. The villages, formerly leased to Pedro were leased to Lazar for 5 years in 1750. But Lazar proved to be an unethical person, lacking in talent and unfit for the office. He took bribes. Dupleix simply called him 'donkey'. He accused him of incompetency and dismissed him as weak and lacking in energy to work.

It was the same with other Europeans. Mahé de Villabague, the brother of Mahé de La Bourdonnais called him a 'boor' and an 'ignoramus'. Delarche, the interpreter of Dupleix considered Lazar no better than a fool. Pedro in his time too was miserly, though he spent sometimes money liberally for the church. But he was not pussilanimous like Lazar, who extracted money at all costs. When a certain Annapurna Aiyan applied for the post of chief *dubash*, Lazar abused him and said that his daughter was unchaste and his wife was lustful, quite intimate with Muslims and Europeans, without the slightest regard for caste and creed. However, the Jesuits still wanted a Christian to be nominated to the post of *diwan*, after the death of Pedro. Lazar vied for the post.[28]

Asarappan, son of Savarimuthu Mudali and Pedro's sister, married Nakshattirammal's sister's daughter. He received a dowry of 15,000 pagodas and other things. His wife once went to the church, decked with all the ornaments that were worn by the women of her caste, in the Hindu fashion. But the French Jesuit priest objected to it. Christians of the 'high' castes immediately boycotted the church. Pedro Canagarayen had to intervene and maintained the staus quo. Asarappan had a younger brother called Dairiyanatha Mudali or Dairyam, who was choultry *dubash*.[29]

But Lazar himself having no issues had to adopt the child of one Tiruchelvarayan, just three days after his birth. Lazar's wife's name was Gnanamuthammal. She donated her properties to the adopted son, Canagaraya Annasamy Mudaliar. As the latter was still a minor, his uncle Roman Mudaliar was authorized to exercise the function of interpreter in the choultry of Pondicherry town.[30]

Ananda Ranga Poullé had to wait till November 1747 or even as late as 1749, according to some sources, for him to be appointed officially as *dubash*, in spite of the fact that Chinnadu Mudali or Lazar, the brother of Pedro was out of reckoning for the post due to his incapacity and incompetency. In the opinion of many Frenchmen, Ananda Ranga Poullé was a good choice as he came from a respectable Telugu merchant family in the service of the French since several decades and was held in respect by the Muslims, the people of the Carnatic, Mysore, Trichinopoly and Tanjore. He was also considered intelligent enough to go as ambassador on behalf of the French to the Indian princes. But the delay in the appointment of Ranga Poullé might be partly due to the hostility of Madame Dupleix and the Jesuits, who did not want to appoint a Hindu as *dubash*. Besides, Ranga Poullé never had a good opinion of Canagarayen and Madame Dupleix. He accused Canagarayen of collusion with Governor Hébert which caused the death of his uncle Nainiappa, the persecution of his family and the banishment of his own father, Tiruvengadm Poullé.[31]

Further Ananda Ranga Poullé blamed Madame Dupleix for trying to sell the post of *dubash* to the one who offered the most. At the same time, he admitted that the delay in his appointment might be due to financial irregularities in his dealings with the Company. Besides, he owed Dupleix Rs. 10,000 at that time. Nevertheless Ananda Ranga Poullé seems to have an aversion for Madame Dupleix due to the fact that she had Paraya blood in her. This has been confirmed by none other than her principal biographer Yvonne Robert Gaebelé. His aversion might also be due to the fact that Poullé never liked women occupying a commanding and authoritative position

The chief of the Jesuits, Father Coeurdoux actually wanted Ananda Ranga Poullé to set an example and convert to Christianity, so that others might convert following him. But Ranga Poullé, a fervent devotee of Vishnu, refused by pointing out that most of the Christians were poor and were servants and coolies, except the family of Pedro Canagarayen and his brother, and those few who were lately *dubashes* of Europeans or who held other jobs, while the Hindus occupied the government posts in the customs office, in the choultry and in the fort, owned godowns, and various shops selling rice, wheat, cloth, etc., and were also the merchants of the Company, farmers and renters in the countryside.

Besides he said that the merchants were all Chettys, Komuttis, Brahmins and Gujaratis, while those in the Company's service were mostly Brahmins and Vellalas. As for his own Idayan or shepherd caste, except for Muthiah Poullé, all the rest grazed sheep and had no other means of livelihood. He added that during Kanagarayen's time, neither Arumbattai Poullé nor other leading Hindus of the Agamudaiyan caste converted. Pedro Kanagarayen himself did not make any converts. But Reverend Coeurdoux insisted that the post of diwan was reserved for Christians alone.[32]

NOTES

1. Misoffe, *Dupleix et La Bourdonnais*, Paris, 1943, p. 17; Vincent, 'Zenith in Pondicherry', Bombay, 1990, p 38.
2. Sridharan, *Papers on French Colonial Rule in India*, Calicut, 1997, p. 39; Naf. 9364, La Vie de Dupleix et sa famille avant Pondichéry, BNF.
3. *RHIF*, I, 1916-17, pp. 81-120; Cultru, *Dupleix, ses plans politiques, sa disgrâce*, Paris, 1901, p. 113; Sridharan, ibid.
4. De Closets d'Errey, *Précis Chronologique de l'Histoire de l'Inde Française, Paris*, 1934, p. 24.
5. Kormocar, *Dupleix et Chandernagore*, Calcutta, 1963, pp. 150, 181; Vincent, op. cit., p. 48; Sridharan, op. cit., pp. 39-40; Manning, *Fortunes à Faire. The French in Asian Trade*, Aldershot, 1996, p. 236; Naf. 9364, p. 140, BNF; cf also Naf, 9357, for further information on Dupleix's commerce; *Correspondance du Conseil Supérieur de Pondichéry avec le Conseil de Chandernagore*, I,

GOVERNORSHIP OF JOSEPH FRANÇOIS DUPLEIX 151

p. 110; II, p. xii) Gaudart, *Catalogue des Manuscrits* . . . , 1931, p. 53; Kormorcar, K.C. *Dupleix et Chandernagore*, Calcutta, 1963, p. 189; Sridharan, op. cit., pp. 39-40.

6. *Correspondance du Conseil Supérieur de Pondichéry avec le Conseil de Chandernagore*, II, pp. iv, v, 209; I, p. 371; Indrani Ray, 'Dupleix private trade in Chandernagore', 1974, pp. 279-94; Gaudart, *Catalogue des Manuscrits*. . ., 1931, pp. 43, 44, 45, 50; *Correspondance du Conseil Supérieur de Pondichéry et de la Compagnie*, III, p. xix; Martineau, *Dupleix et l'Inde Française*, I, 1920, pp. 301, 303, 306, 307, 311, 342-9, 517, 518, 519, 522, 523.

7. Clarins de la Rive, *Dupleix ou les Français aux Indes Orientales*, Lille, 1888, p. 15; RHIF, vol. 3, 1919, 368, 370; Hamont, *Un Essai d'Empire français dans l'Inde aux XVIIIème siècles*, Paris, 1881, ch. I; Cultru, *Dupleix, Ses plans politiques, sa disgrâce*, Paris, 1901, pp. 53, 146; Subramanian, *The French East Company and the Trade of the Indian Ocean*, New Delhi, 1999, pp. 92, 101; Fr. 8979ff, f. 18, 38v-39, f. 40, f. 96, BNF; Manning, op. cit., 1996, pp. 179, 239-41.

8. Cultru, ibid., pp. 131-7, 150, 151, 154, 159, 160, 165, 170, 171, 173, 174; Subramanian, ibid., 107-8, 112-19, 125, 138-9; Lettre de Dupleix à Forestieri, 2/9/1732, Fr; 8979f, 50v, BNF; Lettre de Dupleix à Dumas, 10/1/1740, Fr. 8982ff, ff. 202-3, BNF; Lettre de Dupleix à Groiselle, 12/11/39, Fr. 8982, f. 140, BNF; Haudrère, *La Compagnie Française des Indes au XVIIIe siècle, 1719-1795*, III, pp. 822-4, 825; Malleson, *Dupleix*, 2001, 40; Fr. 8980, ff. 59, 91, 96, BNF; Fr. 8982, ff. 57, 172, Dupleix's letters; Vigie, *Dupleix*, Paris, 1993, p. 134; Fr. 8982, f. 115, BNF.

9. Kormocar, *Dupleix et Chandernagore*, Calcutta, 1963, pp. 183,184; Gaudart, *Catalogue des Manuscrits* . . . , 1931, pp. 38, 42; Gaebelé, *Créole et Grande Dame, Johanna Begum, Marquise Dupleix*, 1934, pp. 7, 59-82 and ch. III; Cultru, ibid., 137f; Martineau, *Resumé des Actes de l'Etat Civil de Pondichéry*, II, pp. 96, 201-2; IV, p. 151; Laude, *Dupleix. Le Siège de Pondichéry en 1748*, 1870, p. 8; Vincent, op. cit., p. 40; *Correspondance du Conseil Supérieur de Pondichéry avec le Conseil de Chandernagore*, I, 364; Sridharan, op. cit., p. 40.

10. *Correspondance du Conseil Supérieur de Pondichéry avec le Conseil de Chandernagore*, II, pp. iii, vi, 1-16, 25; Zay, *Histoire Monétaire des Colonies Françaises*, Paris, 1892, p. 321.

11. Vinson, *Les Français dans l'Inde, Dupleix et Labourdonnais*, Paris, 1894, p. 83f; Naf, 9357, f. 6, BNF; Plan de Pondichéry en 1741, in *Le Petit Atlas Maritime*, tome III, no. 35; Deloche, *Le Papier Terrier* . . . , 2002, pp. 57, 102; ARP Diary, XII, p. 164; VIII, p. 379; Y.R. Gaebelé. *Créole et Grande Dame* . . . , Paris, 1934, p. 58.

12. Cultru, op. cit., p. 141, 196; Martineau, *Resumé des Actes de l'Etat Civil de*

Pondichéry, II, p. 58; *ARP Diary*, XII, pp. 72, 164; Gaebelé, *Créole et Grande Dame, Johanna Begum, Marquise Dupleix*, pp. 88, 95; R. Alalasundaram, *Some Sketches from Ananda Ranga PIllai, 1736-1761*, Pondichéry, 2001, p. 81.

13. Col. C² 80, Lettre de Cossigny au Controleur Général, 25 Janvier 1740, A.N.
14. Cultru, op. cit., p. 196; *Correspondance du Conseil Supérieur de Pondichéry et de la Compagnie*, III, p. xxx; Labernadie, *Le Vieux Pondichéry (1753-1815)*, Pondichéry, 1936, p. 168; Marquis de Nazelle. *Dupleix et la Défense de Pondichéry*, Paris, 1908, pp. 32f.
15. Gaudart, *La Criminalité dans les Etablissements Français de l'Inde*, Pondichéry, 1938, p. 164.
16. Sridharan, op. cit., p. 43; Gaudart, ibid., p. 164, 167; *ARP Diary*, I, pp. 227-30.
17. Gaudart, ibid., pp. xvi, xvii, 168, 170, 172, 186, 227.
18. *ARP Diary*, VII, pp. 197, 213, 220; Sridharan, op. cit., pp. 43-4; cf also. Gaudart, *La Criminalité dans les Etablissements Français de l'Inde*, Pondichéry, 1938.
19. Ibid. VIIII, p. 308; Y.R. Gaebelé, op. cit., pp. 95, 114.
20. *ARP Diary*, V, p. 315; VIII, p. 172; Naf. 9384, f. 141, 142 BNF.
21. Gnanou Diagou, *Arrêt du Conseil Supéreiur de Pondichéry*, I, pp. 188, 189, 202; *ARP Diary*, I, pp. 34, 350; *Correspondance du Conseil Supérieur de Pondichéry et de la Compagnie*, IV, pp. 22, 30.
22. *ARP Diary*, I, p. 347; II, pp. 164, 237.
23. Ibid. I, pp. 311-13, 386.
24. Ibid. I, pp. 13, 310-11, 316, 402; IV, p. 330.
25. Ibid. I, pp. 314-16, 320-1, 324, 343-8.
26. Gnanou Diagou, I, 1935, pp. 178-80; *ARP Diary*, I, pp. 346, 314-19, 402-3.
27. *ARP Diary*, I, pp. 342-3, 358-9, 362-4; II, pp. 11, 14, 15; V, p. 56.
28. Ibid., I, pp. 147, 388, 404-6; II, pp. 149-51, 157, 196, 210, 249; IV, 28; VI, 222 388.
29. *ARP Diary*, I, 286; V, 55, 56; VI, 222; XII, 297-8, Asarappan died in 1748.
30. Gnanou Diagou, *Arrêts du Conseil Supérieur de Pondichéry*, II, 141; III, p. 365; IV, pp. 161, 471; *ARP Diary*, I, 106, 191; II, 24; IX, 216.
31. *ARP Diary*, I, 68, 386; IV, 141, 143f, 238; V, p. iv.
32. Ibid., IV, 147-50; Oubagarasamy, *Un Livre de Compte de Ananda Ranga Poullé*, Paris, 1930, pp. xxvii, xxviii; Gaebelé, op. cit., p. 109.

CHAPTER 6

Rivalries in the Carnatic and the Capture of Madras

CARNATIC TENSIONS AND CONFLICTS

ALL WAS NOT well for Nawab Safdar Ali Khan as the nizam of Hyderabad disliked him and the Tamil people did not relish the prospect of paying more taxes, so that he could pay off his debts to the Marathas. So Khan sent his infant son to Madras to be under the care of the English. He himself sought refuge in the well fortified citadel of Vellore, of which his brother-in-law Murtuza Ali was Governor. But Murtuza Ali, wanting to become nawab, attempted to poison Safdar Ali. The nawab escaped, but later was stabbed and killed by a Pathan. Murtuza Ali became nawab of Arcot in September 1742, but had to flee due to general opposition. The Maratha, Morari Rao at Trichinopoly as well as the English were also against Murtuza, who escaped to Vellore.

After the capture of Trichinopoly and Chanda Sahib, the Marathas made their way towards the north and Bengal. They confined Chanda Sahib as a prisoner in the neighbourhood of Satara.[1] In 1743, the nizam arrived at Arcot with 30,0000 troops. He appointed a general of his army, Coja Abdullah Khan, who was not a Nawayat, as the new nawab. He asked Morari Rao to surrender. Morari Rao withdrew from the Carnatic and the nizam returned to Golconda.

But very soon Abdullah Khan was poisoned and the nizam appointed Syed Muhammad Khan (Sadatullah Khan II), who was still a boy, as nawab. A certain Anwaruddin Khan was nominated as the governor/regent of the province. In 1744, when the nawab of Arcot, Syed Muhammad Khan was murdered, by none other than Murtuza Ali, Nizam-ul-mulk appointed Anwaruddin Khan as the new nawab of Arcot. He too was not a Nawayat. He hailed from Gopamau in northern India. However, most of the forts in the

Carnatic were held by the Nawayats. It seems that the nizam considered the Nawayats as a 'band of vagabonds'.[2]

Dupleix welcomed Nawab Anwaruddin to Pondicherry on 11 September 1745. When Anwaruddin married off his daughter, Dupleix sent him a gift of 3,000 pagodas. But at the same time, a little earlier, in May 1745, Dupleix and his Superior Council decided to lend Rs. 1 lakh to Chanda Sahib, to secure his release from the Marathas, so that he could stake his claim to become nawab of Arcot, with French support. This expenditure was definitely not necessary at this time. But Dupleix had other calculations in his mind. By this act Dupleix, following Dumas, waded into the volatile politics of the Carnatic. He clearly took the side of Chanda Sahib against Anwaruddin Khan, while the latter had the favour of the Nizam as well as the English. This was not a sagacious political move by Dupleix.[3]

During this period, the English were absolutely dominant in the sea. The Anglo-French war had broken out in 1744. The English seized all French ships in the high seas and there was no help coming from France. Trade on the high seas was severely undermined. Arrival of funds to Pondicherry from France was blocked. It was at this time that the Superior Council under Dupleix agreed to lend Chanda Sahib Rs. 1 lakh as soon as he reached Tamil Nadu and asked Raza Sahib, second son of Chanda Sahib to fall upon Anwaruddin Khan at Arcot. Besides, Dupleix knew that Dumas had made use of sepoys for defensive purposes in Mahé and Karaikal. As a result, Sheikh Hassan of Mahé who had stayed back in Pondicherry with 100 sepoys was called by Dupleix and was asked to call his brother Abdul Rahman from Mahé/Malabar to Pondicherry with 500 or 600 sepoys.[4] Thus Dupleix was ready to involve, recruit and use Indian soldiers on his side in future battles in the region.

Dupleix fearing an invasion of Pondicherry also armed all its inhabitants. Besides, on 2 and 27 November 1745, two violent cyclones hit Pondicherry. The small Uppar River overflowed destroying more than 2,000 houses and huts and there were several people and cattle dead. All this added to the financial burden of Dupleix's government. Dupleix also had to complete the fortification of Pondicherry town.

The construction of the wall on the sea-side was finally completed in January 1747. Thus Pondicherry was protected on all sides by walls. A narrow moat separated the fort from the town. All these constructions too involved expenditure. As a result, things were not very bright for Dupleix in the financial and trade front unlike during Dumas' regime. Instead, the French Company directors in Paris accused Dupleix of over-spending which resulted in less sales and less profits for the shareholders. Consequently, Dupleix and the members of the Superior Council volunteered to resign their posts as early as 1745, but the Company would not accept.[5] Thus it is clear that even in 1745, Dupleix had no intention or design to found a French empire in India.

In Karaikal, the situation was no better. Trade was almost at a stand-still. Prakasa Mudali was still the chief *dubash* there. Besides, since the arrest of Chanda Sahib, the raja of Tanjore persistently demanded more money from the French. In April 1744, the king was in need of money. He prevented the French from harvesting the rice in their lands. Dupleix, instead of negotiating with the raja, preferred to use force. He sent 3 ships with soldiers, under the command of Paradis, his trusted lieutenant. After prolonged tension and conflict, peace came about only in 1747. On 20 May 1747, the French, with the consent of Dupleix paid 2,000 pagodas out of 3,000 that the raja demanded with insistence.

As a result there was no trade in Karaikal between 1744 and 1748. But Dupleix managed to obtain a *parvana* from Chanda Sahib confirming the sale of 81 villages by the raja of Tanjore. This cession was ratified by the raja of Tanjore on 31 December 1749. Besides, the raja agreed to forego the tribute of 2,000 pagodas paid to him since 1739. Further he accepted to pay the arrears of tribute due to the nawab of Arcot to Chanda Sahib, which amounted to Rs. 75 lakh.

At the same time, the incursions of the Marathas into Bengal had brought trade to a halt in Chandernagore, which was flourishing when Dupleix was director there. In Mahé though peace prevailed since 1742, the expenditures incurred there absorbed all the profits made out of the pepper trade. Thus the French Company's finances were in dire straits in all the French territories in India during this period.[6]

Capture of Madras, 1746

Madras was the seat of the English in south India. They had obtained it in 1639 from the local ruler, Raja Venkatappa. The name 'Madras' was actually an abbreviation of the Tamil *medurasapatnam*, or *metturasapatnam* which meant 'chief's town on the mound'. It had grown to become a very prosperous city under the English with a lot of Indian merchants settled there, unlike in Pondicherry, which was situated about 150 km south of it. It was known as the city of 'Kubera' or the 'golden city'.[7] It was also known as 'Indian London' among the English. Naturally there was cause for Dupleix, governor of Pondicherry and La Bourdonnais, governor of Isle de France, and the French generally to envy the position of Madras.

In the year 1745, war broke out between the English and the French. Several English warships were sent to India to tame the French. Some French commercial ships and the ships of their allies like those of Imam Sahib were plundered in the Indian Ocean by the English. Naturally the French Superior Council's members including Dupleix incurred heavy losses. A part of Dupleix's private fortunes was also wiped out due to the wars.[8]

In February 1746, Pedro Canagaryen died. In the same month, Dupleix received Maphuz Khan, the son of Anwaruddin Khan to Pondicherry. Dupleix attempted to strike an alliance with him against the English.[9]

But Dupleix was forced to react to the dire financial situation and the loss of revenue due to English attacks. He did not have Pedro Canagarayen to offer advice any more. He felt the need to strike at the English, though the English did not attack him or the French overland. Already in January 1742, Dupleix had sent his engineer, Paradis to Madras, to study the ways and means for attacking the town.

Dom Antonio Noronha, who was officiating as priest at the Luz church of Madras and was related to Dupleix's wife, was also sending reports of Madras to Dupleix. Mahé de la Bourdonnais wanted to intercept the English in the French islands of which he was Governor. Instead, at the request of Dupleix, he sailed to the Cholamandalam Coast with a strong squadron of about ten ships and 2,350 European soldiers, to confront the English. During this time, Chanda Sahib sent message to Dupleix that he would come with the Marathas to capture the Carnatic.[10]

La Bourdonnais and Dupleix though they had business relationships since sometime, never got along well together. Dupleix thought that he was the sole French authority in India to whom everybody were subject. When La Bourdonnais would not accept that and thought that he was an authority in his own right, there was cause for Dupleix to become furious.

La Bourdonnais had a very poor opinion of Dupleix. He thought that Dupleix was vain and jealous, wanting to have an upper hand over him, though they were equal in power, heading their respective governments.[11] Dupleix dismissed La Bourdonnais as a 'dog' and as an indiscreet, messy, talkative and shady schemer.

Even though Pedro Canagarayen had died in February 1746, Ananda Ranga Poullé had not still been appointed as the *dubash*. He indulged deliberately in the art of flattery. He bluntly declared to Dupleix that there was no one in India to equal him and never will the French Company find somebody like him.[12]

But both La Bourdonnais and Dupleix wanted to capture Madras, in spite of the fact that Nawab Anwaruddin was against it. Anwaruddin even threatened to expel the French from Pondicherry in case they attacked Madras. Dupleix countered by promising to restore Madras to the nawab once conquered.[13]

French troops under La Bourdonnais landed in Madras on 15 September 1746. The English never expected the French to attack Madras. The French first entered the Black town, inhabited by rich Muslim, Armenian, Jewish as well as other merchants of Asia, whereas the White town was composed essentially of whites. In just six days, on 21 September 1746, La Bourdonnais took possession of Fort St. George without much difficulty.

Very quickly, 1,000 men including European soldiers and sepoys under Abdul Rahman and Sheikh Hassan were sent to Madras by Dupleix. Bussy was part of the first detachment of French troops who landed in Madras. He was just 26 years old then. All Englishmen of Madras were taken prisoners. Besides, all goods, arms, provisions, gold and silver as well as furniture in the fort and outside, were made over to the French. They were worth 1,85,000 pound sterling. The conquest of Madras entailed a profit of 16,09,920 gold pagodas for the French Company. La Bourdonnais never had the intention of ransacking Madras and his troops never ravaged or robbed the inhabitants of Madras.[14]

It seems that during the occupation of Madras, the Mahé brothers Abdul Rahman and Sheikh Hassan were used by Dupleix to seize palanquins, elephants, horses, etc., which he allowed them to keep for themselves as booty. Otherwise, they seem not to have taken part in any battle to conquer Madras. The Mahé brothers seem to have enriched themselves in this way whenever the opportunity arose.

Later in September 1746, Dupleix remarked: 'These Musliim dogs do not realize their force; as soon as they saw our troops, they panicked'.

Ananda Ranga Poullé immediately retorted that with thousand French soldiers, the entire country of the Muslims, south of Krishna River could be captured. Dupleix then said that with just 500 soldiers and two mortars, he would do that. Thus Ananda Ranga Poullé was openly encouraging Dupleix in his warlike adventures and colonial enterprise.[15]

Such was the poor opinion that Ananda Ranga Poullé and Dupleix hold of the Indian soldiers and the princes of India. Ranga Poullé encouraged him in this line of thinking and contributed his bit to the increasing aggressivity of Dupleix since the death of Pedro Canagarayen. Generally in his dealings with Dupleix, Ananda Ranga Poullé off and on proved himself as a flatterer of the first order and encouraged Dupleix's belligerent attitude. This becomes quite obvious when we go through his diary records. Ananda Ranga Poullé seems to have adopted this strategy of flattery for his own survival, for otherwise he ran the risk of meeting the same fate as his uncle, Nainiappa.

When the English at Madras capitulated, La Bourdonnais thought that Dupleix wanted to return Madras to the nawab of Arcot. He had no intention of annexing it as part of French territory in India. Nor had he any intention of expanding French territories in India through conquest. Instead, due partly to the pressure exerted by Maphuz Khan, the son of Nawab Anwaruddin, on Madras and the intentions of Dupleix, he negotiated an agreement on 24 September 1746 with the English without the knowledge of Dupleix by which he agreed to give back Madras to the English provided they paid him 11 lakh pagodas in two years. This was known as the Treaty of Ransom.

Of this sum, 88,000 pagodas were in gold, silver, diamonds and precious stones and were delivered to La Bourdonnais, while the rest was to be paid later. A special tax was also imposed upon the rich inhabitants of Madras to pay the ransom. It is believed in some quarters that La Bourdonnais received hefty bribes in secret from the English as well as merchandise for the conclusion of the Treaty of Ransom. Ananda Ranga Poullé put the amount made by La Bourdonnais at 10 lakh pagodas while his brother made just 2 lakh.[16]

Dupleix and the Superior Council of Pondicherry had previously engaged to abide by whatever treaty La Bourdonnais would make with the English. La Bourdonnais was not favourable to put Madras under the control of the Pondicherry Council and Dupleix or even Paradis, Dupleix's commandant. La Bourdonnais concluded the Treaty of Ransom with the English and sailed off from Madras to Pondicherry on 23 October 1746 to avoid the terrible monsoon rains, in which he is believed to have lost much of his wealth obtained as ransom.[17]

Dupleix proceeded to nominate a Council of Madras by disregarding the promise made to Nawab Anwaruddin. A provincial council, answerable to Dupleix was set up. Frenchmen close to or related to Dupleix like d'Espresmesnil (son-in-law of Dupleix), Paradis, Dulaurens, Barthélémy and Bruyère were the chiefs of the Madras Council during this period.[18] Thomas Saunders became the Governor of the English factories on the coast subsequently. He operated from Fort St. David, near Cuddalore.

Dupleix then seems to have ordered his troops to ravage the Black town of Madras, inhabited by Tamils, and the Madras country as a sort of revenge act. Several villages of the Tamils were burnt down and looted by the French causing great devastation and misery all around. They, under the French chief Mainville, even plundered the English at St. Thomas Mount and their homes were burnt. Mainville had actually received orders from Dupleix to plunder the country between Madras and Arcot, destroy the harvest and burn the houses, so that the villagers would not pay taxes to the nawab.

Ananda Ranga Poullé backed Dupleix in this matter related to the devastation of Madras and the plundering of the Tamils. It was a sinister design, born in the mind of Dupleix and faithfully executed by his *dubash* Ananda Ranga Poullé and Dupleix's chiefs like Mainville to the great distress of the Tamil population. Muslim houses were destroyed as they fought against the French, along with several other houses for months together. Even those belonging to the nawab's *diwan* and the son of Imam Sahib were not spared. It is noteworthy that when Barthélémy was Director in Madras an attempt was made to destroy a mosque. Dupleix wanted the destruction of this mosque and gave orders to seize the ring-leaders opposing the mosque destruction on the least disturbance.[19]

But the Madras lands were farmed out with great difficulty with the help of a certain Moutiapa, the new Prefect and a certain Papayapoullé. It was here that the French came into contact with Papayapoullé, the notorious farmer, who was imprisoned and whipped cruelly by the English for robbing from the accounts of Petounaiken, the previous prefect of the English. Madame Dupleix was particularly inclined towards him to the great dismay and detriment of Ananda Ranga Poullé. Besides, Dupleix wanted to bring the merchants of Madras to trade from Pondicherry. He even confiscated their properties to pressurize them to settle in Pondicherry. In this attempt Dupleix falied miserably as very few merchants actually accepted to settle in Pondicherry.[20]

Dupleix had other ideas in his mind. He was incurring loss in the trade front everywhere and all was not well with the finances of his government at this time as we have seen precedingly. He seems to have thought of raising the revenues of his settlement somehow. He did not want La Bourdonnais to sign the treaty of ransom. Instead he wanted to occupy Madras and use it to raise the revenues of Pondicherry, even by exchanging it for Vazhudavur and Villianur adjoining Pondicherry. He did not also want to give Madras any more to the nawab of Arcot. So the nawab's troops under Maphuz Khan laid siege to the town and demanded its return to the nawab. The French troops under Paradis and La Tour broke the blockade. Besides, Dupleix and the Council of Pondicherry declared as void the treaty concluded by La Bourdonnais with the English on 7 November 1746, after the departure of La Bourdonnais.[21]

Paradis' victory at Adyar with just 230 Europeans and 700 sepoys (mainly Muslims and Pallis) against the might of the numerous troops of Maphuz Khan was considered as a spectacular victory of European arms and tactics against the numerical superiority of Indian troops. Only two French men were hurt in this battle while the Indians suffered a loss of 500 men.

More than this victory, Paradis got a very big booty, consisting of 100 camels and 600 bullocks, necessary to maintain themselves in Madras. Paradis personally plundered the property of Arunachala Chetty, a leading merchant of Madras. However, what seems to have been decisive in this victory was the role played by the sepoys. Without the sepoys, one cannot imagine Paradis scoring over the troops of Maphuz Khan. Paradis gave Mylapore over to plunder. Pallis, Parayas, Muslims and some other people of the surrounding areas joined the pillaging. Many merchants were ruined. When Paradis left Madras, he and his men, sepoys included took with them a considerable booty to Pondicherry. They were passed duty-free into Pondicherry.

Many like Muthiah Poullé, Arumbattai Poullé and others who went to Madras from Pondicherry, returned with their share of the spoils. Muthiah Poullé, the chief of the Pondicherry police alone came back with Rs. 10,000. The Mahé chief got 2 lakh pagodas. Even the coolies got 100 pagodas each. Freill, son-in-law of D'Auteuil came back with his share of loot. A certain Tamilian called André who was at the service of Mahé de Villebague reaped 50,000 pagodas. Ananda Ranga Poullé thinks that the spoils alone amounted to 10 lakh pagodas.

However, the same Ananda Ranga Poullé, who complained about the loot of Madras in his diary, encouraged Periya Aiyan, son of the polygar of Vettavalam to raid and burn the Tamil country that was under Muslim control. This caused immense misery to the Tamilians and devastation to the Tamil countryside. But Ananda Ranga Poullé was quite insensitive to the sufferings of the Tamils.[22]

Though Paradis and La Tour scored victories in skirmishes, Dupleix was conscious of the numerical superiority of the nawab's forces and concluded peace with him very quickly. Maphuz Khan and his brother Mohammad Ali Khan had actually threatened Pondicherry in January 1747. Ananda Ranga Poullé pacified them by giving them Rs. 10,000 and some objects from Europe. Maphuz Khan himself came to Pondicherry on 19 February 1747 at Ranga Poullé's insistence. Dupleix received him at Mortandi and took him to the town and the Governor's House in a palanquin. Maphuz Khan was lodged in the Council building, located on the eastern side of his residence. There was a grand dinner and Muslim style food was prepared by Avai Sahib, the agent of Imam Sahib. Maphuz Khan stayed in the *Hotel de la Compagnie* (site of the present Governent House).

By 2 March 1747, Dupleix clinched a peace deal by offering huge presents to the nawab amounting to over Rs. 80,000 and by allowing the Mughal flag to fly over Madras for a week to show that the town belonged to the nawab. Dupleix was also awarded the Mughal title 'Nawab Zafar Jung Bahadur Dupleix, Governor of Pondicherry'. Dupleix also received from the French king the title of *Chevalier de l'Ordre de Saint Michel*. All dignitaries of Pondicherry came and felicitated Dupleix for his titles with presents on 7 April 1747. Lazar Tanappa Mudali, the brother of Pedro Cangarayen, prostrated in front of Dupleix, held both his feet in his hands and offered homage to Dupleix, in the most submissive and slavish manner.[23]

At that time, Dupleix had at his disposal only 436 European soldiers, under Schonamille, a son-in-law of Dupleix. La Bourdonnais thought initially of leaving just 150 of his soldiers in Madras. So altogether Dupleix would have at his disposal only 590 European soldiers with which he had to defend both Madras and Pondicherry. Besides, the English held the high seas. This was almost an impossible task because eight English vessels were blocking Madras at sea while the nawab's troops imposed a blockade of Madras on land at that critical moment. No food grains could be imported from the fertile northern coasts into Madras and Pondicherry. But Dupleix somehow thought that he could defend both with such limited number of soldiers. His main aim in holding on to Madras seems to be to raise additional revenues for Pondicherry through acquisition of a territory and that too from the English.

La Bourdonnais accused Dupleix of having intrigued to obtain the commandment of Madras as well as the squadron under La Bourdonnais. Unlike La Bourdonnais, Dupleix was never trained in warfare. Therefore it is not surprising that he took the decision to hold on to Madras, against the will of La Bourdonnais. In the process, the Company lost the ransom of 11,00,000 pagodas too. It also lost the value of the goods seized in Madras which amounted to 5,09,900 pagodas.[24] Probably, Dupleix thought of compensating all this by raising revenues in Madras. The English Governor of Madras, Nicholas Morse and certain members of his Council were brought to Pondicherry as prisoners.

Fortunately for Dupleix, a cyclone on 13 October 1746 ravaged the French squadron and vessels under La Bourdonnais. As a result, the latter was forced to leave back 900 European soldiers and about 300 *Cafres* (Africans) in Pondicherry, who were excellent soldiers. This not only reinforced the troops of Dupleix in Pondicherry, but also his ambitions. If Dupleix did not have these troops, which he secured by chance, it is impossible to imagine him wage his wars later in support of some Indian princes or to defend Pondicherry. Dupleix never acknowledged his indebtedness to La Bourdonnais in this respect.

The French ruled Madras until 1 September 1748. On that date, Dupleix was forced to exchange it for Louisbourg and the island of Cap Breton in North America by the treaty of Aix la Chapelle between the English and the French.[25]

It seems that Dupleix had the intention to arrest La Bourdonnais. Mahé de la Villebague, brother of La Bourdonnais, was in Pondicherry since 1725, and was Councillor since 1743. He had followed his brother to Madras in 1746. Dupleix persistently complained about his activities and that of a certain Desjardins in Madras to King Louis XV, who finally ordered their arrest. Mahé de Villebague was arrested on 4 April in the Isle of France for embezzlement of the funds and goods which included gold coins put into his hand by the English Governor of Madras, Morse. He was treated as a State prisoner and was incarcerated in the dungeon of Fort Louis in Pondicherry (presently Bharathi Park), along with Desjardins. On 1 March 1749, he was dispatched to France by sea. But he died on the way. He was accused of complicity with Mahé de La Bourdonnais for embezzlement of the English company's funds and goods.[26]

Mahé de La Bourdonnais was arrested in Paris on 1 March 1748 and ended up in the Bastille prison for his Madras operation and ransom. He was released from prison for want of evidence in 1751 and the case was decided in La Bourdonnais' favour. The latter demanded from the Company Rs. 20 lakh as compensation for him and the officers involved in the capture of Madras. This was a great setback for Dupleix. La Bourdonnais died on 10 November 1753. When he died he was worth 2.7 million livres.

Dupleix's main aim to hold on to Madras was to prevent it from being the hub of English trade on the coast and increase the economic prospects of Pondicherry. In this he failed. Otherwise there is nothing in the literature that I have consulted that Dupleix had a grand design to create a French political empire in India at this juncture. He never had such ideas before. In any case, he did not have the full backing of the Company in political ventures. If he confronted the English it was rather to prevent them from having an upper hand in trade in the region than anything else. Dupleix was essentially a trader since the time he came to India. He had written a memoir on trade in 1727. He was fully engrossed in trade all throughout his stay in Chandernagore. Unlike La Bourdonnais, he was never a warrior or a seaman. He had never waged any battles, leading his troops from the front.

But Dupleix using his position as Governor of Pondicherry took advantage of the capture of Madras by La Bourdonnais in order to augment the revenues and trade prospects of Pondicherry and never in order to found a French colonial empire in India, as it is popularly believed. His intention rather was to drive the English from south India, the rivals of the French in the trade domain. There is no indication that Dupleix entertained any expansioninst idea during the past 25 years that he had spent in India until then. His intention to hold on to Madras was with intention of exchanging it some day for Vazhudavur, bordering Pondicherry.[27] If he had the desire to found an empire in India, he would not have given back Madras to the English without a murmur, as it was decided by the French king himself. He never argued with the king that he was working for the expansion of French territories in India. Besides, he never broached the topic of French expansion in India with any of the French higher authorities, or with his colleagues, subordinates, friends and relatives in Pondicherry including his wife and his *dubash* Ananda Ranga Poullé, in a sustained and serious manner as a matter of policy.

NOTES

1. Dodwell, *Calendar of the Madras Despatches*, 1920, p. v; Orme, *History of Indostan*, I, pp. 44, 45-50; Castonnet des Fosses, *L'Inde Française au XVIIIème siècle*, Paris, s.d., p. 175; *ARP Diary*, I, p. 202.
2. Dodwell, *A Calendar of Madras Records, 1740-1744*, Madras, 1917, pp. 354-8, 380, 393; Jouveau Dubreuil, *Dupleix ou l'Inde Conquise*, Pondichéry, 1941, pp. 57, 58; *Correspondance du Conseil Supérieur de Pondichéry et de la Compagnie*, III, p. xix; *Correspondance du Conseil Supérieur de Pondichéry avec le Conseil de Chandernagore*, II, pp. 331-3; Orme, *History of Indostan* I, pp. 51-8.
3. *Correspondance du Conseil Supérieur de Pondichéry et de la Compagnie*, IV, p. xii; Dodwell, *Calendar of the Madras Despatches, 1744-1758*, Madras, 1928, p. 21; Dubreuil, ibid., p. 64; *ARP Diary*, IV, p. 125f; Nainar, *Tuzaki-Walajahi*, I, Madras, 1934, I, p. 83.
4. Srinivasachari, *Ananda Ranga Pillai: The 'Pepys' of French India*, New Delhi, 1991, p. 194; *ARP Diary*, III, pp. 140, 157.
5. *Correspondance du Conseil Supérieur de Pondichéry et de la Compagnie*, IV, pp. xi, xii, xiii, xx, lxi; Correspondance du Conseil Supérieur de Pondichéry avec le Conseil de Chandernagore, II, p. 361; Vincent, op. cit., p. 54; Col.c² 82, f. 62, A.N.; Alalasundaram, *The Colonial World of Ananda Ranga Pillai*, 1998, p. 8).
6. Correspondance du Conseil Supérieur de Pondichéry et de la Compagnie, IV, pp. xv, xviii, 24, 48; *ARP Diary*, V, p. 131; Gaudart, *Catalogue des Manuscrits . . .* , Paris, 1933, pp. x, xi, 15.
7. Vinson, *Les Français dans l'Inde, Dupleix et Labourdonnais*, Paris, 1894, p. 157; cf. also, J.B.P. More, *Origin and Foundation of Madras*, Chennai, 2016.
8. Mahé de La Bourdonnais, *Mémoire Historique de B.F. Mahé de la Bourdonnais*, 1890, pp. 60, 61, 104; Dodwell, *Clive and Dupleix*, 1989, pp. 8-9; Haudrère (ed.), *Les Français dans l'Océan Indien au XVIIIe siècle*, 2004, p. 103.
9. *ARP Diary*, I, pp. 305, 309; III, p. 393.
10. Dodwell, *Clive and Dupleix*, 1989, pp. 7, 9, 42; Love, *Vestiges of Old Madras. 1640-1800*, London, 1913, ii, p. 400; Naf. 9357, p. 235, BNF; *ARP Diary*, I, p. 365; II, p. 117.
11. Mahé de La Bourdonnais, op. cit., p. 86; Correspondance du Conseil Supérieur de Pondichéry et de la Compagnie, IV, p. iii; Vinson, op. cit., p. 194; Le Treguilly, 'La présence Française en Inde: aléas politiques et militaires', 1995, p. 38.
12. Vinson, ibid., pp. 16, 95; *Correspondance du Conseil Supérieur de Pondichéry et de la Compagnie*, IV, p. 357; Bourdat, *Les Grandes Pages du "Journal" d'Ananda Ranga Pillai*. p. 137; Naf, 9148, pp. 63, 66, BNF.

13. *ARP Diary*, II, pp. 285, 291, 311; Dodwell, op. cit., 1989, pp. 13, 14.
14. Mahé de La Bourdonnais, op. cit., pp. 120, 135, 139; cs, IV, xiii; Orme, op. cit., I, p. 71; Chassaigne, *Bussy en Inde*, Chartres, 1976, p. 13; Love, op. cit., II, 360-1; Naf, 9357, f. 246v, BNF; Haudrère, ed., op. cit., p. 102.
15. Vinson, op. cit., p. 132; Srinivasachari, op. cit., pp. 174-5, 259f; *ARP Diary*, VII, pp. 169-70).
16. Love, op. cit., II, pp. 360-1, 365-75; Vinson, ibid. pp. 144, 150; Mahé de La Bourdonnais, op. cit., p. 134; Orme, op. cit., I, p. 71; Marquis de Nazelle, op. cit., p. xx; De Closets d'Errey, *Résumé des Lettres du Conseil Provincial de Madras...*, 1936, p. iii; *ARP Diary*, II, pp. 301, 302, 394; viii, p. 152; Manning, op. cit., p. 217.
17. Gaudart, *La Criminalité dans les Etablissements Français de l'Inde*, Pondichéry, 1938, pp. 239-41; De closets d'Errey, ibid., p. iv; I/1/1 *French in India, 1664-1810*, pt. 3, p. 474, IOL.
18. Mahé de La Bourdonnais, op. cit., p. 163; De Closets d'Errey, *Précis Chronologique de l'Histoire de l'Inde Française*, 1934, p. 32.
19. Dodwell, op. cit.,1920, pp. 37-40; Marquis de Nazelle, op. cit., p. 8; *ARP Diary*, III, pp. 104, 108, 163, 168, 170, 171, 197, 227, 238-9; V, p. 337; VI, p. 19; I/1/1, *French in India, 1664-1810*, pt. 3, Memoirs of M. de la Bourdonnais, pp. 472-4, IOL; Vinson, op. cit., pp. 150-1; Mahé de La Bourdonnais, op. cit., p. 141; Manucci, *Storia Do Mogor*, 1908, IV, p. 168.
20. De Closets d'Errey, *Résumé des Lettres du Conseil Provincial de Madras*, 1936, pp. v, vi, 58, 133-8; Dodwell, ibid., p. xii; *ARP Diary*, III, pp. 109, 135; IV, pp. 57, 67; Col.c²81, ff. 4-72, A.N.
21. (I/1/1, *French in India, 1664-1810*, pt. 3, Memoirs of M. de la Bourdonnais, pp. 472-4, IOL; Vinson, op. cit., pp. 150-1; Mahé de La Bourdonnais, op. cit., p. 126; Dodwell, op. cit., 1989, pp. 20, 21; Col.c²81, ff. 4-72, A.N.; *ARP Diary*, II, pp. 255, 376; III, pp. 122, 177; IV, pp. 24-7, 116-17.
22. *ARP Diary*, III, pp. 105, 107, 133-4, 135, 172, 227-8; IV, 65, 67; Castonnet des Fosses, op. cit., p. 267; Malleson, *Dupleix*, 2001, pp. 55-7; Laberandie, *Le Vieux*, Pondichéry, 1936, p. 171.
23. Dubreuil, op. cit., p. 104; *ARP Diary*, III, pp. 322, 324, 365, 376; IV, 16; cf. also Mémoire pour Labourdonnais, pièce, No.230; Laberandie, ibid. p. 173; Manning, op. cit., p. 212; Oubagarasamy, op. cit., p. xxviii.
24. Bourdonnais, op. cit., pp. 114, 134, 172, 204, 212; De Closets d'Errey, op. cit., 1936, pp. 2, 42; *ARP Diary*, IV, p. vi.
25. Bourdonnais, ibid., pp. 163, 206; De Closets d'Errey, *Précis Chronologique de l'Histoire de l'Inde Française*, 1934, p. 32; Vinson, op. cit., pp. 177f.
26. Gaudart, op. cit., ii, 230, 231, 232, 234, 235, 237; Bourdonnais, op. cit., pp. 162-3, 367; Vinson, ibid., pp. 89f; *ARP Diary*, VIII, p. 152.
27. Gaudart, ibid., p. 234; Bionne, *Dupleix*, Paris, 1881, p. 312; Manning, op. cit., p. 77; *ARP Diary*, VIII, pp. 153, 154f; Col.c²81, ff. 4-72, A.N.; Haudrère, *La Compagnie Française des Indes au XVIIIe siècle*, III, p. 982.

CHAPTER 7

Siege of Pondicherry, 1748 and its Aftermath

FORT ST. DAVID or Devanampatnam was located at about 2 miles from Cuddalore. The site was bought by the English in 1690. It was functioning as the headquarters of the English since September 1746. Dupleix thought that unless Fort St. David was also captured, trade in Pondicherry would not flourish. Dupleix sent Bussy Castelnau with 1700 men to conquer it in December 1746. But Mohammad Ali's troops repulsed Bussy. A second attempt was made on 11 March 1747 under La Tour and Louis Paradis. Many Tamils of the Palli caste participated in this assault as sepoys. There was a third attempt in the same year. In 1748, a fourth attempt was made to conquer Fort St. David by Mainville.

Ananda Ranga Poullé never uttered a word against these expeditions. Instead he actively encouraged it and said that God would grant victory to Dupleix. He told Dupleix that he was his 'obedient servant' and did not want any share in his glory. However, all these expeditions which had the blessings of Poullé seems to have resulted in immense damage to the Tamil countryside causing misery to the Tamil population. But Ananda Ranga Poullé, more than Dupleix, was least bothered.[1]

The English were naturally waiting for an occasion to invade Pondicherry and put an end to the repeated attacks of Dupleix to dislodge the English from Fort St. David and probably get rid off them altogether from south India, so that the French could monopolize the trade in the region. Dupleix was conscious of the aggressive designs of the English against Pondicherry, which he himself had provoked, having failed in all his four attempts to drive the English away from Cuddalore.[2] This in itself shows that Dupleix lacked experience and training in military warfare. Besides, he held on to Madras until 1749 due to La Bourdonnais's exploits in 1746 and not because he won it personally through conquest.

The death of Nizam-ul-mulk on 1 June 1748 paved the way for a change in the political scenario of south India. Nazir Jung, the second son of Nizam-ul-mulk became the new nizam. But Muzaffar Jung, a nephew of Nazir Jung contested this succession. Dupleix decided to throw his weight behind Muzaffar Jung, who theoretically had no right to the throne. The English finally decided to invade Pondicherry in August 1748 and put an end to French rule in India. They decided on a naval cum land attack. There is no indication that Dupleix foresaw this revenge invasion, when he repeatedly attacked Fort St. David.

However when Dupleix got wind about the impending invasion, he organized Pondicherry's defence against the English. Dupleix was never trained in military matters. He had never led any army into the battlefield. He never had any military advisors by his side. He was a trader and an official. He did not have any official sanction from the Company Directors in France to wage wars in India. He had been over-stepping his mission since 1745. But in spite of such handicaps and drawbacks, he prepared Pondicherry for war. Ananda Ranga Poullé played a crucial role during the siege by making available the necessary provisions and informing Dupleix about the various movements of the enemy and asking the Tamils to resist the English. His Brahmin astrologer had predicted that Dupleix would shine like the sun in future.[3]

Dupleix had earlier completed the construction of the protective wall on the beach side, east of the Fort. In the southern extremity of Pondicherry region at Ariyankuppam, he had a fort. He had at his disposal European soldiers as well as locally recruited sepoys, mainly from Mahé, trained by French officers. The number of European soldiers was always very limited. They had to assure the maintenance of security and the protection of not only Pondicherry, but also other French territories like Mahé and Karaikal. They were never meant for waging wars against Indian powers.

Most of the recruits when they left France were untrained men, who were generally 'unwanted' in France, recruited by chance and by force. Vagabonds, deserters and murderers were also recruited from prisons and sent to India.[4] There were very few officers who were capable men. On 31st December 1740, during Dumas's governorship there were just 350 white soldiers present in Pondicherry and 117 in Karaikal, of which 30 or 40 were sick and another 30 or 40 were crippled.

Of course, by 1748, Dupleix had succeeded in increasing the number of French soldiers and officers, thanks to La Bourdonnais. However, officers who really received military training were few. Paradis, who rose to become a commanding officer of the French army, was actually a land surveyor in the beginning. There were others like the Count d'Auteuil, Bussy, Jacques Law, de la Tour and La Touche. It was with such European men who formed a rag-tag army that Dupleix had to assure the defense of Pondicherry. If the nawabs and other conquerors and invaders like the Marathas had wanted to drive the French out of south India, they could have easily done it but fortunately for the French, the Indian rulers wanted to keep them in India for trade reasons and to augment their revenues.[5] They never foresaw the impending danger to their own rule in the long run. This was a fatal error on their part.

Besides the European soldiers, Dupleix had at his disposal the south Indian sepoys, who have been used for defensive purposes since François Martin's time. It was not Dupleix who raised the regiment of Indian sepoys. He simply followed the tradition established by his predecessors, as there was always an acute lack of trained European soldiers in Pondicherry. During the war waged by the French under Mahé de La Bourdonnais against the troops of the Vazhunavur of Badagara in 1740-1, many locally recruited troops fought alongside the French troops.[6] Many of them were Muslims of Mahé and Malabar.

These soldiers passed over to Pondicherry during Dupleix's governorship. In the beginning they were undisciplined. Dupleix created separate regiments out of them since 1746, gave them uniforms and got them trained by French officers. They were put under a European officer who was assisted by Indian subaltern officers. Among these subalterns, there were two or three officers who were the most distinguished. They were Sheikh Ibrahim of the Infantry regiment and Abdul Rahman and his brother Sheikh Hassan of the cavalry. All hailed from Mahé and were originally fishermen. The soldiers of their regiments called *sipahis* or sepoys were composed mainly of the Muslims of Mahé and Malabar. It seems to have consisted also of Paraya and Palli castemen. Ananda Ranga Poullé frequently refers to them as 'Paraya sepoys' in his diary.

The Company paid Rs. 6 for every sepoy soldier to Abdul Rahman. But Abdul Rahman used to pay every soldier just Rs. 3 and kept the rest for himself. It has been noted in the records that the sepoys had a predilection for robbing indiscriminately rather than fighting the enemy. It has been also noted that they were not like the Marathas or the Mughal Muslims. Instead they were groups of coolies, miserable and ugly coolies, though they passed off as the best foot soldiers and cavalrymen in the whole of India. However, it seems that Abdul Rahman was not happy with his pay. He complained to Dupleix that it was not enough. Dupleix raised his pay by Rs. 2. Sheikh Hassan too was poorly paid, which pushed them to steal the money given as pay to the sepoys under them.[7]

Sheikh Ibrahim was actually employed in the beginning as a servant by one Musafer Khan, chief of a small number of sepoys at Masulipatnam. Gradually, he became sepoy and then corporal and sergeant of the sepoys, until he was appointed as captain by Dupleix. He was in the good books of Madame Dupleix too. There were other Muslim chiefs like Ali Khan employed by Dupleix. It is noteworthy that during this period the French nicknamed the sepoys as 'brown dogs' or 'Madras sepoys'. It is also quite noteworthy that during this period Jamedar Sheikh Hassan, the younger brother of Abdul Rahman, who was originally a fisherman from Mahé, married the daughter of Muhammad Kamal, Nawab Anwaruddin's son by a concubine and became part of the Muslim nobility.[8]

Sensing an impending attack, the Tamil people began to leave the town. Father Coeurdoux removed the doors and timber of the churches in the Ozhukarai and the Ariyankuppam churches as well as the statues and other cult objects to a safer place. This caused panic among the Tamils who started fleeing. Families of landowners and merchants like the wife of Tandavaraya Mudali, the wife of his brother Tanappa Mudali and all their children, the women and the children of Arumbattai Poullé's house, the women and children of Chanda Sahib, Dost Ali Khan's wife, all the employees of the fort and all others, except Ananda Ranga Poullé's family, had hidden their furniture, precious objects, jewels and money and had left with some of their goods, leaving behind some old persons. It seems that under the influence of his wife, Dupleix extracted Rs. 10,000 from Chanda Sahib's son and sent soldiers to stop the Muslim noble women in their flight, made them stand in the sun and humiliated them. When Dupleix asked why the Tamils were leaving the town, Ananda Ranga Poullé who was a Telugu, replied that they were 'cowards' and 'ignorant', unlike the Europeans. He added that it was good that they left as there were not enough grains to feed them.[9]

During the siege, Dupleix gave orders to burn down all the villages neighbouring Pondicherry like Singirikovil, Kijanipet, Bahur and Kirmampakkam which were in the hands of the English. Ananda Ranga Poullé executed these orders meticulously. This put the Tamils inhabiting those villages to great hardships. But Dupleix or Ananda Ranga Poullé never cared about that. Both were insensitive to the sufferings of the Tamil population.

Dupleix just wanted to defeat the English by all means and Ananda Ranga Poullé was there to execute his orders. He even gave orders to destroy the feeble wall of defence that surrounded Pondicherry and the whole town, i.e. the black town was almost razed to the ground, except the fort which was well protected. The people were unhappy with Dupleix over this unnecessary destruction. Ananda Ranga Poullé never seems to have opposed such destruction. In fact, he was complicit. However, Dupleix never seems to have resisted the siege from the front. He never came to the ramparts or led his combat troops against the English all throughout the siege. He was content with issuing orders which was executed by his commanders and chiefs.[10]

A local militia had created in 1743 consisting of hundred Tamil men, made up essentially of the Pallis. They were under Saverimuthu, a lame man of the Palli caste, who was a Christian. Viraraghava Nayakar and Ponnan were the subordinate chiefs of the militiamen. Every one of them was paid Rs. 6 per day, apart from the rice given to them daily.

Madame Dupleix used these men, during the siege to rob the town for her own benefit. These men set fire to Kosapalayam (potters' village), Saram and other places along the bound-hedge. She used to send low caste people and Parayas to inhabit the empty houses of the higher castes, while the outcastes used the ustensils of the higher castes. Santappan, the head peon caught Apu Mudali's brother trying to leave the town with 100 pagodas, and other goods and jewels. Dupleix imprisoned Apu Mudali at the choultry.

Ananda Ranga Poullé claimed that Madame Dupleix favoured the Christians and beat and imprisoned the Hindus unjustly. Apart from the Pallis under Saverimuthu, the sepoys who numbered about 300 foot soldiers and 60 to 70 cavalry men under Abdul Rahman robbed the people and took away all their furniture, cloth, rice, sarees of women and other objects to the town. They even molested poor women. The complaints of the various inhabitants of Pondicherry against this robbery and molestation done with the approval of Madame Dupleix fell on deaf ears.[11]

Ananda Ranga Poullé had appointed Vira Nayakkan as the chief of the Pallis in March 1747. Vira Nayakkan was formerly banished from Pondicherry for thievery. But Poullé justified this appointment with Dupleix. Madame Dupleix retained these Pallis at her service until 1752.[12]

Ananda Ranga Poullé concurred with Dupleix on the necessity of driving away the Brahmins from the town. Dupleix issued orders on 4 November 1748, which was pasted at six places in the town in French, Tamil and Persian announcing that the lands of those who had left the town or joined the enemy would be forfeited, sold at public auction and the proceeds would be taken over by the Company. As a result many Brahmin houses in Brahmin Street were bought by low caste Christians and Frenchmen. The caste headmen could do nothing about it and were driven away by the guards. When the Vedapuriswaran temple garden was taken over, brass and copper vessels, besides jewels were found there. Dupleix ordered them to be sent to him. Ananda Ranga Poullé hardly objected.[13]

When the English under Admiral Boscawen besieged Pondicherry by sea and by land in August 1748, Dupleix made use of not only European soldiers but also the Indian soldiers under Abdul Rahman and Sheikh Hassan to repulse their attacks at the various gates. It seems that the Vedapuriswaran temple tower served as a landmark for the English to bombard the town in the night. Five thousand bombs were hurled on Pondicherry and 40,000 cannon shots were fired at it in 42 days. French officers like the Count d'Auteuil, Paradis, La Touche, de La Tour, Mainville, Bussy and Jacques-François Law were deployed to defend Pondicherry along with European soldiers and the sepoys under the Mahé chiefs to thwart any English incursion into Pondicherry through Ariyankuppam and Archivac.

It seems that the English had paid the Nizam 1,00,000 pagodas during this period in order to acquire his support and that of his vassals in the Carnatic in their fight against the French in Pondicherry. Ananda Ranga Poullé, however, held that the English under Boscawen were benevolent, who treated well the people captured, while his master, Dupleix was cruel and money-minded even in the thick of war.[14]

As many as 3,000 English soldiers and 10,000 sepoys marched from Fort St. David in Cuddalore and camped near Archivac. Ariyankuppam and its five-faced fortress surrounded by a pit, with the Ariyankuppam River flowing by on its north, the village in the east, the Chunambar River in the south and an open field in the west, had to be protected at all cost, as it was the entry point towards Pondicherry town. Eleven days were spent in capturing the fort at Ariyankuppam. It finally fell on 20 August 1748.[15] The English even hoisted their flag at Singarikovil and reached the Ariyankuppam Church and Pedro Canagarayen's garden behind it. The English did not molest the farmers of Ariyankuppam or destroy their fields. Instead they asked them to return to their fields.

Many records related to the siege point to the crucial role played by the local chiefs, Abdul Rahman, Sheikh Hassan and Ali Khan who defended valiantly at the Ariyankuppam front, by inflicting severe losses upon the English. Without them, the French would have definitely capitulated to the English. It was largely due to the valour of the sepoys that Ariyankuppam was saved for the French and the English suffered a loss of 1,000 men.

Dupleix himself was conscious of this historical fact when he chose to honour both the Mahé brothers and others for their bravery in defending Pondicherry. Even Madame Dupleix showered the Mahé chiefs with presents. As a matter of fact, Paradis, the French officer, most trusted by Dupleix, lost his life during the siege on 14 September 1748 due to a gunshot. He was buried in the chapel of the old hospital. Consequently it was largely to the credit of the Mahé chiefs and the men under them to have withstood the onslaught of the English until the latter withdrew, unable to make any headway into Pondicherry. On the whole, the English lost at least 1675 men in this siege, while the French lost 353.[16]

The nawab of Arcot, Anwaruddin Khan's troops, commanded by Abdul Jalil, son-in-law of the nawab, was camping at Villianur during the siege. But they did not intervene in the battle, on the side of the English. Dupleix appreciated the valour of Abdul Rahman. He praised the heroic resistance put up by Abdul Rahman and his sepoys against the 'black English' or the sepoys of the English, without much loss. He wanted the French nation to show outward signs of gratitude towards Abdul Rahman and his brother Sheikh Hassan for their faithfulness and courage during the siege and to keep them tied with the French by addressing letters of the minister to them and making them commandants of the sepoys and Moors and such 'species' which would flatter them and offer them medals of recognition. Further the Company could offer them presents that were suitable to Asiatics like swords, pistols and guns.

It was under these extraordinary circumstances that Dupleix complimented Abdul Rahman and gave him the title of 'Nawab of Arcot'. Abdul Rahman asked Dupleix to provide him with 1,000 Indian soldiers and horsemen, four mortars and four big canons so that he could subdue not just Arcot but also all territory, south of the Krishna River. Abdul Rahman was no doubt brimming with confidence at the end of the siege and Dupleix was certainly considering a greater role for him and his sepoys in future. Ananda Ranga Poullé himself was jealous of the growing closeness of the sepoy chiefs with Dupleix, whom he usually dismissed due to their humble 'fishermen' origin. Dupleix on the other hand held that the Tamil inhabitants did nothing to help him during the siege. Instead, they hid the paddy and caused food scarcity in the town.

Nevertheless, Dupleix even apprised the Company Directors in Paris of the valour of the Mahé chiefs. He wrote: 'The person known as Cheik Abdoul Rahman, who during the war in Mahé had demonstrated his fidelity and his bravery, and who commands the sepoys here, has distinguished himself with his brother Cheik Assem in a notable manner (in the war with the English)'.

Nevertheless, in July 1749, a *parvana* was received from the Mughal emperor granting Dupleix a *mansab* of 4500 horses, with the seal of the vizir Qamaruddin Khan.[17]

In 1750, the Mahé brothers were presented with medals and were made Captains. In the light of all this, there is no doubt that the Indian soldiers collaboration with Dupleix during this period, had led to the consolidation of French colonial power in Pondicherry and vetted the political appetite of Dupleix. These soldiers, as well as the Indian merchants like Ananda Ranga Poullé who collaborated with Dupleix primarily out of self-interest, had no idea of what was nationalism, which was born in the European countries since the fifteenth century at least.

Nationalism is an idea or feeling of belonging to one territory, on the basis of language, culture, religion, race or a common shared legacy. Dupleix and the French were imbued with French nationalist spirit that cut across class lines. It was the same with the English, Dutch and the Portuguese. On the other hand, Indians were split on linguistic, caste, class, religious, racial and sectarian lines that prevented the emergence of European type nationalism, based on the feeling of a certain oneness during this period.

According to the Treaty of Aix la Chapelle of 3 October 1748, Madras was returned to the English in 1749, even after Dupleix had successfully repulsed the English attack on Pondicherry in 1748, while still holding on to Madras. Barthélémy was its last French administrator. Dupleix had to abide by the treaty. He could do nothing about it. If Dupleix had not been forced to relinquish Madras by the Anglo-French treaty of 1748, probably the history of south India, Madras and Pondicherry would have taken a different turn. But that was not to be.

In any case it seems that Dupleix himself wanted to exchange Madras for Vazhudavur and Villianur at that time with Anwaruddin Khan, nawab of Arcot. Actually, in November 1748, Dupleix wrote to Imam Sahib asking him to get for the French a *parvana* from the nizam granting Koonimedu and its 75 villages, Vazhudavur, Bahur and Villianur with their dependent villages. Dupleix even sought Masulipatnam and the country around it from the Nizam, promising to help him in return to conquer lands up to Delhi.[18]

On 11 October 1749, the French king awarded the title of *Chevalier de Saint Louis* to Dupleix, for his defense of Pondicherry. The Company was happy with Dupleix and disapproved of the actions of La Bourdonnais.[19]

Due to the wars with the English since 1745, trade was completely ruined in Pondicherry. No French ship could ply on the high seas safely. Besides, the detruction of the Vedapuriswaran temple during the siege had sent a message to the Hindu merchants and others not to settle in Pondicherry as their religion, culture, customs and traditions were not safe there. As a result the population of Pondicherry stagnated and even dwindled.

Ananda Ranga Poullé seems to have contributed considerably to such a state of affairs, as he never used his position and influence to stop the destruction of temple, unlike his uncle Nainiappa Poullé. Instead, he never was tired of flattering Dupleix and his greatness. He most certainly knew that Nainiappa's fate would befall him, if he did not toe the line of the Governor. So out of pure self-interest, he preferred to sacrifice the interests of many Tamils of Pondicherry. This despite the fact that Ananda Ranga Poullé was not still nominated officially as the *dubash* of the Company. However, the French were convinced that he was the only person capable of succeeding Pedro Canagarayen. His brother Lazar was considered as an imbecile and was looked down upon by the Tamils. Ananda Ranga Poullé himself blew his own trumpet off and on, extolling his diplomatic and negotiating skills, which he claimed was known to the whole of India and would also be known in Europe.[20]

Dupleix had started as a trader in Pondicherry. He multiplied his trade operations for ten years in Chandernagore. Naturally when he returned to Pondicherry as governor, he was very much interested in promoting trade in Pondicherry. It was with this objective that he occupied Madras. But trade never flourished in Pondicherry. In order to augment trade as well as the revenues, he took some measures.

For example, he brought in weavers from various parts of Tamil Nadu and settled them in areas south of Villianur near the river. He even gave a loan of 10 pagodas to be re-imbursed in ten years, to every migrant to establish their looms and build their houses. At Kurumampet near Villianur 1,200 weaver families were settled. They worked for the Company until 1752 when they left due to non-payment and due to English incursions. Tax was imposed on every loom by the customs house. Besides, all artisans were subjected to pay professional tax to the Company. But the production and stocking of the products was in the hands of merchants like the *de facto dubash* Ananda Ranga Poullé. The latter had his own looms at Lalpettai and Arcot. He as well as other merchants like Muthiah Poullé and Sunguvar Seshachala Chetty had their own arecanut and tobacco or cloth godowns in the town. Seshachala Chetty supplied cloth to the Company at wholesale rates on the basis of a contract with the Company.[21]

Liquor was big business in Pondicherry. Merchants like Tiruvengadam Poullé, father of Ananda Ranga Poullé had dealt with the manufacture and sale of toddy and arrack *patté*. The latter was locally produced by coolies and stored in the godowns. Actually the sale of liquor in Pondicherry was the Company's monopoly. The Governor leased out the right to manufacture and sell toddy and arrack against an annual payment.[22]

Among the other prominent merchants of Pondicherry during this period there were Lakshmipathi Chetty, Chidambara Chetty, Sungu Muthurama Chetty, Salatu Venkatachala Chetty, Petachi Chetty, Vira Chetty, Tillai Mudali, Ariyappa Mudali, Chinnadu Mudali, Nallathamby Mudali. Tiruviti Balu Chetty was another merchant, who according to Ananda Ranga Poullé was quite liberal-minded, in the sense that he who would offer any material help to any Brahmin or anyone, provided they pandered to his lust with their wives, sisters or some other suitable women. But the most prominent of the business men was of course Ananda Ranga Poullé, who enriched himself enormously through various operations. He was tax-farmer, money-lender, revenue manager, caste chief, enjoyed commissions on exports and imports, in the buying and sale of goods and on coinage and was also the chief of the Indians. He lent money even to Dupleix and the Company officials.[23]

Ananda Ranga Poullé had taken to flattering and showering

encomiums on Dupleix more and more thenceforth, for his own survival as *dubash* and his own economic well-being. He told Dupleix that 100 French soldiers were equal to 1,000 Indian soldiers. He praised Dupleix, instead of La Bourdonnais, for capturing Madras from the Englishmen without the loss of a single soldier. He later told Dupleix that his glory was even greater than that of the Mughal emperors and that the war had happened so that his glory could spread throughout India.

Besides, Ananda Ranga Poullé was a great believer in astrology. He told that all his predictions would be precise and correct. He was assured that his master, Dupleix's future would be great and glorious. Even Madame Dupleix, who disliked him, believed in astrology and predictions. In this she was no different from Ananda Ranga Poullé, though she had a visceral hatred for him as a person.[24]

NOTES

1. De Closets d'Errey, op. cit., 1934, p. 29; *ARP Diary*, III, pp. 44, 138, 143-4, 215-16, 226, 394-5; IV, 24-27; I/1/1, *French in India, 1664-1810*, pt. 3, 474, IOL; Malleson, op. cit., 2001, pp. 59-63.
2. Marquis de Nazelle, op. cit., pp. 62-80, 99-106, 145.
3. Oubagarasamy, op. cit., pp. xxviii, xxix.
4. Cultru, op. cit., p. 301.
5. Martineau, *Dupleix et l'Inde Française, 1742-1749*, 1923, pp. 75, 77, 82; J.B.P. More, 'Some Maritime Aspects of the Indian Ocean Region (1600-1760)', 1996, pp. 130-48.
6. Martineau, ibid.,p. 82.
7. *ARP Diary*, IV, pp. 134, 266; Asie 12, f. 54, Relation du siege de Pondichéry, AMAE; Cultru, op. cit., pp. 311-12; Alalasundaram, op. cit., 1998, p. 228.
8. *ARP Diary*, IV, 252; Martineau, op. cit., pp. 83-4; Naf, 9359, f. 126, BNF; Naf 9357, f. 232, BNF; Col.c²83, ff. 186-233, A.N.
9. Vinson, *Les Français dans l'Inde, Dupleix et Labourdonnais*, op. cit., pp. 183, 186, 219; Martineau, ibid., pp. 481, 487; *ARP Diary*, V, pp. 188, 278, 292, 316, 283, 287, 291, 292, 295-7.
10. *ARP Diary*, V, p. 421; Vinson, ibid., p. 193; Marquis de Nazelle, op. cit., p. 19.
11. Laude, op. cit., pp. 44, 49, 53; Vinson, ibid., pp. 237-9, 245; Naf 9364, f. 141, BNF; Marquis de Nazelle, ibid., pp. 174, 221; *ARP Diary*, I, p. 261; V, pp. 286, 294, 295, 298, 299, 333, 334, 335, 386; VI, p. 51.

12. E 3751, 76, A.V.; Cultru, op. cit., p. 331; *ARP Diary*, V, pp. 284, 294-5, 335; VI, pp. 50-1; IV, p. 24.
13. *ARP Diary*, V, p. 100; VI, pp. 73, 75, 76, 87, 122-3.
14. Ibid. V, p. 282; *Country Correspondence*, 1748, pp. 3, 4, 5; Dubreuil, op. cit., p. 136.
15. *ARP Diary*, V, p. 250; VI, pp. 50-1.
16. Chassaigne, op. cit., p.15; Law de Lauriston, *Mémoire sur quelques affaires de l'Empire Moghole, 1756-1761*, Paris, 1913, p. xx; Vinson, op. cit., pp. 191f, 199, 204, 211, 212, 239; Correspondance du Conseil Supérieur de Pondichéry avec le Conseil de Chandernagore, III, pp. 28, 29; Laude, op. cit., pp. 48fn, 56; Le Treguilly, op. cit., p. 39; Marquis de Nazelle, op. cit., pp. 156-7, 176-201; Vincent, op. cit., p. 53; Castonnet des Fosses, op. cit., p. 291; *Relation du Siège de Pondichéry, 1749*; Martineau, op. cit., 1923, pp. 84, 442, 481 491, 494, 496, 504; Gaudart, *Catalogue des Manuscrits . . .* , 1931, pp. 64-5; *ARP Diary*, IV, pp. 266, 315, 317, 318; V, 219, 239, 243, 281, 331, 332.
17. *ARP Diary*, III, p. 200; V, 201, 327-8; VI, pp. 9, 10, 55, 144; Martineau, ibid., pp. 491, 494, 496, 501, 504, 481, 442; Laude, ibid., pp. 84-5; Marquis de Nazelle, op. cit., pp. 328-9, 336, 338-40, 336-40 (letters of Dupleix to Company Directors).
18. Labernadie, op. cit., p. 189; Col.c²81, ff. 4-72, A.N.; Fr.8983, ff. 31, BNF; Naf, 9144, ff. 119, BNF; *ARP Diary*, III, pp. 121-2, IV, pp. 116-17; VI, pp. 22, 48, 55, 147-8; *Correspondance du Conseil Supérieur de Pondichéry et de la Compagnie*, IV, pp. xii, xiv; Srinivasachari, op. cit., p. 173.
19. Col c²32, f. 18v, A.N.; Haudrère, op. cit., III, pp. 985-6.
20. Correspondance du Conseil Supérieur de Pondichéry et de la Compagnie, IV, pp. xix, 357; *ARP Diary*, III, pp. 366, 370, 371, 376, 380, 381.
21. *ARP Diary*, III, p. 24; VI, 157, 190; VIII, p. 106; Srinivasachari, op. cit., pp. xii, 3,4, 135,136; Col.c²102, f. 184), A.N.; Manickam, *Trade and Commerce in Pondicherry*, 2001, p. 43; De Closets d'Errey, *Histoire de l'Inde Française*, 1940, p. 64.
22. *ARP Diary*, IV, p. 249, Gaudart, *Catalogue des Manuscrits . . .* , I, p. 46.
23. Ibid., I, 56-8, 315, 426, 322, 323, 330), IX, pp. 25, 45, 46, 84, 112, 122, 257, 318; Arasaratnam, *Maritime Trade, Society and European Influence in Southern India*, 1995, pp. 142, 143.
24. *ARP Diary*, III, pp. 73, 96, 97-8; IV, pp. 56, 237, 241.

CHAPTER 8

Vedapuriswaran (Shiva) Temple Destruction and Related Events

THE STUDY OF the siege of Pondicherry by the English will not be complete, if we do not evoke the destruction of the famous Hindu temple caused by Dupleix. This temple dedicated to Lord Shiva, in the form of Vedapuriswara, stood exactly at the site of the present Mission Press which jutted into the Mission Street. The sacred tank of the temple extended from the Mission Street eastwards down the present Nidarajapayer Street upto the premises of the Sisters of Saint Louis de Gonzague. This temple seems to have come into existence in the seventeenth century or a little before. There is no evidence that it existed before that, though some scholars like Jouveau Dubreuil claim that it existed since the second century and that it was a seat of learning or *Vedapuri* and all that. Most of Jouveau Dubreuil claims with regard to the Vedapuriswaran temple can be reasonably relegated to the realm of fantasies, in the present state of our knowledge.[1]

The French Jesuits, whose residence and church was located on the southern side of the temple, had been trying to dislodge this temple since François Martin's time, as we have seen. Already in May-June 1743, Dupleix tried to get the *polygar* Muthiah Poullé to destroy the temple. Dupleix threatened to cut off his ears and beat him publicly and even hang him. But Muthiah Poullé escaped to Venkatammalpettai by promising Dupleix that he would bring a Brahmin saint from Tirupapuliyur who would tell the caste headmen to remove the *lingam* and build another temple. Fortunately for Poullé Dupleix believed in him and let him go.

In 1744, the French Jesuits were very much exasperated by the numerous 'magnificent' ceremonies of the Hindus, near their residence and church. They regretted that in Pondicherry, there were temples and mosques and the 'cult of the demons' was dominant and the cult of the 'true God' was obscured by that of the demons.[2]

In March 1746, the Vedapuriswaran temple Nandi (sacred bull) was desecrated by some miscreants. On 22 September 1746 some caste headmen of Pondicherry had approached Dupleix asking him to grant permission to build a wall at the Vedapuriswaran temple to protect it. Ananda Ranga Poullé was in favour of the construction of the protective wall. But Dupleix did not grant any such permission.

Again in December 1746, a jar of filthy stuff was thrown into the Vedapuriswaran temple from the neighbouring St. Paul's Church of the Jesuits. It almost fell on the head of Sankara Iyer, who was doing his religious duties around the shrine of *Pillaiyar*. When the jar broke, the stench was unbearable. Ten caste headmen including Tillai Mudali, Peddu Chetty, Arumugattan Mudali and Andanayakkan Mudali reported the matter to Dupleix. Dupleix sent two officials with Tanappa Mudali and Paradis to inspect the place. Father Coeurdoux rejected the accusation. Dupleix evaded the issue by promising to write to France, though Ananda Ranga Poullé felt that the incident might tarnish Dupleix's image, at a time when people were extolling his fame and valour.[3]

Even when the siege was going on, Dupleix did not consider it necessary to obtain the cooperation of the Hindus, who were the majority population in Pondicherry. Most of the merchants, weavers, artisans and workers were also Hindus. Dupleix knew that the rulers of India were the Muslims of foreign extraction who spoke Persian, and the Marathas, who spoke their own language. So he hardly sought Tamil cooperation, in spite of the fact that the *dubash* of the Company was a Hindu albeit a Telugu one – Ananda Ranga Poullé.

Generally Dupleix seems to have had a very poor idea about the fighting capabilities and morality of the Tamils. Besides, Dupleix knew that Hindus were a house divided on caste basis, where the higher castes alone were 'Tamizhars' while the rest were lowly placed in the Hindu social scale or were outcastes. It should not be forgotten at this juncture, in the eighteenth century the term 'Hindu' was not still in vogue in Pondicherry to denote the non-Muslim Indians. Instead, the French used the term 'Malabar' to designate all Tamils, whether high or low caste, unlike Ananda Ranga Poullé, who used the term 'Tamizhar' to signify only the higher castes.[4]

The low castes and the outcastes were not even allowed to enter the main Hindu temples of Pondicherry including the Vedapuriswaran temple, as they were considered as polluting castes due to their lowly occupations, food habits and traditions. Ananda Ranga Poullé himself looked down upon them, as revealed by his accounts in his *Diary*. Naturally they were not very much bothered about the temples of the 'soft' or 'good' castes, i.e. the castes who did not take to menial work.

However, instead of seeking the general Hindu cooperation during the siege, Dupleix seems to have done everything to displease them during this period. Many of the Hindus including the Brahmins had left the town. It was thought to be good as the Brahmins could have hindered the destruction of the temple. The four gates of the fort were closed. But ten caste headmen were still in the town. Dupleix did not consider it necessary to consult them before giving orders for the destruction of the temple.

Under the influence of the French Jesuit fathers and the prodding of his wife, Johanna Begum, as well as Paradis, the French commander, Dupleix during the thick of the siege, issued orders to demolish the Vedapursiwaran temple, which stood adjacent to the Jesuit Church, just outside the White town towards the west, on the pretext that it obstructed the defence of the town. The Jesuits had been demanding its destruction since François Martin's time. Their demand was finally fulfilled by Dupleix.

Paradis actually incited Dupleix to issue orders for its destruction. He told that he had destroyed one in Karaikal and the Dutch had destroyed another temple called *Naduvarkovil* in Nagapattinam in the middle of the town. He added that in Karaikal they had crushed a statue of the temple and put it in the wall of the Karaklanchery fort. As a matter of fact, several temples of Karaikal were destroyed by Paradis during the wars of 1744 when he was commandant of Karaikal. The stones of these temples were used for the construction of the fort. There was a very big temple in Karaikal which he converted to a fortress for the defence of Karaikal. Another small temple on the north-west, near the river Arsalar was also converted into a small fortress. All this Paradis did in order to protect Karaikal from the 'blacks' (Indians/Tamils).

In April 1748, there were differences of opinion between Paradis and the Jesuit priests with regard to the reparation of temples in Karaikal and the re-construction of some of these temples. The matter was taken to the Superior Council of Pondicherry. It was decided that the destroyed temples might be reconstructed if they were not bigger than the older ones. Besides the Council decreed that Paradis could not oppose reparations of the existing temples.[5]

The role played by Madame Dupleix in the destruction of the temple and the propagation of Christianity during this period is quite amazing. It should not be forgotten that she was of Indo-Portuguese descent and her grandmother was actually a Tamil lady. Though we do not have any records to prove the caste origin of this lady, yet it appears quite probable that she was a Paraya woman. Madame Dupleix would have definitely known about the caste affinity of her Tamil ancestor though she had never spoken a word about it.

But her actions prove that she was vehemently against the caste Hindus including the *dubash* Ananda Ranga Poullé, when Dupleix was Governor. She was naturally hell bent to propagate Christianity, to be in the good books of the Jesuits and to get rid of the hold of the 'higher' caste Hindus of Pondicherry in the society, at least to some extent. That is why she stood in the forefront of the move to destroy the Vedapuriswaran temple during the siege.

It is noteworthy that during the siege Madame Dupleix and her children and some relatives had found refuge in the missionary church that stood right in front of Ananda Ranga Poullé's house. She was never seen on the ramparts, encouraging the soldiers.[6]

Following the orders of Dupleix, on 8 September 1748, the priests and the French chief engineer, Gerbault, 200 coolies, 200 soldiers and 67 cavalry men, armed with pickaxes, spades and tongs arrived at the temple. They started the demolition of the temple from the southern wall of the temple and the out-houses. The managers of the temple ran to Ananda Ranga Poullé's house, which was situated just nearby in the next street towards the north, to ask him to intervene. But Poullé, for reasons that we do not know, did not budge from his house. The scholarly chief of the Jesuits since 1744, Father Coeurdoux, who had first pointed out the relationship between Sanskrit and Latin/Greek, kicked the idol in the *sanctum santorum* and exhorted the Africans to break the doors of the temple.[7]

Ananda Ranga Poullé was hardly bothered about the destruction of the temple. He went about his daily business as usual. When Ananda Ranga Poullé was in his areca nut shop, near the Governor's house, some Tamil caste headmen like Tillaiyappa Mudali, Uttira Peddu Chetti, Ammayappan, Pichandi, Devanayaka Chetty of Nagapattinam, the mason Venkatachalam, his brother Latchigan, Kuttiya Pillai, Chinnadu Mudali, Andanayaka Mudali, Muthu-kumarappa Mudali, son of Ariyaputhiri Mudali, husband of Sadagopa Mudali's sister-in-law, two weavers, three or four cultivators and the managers of the temple met him again, as he was theoretically the chief of the Hindus, though he was still not appointed officially as *dubash* or *diwan*, and expressed their desire to meet Dupleix and also asked Poullé to intervene to sort out the problem. But Ananda Ranga Poullé pacified them and dissuaded them in their efforts. Instead he asked them to remove the temple objects, the images, etc., to the Kalatiswaran or Perumal temple. In other words, he was actively and indirectly supporting the destruction of the temple.

Ananda Ranga Poullé also pointed out that some among them were always telling that the *lingam* was *swayambu* (self-existent) and so it could not be removed. Other Temil men like Arumugattu Mudali and Lachigan were in favour of the destruction of the temple and rebuilding it elsewhere, if Annapurna Ayyan was made the choultry *dubash* and if Malayappa Mudali, son of Tambuswami Mudali, was appointed as the chief *dubash*. They had even affirmed that they would get the people's consent for the purpose. Even Annapurna Ayyan had told the Jesuits that he would get the people's consent if he and Malayappa Mudali were appointed.

Dupleix saw the contradictions in the stand of the Hindus, with regard to the temple. So Dupleix himself urged them to build the temple elsewhere as the present one was in the middle of the road and by the side of the church. He even promised them to pay the cost for erecting a new temple and provide them with a good site. Thus it is clear that Ananda Ranga Poullé, who was a Telugu did not intervene in the affair due partly to the divisions among the Tamil Hindus with regard to the destruction of the temple and also because some Hindus, especially those of Tamil descent, opposed his nomination as *diwan*.[8]

As a result Ananda Ranga Poullé insisted that the headmen should go immediately to the temple and remove the cult objects, before the *arthamandapam* (the court next to the shrine) and the *Mahamandapam* (the main court) were pulled down. He warned that soldiers, Coffrees (Africans), topasses and even Paraya Christian converts would carry away the images of Pillaiyar, etc.

Then Ananda Ranga Poullé met Dupleix in his mansion nearby. The Tamil caste headmen Arumugattu Mudali, Peddu Chetty, Tilaiyappa Mudali and others came to see Dupleix too. They were given permission to remove the cult objects, but not before Dupleix ordered the peons to beat and disperse them like riff-raff.[9]

When some 'higher' caste Tamil headmen went to the temple to remove the cult images and objects to the Kalatiswaran temple, the French Jesuit priests incited the Africans, the soldiers and some Paraya Christians to hit them. The priests themselves seized some sticks and hit each one of the headmen twenty times. The headmen were able to save only the Ganesh statue and the chariot idol. When they were removing the ornaments of the idols, Rev. Coeurdoux came on the scene and kicked forcefully the big *lingam*. He took a big hammer and broke the *lingam* into pieces. He then excited the Africans and the whites who broke the statue of Vishnu, vehicles and other idols and removed the doors. Dupleix himself came to the temple and asked the priests to break whatever they wanted. The Jesuits praised Dupleix and told him that they would make him famous the world over. Just then the Tamil servant of Madame Dupleix, Varlam Mudali came and kicked eight or ten times the great *lingam* with his sandals and spat on it. Madame Dupleix herself spat on the *lingam*.[10]

Strangely at the same time Dupleix and his wife also gave orders to demolish the mosque which stood on the southern side of the fort in the White town, on the right side of the Capuchin Church. It was actually situated on the Mosque Road called rue de la Mosquée. This, in spite of the fact, that most of his sepoys were Mahé Muslims. Probably he thought that the mosque belonged to Tamil-speaking Muslims and therefore the Muslim sepoys who were mostly Mahesians would not react. But he was proved wrong very soon. When the French went to destroy it, Abdul Rahman, the chief of the sepoys met Dupleix personally and issued a stern warning that his men would rise in revolt against the demolishers and would cease to serve the French. He defied Dupleix and said: 'Barking dogs seldom bite; but who will dare to insult Muslims as long as I am here'.

Dupleix realizing that he was not in a position to manage or quell a revolt of his Muslim sepoys, who were defending Pondicherry, meekly submitted to the threat of Abdul Rahman and refrained from going ahead with the destruction of the mosque. This mosque was nevertheless destroyed by the English in 1761, when they razed the White town to the ground.[11]

Abdul Rahman himself came to relay this information to Ananda Ranga Poullé in his areca nut shop. But the same Abdul Rahman was least bothered when the Vedapuriswaran temple was destroyed. This shows that even in those early days there was a clear divide between Hindus and Muslims in Pondicherry on the basis of religion. On his part Ananda Ranga Poullé lamented: 'If there were courageous people among Tamils, one would not have touched the temple.'

Thus Ananda Ranga Poullé, a Telugu himself, admitted that there were no courageous people among Tamils, unlike among the Muslims, forgetting that he himself represented them as their chief spokesman and leader. He simply failed to defend Tamil interests by allowing the destruction of the temple, which hurt the feelings of the Hindus very much. He did not even flee Pondicherry like his father earlier. He did not even ask the Hindus to revolt non-violently or lead them out of Pondicherry non-violently as it was the case earlier on several occasions. He stayed put in Pondicherry so that Dupleix could accomplish his designs without the least obstruction. In short, Ananda Ranga Poullé failed to protect the interests of the Tamils during this period.

Some advance the reason that the temple was an obstruction for the defence of the town and therefore it had to be destroyed by Dupleix. If this reason was genuine, then the adjacent Jesuit Church which was not less obstructive than the temple, had to be destroyed too. Instead, it was spared and even protected with coconut trunks and with bundles of humid cotton. Dupleix himself never advanced defence reasons to the caste headmen for destroying the temple.[12]

Some others hold that some Hindus sided with Dupleix when he wanted to shift the Vedapuriswaran temple to a different site. In any case, some prominent Pondicherrians like Varlam Mudali, Madame Dupleix's asssistant were against Ananda Ranga Poullé for their own reasons. Thus there was division in the ranks of Hindus with regard to the temple. Dupleix probably took advantage of it. Ananda Ranga Poullé, on his part, was most certainly in the camp of the Hindus who agreed with Dupleix to shift the temple.[13] Besides, at that time he was also angling to be officially nominated as the *diwan*. He could not afford to anatagonize Dupleix and protest against the destruction of the temple like his uncle Nainippa Poullé earlier.

So it is not surprising that Ananda Ranga Poullé never interceded with Dupleix to stop the destruction of the temple, in spite of the requests of many of the caste headmen. He never even went to the temple to see what was happening, though his house was located just one street away. He advised the caste heads who pleaded with him to stop the demolition to remove the idols and other objects of cult from the temple, with the permission of Dupleix. He did not want them to leave the town like during the period of François Martin or Hébert. It was quite obvious that Ananda Ranga Poullé as chief of Malabars (Tamils) had failed to protect Tamil interests.

It appears quite certain that he had an understanding with Dupleix with regard to the demolition, which prevented him from intervening energetically to stop the destruction of the temple. Instead, he lamented that Dupleix and the Councillors had lost control of power and it was Dupleix's wife who ruled. In this way, he had tried to disculpate Dupleix and shift the blame for the temple destruction on Dupleix's wife. This sounds unreasonable. He further lamented in his diary the following:

> It has been prophesied that, at the end of the Kaliyuga, all religion will decay, all castes will be mingled together and the caste people will cease to observe their customs. . . . Hundreds of people, coffrees, sepoys and Europeans enter the houses pretending to be Madame's spies and steal what they could. Parayas go and live in the houses of the Brahmans, Komattis and Vellalas. Women are ravished and none complains. . . .[14]

Ananda Ranga Poullé had thus tried to shift the blame for the destruction of the temple on Dupleix's wife. Ananda Ranga Poullé's hatred for Dupleix's wife might stem from the fact that she had lower caste Tamil blood in her. He could not digest the fact that he was at her service too. Ananda Ranga Poullé knew about Dupleix's close relationship with the Jesuits and his desire to promote Chrisitianity in Pondicherry at their bidding. Dupleix knew that the Jesuits had a powerful influence in the Court of Versailles. He seems to have wanted badly to be in their good books, probably fearing that he might be pulled up like Governor Hébert earlier. He knew also about the influence that the Jesuits wielded in Pondicherry society. Therefore it is quite reasonable to conclude that Dupleix in order to achieve his ends, decided to please the Jesuits as well as the king of France by destroying the temple, though it was not conducive to the trade interests of his Company. [15] Ananda Ranga Poullé on his part chose to play down the affair.

Besides, Ananda Ranga Poullé had trade dealings with Dupleix since the 1720s. He had enriched himself due to his business relationship with Dupleix, who too had benefitted enormously by such dealings. Though one was French and the other Tamil, both belonged to the same trading class that came into existence due to Euro-Indian interactions during this period. It was quite natural to assume that Ananda Ranga Poullé would not want to jeopardize this profitable relationship by antagonizing Dupleix, as that would have invited the latter's wrath and he would have probably ended up in the fort dungeon like his uncle Nainiappa earlier. So he simply skirted the issue and tried unconvincingly to accuse Dupleix's wife and on *Kaliyuga* and all that stuff, for the destruction of the temple.

It is also quite possible that Ananda Ranga Poullé was swayed by sectarian interests at that time. He was a Vaishnavite, whereas the temple that was destroyed was a Shiva temple. It may very well be because of this sectarian aspect too that Ananda Ranga Poullé failed to stop the destruction of the temple. But that might not be the only reason. From what we have seen above, the main reason might be purely material and his special relationship with Dupleix.

Further Ananda Ranga Poullé had written a lot about the wealth acquired by others, both French and Indian. But he hardly talks of his own wealth, acquired before Dupleix became Governor and after. However, various sources at our disposal point to the immense wealth accumulated by Poullé since the 1720s in various capacities. First of all, Ananda Ranga Poullé like Dumas and Dupleix possessed various *jagirs*, given to him by the various Muslim rulers, for the services that he rendered them.

Ananda Ranga Poullé had gardens in Saram, Kosapalayam and Kattumedu, between Pondicherry and Ozhukarai, and beyond Kottakuppam, a plantation in Kilinjakuppam and a garden house in Koodalur. On the banks of the Uppar he had a Thopu (wood). He also had a large house which opened on Vellala Street. He had also farmed out lands in Villupuram, Tindivanam, Nallatur, Mandagapattu, Vanamadevi, Annavalli, Tittakudi, Viramaperunallur, Pudupattu, Acharapakkam and around Devanampatnam as well as in Karaikal. He brought the paddy from Karaikal in boats and sold it in Pondicherry. He was entitled to commission on purchases of goods imported by the Company and from the local suppliers of goods for export. He had a commision on minting money in Pondicherry. He had numerous godowns where he stocked various goods from textiles to timber. He had a monopoly in the manufacturing and selling of arrack. He had factories at Porto Novo and Lalpettai. He possessed a small ship called *Ananda Puravi* for sometime. He was farmer's general of some lands in the Carnatic including Pondicherry for sometime, with power to collect rent and forward a fixed amount to the Company. He laded several ships with his goods bound to foreign countries. He also stood to profit enormously by cooperating with the Company officials in their private trade.[16]

However in 1750 Ananda Ranga Poullé complained that he had lent much money to the Company and his *jagirs* were made over to the Company. Poullé further held that the Company had only one objective, i.e. to make profits and if that was not feasible he would lose all his money and would be also blamed for it.[17] It is, however, quite obvious from the preceding that Ananda Ranga Poullé had gained enormously by his relationship with the Company servants and especially with Dupleix. Naturally he would not want to jeopardize his comfortable economic position and power, just because Dupleix was intent in bringing down the Vedapuriswaran temple to please the Jesuits and the French king.

On 21 October 1748, Dupleix wrote the following to the Directors of the Company: 'One of the most happy events of the siege was the destruction of the temple which since many years was a continuous scandal. It is finally destroyed . . . this event comforts the Jesuit fathers'.

In another letter of the same date, Dupleix wrote to Barthélémy, a member of the French Council at Pondicherry: 'The Jesuits sang the Te Deum yesterday. . . . The demolition of the temple flatters them immensely and I am in fact very satisfied for having ended a scandal so close and so continuous. God be praised.'

These two handwritten letters of Dupleix, which were in the private archives of Marquis de Nazelle, a descendant of the former's brother, were published in 1908.[18]

In a third letter written by Dupleix to his brother on 26 January 1749, available at the National Library of Paris, we read: 'I am better with the Jesuits since I got a certain temple demolished, which was truly a continuous scandal. This action is worth a passport for me to the other world. . . . These good Fathers will always be an obstacle in the development of this colony and by the next fifty years, the Jesuits will own half of the houses and lands in Pondicherry. . . .'[19]

This letter establishes that Dupleix was fairly pleased about the destruction of the temple. In this way he had satisfied the desires of the Jesuits and was in their good books. But he was also conscious of the economic influence wielded by the Jesuits in Pondicherry, due mainly to the fact that they owned a good part of the town.

It is wrong on the part of Ananda Ranga Poullé to try to cover up Dupleix's actions, by putting the blame on his wife. Dupleix had a mind of his own, as far as I could see and he need not be influenced by his wife in such sensitive matters as the destruction of the temple. At the most, it could be said that his desire to get rid off the temple coincided with that of his wife as well as the Jesuits at that time. However, the fact remains that Ananda Ranga Poullé did nothing to prevent the destruction of the temple. There is no evidence for it even in his diary.

Dupleix was also in full praise of his wife, for the role that she played during the siege. On 3 October 1748, he wrote: 'My wife is a heroine who has given such a good example that no other woman in Pondicherry could give.'

VEDAPURISWARAN (SHIVA) TEMPLE DESTRUCTION 191

On 5 October 1748, he wrote again the following: '... I can assure you that this lovable lady is truly worthy of the respect of the nation for her conduct during the siege of this place. She had rendered the essential assistance and had pronounced words worthy of ancient Rome'.[20]

All this he seems to have written knowing fully well that she, like him, was never on the ramparts, but mostly within the walls of the church or the fort.

Apart from the preceding remark about his wife, Dupleix had never to my knowledge referred to her in his letters about his political adventures in south India or his policies. She was most of the time content in receiving presents and jagirs from the various princes, in her capacity as the wife of Dupleix, but never had she seemed to have interfered directly in political matters, except perhaps when she recommended her nephew Noronha to the post of governor of San Thomé. However, unlike Ananda Ranga Poullé whom she disliked, she had definitely wielded some influence over Papaya Poullé and also had a soft corner for the Mahé chiefs Abdul Rahman and Sheikh Hassan.[21]

Immediately after the destruction of the temple, there was a rumour that the Superior Council of Pondicherry had allowed the rebuilding of the temple in a different site. Actually the question of the reconstruction of the temple in some other place was already raised when Dupleix consulted all the missionaries with regard to the destruction of the temple. In the year 1750, the Archbishop of Mylapore permitted the reconstruction of the Vedapurisawaran temple at another place in the Madras road.[22]

Later the Jesuits set up their press called the 'Mission Press' on the site of the destroyed temple. This Press exists even today. But the construction of the new temple took time. In 1754, Godeheu was not favourable to the idea that the Company should contribute to its rebuilding. But Ananda Ranga Poullé pointed out that European companies had given money for reconstruction of temples in Nagapattinam, Madras and other places, where temples were pulled down.[23]

While the Vedapuriswaran temple was flattened during the siege under Dupleix's orders, the Kalatiswaran temple and the Perumal temple were only damaged. Dupleix ordered them to be repaired. He also ordered the Villianur temple to be repaired.[24]

Much later, French scholar Julien Vinson opined: 'the destruction of the Vedapuriswaran temple on 8th September 1748, was an an act of stupid fanaticism which stained awkwardly the memory of Dupleix, as this temple, like all others in the country, contained very precious inscriptions for the history of South India'.[25]

This statement throws light however on the fact that even as late as nineteenth century, French intellectuals and scholars like Julien Vinson who believed in the superiority of European culture and civilization never really regretted about the destruction of the temple as it would have hurt the religious feelings of the Tamil Hindus. Instead they were deeply concerned about the destruction of the inscriptions in the temple, which would have shed light on the history of Pondicherry and south India.

NOTES

1. See J.B.P. More, *From Arikamedu to the Foundation of Modern Pondicherry*, Chennai, 2014.
2. Lettre de Père Mathon, du 19 Oct. 1744, p. 370, vol. 993, AME; *ARP Diary*, I, pp. 188, 299, 301.
3. Vinson, *Les Franças dans l'Inde. Dupleix et Labourdonnais*, Paris, 1894, pp. 157; *ARP Diary*, I, p. 332; II, p. 321; III, pp. 220, 224, 225.
4. Vinson, ibid., 71f.
5. Ibid., p. 229; Lettre du Conseil Supérieur de Pondichéry à la Compagnie à Paris, 31 Janvier 1744, in Vinson, ibid., p. 54; Rev. Père X de Saint Estevan, Missionarie de la Compagnie de Jesus à M; le Comte de . . . , Karikal, 15 Nov. 1755, LEC, 1810, XV, 123-6; Laude, *Dupleix. Le Siège de Pondichéry en 1748*, Pondichéry, 1870, p. 39; Gaudart, op. cit., Paris, 1933, p. 13; *ARP Diary*, V, p. 314.
6. Vinson, ibid., p. 229; Laude, ibid., p. 39; Gaebelé, op. cit., p. 200.
7. Vinson, ibid., pp. 89f; *ARP Diary*, V, p. 299; Laude, ibid., p. 38.
8. *ARP Diary*, V, pp. 304-5.
9. Ibid., V, pp. 306-8.
10. Vinson, op. cit., p. 229; Naf.8871, Père Coeurdoux sur la religion et langue hindoue, BNF; Fr.17240 Père Coeurdoux sur la Chine, BNF; Bourdat, *Eighteenth Century Pondicherry*, 1995, pp. 185-6; *ARP Diary*, V, pp. 306-7, 310-11.

VEDAPURISWARAN (SHIVA) TEMPLE DESTRUCTION   193

11. Martineau, op. cit., 1923, p. 490; Vinson, ibid. p. 227; *ARP Diary*, V, p. 308; Oubagarasamy, op. cit., p. xix; Gaebelé, op. cit., pp. 198f.
12. LEC, Paris, 1781, XIV, pp. 252-3; Vinson, ibid., 55, 55f; Launay, *Histoire des Missions de l'Inde*, I, p. lxiv; Martineau, ibid., 1923, p. 490; *ARP Diary*, V, pp. 311-12.
13. *ARP Diary*, II, pp. 365-70; IV, p. 172.
14. *ARP Diary*, V, pp. 309, 335, 336 (entry 19th September 1748).
15. Gaebelé, op. cit., p. 109.
16. *ARP Diary*, I, pp. 221, 327, 408; II, p. 41; III, p. 268; V, 17-18, 294; VI, pp. vi, 116, 221, 265, 400; VII, pp. 4, 116, 405; IX, 401; XII, pp. 178, 376, 382; Gaebelé, 'Enfance et Adolescence d'Anandarangapoullé', 1955, pp. 101-34; Gaudart, *Catalogue des Manuscrits* . . . , I, p. 10; Manning, op. cit., 1996, p. 137; Alalasundaram, op. cit., 1998, p. 219.
17. *ARP Diary*, VII, p. 4.
18. Marquis de Nazelle, op. cit., pp. 341, 357.
19. Lettre de Dupleix à son frère, 26 Jan. 1749, Naf 9357, f. 336, BNF.
20. Naf, 9357, Lettre de Dupleix à Mr. George, 5 Oct. 1748; Lettre de Dupleix à M. D'Arboulin, 3 Oct. 1748, p. 318, BNF; Gaebelé, *Créole et Grande Dame*, 1934, pp. 200, 211.
21. Naf, 9165, f. 100, BNF; Cultru, op. cit., pp. 333, 334; *ARP Diary*, IV, p. 466; Col. C², 85, ff. 88, A.N.
22. Vinson, op. cit., p. 56; vol. 993, pp. 657, 672, AME.
23. *ARP Diary*, IX, pp. 62-64; Bourdat, op. cit., 1995, p. 172.
24. *ARP Diary*, VI, pp. 157-8.
25. Vinson, RHIF, 4e vol, 2e partie, p. 115.

CHAPTER 9

Carnatic Wars, Promotion of Christianity and Senji Temple Destructions

WITH THE SUCCESSFUL repulsion of the English from Pondicherry, the prestige of Dupleix and the French rose very much in Hindustan and even in France. Besides, he was still holding on to Madras. But was unsuccessful in capturing Fort St. David. Even at this stage there is nothing in the literature that I have consulted to indicate that Dupleix really wanted to establish a French empire in India, at the expense of the English. If he had really wanted to do that, he must have invaded the territories of the Indian princes and annexed them outrightly, which he never did.

DUPLEIX TRAPPED IN CARNATIC WARS

It was during the year 1748 that Chanda Sahib was set at liberty by the Marathas. This release took place after the death of the nizam on 2 June 1748. The Maratha general, Raghoji Bhonsle announced that he was returning to Tamil Nadu to re-establish Hindu rule. One of the conditions for Chanda Sahib's release was the restoration of Hindu rule in Trichinopoly. On his part, Dupleix had raised his offer to Rs. 3 lakh for the release of Chanda Sahib. Actually a ransom of Rs. 4.5 lakh was paid for the release of Chanda Sahib alone.[1]

At the death of Nizam-ul-mulk, his second son Nazir Jung succeeded him to the throne as Nizam. The Nizam was virtually independent of the Mughal Empire since at least the death of Aurangzeb in 1707. Muzaffar Jung, the son of a daughter of Nizam-ul-mulk also aimed to become the nizam of Hyderabad. He was thought to have a firman appointing him as nizam from the Mughal emperor, who disliked Nazir Jung because he was a debauchee. Muzaffar Jung was a young man, aged 25, was of medium height, as white as an European, a pleasing and an extremely polite personality. In the year 1744, Anwaruddin Khan, who had no blood relationship with the previous Nawayat nawabs of Arcot and was a stranger to the Carnatic, was declared nawab of Arcot by Nazir Jung.[2]

Chanda Sahib did not take things lying down. He came to an understanding with Muzaffar Jung. He conspired to cut off the new nawab of Arcot. In order to achieve his objective he decided to make use of Dupleix and the French in Pondicherry. It seems that he promised the French the town of Vellore with its dependencies consisting of 45 villages as well as Villianur and 80 villages around Karaikal, if Dupleix could extend his help to him. Dupleix fell for Chanda Sahib's offer, for his own reasons of raising the revenues of Pondicherry somehow. Dupleix knew that Anwaruddin Khan had supported the English during the siege of Pondicherry. So he threw in his lot with Chanda Sahib and tried to prop him up with the soldiers and sepoys at his disposal. The English historian, Henry Dodwell had asserted that Dupleix began selling his mercenaries to pretenders like Chanda Sahib thenceforth, with the objective of augmenting his revenues.[3]

The French troops consisting of 420 Europeans, 100 *topas* and 2,000 sepoys were deployed against Anwaruddin's troops. Raza Sahib joined his father's troops with his forces. The French troops were under the command of Combault d'Auteuil, brother-in-law of Dupleix, while the sepoys were under Sheikh Hassan and Abdul Rahman. They together cut into pieces the troops of Anwaruddin Khan consisting of 12,000 cavalry, 6,000 infantry and 220 elephants. Anwaruddin Khan himself was defeated and slain in the month of July 1749 at Ambur. His son, Maphuz Khan was imprisoned. It was none other than the Mahé sepoy, Sheikh Hassan who had risen to become *jamedar* or second officer, who killed the aged Anwaruddin. On the whole, only 10 Europeans died in the war, while 500 Indian sepoys as well as 1,000 soldiers of Anwaruddin lost their lives.

However, a considerable booty was acquired by the French after the war, due partly to the generosity of Chanda Sahib. This included Rs. 17 million in cash, 60 elephants, horses, camels, jewels, arms and ammunitions. The French officers benefitted largely from it, though it is certain that a good part of it was sent to Dupleix. Dupleix was very much interested in the acquisition of this booty, rather than consolidating French political power or glory in south India, in the aftermath of the war. He asked his officers from Combault d'Auteuil down to the chief of the sepoys, Abdul Rahman to gather as much booty as possible, in cash or in the form of villages. D'Auteuil had received Rs. 100 as payment for every soldier. He gave just Rs. 6 out of it to every soldier and kept the rest for himself, under orders from Dupleix himself.[4] During the whole operation, Dupleix seems to have behaved more like the chief of a gang of mercenaries, out to make the maximum profit through loot rather than somebody imbued with the interests of the Company or France.

Chanda Sahib made a triumphant entry into Arcot on 7 August 1749. He was re-instated as nawab of Arcot. Dupleix was of course instrumental in Chanda Sahib becoming nawab again. However, Anwaruddin's second son, Mohammad Ali Khan, the rightful heir to the throne, escaped to Trichinopoly, from where he supplicated the English to assist him.[5] The English accepted to help Mohammad Ali Khan with troops in exchange for some commercial concessions. A force under Major Lawrence was sent to help him.

But Dupleix seems to have been also interested in pecuniary matters related to the war. He wanted a share of the booty for himself and his troops. He ordered his troops to attack the forts and retrieve the treasures hidden there. He told the French commander Combault d'Auteuil, not to give up the prisoners till he received a share in the booty. In spite of such efforts, Dupleix got only a donation of Rs. 50,000 for his troops and a promise of Rs. 1,40,000 for his officers.

But Dupleix, his wife and her relatives were rewarded with a village apiece. However later in July 1749, Dupleix received a *parvana* from Raza Sahib, son of Chanda Sahib conceding the French, Villianur and Bahur with 80 dependent villages, bordering Cuddalore and Fort St. David, which were farmed out for Rs. 96,000. Even Vazhudavur and Masulipatnam were handed over to the French on certain conditions. According to one estimate, the operations against Anwaruddin had cost the French Rs. 6 lakh. They could not compensate it with the loot after the battle of Ambur. The Muslim potentates had granted a few villages around Pondicherry as compensation, but the revenues derived from them were quite limited or inadequate.[6]

Nevertheless, the victory at Ambur was celebrated by Dupleix in Pondicherry in great pomp and splendour. Chanda Sahib left Arcot on 14 September and reached Pondicherry on 28 September 1749. Chanda Sahib made a triumphant entry into Pondicherry with all his troops, elephants and camels. Dupleix welcomed Chanda Sahib at the heights of Mortandi Chavadi, where he had a luxurious mansion. He and Chanda Sahib came in a procession into Pondicherry on palanquins as far as Dupleix's mansion.

Two days later, it was the turn of Muzaffar Jung to enter Pondicherry with thousands of his troops and elephants, retinue and family. Pondicherry witnessed a never-ending feast for several days. Dupleix, who was always lavish in throwing gastronomical parties, saw to it that the Ambur victory and the celebrations that ensued excelled all the rest in food and gastronomy, both of the Indian or Hindustani Muslim and French varieties. Both Muzaffar Jung and Chanda Sahib dined at the Governor's House (presently Villa Aroumé). Chanda Sahib left Pondicherry in three days. He as well as other nobles gave rich presents to Dupleix.[7]

Dupleix got Chanda Sahib to appoint Dom Antonio Noronha as governor of San Thomé, which was about 3 miles from Fort St. George. He also received some concessions like Villianur and Bahur for the Company, Covelong for himself and Porto Novo for his wife, Alamparai for his relative Combault d'Auteuil and San Thomé for Noronha. The lame man, Savarimuthu, the chief of the peons, was appointed polygar of Villianur.

Ananda Ranga Poullé showered encomiums on Dupleix. He called him 'badshah', i.e. emperor, while Muzaffar Jung and Chanda Sahib were mere *mansabdars*. Besides he said that Dupleix's glory shone from the Himalayas to Rameswaram and had the power to raise or cast down nizams and nawabs. He told Dupleix that even Louis XIV, the king of France with all his might had not won greater victories and conquered more lands than him with just 1,000 soldiers. This was pure unadulterated flattery.[8]

However, Dupleix knew that the victory was not complete as Mohammad Ali Khan had escaped to Trichinopoly and he had the help of the English. Mohammad Ali Khan was a threat not just to Chanda Sahib but also to Dupleix and the very existence of French territories in Tamil Nadu. Dupleix had no other alternative except to get rid of him somehow, even by allying with the devil. This is what Dupleix did in the course of time by involving himself more and more in the conflicts of the Indian princes. He did this not with the intention of establishing a French empire, but with the desire to safeguard French trade and financial interests and protect Pondicherry.

Chanda Sahib on his part had emerged all powerful during this period. He would not take orders from Dupleix. At the most, Dupleix could only offer advice and put his troops at the service of Chanda Sahib for hire and get paid for it. There is no evidence in the records that Chanda Sahib consulted Dupleix or even associated him in his plans or considered Dupleix as a sort of master. As a matter of fact, when Chanda Sahib left Pondicherry with 20,000 men, accompanied by Muzaffar Jung, Dupleix provided him with 800 French soldiers. Contrary to the advice of Dupleix to attack Trichinopoly first, Chanda Sahib went after the raja of Tanjore and had to fall back to Pondicherry when Nazir Jung entered the Carnatic with an immense army.[9]

Towards the end of 1749, the French settlement at Yanam was ransacked and ruined. The French were expelled from Masulipatnam in May 1750. The English were behind this expulsion and the arrests of the French factory chiefs at Yanam and Masulipatnam. In July 1750 Divi Island on the Andhra coast was given to the French by Muzaffar Jung, though the English were in possession of it.[10]

Dupleix immediately swung into action. He sent his forces in two ships with 200 Europeans and 300 sepoys under the Frenchmen Guillard, Coquet and others and re-occupied Masulipatnam in July 1750 and the island of Divy in February 1751. This was only a defensive move by Dupleix to protect the territories given to him.[11]

Around the same time, French troops under Duquesne defeated the king of Tanjore, Pratap Singh. The latter entered into a treaty with the French by which he agreed to pay Chanda Sahib and Muzaffar Jung Rs. 7 million, to reduce the tribute paid by the French Company to him since 1738 by Rs. 3,000 and concede 81 villages which was added to Karaikal and pay Rs. 2 lakh for the upkeep of the French troops in the region.[12]

PROMOTION OF CHRISTIANITY UNDER DUPLEIX

The Christian population in Pondicherry grew slowly since the establishment of the French there in 1673-4. In 1709, there were about 1,000 to 1,100 Christian converts in Pondicherry. By 1725, there were 3,000 Tamil Christians out of a total population of about 30,000.[13]

From the time when Dupleix arrived in Pondicherry, things were not very rosy in the economic front for the people of Pondicherry. The French missionaries have attested to this fact quite amply in their records. Whenever there was scarcity of food or when the cost of food was quite high, there were numerous conversions to Christianity. Father Mathon had actually written that during such periods of scarcity and high cost in the 1740s, many Hindus died and went to hell, but many others converted and gained Paradise. During this period, conversions to Christianity were very slow. Actually there was a demand at that time by the missionaries to prohibit all Hindu manifestations and ceremonies outside their temples.[14]

During Dupleix's period, the Superior of the Jesuits in Pondicherry was Father Coeurdoux. He was a fervent Catholic, but a scholar of great learning. It was Father Coeurdoux who first pointed out the relationship of Sanskrit with Greek and Latin and the similarities between them well ahead of British scholars like William Jones. He also wrote a report about the secrets related to the manufacture of textiles in Pondicherry and Tamil Nadu.

On his part, Dupleix himself was religiously inclined, due to his upbringing and early education in France. He never missed the Sunday mass. The Ariyankuppam Church was frequented by him and his wife quite often.[15]

Pedro Canagarayen's son André had died on 22 October 1739 during Dumas' governorship. Pedro asked for land in Oulgaret or Ozhukarai in the year 1740-1 from the French Government, as a reward for the services that he had rendered to the Company. Land was allotted to him on 24 July 1741 at the *paracheri* occupied by the depressed castes, on the express condition that a church would be built in that place. This place stood to the east of Ozhukarai at Reddiarpalayam, which was then called Tambi Reddipalayam or simply Reddipalayam.

On the 29th of the same month, Pedro donated this land to the Jesuits, along with 3,000 pagodas, for the construction of a church in honour of Saint André and a presbyter for lodging a resident missionary. It must not be forgotten that Pedro's son was also known by the name André. However, it is quite surprising that the high caste Christian *dubash* of Dupleix had accepted to build his church in honour of André at the site of a *parachery*, which for the high castes was generally a polluted place. Besides, the government had to find a place to lodge the depressed caste persons displaced from the *parachery* to make way for Pedro's church.[16]

The church was completed in the year 1745 when Dupleix was the Governor. There was a stone inscription engraved in French and Tamil on the northern side wall of the church. However the present church is not the same as the original one.[17] Canagarayen organized a lavish feast on 30 November 1745 at Oulgaret when the church was consecrated on 30 November 1745. During this feast, food for Brahmins was cooked by Brahmins, food for the Vellalas was cooked by the Agamudaiyas and so on.

Ananda Ranga Poullé, who was most certainly present at the feast, opined that as a Christian, Pedro Canagarayen should have entertained only those belonging to his faith like the Europeans, and the native Christians of the various castes including the Parayas. At this church, Christmas was celebrated with great pomp for 10 days. The images of Mary and Jesus were carried in a procession from the Jesuit Church in the town with torches, fireworks and music, first to Canagarayen's house in the town and then to the new Ozhukarai Church and then back to the Jesuit Samba Kovil Church on the last day. But Canagarayen himself passed away on 12 February 1746 and his funeral took place the very next day.[18]

It must not be forgotten that it was during Dupleix's governorship on 16 October 1745 that a line was drawn or a wall was put up in the St. Paul's Church of the Jesuits according to the decree of Pope Benoit XV, in order to keep the low castes separate from the higher castes. At that time, the French priests of Karaikal instigated the Paraya Christians living in Panni *parachery*, Periya *parachery*, Sudukattu *parachery* and Ozhandai *parachery* of Pondicherry and the *thotis* (scavengers) to remonstrate with the senior priest of Pondicherry.

Pedro Canagarayen intervened and chairs appeared to separate the Parayas from the others. It was during this period that Father Artaud was converting a good number of Parayas to Christianity.[19]

On 14 November 1746, the Superior Council under Dupleix prohibited by decree the whites (Europeans) and the blacks (Indians) to make the workers toil, without permission during Sundays and Feast days. Whoever failed to abide by this decree was fined 10 pagodas, half payable to the denouncer and the other half to the poor. On 12 January 1747, another decree was adopted, forcing the owners of slaves to teach them the Christian religion and get them baptized within one year.[20]

The wife of Dupleix, Johanna had played a significant role in the promotion of Christianity in Pondicherry and its surroundings. Her servant was the Christian Varlam, who was the son of Malaikozhundumudali.[21] She had given the French Jesuits a site, just outside Pondicherry town towards the west, called Nellithope. Poor converted Catholic families who were unable to find a place to stay within the precincts of the town, were allowed to establish themselves at Nellithope. In the year 1750-1, a church was built there by the Jesuits for these Christians.

In the beginning Nellithope village was inhabited only by Christians. Gradually Hindus came to the area and established themselves principally in the northern portion of the village called Velipalayam.[22]

In the year 1751, Jeanne Dupleix gave the villages of Marakkanam and Cheyur, not very far away from Pondicherry, which she had received as a reward from Muzaffar Jung to the Jesuit missionaries, on condition that they utilize the income from the villages for the upkeep of 24 catechists who would preach among the Hindus and baptize their children. At the same time, she donated the village of Kadapakkam to the Capuchin missionaries and even helped them to construct a church there.

On account of such moves by Jeanne Dupleix, with the concurrence of her husband, there were more and more conversions in these areas during this period, both among the higher caste Shudras as well as the depressed caste Parayas. The Jesuits brought them to Christianity from separate places within the church.[23]

On his part, Father Coeurdoux, after several attempts finally succeeded in displacing the cremation ground of the Hindus, situated near their church of Immaculate Conception to the other side of what is today the Cathedral or Mission street. In the land thus obtained, a hospice came up.[24]

In the last quarter of 1752, Madame Dupleix insisted upon the conversion of a Hindu by the name of Muthian, at his death bed. Muthian was the younger brother of the writer of Dupleix. Madame Dupleix stressed that she wanted to save the soul of Muthian, in spite of opposition from his relatives and the refusal of most Christian priests to perform baptism and the last rites or even simply receive the sick man. Even Lazar Tanappa Mudali, the brother of Pedro Cangarayen would not receive him in his house.

Madame Dupleix then got him carried in a palanquin to the catechist Arulanandam's house in Mirappali. There she got the Bishop of Mylapore to perform the customary rites and buried him in the Christian way. Besides, during the Holy Week of the same year, Dupleix became suddenly very religious. He half-masted the flag and distributed unusual sums in charity during the week.[25]

During Dupleix's rule and even earlier, famine and epidemic played a crucial role in the conversion of some Hindus to Christianity. The lower castes were the most vulnerable during periods of famine and epidemics. The missionaries deployed their zeal during such periods and obtained numerous conversions since the beginning of the eighteenth century. In the years 1744 and 1745, Hindu parents brought their children to the hospital which was built then by the missionaries in Chandernagore and sold them for just Rs. 2 per child and a piece of cloth. Sometimes mothers came with their children and became Christians. During this period, in Pondicherry too there was famine, which brought about a lot of conversions.[26]

Besides, the failure of the north-east monsoon in 1746 and the fact that no ships could bring grains to Pondicherry due to the war with the English, made life miserable for the people of Pondicherry. As a result, famine once again struck Pondicherry. This brought about several conversions to Christianity. Many dying children were baptized then. Governor Dupleix and his wife helped the missionaries financially to bring about these conversions.[27] As both were favourably disposed towards the missionaries, conversions continued in Pondicherry.

The French father Artaud was considered as the apostle of the Parayas. He converted at least seven or eight persons or sometimes more during this period. Special catechism classes were held for them in the courtyard of the Cathedral church, while the Shudra converts were instructed in Christianity separately.[28]

During this period there was an epidemic which broke out in Karaikal. More than 4,000 Hindus died in it. A few of them had converted to Christianity at the time of death. Three hundred Christians including several children whom the missionaries had baptized succumbed to the epidemic. During 1755, the missionaries had baptized more than 150 adults in Karaikal as well as several children.[29]

Though there was official patronage in favour of conversions to Christianity, especially when Dupleix was governor, there were always various obstacles for conversion. For example, if a convert belonged to a caste where there were only a few converts, there was almost no chance of founding a family. This factor continued to deter many a Hindu from converting.[30] Besides in some localities, the converts were mainly Parayas. As a result the 'good' castes associated Christianity with *parayanism*, which proved to be an obstacle to obtain converts from these castes.

Sometimes the converts were excommunicated by the Brahmin priests and driven out of the town. Caste meetings were held to identitify the converts and drive them out of the caste and the town, so that the convert would have no other alternative except to join the ranks of the Parayas or Perish or if he had a family, he would be unable to find a suitable match for his daughter or son. This was a great deterrence for people to convert to Christianity.[31]

The Hindus always had a bad opinion of the European colonizers, due to their 'immoral' behaviour, sexual scandals and bad conduct and habits like having concubines and drinking alcohol. Generally they dismissed them as 'firangis'. The missionaries had to take great care not to identify themselves with these Europeans, so that the Christians were not subjected to ostracism and persecution.[32]

The missionaries held that the Hindus of the higher castes venerate their gurus and Brahmins and think that they have the obligation to enrich the Brahmin priests and gurus by giving them alms in order to be happy and wipe off their sins. They were flabbergasted to note that in some temples the Brahmins chose every year a girl, married or unmarried, to be consecrated as the wife of God. They noted that the Brahmin's authority in religious matters was absolute as they were the authors of the Hindu holy books. The missionaries even hold that there existed no nation in the world more arrogant, more rebellious against truth and more obstinate in their superstitions and their nobility than the Brahmins and those of the 'good' castes.

The missionaries considered the Brahmins as the principal obstacle to their mission and the expansion of Christianity, as the latter think that the missionaries were out to destroy their religion. They employed vile means to discredit the missionaries and incite the people against them. The missionaries generally believed that it was the Brahmins who inspired the people to hate the Christians. Other missionaries opined that Banaras like Sodom would be destroyed and that the 'yogi' was a vulgar gangster, while the phallus/lingam the Hindus venerated was obscene and repulsive.[33]

The missionaries had also noted that unlike the Europeans, the Muslim rulers, who were of foreign or north Indian origin, hardly interfered in the customs and traditions of Hindus and allowed them to celebrate their ceremonies and perform their rituals in liberty, though the Hindus were subject to them and were considered by them as their 'slaves' and looted off and on whenever opportunity arose. Besides, through conversions of Hindus and mixed marriages (Indo-French), the French, following the policy of the Portuguese since the sixteenth century, attempted to create an intermediary society between themselves and the Indians, who would be totally subservient and loyal to them.[34]

In any case, it could be affirmed without a semblance of doubt that Dupleix had done more to the propagation of Christianity in Pondicherry and the Tamil country than many of his predecessors. Dupleix's wife especially was an over zealous Christian who continuously supported the Jesuits in their proselytizing activities and came to their help many a time financially. She had no regard or sympathy for any other religion other than her own and in this she even surpassed Dupleix. It was for this reason also that Ananda Ranga Poullé hated her. But he never did anything that would constitute an impediment to her in her actions in favour of Christianity. Ananda Ranga Poullé never adopted the line of Nainiappa Poullé. He never criticized openly the policies of Dupleix and his in matters of religion, as he knew that it would cost him dearly in the changed political and social situation. He did not want to undergo the sufferings that his uncle Nainiappa underwent due to his rebellious attitude.

DUPLEIX'S RELATIONSHIP WITH HINDUS AND MUSLIMS

It is worthwhile to note here that during his tenure as Governor, Dupleix had mostly to deal with the Muslim potentates, who did not belong to southern India but were only there in their capacity as conquerors, invaders and migrants. The Tamils had lost political power to the outsiders since the fourteenth century. Dupleix knew them as an enslaved race, who were only fit to be converted.

Dupleix had a very high opinion of his own values, language, religion and culture. He never learnt the Tamil or Bengali language or even Hindustani though he was in India for three decades. He never was interested in the Hindu religion and culture. Naturally Dupleix had a very poor opinion of the Hindus. He disliked their habits and customs, especially their food. He was surprised to learn that Ananda Ranga Poullé, probably the richest Indian in Pondicherry at that time ate for breakfast, just some old rice of the preceding evening with butter milk and some pickles. He thought that the Tamils ate very badly. He also thought that what the Tamils ate was not fit for human consumption. He disliked their vegetarian dishes and curry.

Dupleix thought that the Muslim *pulao* was better than those of the Hindus. He considered that European dishes were far superior in their preparation and in the usage of the ingredients, to Indian food. That is why, according to him, both Muslims and Hindus wanted to eat European food, while the Europeans disliked Indian food.

Dupleix also was in full praise of the European habit of sitting around a table, with ladies and gentlemen, relatives and friends and enjoyng a good meal, unlike the Tamils who squatted on the floor to eat. He told Ananda Ranga Poullé who had taken to the European habit of eating on the table, that he was not doing anything against his customs by doing so.

He added that the Tamils generally think that it is wrong to adopt customs that were contrary to their own customs and they talk ill of the Europeans thinking in their terrible ignorance that they were Parayas, probably because the Europeans ate beef like the Parayas. This was actually a dominant opinion prevailing among Tamils about Europeans during this period.[35]

However this did not prevent the Tamils from calling the whiteman as 'durai', which literally meant 'lord' and from being subservient to him. It also did not prevent Dupleix from throwing lavish parties and dinners in his residence off and on. Generally speaking Dupleix had a very poor opinion of Indians, whether they were high officers of the empire or merchants and employees of the Company. He thought they were untrustworthy and venal.[36]

But Dupleix did not reject the Tamil Hindus altogether. He participated in their festivals and marriages whenever occasions arose, especially when he was bestowed with costly presents. He watched dancing girls known as *devadasis* perform. The *dasis* performed even at the marriage of his wife's daughter. In December 1744, he even visited Balaya Swamiyar *mutth* in Bommaiyapalayam. Above all, he tolerated the caste system and hierarchy that was prevalent and the traditions that went along with it.[37]

Actually Dupleix got along better with the Mughal Muslims who ruled India, and who ate beef like himself and the Europeans and drank wine. Nazir Jung himself was a great wine drinker. Besides all Muslim rulers were of foreign extraction or descendants of foreign invaders/migrants, ranging from the Mughals to the Pathans, from the Persians to the Arabs, very much like the Europeans.[38] This aspect made Dupleix to view the Muslims in a better light than the Tamil or Telugu Hindus, who were a subject race.

DESTRUCTION OF THE SENJI NAYAK HINDU TEMPLES

In July 1750, Sheikh Hassan captured the Tiruvadi fort, near Cuddalore. On 11 September 1750, Dupleix dispatched 500 Europeans and 1,200 sepoy troops under Captain Bussy and La Touche to capture the hill fort of Senji, located at 67 km to the north-west of Pondicherry, reputed to be impregnable. Captain Sheikh Hassan, the Mahé chief of Dupleix was also dispatched with Bussy. Bussy succeeded in this venture with ease. From this time Senji fort complex became a French possession and it remained so until 1761. The victory of Bussy at Senji added very much to the reputation of the French as redoubtable fighters and conquerors all over India. Dupleix awarded Bussy the grade of Captain after this victory. For some French scholars, Bussy was the incarnation of the dominating genius of Europe.[39]

However Bussy did not stop with conquering Senji. In the process, following Dupleix, he gave orders to destroy two remarkable Hindu temples within the plains of the fort complex dedicated to Lord Venkatarama and Lord Pattabhirama, according to Gnanou Diagou and Frère Faucheux. These temples seem to have been built during Vijayanagar rule at Senji. They contained a huge *mandapam* with twelve identical huge sculpted pillars and exquisitely decorated walls. There were most certainly also many inscriptions found in the temples which would have shed valuable light on the history of Senji and its region. But Bussy did not care much about all that. He was just executing his master's orders at Senji and was most certainly interested in looting the wealth of these temples. The temples were accordingly pulled down.

Dupleix himself visited the fort of Senji with the chief of the Jesuits, Father Lavaur and also Chanda Sahib during April 1751. Dupleix gave orders to transport the temple pillars to Pondicherry. Thus twelve single-piece granite sculpted pillars, which was an architectural marvel, supporting the roof of the temple *mandapam* were transported to Pondicherry in hundred ox-carts under the orders of Dupleix, as he needed them as sort of victory trophies to be installed in the garden and the avenue in front of his newly built Government Palace within the fort.

There was particularly one magnificent sculpted pillar 27 feet long which was dragged to Pondicherry in bullock carts, along with some magnificent canons. Once the temples were desecrated and pulled down, the stones seem to have been carried away by the neighbouring villagers for construction purposes. The huge granite chariot of the temples was carted away by the Jains of the neighbouring village of Sittamur and was put to use in the procession of their divinities. We do not know what happened to the idols of Venkatarama and Pattabirama. They were probably looted or broken to pieces by Bussy's soldiers. We do not know either what happened to the ornaments of the idols and other jewels and riches belonging to the temple. It is quite possible that Bussy might have laid his hands on them or sent at least part of the booty to Dupleix.[40] In 1761, the English destroyed the new palace in Pondicherry. Many of the granite pillars and other statues brought from Senji were also not spared. Some of them at least might be buried still in the 'Place du Gouvernement' (presently known as Bharathi *Poonga*).

Many Indian writers and historians of the French and post-French periods in Pondicherry and elsewhere have never seriously taken note of the destruction of the Hindu temples in which Dupleix himself indulged. The French historian, Henri De Closets d'Errey imagined that the king of Senji gave the sculpted columns as a gift to Dupleix. But there is no corroborating evidence to this assertion. Even the author of the *Pondicherry Gazetteer*, Cyril Antony, at the service of the Pondicherry government had preferred to gloss over Dupleix's and Bussy's complicity in the destruction of the Senji Nayak temples. Instead, he simply noted that the sculpted columns were erected at the Pier as well as in the open ground in front known as Place Dupleix.[41]

It seems that much later Dupleix regretted the pillage of Senji. But that was no atonement for the damage done under his orders. Even the French scholar Jouveau Dubreuil admitted that the French glory at Senji was mixed up with the ruins caused by the French there.[42]

It is nevertheless quite strange to note that Ananda Ranga Poullé, the devoted *diwan* of Dupleix, had not a word to say about the destruction of these temples by the French and the transportation of the temple pillars to Pondicherry to embellish the newly built governor's palace. Perhaps he did not want to offend Dupleix during this period, when he was enjoying the *diwanship* and other advantages given to him by Dupleix. Therefore he preferred to close his eyes once again as he did when the Vedapuriswaran temple was destroyed. In fact, Ananda Ranga Poullé's actions or non-actions during this period were determined by pure self-interest.

NOTES

1. Marquis de Nazelle, *Dupleix et la Défense de Pondichéry*, Paris, 1908, pp. 268-9; Clive Dodwell, and Dupleix, 34-5; Jouveau Dubreuil, *Dupleix ou l'Inde Conquise*, Pondichéry, 1941, pp. 84-5; *ARP Diary*, IV, p. 120; Lehuraux, *La Découverte de Dupleix-Fatheabad*, Pondichéry, 1944, p. 41.
2. Orme, *History of Indostan*, Madras, 1913, I, p. 54; Le Mascrier, *Histoire de la Dernière Révolution des Indes Orientales*, Paris, 1757, I, p. 192; Marquis de Nazelle, ibid., p. 269; LEC, vol. IV, 1810, Toulouse, p. 321.
3. Dodwell, *Clive and Dupleix*, 1989, p. xvi; Col.c², 82, f. 236, A.N.; Gaudart, *Catalogue des Manuscrits...*, V, p. 15; Marquis de Nazelle, ibid., 118, 119; Malleson, *Dupleix*, 2001, p. 73.
4. Castonnet des Fosses, *L'Inde Française au XVIIIème siècle*, Paris, s.d., p. 303; Srinivasachari, *Ananda Ranga Pillai: The 'Pepys' of French India*, New Delhi, 1991, p. 259f; Haudrère, *La Compagnie Française des Indes au XVIIIe siècle*, III, p. 989; *ARP Diary*, VI, p. 131; V, p. 127; *Mémoire pour le sieur Dupleix...*, Paris, 11 Mars 1758, ff. 90, 91; Naf, 9156, pp. 15-18, 45, Dupleix's letters, BNF; Cultru, *Dupleix, ses plans politiques, sa disgrâce*, pp. 241, 242, 243; 95 AP-4, Dossier 8, Relation de la Victoire emportée par l'armée française sur celle du nabab d'Arcate Anaverdikan, le premier Août 1749; du milieu du camp de Mafouskhan, le 1ᵉʳ Aout 1749, A.N.
5. *A Complete History of the War in India from the Year 1749 to the taking of Pondicherry in 1761*, p. 3; Le Treguilly, 'La présence Française en Inde: aléas politiques et militaires', pp. 39-40; 95 AP-4, dossier 8, ibid.
6. Dodwell, op. cit., 1989, pp. 38, 39, 42, 48; *ARP Diary*, V, pp. 127, 163; VI, p. 146; Lettre de Dupleix à d'Auteuil, Août 5 & 6, 1749, in Cultru, op. cit., p. 239; I/1/1, French in India, 1664-1810, pt. 1, 125, based on the Memoirs of Dupleix, IOL; Clarins de la Rive, *A. Dupleix ou les Français aux Indes Orientales*, Lille, 1888, p. 84; *Mémoire pour le sieur Dupleix...*, 1758, f. 47.
7. Favier, *Les Européens et les Indes Orientales au XVIIIe siècle*, Paris, 1997, p. 88; LEC, vol. 14, p. 382 sq; Weber, 'La Vie Quotienne dans les Comptoirs', 1995, pp. 97-8; Guénin, *L'Epopée Coloniale de la France racontée par les Contemporains*, Paris, 1931, pp. 152-3; *ARP Diary*, VI, pp. 200, 204-8; 95 AP-4, dossier 8, op. cit.
8. *ARP Diary*, I, p. 243; VI, pp. 192, 197, 229, 310, 353; VII, pp. 4, 66,112; IX, p. 34; Love, *Vestiges of Old Madras*, II, p. 400; the English seized Noronha and San Thomé in 1750.
9. Malleson, op. cit., 2001, pp. 80-1.
10. I/1/1 French In India 1664-1810, pt. 2, pp. 337, 339, IOL; Naf 9359, Mémoire sur l'Inde, f. 281, f. 293, BNF; Arasaratnam and Ray. *Masulipatnam and Cambay*. New Delhi, 1994, p. 98.
11. *Annuaire des Etablissements Français dans l'Inde*, 1934, pp. 25, 66-68; 1884,

19, 21, 75; Martineau, *Bussy et l'Inde Française, 1720-1785*, Paris, 1935, pp. 20-1, 123-4; Naf 9359, Mémoire sur Mazulipatam . . . , ff. 6-7, 68, BNF.
12. De Closets d'Errey, *Précis Chronologique de l'Histoire de l'Inde Française*, 1934, p. 32.
13. Launay, *Histoire des Missions de l'Inde*, I, p. xxxii; LEC, tome 13, Paris, 1781, pp. 335-6
14. Mathon à Dufau, 1744, Pondichéry, p. 371, vol. 993, AME; Lettre de Mathon, du 21 déc 1744, p. 518, vol. 993, AME; Mathon à M.Collet, 1947, Pondichéry; M. Cama à M. Dufau, 21 Oct. 1743, Pondichéry, p. 324, vol. 993, AME.
15. *ARP Diary*, II, p. 291; Vinson, *Les Français dans l'Inde, Dupleix et Labourdonnais*, p. 89f; Isabelle and Jean Louis Vissière. Lettres Edifiantes et Curieuses . . . , S-Seine, 2000, pp. 142-6.
16. *ARP Diary*, I, p. 86; XII, 230.
17. Launay, op. cit., I, p. xlvii; Gnanou Diagou, *Arrêt du Conseil Supérieur de Pondichéry*, 1937, III, p. 54: *Correspondance du Conseil Supérieur de Pondichéry et de la Compagnie*, III, 1920, pp. 121-2.
18. Naf, 9364, pp. 142-4, BNF; *Correspondance du Conseil Supérieur de Pondichéry et de la Compagnie*, IV, pp. xii-xiii; *ARP Diary*, I, 293-4; IV, 330, 352; XII, 230.
19. Launay, op. cit., I, pp. xviii, xxxix; *ARP Diary*, I, p. 285; K.S. Mathew, 'French Missionaries, Tamil Catholics and Social Changes in Pondicherry', 2006, pp. 301-2; Vinson, op. cit., p. 21; Sridharan, *Papers on French Colonial Rule in India*, 1997, p. 45.
20. Gaudart, *Catalogue des Manuscrits* . . . , I, p. 9.
21. Vinson, op. cit., 89f.
22. Launay, op. cit., I, p. xlviii.
23. Launay, op. cit., I, xxxix, xxxviii; LEC, t. viii, p. 324, Pondichéry, 7 Dec 1754; Lettre du Vicaire Apostolique au Gouverneur à propos de deux villages donnée par Jeanne Albert, 6868, AOM.
24. Launay, op. cit., I, p. xl.
25. *ARP Diary*, VIIIi, pp. xxiii, 248-51.
26. Lettre de Mathon, prêtre, 21 Dec. 1744, Pondichéry, vol. 993, AME; LEC, tome 14, Paris, 1781, pp. 10, 173, 249-51; More, 'Hindu-Christian Interaction in Pondicherry, 1700-1900', 1998, p. 104.
27. Extrait d'une lettre de Père Poissevin au Père d'Irlande, Chandernagore, 11 Janvier 1749, LEC, 14, pp. 249-52; Launay, op. cit., I, pp. xxxviii, xxxix; LEC, VIII, Lyon, MDCCCXIX, pp. 150-1, 11 Jan. 1749; LEC, XIV, 1810, pp. 207-8.
28. Lettre du Reverend Père X de Saint Estevan, Pondichéry, 7 Dec. 1754, LEC, vol. 15, p. 149; *ARP Diary*, IV, p. 237.

29. Seconde lettre du Père x de saint estevan, jésuite à M. le comte--, Karikal 15 Novembre 1755, vol. 15, MDCCLXXXI, pp. 165-9.
30. Lettre du Père Bouchet, Jésuite au Père Baltus, Jésuite, LEC, II, Paris, MDCCLXXXI, pp. 42-4; LEC, tome 11, Paris, 1781, pp. 216-18; tome 13, 1781, pp. 201, 210-11.
31. Ibid., Lettre du Père le Caron à Mesdames les soeurs religieuses d'Ursulines, de la Mission de Carnate, 20 Nov. 1720, pp. 201, 210, 211, LEC, vol. 13, Paris, MDCCLXXXI; Seconde lettre du Père Martin, Jésuite, au Père de la Vilette, Jésuite, LEC, II, Paris, MDCCLXXXI, pp. 164-5; Lettre du Père Etienne Le Gac, Jésuite au Père Charles P., Chinnaballaparam, 10 Jan. 1709, pp. 202, 208.
32. Lettre du Père Bouchet au Père de la même Compagnie, LEC, 13, Paris, MDCCLXXXI, p. 24; LEC, tome, 10, Paris, 1781, pp. 44-46; 66-71, LEC, tome, 12, Paris, 1781, p. 77; tome 10, 1781, Preface; LEC, tome 13, MDLCLXXXI, pp. 45, 50; LEC, tome 14, Paris, 1781, p. 41; More, op. cit., pp. 114-15.
33. Lettre du Père de la Lane, Jésuite au Père Mourgues, Jésuite, Pondichéry, 30 Jan 1709, LEC, tome 11, Paris, MDCCLXXXI, pp. 210-30; Lettre du Père Bouchet au Père de la même Compagnie, LEC, 13, Paris, MDCCLXXXI, pp. 22, 23, 45; Lettre du Père Calmette à M. Le Marquis de Coetlogon, Vice Amiral de la France, Ballabaram, 28 sep 1730, LEC, 2000, pp. 53-9, 63, 64, 69.
34. Lettre du Père de la Lane, ibid., p. 216; Lettre du Père Saignes, Jésuite à Madame de Saint Hyacinthe, Religieuse Ursulines à Toulouse, Attipakkam, 3 Juin 1736, LEC, 14, Paris, MDCCLXXXI, pp. 57-8; see also J.B.P. More, *Offerings to the Muslim Warriors of Malabar.*
35. *ARP Diary*, VIII, pp. 296, 297; Lettre d'un missionaire, p. 127, LEC, vol. 15.
36. Manning, *Fortunes à Faire, The French in Asian Trade*, 1996, p. 104; *ARP Diary*, XII, pp. 62, 69.
37. *ARP Diary*, I, pp. 177, 214; II, p. 32; III, pp. 29-30, 41, 72; IX, p. 149.
38. Jouveau Dubreuil, op. cit., pp. 11, 112.
39. Naf. 9357, f. 374, BNF; Hamont, *Un Essai d'Empire français dans l'Inde aux XVIIIème siècles*, pp. 130, 139.
40. Introduction of Gnanou Diagou in Poullé, *Histoire Détaillée des Rois du Carnatic*, Pondichéry, 1939, p. 5; Sridharan, op. cit., p. 35; LEC, vol. xv, 1810, p. 84: Jouveau Dubreuil, 'Les Colonnes du Pier', pp. 250-3; De Closets d'Errey, op. cit., p. 33; De Closets d'Errey, *Histoire de l'Inde Française, 1664-1814*, 1940, p. 51; Srinivasachari, op. cit., pp. 259f; LEC, vol. XIV, p. 265, 1781; Jouveau Dubreuil, *Dupleix ou l'Inde Conquise*, p. 167; Lehuraux, op. cit., p. 82; *ARP Diary*, XII, p. 318; Interview with Frère Faucheux in *Le Trait-d'Union*, Janvier 1945.

41. Antony, *Gazetteer of Pondicherry*, II, p. 1196, Sridharan, ibid., p. 35; De Closets d'Errey, op. cit., 1940, p. 33.
42. Jouveau Dubreuil, 'Histoire Ancienne et Moderne: Les Soldats Français à Gingi', 1955, p. 275; Thompson, *Dupleix from his Letters, 1742-1754*, 1933, p. 264.

CHAPTER 10

Further Carnatic/Deccani Conflicts and Related Affairs

WARS, DEVASTATIONS AND ACQUISITIONS

THE CONQUEST OF Senji by Bussy brought Nazir Jung to move his troops further into the south. His troops devastated the whole country of Tindivanam, Acharpakkam, Villupuram, Tiruviti, Venkatammalpettai, etc., and plundered all that the Tamil cultivators had in their houses, their grains and crops were stolen or cut down and their bullocks and cows were driven off. Sadras, Covelong, places around Madras like Poondamalee, Manimangalam, Uttiramelur, Salavakkam, Chinglepet, Kanchipuram, etc., were plundered and their women ravished by 4,000 Marathas.

In March 1750, Mohammad Ali Khan had left Trichinopoly to join Nazir Jung at Vazhudavur. Nazir Jung was camping at Vazhudavur, about 15 miles north-west of Pondicherry on the road to Senji, on the right bank of the Senji River, near Matour (which was still under the French). His camp spread from Mangalam beyond Villianur to Tiruvakkarai. Nazir Jung had the intention of punishing Muzaffar Jung, who surrendered to him eventually.[1] His army is believed to have consisted of 3,00,000 men. Besides, he had the Maratha cavalry, commanded by Morari Rao and a detachment of sepoys from Fort St. David. Major Lawrence joined Nazir Jung with 600 Englishmen.

Muzaffar Jung's and Chanda Sahib's troops were less in number. But they had the French regiment, commanded by Combault d'Auteuil. However, the French were terrified by Nazir Jung's army of 25,000 men, camping from Tiruvakkarai to Villianur. The tent of Nazir Jung was at Vazhudavur, near the mosque (presently this mosque is abandoned and dilapidated and is found within the ruined fort of Vazhudavur). A little way from the tent, Muzaffar Jung was held prisoner. Mohammad Ali, the English and the Pathans were all present.

However, Combault d'Auteuil seeing the immensity of Nazir's army ordered a retreat. They left Matour and hastened back to Pondicherry, where they were put under arrest for interrogation by the Superior Council, headed by Dupleix, but not before 13 French officers had deserted them.[2] Dupleix tried to reason out with Nazir Jung that the Carnatic did not belong to Anwaruddin's sons. By then, Nazir Jung and his troops had pulled away from Vazhudavur to Arcot, after being attacked in the darkness of night by the French and suffering heavy casualities.[3]

In the meantime, La Touche came with 800 Europeans, 3,000 sepoys and 10 cannons from Senji. After the conquest of the fortified temple of Tiruvadi by Combault d'Auteuil, Mohammad Ali Khan fled to Arcot.[4]

In the meantime, Nazir Jung's troops were corrupted by Dupleix himself and Muzaffar Jung was taken out of Nazir Jung's prison and proclaimed as the Viceroy of Deccan. There was a general massacre that followed and Nazir Jung was killed in battle by the Pathan Nawab of Kadappa, Abdul Nabi Khan. He cut off the head of Nazir Jung and stuck it on a pole. Abdul Rahman was present at that time. Maphuz Khan was also killed in the battle. But Mohammad Ali, his younger brother escaped to Trichinopoly. He was the legitimate successor of Anwaruddin Khan. Dupleix confessed that he laid the plan for the destruction of Nazir Jung.[5]

The French laid their hands on the immense treasures of Nazir Jung in money and jewels, inherited from his father Nizam-ul-Mulk. They consisted of Rs. 2 or 3 crore of jewels, Rs. 10 or 15 crore of money, 1,000 elephants, 5,000 horses, etc. Dupleix benefitted largely from the loot of Nazir Jung's treasures, along with other Frenchmen. Sixteen chests of jewels, diamonds, precious stones and Rs. 1 crore, besides bullion, belonging to Nizam-ul-mulk seems to have been carried away to Pondicherry. The total value of the treasure was estimated at Rs. 200,000 lakh. Soldiers and officers, councillors and junior servants all had their share of the booty. Dupleix of course received an unknown amount. It would not be an exaggeration to conclude that Dupleix had developed a special liking for loot and booty since 1748 at least.[6]

Muzaffar Jung, the son of a daughter of Nizam-ul-mulk annointed himself as the new Nizam on 5 December 1750. Muzaffar Jung was just 25 years old, and had an extremely pleasing and polite personality. Muzaffar Jung was only a nephew of Nizam-ul-mulk and therefore had no legitimate right over the throne. But with Dupleix's help, he declared himself as the Nizam. The Mughal Emperor did not endorse this succession.

Muzaffar Jung declared Chanda Sahib as the nawab of Arcot and associated Dupleix in the government. Besides, he issued a *parvana* which gave Dupleix theoretically the commandment of the coast as Governor-General of all provinces and kingdoms from Krishna to Cape Comorin. Dupleix also acquired some territories in the process, including Vazhudavur on 14 December 1750. Chanda Sahib was also not the legitimate heir to the throne at Arcot.[7]

Thus Dupleix had thrown in his lot to prop up Muzaffar Jung and Chanda Sahib as the rulers of the Deccan and the Carnatic, though they had no natural right to it. On the other hand, it could be said that Muzaffar Jung and Chanda Sahib had benefitted largely from their dealings with Dupleix, by which they became nizam and nawab respectively. In fact, they had made use of Dupleix to achieve their own ends. French troops were put at their disposal by Dupleix for pecuniary benefits and in order to execute the plans of Muzaffar Jung to occupy the throne at Hyderabad.

In order to commemorate the victory over Nazir Jung and the massacre that ensued, a town called Dupleix Fathiabad was to be built at the Vellimedupet site, not far from Pondicherry. It seems a pillar was erected in Pondicherry market place with Latin inscriptions recounting the exploits of the French against Nazir Jung. Muzaffar Jung himself came to Pondicherry with his large retinue and was welcomed by Dupleix at Mortandi and was taken in a procession on an elephant. In his capacity as the future nizam, as he was not yet enthroned in Hyderbad, he conferred the title of 'General Nabob' on Dupleix.[8]

Dupleix probably thought that he was anointed as nawab or an Indian prince by Muzaffar Jung. He never realized that it was just a title that was conferred on him. He was still only the French governor of Pondicherry, at the service of the Company. Instead, Dupleix seems to have wanted the title of nawab of Carnatic conferred on his friend,

Chanda Sahib. But he accepted the title of *mansabdar* commanding 7,000 horses and the persmission to carry the fish emblem, which was a very high distinction. Like Dumas before, Dupleix had accepted to be the local lord or vassal of Muzaffar Jung.

However thenceforth he seems to have adopted the practices and formalities of an Indian prince. Nobody could approach him without a present. Not only him, but also his wife received costly presents on various pretexts like attending a marriage or solving a dispute. Ananda Ranga Poullé himself helped Dupleix to procure many of those presents through his contacts. Generally Dupleix received more than what he gave or bought. Thenceforth, Dupleix mounted his elephant after the eastern fashion and held his *durbar* in his palace at Pondicherry.[9]

All this he did without the consent or sanction of the French Company Directors in Paris, to whom he was still answerable as he was just their employee in Pondicherry. He had no right to receive presents since the year 1750-1. He had even no right to wage wars in India given to him by the Company. Compliments addressed to Dupleix off and on for winning some battles can in no way be taken as a legal authorization given by the Company to wage war in India. Even the Company warned Dupleix that for trade to flourish peace was necessary and not war.

St. Priest who was the king's Commissioner for the French Company actually wrote a letter to Dupleix in early 1751, advising him to desist from war. He said:

Nothing is more contrary to commerce than war; and because commerce is the soul of the Company, the unique aim of its formation, that which is of greater interest to the State, it follows as a necessary consequence that we can go to war only when it is absolutely impossible to do anything else. All news that we receive from India speak of the flight of weavers, of the desolation of the country; how can commerce develop thus?[10]

It is impossible to imagine that when the French Company had no interest in conquering India and wanted to indulge only in trade, how can an employee of the Company have desires well and above the objectives of the Company? Besides, the Company had stated in clear terms its objectives and warned Dupleix not to indulge in any unnecessary wars. But Dupleix had never really and rightly argued his case for wars to convince the Company that his actions were well thought out. In this context, it is really an exaggeration on the part of many French historians to assert that Dupleix was in the process of founding a French colonial empire in India or had the intention or desire to found one. If that was so, it was not reasonable on the part of Dupleix to accept Muzaffar Jung's overlordship of the territories from the Krishna to the Cape.

Muzaffar Jung gave the French Company 1,25,000 *livres* on account and the fort of Alamparai. On his part, Chanda Sahib presented Dupleix with the fort of Vazhudavur and some dependent villages on an annual rent. The revenue from Vazhudavur was 3,50,000 pounds every year according to one estimate. Jung also gave him a *jagir* or present of Rs. 100,000. In 1750, Pondicherry region under French control was made up of 29,000 hectares, split into 14 enclaves. Dupleix's wife received 3 villages as presents, while Combault d'Auteuil, Dupleix's brother-in-law was given one village yielding 10,000 pounds every year. Ananda Ranga Poullé and Bishop Noronha, related to Jeanne Dupleix received one village each. Dupleix also took loans from men like Ananda Ranga Poullé at 8 per cent interest.[11]

Besides, Dupleix himself continued to accept presents or money or demanded loan on various pretexts like for restoring a dismissed official to a post, for the release of left-hand caste *devadasi* girls, who disrespected right-hand caste men, for giving a favourable award in an inheritance suit, for attending a Tamil wedding, for the release of a person, for settling a problem, and for the appointment to a post. Besides, it is clear from Ananda Ranga Poullé's accounts that Dupleix induced the Indian princes to offer him gifts of jewels, elephants, horses, brocades, etc., in return for rice, provisions and protection. This was a form of corruption, which had become an institution during Dupleix's period.[12]

Dupleix himself asked Poullé to tell the merchants to present him with gold coins rather than clothes and to instruct the merchants, *amaldars* and Muslims to come to see him with presents. Even Turaiyur Pachai Kandappa Iyer, the new Balaiya Swamiyar of Bommaiyarpalayam sent gifts to Dupleix. Dupleix did not even spare Frenchmen in such matters. We do not know how much money Dupleix made out of the Carnatic wars, especially in cash and jewels and gold got as booty.

Madame Dupleix also meddled in disputes and got her share. She was known for boundless greed. Ananda Ranga Poullé had accused her for selling public office and lending money at 10 per cent interest and more.[13]

Muzaffar Jung confirmed the grant of Villianur and 40 dependent villages with revenue of 20,000 pagodas yearly. He also granted Bahur and the dependent villages. On his part, Dupleix agreed to provide Chanda Sahib with 400 European soldiers and 2,000 sepoys. Poullé claimed in his *Diary* that Bahur and Vazhudavur along with nine villages were already granted to him as *jagir* by Muzaffar Jung, but Dupleix took them for himself.

Further through a treaty on 12 January 1750 with the Raja of Tanjore, Pratap Singh, the French were exempted from the payment of 2,000 pagodas annually for the villages around Karaikal. Besides they got 81 villages dependent on Karaikal. This seems to have been confirmed by Muzaffar Jung. These were farmed out for Rs. 1,05,884. Thus, Dupleix received more than whatever he demanded from Chanda Sahib in return for his services.[14]

Dupleix also pressed Muzaffar Jung to cede Masulipatnam and the dependent districts. Besides all this, Muzaffar Jung gave Dupleix Narsapur, Nizampatam, Devracottah and Condavir producing revenue of Rs. 14,41,208 for the Company. The Mughal Emperor honoured Dupleix with the title 'Captain Governor-General Bahadur Zafar Jung'. Jung was the equivalent of Count in English. Muzaffar Jung liked Dupleix very much. He used to call Dupleix endearingly as, 'My uncle, Zafer Jung'. So thenceforth, Dupleix was a Count or Jung. In his turn, the king of France made a *Marquis* of Dupleix in 1753. Dupleix's power and influence in southern India was at its height at this moment. Muzaffar Jung also gave the title of Muzaffar Khan to Abdul Rahman at that time, *khan* meaning *knight* in English. Thus the poor fisherman of Mahé of very humble origin became a Khan.[15]

One should not forget that it had always been the tradition of the Mughal emperor and the nawabs to concede lands to the French under certain conditions since François Martin's time. This was how François Martin got Pondicherry and added several bits of territories adjoining it like Kalapet given by the nawabs. This did not make François Martin into a 'jagirdar' for the territories belonged to the Company and as Governor François Martin represented the Company.

Following François Martin, the other governors of Pondicherry from Hébert to Lenoir had added several territories to French Pondicherry, given by the nawabs and rajas under various conditions. This never made them into 'jagirdars' as they were only acting on behalf of the Company. Even Dumas had acquired several territories from the rajas and nawabs of south India. But he did not become a 'jagirdar' in the strict sense as he transferred all these territories to the Company. Dupleix simply followed the trend set by François Martin and acquired several territories under various conditions in south India. As he acquired these territories in the name of the Company, Dupleix cannot be deemed as a 'jagirdar' either, as he transferred the revenues of these territories to the Company. Dupleix's main aim in the acquisition of these territories seems to be to augment the revenues of the Company, so that he need not depend fully on the funds coming from France.

Besides, the term 'jagirdar' did not confer ownership of the land. Instead, it conferred only usufructuary rights over the land, while the ownership rested with the king or nawab. As a result, it is simply not right to think or assume that Dupleix was in the process of setting up a French empire in India through the acquisition of territories, which the English would emulate later. Generally these territories were not acquired by conquest. They were either donated or conceded by the nawabs and rajas under certain conditions.[16] In order to continue with his policy of supporting one prince against another in India, with the objective of deriving certain territorial and pecuniary benefits, Dupleix needed more troops. He did not fail to demand them from the Company since 1750.[17]

Muzaffar Jung did not forget Ananda Ranga Poullé, who had played a crucial role in advising Dupleix and executing his orders. He honoured him as a *mansabdar* of 3,000 horses. Thus Ananda Ranga Poullé like Dumas earlier and his own master Dupleix had the title of a local lord or vassal of Muzaffar Jung. He was also made *jagirdar* of the fort and the district of Chingleput, which gave him the right to enjoy the revenues of the land, which amounted to Rs. 1 lakh per year.

His father-in-law Seshadri Poullé was the polygar of the region since several years. Ananda Ranga Poullé was called thenceforth by the honorific name *Maharaja Rajshri Ranga Poullé Avargal*.[18] Ananda

Ranga Poullé as *diwan* had been consistently encouraging Dupleix to capture Fort St. David and bring the nawab of Arcot and the nizam under his control. Dupleix of course succeeded with regard to the latter two in a certain sense, but he failed miserably against Fort St. David.

Ananda Ranga Poullé always excelled in the art of flattery in order to be in the good books of Dupleix. He once told Dupleix that the French king would appoint him as his prime minister. At another instance he told Dupleix bluntly that no one in the world could excel him in genius. Just after the failure of the English siege, Ananda Ranga Poullé told Dupleix that his glory had reached Delhi and shone all over India and Europe. However, since 1751, Ranga Poullé's influence on Dupleix in political matters especially and his power in the region and influence on the whole was on a decline.[19]

FRENCH IN THE DECCAN

On 13 January 1751, Muzaffar Jung made his way to the Deccan, accompanied by the French commandant Bussy. Heeding to the request of Jung, Dupleix provided 2,000 sepoys and 300 European soldiers with six canons under Bussy to install the former as the Viceroy of Deccan. Bussy was given Rs. 4 lakh. He paid the other officers handsomely for the operation. Besides, every soldier received Rs. 700. Abdul Rahman accompanied Bussy. Abdul Rahman was recommended by Madame Dupleix herself to Bussy. He was earlier conferred the title of Muzaffar Khan by Chanda Sahib. Thus he gained in prestige and esteem among the Muslim nobility and the Indian princes. His humble Mahé origin would have been obscured and he would have passed off for a Pathan, but for the entries made by Ananda Ranga Poullé about him in his diary and the entries in some French records.[20]

But on the way to the Deccan, Muzaffar Jung was killed in an engagement with the nawabs of Cuddapah and Kurnool on 14 February 1751. On 15 February 1751, the Council of Pondicherry under Dupleix decided to give Chanda Sahib land for him to build a palace, as well as a garden and rice fields in Ozhukarai, in exchange for the presents made by the latter to the French.[21]

In the Deccan, it was Bussy's troops who backed Salabet Jung, the third son of Nizam-ul-mulk to become the nizam of Deccan, after the death of Muzaffar Jung. We do not know the exact conditions under which Salabet Jung was chosen to be nizam. But Bussy seems to have had his say in this choice. Salabet Jung readily confirmed all the donations made to the French by his predecessors including Masulipatnam and the districts dependent on it. Salabet Jung reached Aurangabad with Bussy on 29 June 1751. Meanwhile Abdul Rahman ravaged and robbed Cuddapah. Bussy arrested him. But Sheikh Hassan intervened. As a result Abdul Rahman was not only released but also was made the governor or *faujdar* of Kurnool.[22]

Thus Dupleix was theoretically in control of the Deccan through Bussy, Salabet Jung and Abdul Rahman. He was also in control of the Carnatic through Chanda Sahib, with the exception of Trichinopoly held by Mohammad Ali, and Tanjore, held by the Marathas as well as Madras and Fort St. David. Dupleix's moment of glory had come. One cannot say at this juncture if Dupleix acquired this glory in the name of France or in the name of the Company or simply in his name, though many later day French historians as well as G.B. Malleson hold that Dupleix worked for the glory of France. Working for the glory of a bigger entity like the nation has always been the trick played by the politicians to stake their claims for power and leadership. Dupleix might not be an exception to this rule.

Very soon, Salabet Jung unable to pay the agreed amount towards the maintenance of the French forces issued a *parvana* conceding the entire northern Circars of Rajamundry, Ellore, Mustaphanagar (Kondapalli) and Chicacole for the maintenance of the troops under Bussy. They produced yearly Rs. 5,48,865, which was over and above the expenditure for maintenance. These territories were until then under a certain Niyamatullah Khan who had earlier worked for the expulsion of the French from Yanam and Masulipatnam. Besides after the defeat of Balaji Rao in 1752, Salabet Jung gave Kondaveedu, Guntur and other places to Bussy, which he made over to the French Company.

Thus a part of the Deccan came under French control, and Masulipatnam became their military, revenue and administrative headquarters. On 14 May 1753, a *firman* emanating from the Mughal emperor confirmed all the territories ceded to the French by Salabet Jung. Bussy, the French commander in the Deccan extracted every single rupee the land could yield for the maintenance of his troops in Hyderabad. The total revenue amounted to Rs. 1,10,897 in 1753.

It should nevertheless be noted that these territories were ceded to the French to pay for the maintenance of the French troops in Hyderabad. It was not got through conquest by Dupleix or Bussy. If the French troops were no more needed by the nizam, Bussy had to revert those territories back to the nizam. It is clear that these territories were not conceded in order that the French or Bussy or Dupleix could establish their empire in India. Instead, the French were always at the service of the Nizam. Salabet Jung made use of French troops to extract payments from creditors. It should also be noted that Dupleix did not actually incur much expenditure due to the sending of troops under Bussy as it was the nizam who paid largely for it. Still the French owed Rs. 14 lakh to Morari Rao.[23]

In order to collect revenue in the ceded territories and also probably to repay the debts, Dupleix sent Léon Moracin, a nephew of Madame Dupleix as commandant of Masulipatnam. But some zamindars and *faujdars* refused to pay taxes to the French. The French took measures against them. The most powerful zamindar of the Godavari delta, Vijayaram Razu made peace with the French. Abdul Rahman alias Muzaffar Khan found himself as the chief of all the sepoys at Masulipatnam. He held several *jagirs* in the Deccan, thanks to Salabet Jung. Muzaffar Khan had a son called Baqir Miyan, brought up by his brother in Pondicherry, Sheikh Hassan, who had styled himself as Hasanuddin Khan. They too possessed *jagirs*. By then Muzaffar Khan had become known for his extravagant spending at the cost of the sepoys whom he robbed. He spent about Rs. 5,000 per month for his residence alone. When Bussy left Hyderabad for Aurangabad in 1753, he accused him of meanness and dared even to think of removing Bussy as commandant of the sepoys. He wrote to Dupleix that Bussy and a certain Rumi Khan had robbed him of Rs. 5 lakh of his property and that Bussy had also made Rs. 30 or 40 lakh in other ways.

However, Muzaffar Khan accompanied Bussy to Aurangabad and won his confidence as the best servant of the French Company. He was entrusted with the management of the four provinces of the northern Circars by Bussy. But Muzaffar Khan never collected a single rupee from the farmers. Instead, he raised a cavalry regiment that cost him Rs. 91,000, which was disbanded very soon as he was not able to pay the arrears, that accumulated since the departure of Bussy. Besides, Bussy had appointed him as the commander-in-chief of the province of Chicacole. He employed his sepoys to extract taxes from the zamindars. As his troops were squarely defeated by the latter, he ravaged and pillaged the entire northern Circars. But he never was able to extract revenue from the zamindars.

As a result, Dupleix complained that the factory at Masulipatnam was not profitable and was a liability to the colonial budget. Thus though the French and Dupleix were theoretically in possession of vast territories in the Deccan including Masulipatnam, spread over 13,00,000 sq. km with a population of 30 million, they could not reap the required revenue from those areas. Their hold on these territories was quite uncertain. Bussy was not in a position to hold such vast territories under his control with just 300 Frenchmen and 3,000 sepoys, without the cooperation of the nizam and his vassals. This situation remained unchanged until about 1756, well after the departure of Dupleix from Pondicherry, when war broke out between the English and the French. Muzaffar Khan, whom Dupleix had sent to the Deccan to assist Bussy, finally passed over to the Marathas and took service under the Maratha chief, Baji Rao. This was a blow to Dupleix personally. It proved that his Mahé sepoy chiefs were not completely subservient to him or Bussy or the French.[24]

It is simply an exaggeration and over estimation to call these territories held by the French in the Deccan under certain conditions like catering to the maintenance of their troops in the Deccan, as part of a grand empire that Dupleix had established in India. Besides, these territories did not belong to Dupleix. Theoretically it belonged to the French Company, which never benfitted from such acquisitions.[25]

It is also quite obvious that Bussy, one of the best commanders of Dupleix and Abdul Rahman, the most experienced chief of the sepoys was sent to the Deccan, not to conquer territories for the French, but to help a descendant of Nizam-ul-mulk to enthrone himself as nizam, by keeping at bay all enemies, especially the Marathas. Bussy and his troops were actually at the service of the future nizam. They were amply paid for it. They were given territories in the Deccan to meet the expenditures incurred for the upkeep of their troops, and definitely not because Dupleix had the secret intention of establishing a French colonial empire in India or a protectorate in the Deccan or the Carnatic. Dupleix's main aim in acquiring territories seems more to be with the objective of deriving adequate revenues for the survival and prosperity of the Company in India, without relying completely on funds from France, which were uncertain or inadequate due to various reasons. Even in this he signally failed.[26]

The Company and the king coming to know of the various gifts and presents being made to Dupleix and the officers and the employees of the Company by Muzaffar Jung and others got the State Advisory Board of the king of France through the decrees of 6 June 1750 and 10 December 1751 to prohibit everyone of the Company employees including the Governor from accepting donations, and gifts from the local princes in their personal capacities and in case they accept they were under the obligation of reverting them immediately to the Company.[27] But all such decrees had not prevented the Company officials and employees and their relatives from accepting presents and donations and amassing huge fortunes.

However, it is clear that Bussy and the other French officers including Abdul Rahman made immense personal fortunes in the Deccan through gifts and donations especially. Bussy rose from rags to riches in no time. He had got Rs. 4 lakh from Muzaffar Jung to accompany him to Hyderabad. In July 1751, he sent Rs. 3 lakh to Masulipatnam. He got Rs. 80,000 to accompany Salabet Jung to Aurangabad. Bussy bought an estate in France worth 8 lakh livres and married the daughter of a Duke. According to Ananda Ranga Poullé, Bussy had made Rs. 30 or 40 lakh. Besides, Poullé always had an axe to grind against Abdul Rehman and his brother Sheikh Hassan. He dismissed them as former 'coolies' who had amassed a huge fortune and called themselves nawabs.[28]

Dupleix of course had his *jagir* of Vazhudavur and the dependent villages, which produced Rs. 1.5 lakh per year, apart from the numerous presents and gifts given to him by the local princes and notables from time to time. His wife also received several presents, advantages and jagirs, some of which she made over to the Company or the Jesuits. Papaya himself administered 32 villages of the Company officials.

Vincens, a son of Madame Dupleix possessed Rs. 2 lakh while Bussy and Kerjean, related to Dupleix, possessed 4 to 5 lakh. Madame Dupleix boasted that her son had killed 2,500 or 3,000 Indians single-handedly. Vincens and Kerjean received Rs. 1 lakh each in the Deccan on their arrival. From March to October 1751, Kerjean sent to Pondicherry Rs. 3,80,000. Vincens came back to Pondicherry with 40,000 gold coins, a quantity of pagodas, silver and gems. Kerjean, Dupleix's nephew, made at least as much. Captain Godeville in the Deccan earned Rs. 40,000 in one year, though he never robbed. Mainville and Goupil, two captains had received Rs. 25,000 each on their arrival in the Deccan. They never paid their sepoys and pocketed the money advanced to them for paying the sepoys. Even the officers of inferior rank exacted as much money as they could.[29]

These Frenchmen, especially those on service in the Deccan, had no idea of founding a French empire in the Deccan. They were more worried about amassing fortune, as they knew that their stay in Deccan depended upon Salabet Jung and his requirements. Nevertheless at this stage, it appeared that the whole of south India was at the feet of the French or under a certain French control, except Trichinopoly and a few local lords.

NOTES

1. Love, *Vestiges of Old Madras*, II, p. 427; Vinson, *Les Français dans l'Inde. Dupleix et Labourdonnais*, Paris, 1894, pp. 195f; *ARP Diary*, VII, pp. 74-5.
2. Gaudart, *La Criminalité dans les Etablissements Français de l'Inde*, p. iii; Col.c²82, f. 234, A.N.; *ARP Diary*, VI, p. 431; VII, pp. 72, 153, 160, 431; Malleson, *Dupleix*, London, 2001, p. 81.
3. Naf, 12087, f. 1033, BNF; Malleson, ibid., 2001, p. 81; *ARP Diary*, VII, pp. 38, 85, 420.
4. Malleson, ibid., 2001, pp. 85-9.
5. *ARP Diary*, VI, p. 416; VII, pp. 298, 343-4; Naf, 9359, f. 7, BNF; Naf, 9356, f. 45, BNF; Malleson, ibid., 2001, p. 91; I/1/1, French in India 1664-1810, pt. 1, p. 101; De Closets d'Errey, op. cit., 1934, pp. 33-4; Col.c²82, f. 370, A.N.

6. *ARP Diary*, II, pp. 35, 37, 106; V, p. 107; VII, p. 83; Cambridge, *An Account of the War in India between the English and the French on the Coast of Coromandel for the Year 1750 to the Year 1760*, London, 1761, p. 11; *Mémoire pour la Compagnie des Indes* . . . , pièce no. 4; Dodwell, op. cit., p. 13.
7. Cambridge, ibid. p. 11; Vinson, op. cit., pp. 192f; DE Closets d'Errey, op. cit., 1940, p. 17; Col.c²82, f. 356, A.N.; Gaudart, *Catalogue des Manuscrits* . . . , I, pp. 12-13, 69-70, 180; LEC, 1810, xiv, p. 321.
8. Naf 9359, f. 8, BNF; Cambridge, ibid., p. 11; cf. also, Lehuraux, op. cit.,
9. Cambridge, ibid. pp. 11, 12; David, *Pondichéry. Des Comptoirs Français à l'Inde d'aujourd'hui*, Paris, 2004, p. 30; Gaebelé, *Créole et Grande Dame, Johanna Begum, Marquise Dupleix*, Pondichéry, 1934, pp. 111, 113, 163, 166, 167-71, 213-14, 234, 247; Malleson, op. cit., 2001, pp. 92-3.
10. Cited in Sridharan, op. cit., pp. 45-6; A. Martineau, *Les Dernières Années de Dupleix, Ses Dettes et ses procès avec la Compagnie des Indes*, Paris, 1929, p. 89.
11. *ARP Diary*, II, pp. 86, 221; Vinson, op. cit., p. 62; Favier, op. cit., p. 86; Dodwell, op. cit., 1989, 79, pp. 109, 110; Gaudart, *Catalogue* . . . , 1931, p. 79; Gaudart, *Catalogue des Manuscrits*. . . tome. 6, pp. 1-2; Col.c²102, ff. 5-39, A.N.: Haudrère, *La Compagnie Française des Indes au XVIIIe siècle*, III, pp. 822, 990.
12. *ARP Diary*, I, pp. 150, 346; II, pp. 6, 14, 35, 341-2, 343, 53; III, pp. 74f, 385-9; IV, pp. 14, 21, 22, 219-220, 221, 229, 230, 413-14, 441, 444-5; V, pp. 3, 4, 26, 27, 170-1; VI, pp. 141, 143, 199, 200, 295; VII, pp. 109, 204, 214, 220, 434; VIII, pp. 307-8.
13. *ARP Diary*, II, 114, 121, 245-6; III, 72; IV, pp. 105-6; 223, 225-6, 258, 365; VI, pp. 191, 339; VIII, pp. 206-10; Bourdat, *Les Grandes Pages du "Journal" d'Ananda Ranga Pillai*, p. 435; Gaudart, *Catalogue des Manuscrits* . . . , I, pp. 14, 72; Col.c²83, ff. 27-8, A.N.
14. I/1/1 French In India 1664-1810, pt. 2, pp. 337, 339, IOL; Antony, op. cit., I, p. 3; *ARP Diary*, V, p. 20; Col c² 93, f. 215, A.N.; I/1/1, French in India, 1664-1810, pt. 1, pp. 101,125, IOL.
15. Law de Lauriston, *Etat Politique de l'Inde en 1777*, Paris, 1913, p. 75; Srinivasachari, p. 194; *ARP Diary*, IV, pp. 16, 20, 48; V, p. 421; VI, pp. 357, 389; VIII, pp. 206-10; De Closets d'Errey, op. cit., 1934, p. 34; Naf, 8993, f. 30v, BNF; Col. C² 41, f. 283, A.N.
16. Vincent, 'Zenith in Pondicherry', p. 58; Dodwell, op. cit., 1989, p. 53.
17. Cultru, *Dupleix, ses plans politiques, sa disgrâce*, 1901, p. 300.
18. Oubagarasamy, *Un Livre de Compte de Ananda Ranga Poullé*, pp. xxix, xxx; Vinson, op. cit., p. 62.
19. *ARP Diary*, II, 129, 305-6; III, pp. 137-8, 224; V, pp. 36, 371.
20. *ARP Diary*, VI, 115f; IX, pp. 123-6; Fr. 12087, f. 112, BNF; Cultru, op. cit., p. 261.

21. De Closets d'Errey, op. cit., 1934, p. 35; *ARP Diary*, VIII, pp. 416-17.
22. E 3748, 80, 86, A.V.; Cultru, op. cit., p. 212; I/1/1, French in India, 1664-1810, pt. 1, pp. 101-8, IOL; Chassaigne, *Bussy en Inde*, pp. 27-9; Arasaratnam & Ray, op. cit., pp. 22, 98; Naf, 9359, f. 126, BNF.
23. Martineau, *Bussy in the Deccan*, 1941, pp. 230-6; Martineau, *Bussy et l'Inde Française, 1720-1785*, Paris, 1935, p. 127: Gaudart, *Catalogue des Manuscrits* . . . , Tome VI, 1669-1793, Pondichéry, 1935, p. 2; *ARP Diary*, VIII, p. 290.
24. *ARP Diary*, VIII, pp. 416-17; IX, pp. 123-6; Arasaratnam and Ray, op. cit., pp. 98-100, 103; Naf 9359, Mémoire sur Mazulipatanmi, ff. 65, 68, 69, 71, BNF; Martineau, *Dupleix et l'Inde Française*, II, p. 148; Naf 9359, f. 126, BNF; Martineau, *Bussy et l'Inde Française*, pp. 124, 133, 140-1; Deloche, 'La Mémoire de Moracin sur Masulipatnam', pp. 125-49; Gaudart, *Catalogue des Manuscrits* . . . , VI, p. 2; Sarma, *History and Culture of the Andhras*, Hyderabad, 1995, p. 129; Martineau, *Dupleix et l'Inde Française*, IV, pp. 1-37; col. C² 83, f. 144, A.N.
25. Martineau, op. cit., 1929, p. 126; Martineau, *Bussy in the Deccan* . . . , pp. 187-94, 250; Martineau, *Bussy et L'Inde Française*, 1935, pp. 50, 51, 59, 127, 159, 160, 163, 208, 210, 214, 220.
26. Memo of Dupleix of 1753; Asie. Inde. 10, 4 & Asie.inde. 10, 4, f. 44, 53, AMAE; Cultru, op. cit., pp. 278, 281-3.
27. Gaudart, *Catalogue des Manuscrits*. . ., I, p. 11; Dernis, *Recueil des titres, édits, déclarations, arrêts,. . .*, Paris, 1755, IV, p. 656; Cultru, ibid., p. 344.
28. *ARP Diary*, IX, pp. 123-6, 415.
29. Cultru, op. cit., p. 346; E. 3748, 58, A.V.; Cultru, op. cit., pp. 345, 346, 446; *Journal de Godeheu*, C²85, A.N.; E 3749, f. 17, A.V.; Naf, 9159, f. 250, BNF; Dodwell, op. cit., 1989, p. 109; Fr. Naf, 9159, ff. 124, 130, BNF; Dodwell, *Clive and Dupleix*, 1989, p. 109.

CHAPTER 11

Decline of Dupleix

FURTHER WARS AND DEVASTATIONS IN TAMIL NADU

MEANWHILE MOHAMMAD ALI holed up in Trichinopoly had opened negotiations with Dupleix. At the same time, he sought the help of the English. In March 1751, Dupleix sent 400 Frenchmen, a few Africans and some guns, under Combault d'Auteuil to help Chanda Sahib to conquer Trichinopoly. Chanda Sahib had also at his service Sheikh Hassan and his sepoys. Sheikh Hasan was handsomely rewarded by Chanda Sahib to the tune of Rs. 2 lakh and it was decided also to confer the Fort of Chetpattu and a jagir yielding revenue of Rs. 2 lakh to him. Sheikh Hassan and his sepoys launched several attacks on the English and Mohammad Ali's troops.[1]

It was at this stage that Dupleix decided to convert the famous Villianur temple into a fort and raise batteries. The Hindu merchants told Dupleix that if this plan was executed, all Hindus would quit the town. But Dupleix retorted that the Hindus could use the inner court of the temple, while the soldiers and sepoys would only use the outer areas. However, after a visit to the temple, Dupleix found that the temple was unfit to be converted into a fort and asked Tillai Maistry to build a fort around the *mandapam* (court) in the mango grove.[2]

On 5 April 1751, 400 European soldiers under Captain Rudolf Gingen were detached towards Trichinopoly to help Mohammad Ali. Chanda Sahib's troops besieged Trichinopoly. He demanded further help from Dupleix. A detachment of French troops under a 28 year old young officer, Jacques Law, marched on Trichinopoly on 25 September 1751. He did not storm the fort for three months, as wanted by Dupleix. Instead he blockaded it, thinking that he could starve his enemies out. The Mysore Prince and Morari Rao allied with the English at that time.[3]

Meanwhile Robert Clive, another young Englishman, who was only 26 years old and 29 years younger to Dupleix, entered the fray. He marched to Arcot, the capital of the Carnatic, which was undefended, with a slender force and took it over, in the name of Mohammad Ali. The Tamil inhabitants of Arcot offered him large sums of money to spare the town. But Clive was not made of the same stuff as Dupleix. He did not order his troops to plunder the town. He even refused to accept the money offered to him. As a result, the people sympathized with Clive and the English as well as Mohammad Ali.

Chanda Sahib, hearing about the fall of Arcot, rushed his son to besiege it with a considerable force. Clive received reinforcements under Captain Kirkpatrick. Two thousand Marathas also joined this force. There was a pitched battle between Clive's troops and those of Chanda Sahib's at Arani. Clive emerged victorious. On 17 March 1752, Clive set out from Fort St. David at the head of 400 Europeans and 1,000 sepoys to relieve Captain Gingen who had been blocked up in Trichinopoly since last year by a strong party of Chanda Sahib's forces. Clive dislodged Chanda Sahib's troops at Samayavaram, situated on the river Kollidam.

Chanda Sahib stormed the island of Srirangam with an army of 20,000 men. Srirangam was about 6 miles north-west of Trichinopoly. It was an island formed by the Cauvery River and its branch called Kollidam. The French sent a strong detachment under Count d'Auteuil, the old French commandant, to assist Chanda Sahib. Clive confronted d'Auteuil's troops. Twenty-one Frenchmen died, jumping into the river. Six hundred Europeans were taken prisoners by the English. D'Auteuil himself surrendered with 53 European soldiers and 300 sepoys at Valikondapuram to Robert Clive on 9 June 1752 and was taken to Trichinopoly as prisoner of war.[4]

Meanwhile the Raja of Tanjore as well as Morari Rao Ghorpade, the Maratha free-booter, had espoused the cause of Mohammad Ali. His forces along with that of the English at Trichinopoly marched to Srirangam. The place was completely cut off at a very short time. Chanda Sahib's provisions were exhausted. On 2 June 1752, Jacques François Law who commanded the French forces retreated to

Srirangam, instead of Pondicherry as desired by Dupleix. They were completely cut off from Pondicherry. Law and Sheikh Hassan surrendered with 35 officers, 785 French soldiers, 2,000 sepoys, and 41 artillery pieces on 13 June 1752. Law also gave up Chanda Sahib. Law's troops and those of his allies were taken as prisoners of war. Four hundred of them including Sheikh Hassan were sent to Fort St. David and the rest to Trichinopoly. Sheikh Hassan escaped from the fort by hiding inside a box after 10 months and joined Dupleix.[5] Law was reproached for the downfall of the French and was put in prison by Dupleix. But Law claimed that he followed the orders of Dupleix and had acted according to the circumstances. The very next year, Law joined Bussy in the Deccan.

Chanda Sahib was actually detained at the Dalavai's *mandapam* and taken to Monaji Appa's tent. Monaji was the Maratha minister of Tanjore. The raja of Tanjore ordered his head to be cut off and exposed in the camp. When Chanda Sahib was saying his prayers at Monaji's tent, a Pathan in the service of Monaji cut his head off on 14 June 1752. The head with the body was sent at once to Nawab Mohammad Ali Khan in the fort of Trichinopoly. After his courtiers had a look of it, it was tied to the neck of a camel and was carried five times around the walls of Trichinopoly, with about hundred thousand spectators insulting it with all the obscene and indecent invectives. Thus Mohammad Ali Khan wreaked vengeance for the death of his father, Anwaruddin Khan at Ambur. Dupleix was so flabbergasted by the news, that he could neither go to church nor eat his dinner. He knew that one of his staunchest allies in the Carnatic had passed away. That was going to have great implications for his whole future. Dupleix was not happy that Law had given up Chanda Sahib, without insisting on a Maratha nobleman as hostage.[6]

In the autumn of 1752, Major Lawrence destroyed another French force at Bahur under de Kerjean, who was related to Dupleix. After the French debacle at Trichinopoly, Mohammad Ali was installed as the nawab of Arcot. This was a terrible blow to Dupleix and the French prestige. Thenceforth Pondichery and Karaikal became vulnerable and were unprotected. Mohammad Ali's troops encamped near Tirukanji and had plundered Puranankuppam, Alisapakkam (Archivac), Villianur, Othiampattu and other villages and driven off the cattle. Mohammad Ali would not accept Dupleix's claims that he had a *parvana* from the Mughal emperor commanding all to obey him. Instead he asserted that he had *parvanas* confirming him as nawab of Arcot. Besides, he would not confirm the *jagirs* given to Dupleix and his people by Muzaffar Jung and Salabet Jung.[7]

The success of Bussy, 1,000 km away in the Deccan was a poor compensation and consolation for the defeat at Trichnopoly. Bussy was certainly the best French general at the disposal of Dupleix. But he had sent him off to the Deccan thinking that he would increase his revenues through territorial acquisitions in order to finance his interventionist policies, without counting on the finances provided by the Company. But that was not to be as we have seen, as no additional revenue from the Deccan was forthcoming to prop up his sagging finances. Dupleix had no doubt miscalculated all along. Besides, he was quite unaware that the Muslim potentates right from Chanda Sahib to Salabet Jung had used him and the French to a great extent in order to consolditate their power in the Deccan and the Carnatic, while Dupleix himself was restricted to Pondicherry, with the title of 'General Nawab'.

It was during that time when Dupleix was staring at defeat that the new palace whose construction had begun in 1738 under Dumas was finally completed by French engineers like Gerbault and Sornay, at the cost of Rs. 42,000. It seems that this palace was a monument of excellence and extravagance with a typical French touch. It was the most splendid palace of the whole of south India, with its gilded chambers, wide cool verandahs and snow white pillars. But it also had come at a time when Dupleix's fortunes were not bright. Of course, Dupleix moved to the palace with his wife from Villa Aroumé. But this palace, the Fort as well as most of the White town including churches was razed to the ground in 1761 by the English under Eyre Coote, as a sort of retaliation to the occupation and looting of Madras city in 1758 by the French forces of Count de Lally. It seems that Mohammad Ali bought the ornaments of the palace and probably used them in his new palace of Chepauk in Madras.[8]

During this period and later, Dupleix sought the help and advice of the Jesuit fathers like Rev. François-Louis de Lavaur, chief of the Jesuits since 1751 and Rev. Costes in his dealings with the Indian princes. The French priests were very much involved in the wars. They believed that the English were stronger than the French as the latter had a less number of white soldiers. Actually eight hundred of them had gone over to the Deccan with Bussy. Besides, the English held about 1,000 Frenchmen as prisoners in the name of Mohammad Ali Khan.

The French priests however believed that the English wanted to replace Mohammedan power by Hindu power. This they held gave hope to the possibility of converting the Hindus in future to Chrisitianity while the Muslims were completely opposed to the Christians. Dupleix also had close contacts with a Franciscan priest called Dom Antonio Noronha, who passed off for the nephew of Jeanne Dupleix. Dupleix had intervened in his favour with the Viceroy of Goa and got him nominated as the Vicar of the Luz Church in Madras. When in 1749, Dupleix gave back Madras to the English, he obtained a firman from Chanda Sahib, naming Dom Antonio as the governor or *faujdar* of San Thomé. But he was soon arrested by Boscawen and sent to England as prisoner.[9]

While Dupleix was losing all his wars, his *dubash* Ananda Ranga Poullé continued with his terrible flattering mission. On 11 July 1752, he told Dupleix:

Through Nazir Jung you got jaghir for the Company, Masulipatnam (with revenue of 10 or 12 lakhs of rupees), and Devanakottai, Nizampatnam, Divi Island and other places. Besides these, the Vazhudavur and Karungali countries, and the Nao Mahal (nine countries, a revenue district near Pondicherry), which yield 10 or 13 lakhs of rupees were also given in jaghir with a mansab of 7000 horses, the Fish standard and other marks of honour. You had received the suzerainty on the country which spreads from the Krishna to Cape Comorin and the possession of Carnatic. . . . With the help of God, Mysore, Tanjore, Trichinopoly and all the land on the coast of Krishna will fall under your power and your flag will fly in Delhi.

Dupleix overcome by emotion took off his hat, bowed towards Poullé and said: 'Thank You very much, Monsieur Ranga Poullé'.[10]

Thus even when Dupleix was staring at defeat, Ananda Ranga Poullé put into the mind of Dupleix things which he would have never thought of like subjugating Mysore and the whole of Tamil Nadu. Dupleix wanted to destroy Mohammad Ali at all costs. He devised a method for it as he could not take on him directly. He thought that with his soldiers, sepoys and horsemen, he could create disturbances and ruin the country, so that the Tamil cultivators would not till the land and no revenue could be paid into the coffers of Mohammad Ali. This was a sinister design. Ananda Ranga Poullé on his part insisted that all Mohammad Ali's good fortune would be over by June 1753. Poullé bluntly told that he was fortunate to be the 'slave' of Dupleix. Dupleix probably believed in all this undiluted flattery and in Poullé's astrological predictions.[11]

During September and October 1752, Maratha horsemen plundered Karuvadikuppam, Bommaiyarpalayam, Kalapettai, Kunimedu and other places and drove away the cattle. But by the last months of 1752, Dupleix tried to strike an alliance with Nandi Raja, the General of the Mysore king and Morari Rao, as well as with Murtuza Ali, the governor of Vellore, and the killer of Safdar Ali Khan and brother-in-law of Chanda Sahib. Dupleix wanted Murtuza Ali to be nawab of Arcot. Sheikh Hassan was not happy with it as he was coveting that post. He told Dupleix that he would pay the revenues from it to him, if he was made Nawab of Arcot. He added that he had the *parvana* from Muzaffar Jung and Salabet Jung for the Vellore fort. Dupleix offered him instead the Chetpattu fort and the jagir which had been given to him. Thus the Malayali fisherman from Mahé aimed to become the nawab of Arcot. But Dupleix stood in his way.[12]

On his part, Murtuza Ali who would not contend for nawabship with Mohammad Ali Khan promised Dupleix his neutrality in the war. Raza Sahib, the son of Chanda Sahib, on the other hand lacked the resources to ally with the French and defy the English. Dupleix then negotiated with Morari Rao to obtain 4,000 horsemen and 2,000 foot soldiers, by paying him Rs. 1 lakh in cash and promising him another 2 lakh in two months, in order to defeat Mohammad Ali Khan. According to another account, Dupleix promised Morari Rao Rs. 2 lakh in cash and 2 lakh after the downfall of Mohammad Ali Khan. Dupleix also promised to hand over Trichinopoly to the king of Mysore for Rs. 30 lakh.[84] Morari Rao himself came to Pondicherry to conclude the alliance. Dupleix received him with great respect. The campaign against the English and Mohammad Ali Khan was to begin at the end of 1752. The French forces were led by Jacques Maissin while Morari Rao was at the head of the Marathas.

Since the end of December 1752, Nandi Raja was in Srirangam. He promised to give some jewels to the French chief Astruc to repay the debts that he owed Dupleix. But at the same time, Dupleix came to know that Morari Rao was not in a hurry to lay waste the Tanjore region, most certainly because he had not yet been paid what was promised to him. However, a chief of Nandi Raja of humble Tamil/Kannada origin, known as Hyder Naik (the future Hyder Ali, Sultan of Mysore) compensated to some extent the inaction of Morari Rao by ravaging and devastating the Tanjore region. Besides, Nandi Raja and Morari Rao did not see eye to eye. This was a cause of worry for Dupleix. In July 1753 Srirangam was ceded by the king of Mysore to the French to discharge the sum he owed them. The Frenchman Leyretat farmed it out for Rs. 4,80,000.[13]

At the same time, with fresh troops coming from France, Dupleix mounted another mission to capture Trichinopoly. He sent his nephew Desnos de Kerjean with troops to besiege Trichinopoly, which Dupleix had promised to hand over to the Mysore king. The latter had promised the French Rs. 4 lakh in cash and Rs. 11 lakh when Trichinopoly would be handed over to him. Very soon, Trichinopoly reeled under famine as the Marathas had cut off all the routes to the town.[14] In the year 1753, Dupleix also sent a large force under Sheikh Hassan who had long been commander-in-chief of sepoys after the departure of Abdul Rahman to the Deccan, accompanied by some Marathas, to attack the Hindu temple at Vriddachalam. The French king had honoured Hassan with a gold medal in token of his services. In May 1753, Dupleix himself was honoured with the title of *Marquis* by the king of France.[15]

Even during this trying period for Dupleix in 1753, Ananda Ranga Poullé was never tired of extolling Dupleix's virtues. He bluntly told Dupleix:

. . . You will mount his throne (Mughal) and as our destinies are entwined, when you become Emperor, I will become your prime minister.
Dupleix told:
Ranga Poullé is very intelligent. He has no equal in India or in Europe.
Ranga Poullé retorted:
Emperor Aurangzeb, Louis XIV and other monarchs have conquered with great difficulty only one country with all their power and after several

years of efforts. Auragnzeb took twelve years to conquer Bijapur, Zulfiqar took as much to capture Gingi at the head of a big army. But in spite of the power of Gingi, you took it in one hour with 1000 Europeans and 2000 sepoys . . . Nazir Jung fell __, though he was viceroy of Deccan, at the head of an army of 100000 horsemen and one million of foot soldiers, as that are our power. The other kings are not to be compared with the dust of your shoes.[16]

Dupleix told that he did not deserve such praise. He returned the compliments by telling Ananda Ranga Poullé that he was very clever and there was not one his equal in India or in Europe, in giving timely advice.[17]

THE FALL OF DUPLEIX

Since 1751/2 Ananda Ranga Poullé was losing ground in Pondicherry politics. Dupleix's wife, Jeanne got the upper hand. She had got Papayapoullé nominated as the revenue collector of the Carnatic. Dupleix began to rely more and more on Papayapoullé to collect the revenues of Arcot during this period. He was tyrannical and robbed with ease. We do not know the exact origin of Papaya.[18]

It appears that since 1751 Dupleix did not consult Ananda Ranga Poullé on political and social matters. Instead he consulted him only with regard to the farming out of lands, the lading of ships, etc. His trade contracts with the Company also diminished drastically since 1751.[19] However, this did not deter Ranga Poullé to continue to exercise his art of flattery towards Dupleix and encourage him in his warlike designs.

Papaya was stricken with leprosy and in 1753 developed boils and sores all over his body. In spite of his ill-health, Dupleix relied on him blindly for the collection of revenues since 1751, not only from lands in the Carnatic, but also from Bahur, Villianur and the Karaikal region. He was the one who farmed out the lands, nominated the chiefs of the villages called *amaldars*, who received the taxes and forwarded it to Dupleix. Dupleix waged his wars with the money derived in such a way. But it has been recorded that Papaya was an opportunist of the first order, and made the maximum out of his position and his closeness to Dupleix and his wife.

Papaya was also a robber of first order through various means. Dupleix probably turned a blind eye to his nefarious activities through his men, who imprisoned the *amaldars* or village chiefs to extract revenues from them and robbed the villagers and destroyed their houses to take away even the wood. Besides, Papaya seized people dressed in white attire like the Komuttis, the Vellalas, the Agamudaiyans and other merchants like the Chetties, demanding loans and extorting money in order to pay Morari Rao. Some were made to stoop and stones were placed on their backs, others were tied by the wrist to a tree and flogged, while many others suffered other diabolical tortures like being kicked and beaten up with the fists, which made the merchants flee the town.[20]

Papaya extracted money not only to pay off the debts incurred by Dupleix, but also to enrich himself. For one who had started off as a domestic in Madras, in no time under Dupleix and his wife, he had become the owner of nineteen houses in Pondicherry town alone. He possessed rice fields in Cuddalore and 50 houses in Madras.[21]

However, the misfortunes that befell the French in 1752-3 caused Dupleix to ponder. His armies were most of the time defeated everywhere. Nevertheless Dupleix was no more in a position to wage wars. He proposed peace to Mr. Saunders. Negotiations took place at the Dutch factory in Sadras during 22-5 January 1754 and later. The French wanted the release of all their prisoners. They also wanted the English to recognize Salabet Jung as the nizam and the recognition of all the concessions obtained by the French till then. But the English would not. The French produced *sanads* or *parvanas* from the Mughal emperor and the nizam appointing Dupleix as commander or governor of the territories south of Krishna and confirming Murtuza as his deputy in Arcot. But these *parvanas* might be fake. The English would have nothing of it. They accused Dupleix of killing the lawful nawab of Arcot, Anwaruddin and the lawful nizam, Nazir Jung. The French would have nothing of it. So naturally peace did not come about. Besides, it is doubtful if Dupleix really wanted to become the nawab of Carnatic. It seems more as a belated attempt to justify his claims.[22]

In May 1754, Morari Rao tired of asking Dupleix his dues for the services that he rendered him, retreated from Tanjore, accepting Rs. 3 lakh as the price for abandoning Dupleix. This was a terrible blow to Dupleix's designs. Dupleix vented his anger on Papaya whom he accused of failing to collect the revenues to pay Morari Rao his monthly allowance of Rs. 1.5 lakh. Dupleix kicked him, beat him, spat on him and insulted him for this on a daily basis. Papaya meekly submitted to this treatment by Dupleix. Earlier in his attempt to extort cash from a certain Periya Perumal Pillai to the tune of Rs. 4.5 lakh in order to pay his debts, Dupleix lost his cool and thrashed him 40 or 50 times with a cane and then some Africans dealt him another 40 or 50 blows until he fainted and almost died. He was then thrown into the fort's dungeon. Periya Perumal Pillai unable to bear the atrocity, promised Dupleix Rs. 1 lakh.[23]

Morari Rao on his way back home, not content with Rs. 3 lakh, plundered various towns and villages like Tiruvannamalai, Vellore, and Arani extracting whatever money and valuables he could from the Tamil people, seizing Tamil women and burning and destroying the villages and country that refused him ransom.[24]

At the same time, under orders from Dupleix, his chief Mainville ravaged the Pudukottai region from where the English got their provisions. Following Dupleix's orders he also demolished the dam on the Cauvery, which was an architectural feat of the Chola king in the eleventh century, which irrigated the Tanjore region through a system of canal network. This grand dam situated about 60 km to the north-east of Trichinopoly regulated all the canal networks of the delta. The destruction of this dam was done as a sort of retaliation to punish the Maratha king of Tanjore who never wanted to ally with Dupleix, in spite of the latter's efforts to get him to his side against the English.

However the destruction or partial demolition of the Chola dam by the French had caused immense misery and deaths to the Tamil people of Tanjore due to inundation of the villages and the fields. The destruction, planned by Dupleix and executed by Mainville, instead of bringing the raja of Tanjore towards the French, pushed him in a definitive manner into the arms of the English.[25]

When the successive reverses of Dupleix, his continuous aggressive policy, the precarious financial situation of the Company due to the wars and the gross abuses of Papaya, came to the knowledge of the Directors of the French Company in Paris, they sent Mr. Duvalaer as their commissary to restore peace. Peace was necessary for the Company shareholders to make profits. Dupleix's adventures on behalf of the Indian princes had been having a telling effect on the profits of the Company. The Company Directors were worried about the mounting expenditure caused by Dupleix. They were simply flabbergasted when Dupleix asked for more troops and money. They were surprised that all the funds that they sent to Pondicherry had simply disappeared.[26] Nevertheless, the French Company had made a profit of 5,82,69,331 livres through the sale of goods from India, in spite of Dupleix's wars. But this profit was no doubt reduced due to the expenses incurred.[27]

It is believed by some that Dupleix's wars in India was waged mostly with the money provided by the Indian princes and moneylenders and Dupleix's own money, which he got mostly as presents and *jagirs* from the Indian princes. This contention is of course true in the light of what we have seen above. But Dupleix demanded the re-imbursement of his money spent for the wars from the Company. This amounted to 28,90,616 pounds as well as the money he borrowed from friends and relatives including his wife and others that rose to 70,22,296 pounds on the whole. The Company officials would not listen to him. His creditors were after him in Paris.[28]

The officers lived in great luxury and opulence during Dupleix's period. They constructed big houses with gardens and had elephants and horses in their stables. Barthélémy was worth Rs. 3 or 4 lakh while Delarche, Dupleix's interpreter was worth ten and Guillard three. Barthélémy also owned houses and an estate. They went about in richly decorated palanquins. They possessed exquisite furniture in their salons. A simple writer earned about 600 livres in Pondicherry per year, which allowed him to live in luxury, with servants and chairs to carry them. Ananda Ranga Poullé admitted that Dupleix's wealth knew no limits, while the Company was impoverished. Every officer had made lakhs. During Papaya's time even country writers like Arumpattai made lakhs, not to speak of Papaya who made the most.[29]

From the time, Dupleix stepped into Pondicherry, it was a harvest of gold for his relatives and his wife. Many other capable men were overlooked or sidelined, due to the nepotism that prevailed during Dupleix's governorship. Combault d'Auteuil, his field commander, was the second husband of Marie Madeleine, the sister of his wife. Louis d'Argoulin member of the Superior Council had married another sister of his wife. His wife's daughter Anne Christine was married to Jacques d'Eprémesnil, who was director of the provincial council in Madras. Another daughter of Madame Dupleix known as Chonchon was supposed to get married to Marquis de Bussy whom Dupleix sent to the Deccan, where he made several crores. Jacques Vincens, son of Madame Dupleix left behind a large fortune for his mother when he died in 1752. Kerjean, brother-in-law of Dupleix made several lakhs. Friell, a nephew-in-law of Madame Dupleix was nominated as chief of Masulipatnam factory. Another nephew-in-law, Léon Moracin followed Friell to Masulipatnam as chief. Noronha, related to Madame Dupleix became governor of San Thomé. The wife of Combault d'Auteuil and sister-in-law of Dupleix possessed a village, yielding Rs. 4,000 per annum.[30]

At the same time, since at least the death of Pedro Canagarayen, there was no religious tolerance, the great Vedapuriswaran temple was destroyed, Senji Nayak temples were destroyed and looted, age-old caste rules and customs were flouted, poverty increased and prosperity decreased. People stopped coming to Pondicherry. Instead they left Pondicherry. The incessant wars since 1746 left the people in total disarray, not just in Pondicherry, but also in places where Dupleix sent his troops and ravaged the Tamil towns and countryside. The population of Pondicherry naturally decreased. Ananda Ranga Poullé put it at just 22,000.[31]

The English and the French finally concluded a convention, whereby it was stipulated that the two Companies should reciprocally restore the territories taken by their troops since 1748, except certain districts which the English retained for the convenience of their trade; that the nawabs advanced by the influence of either should be acknowledged by both and that for the future neither should interfere in any dispute which might arise among the princes of India.[32]

The Company finally decided upon certain guidelines to put an end to the governorship of Dupleix in the following words:

The role that the Company had played in the wars of the Moors and the immense profits and possessions which some individuals had obtained from them are the causes and source of the impoverished conditions in which the

Company is reduced. The recall of Dupleix as well as of some persons who have taken part in the turmoils in India has become indispensable. It is necessary to arm M. Godeheu with orders to supersede M. Dupleix and to ship him home with his family. It is also necessary to provide orders to arrest him if he disobeys. M. Godeheu is instructed to take measures to obtain the Company's documents from M. Dupleix and to get the clarifications and explanations about the disbursement of large sums which reached Pondicherry, the benefit of which Dupleix and many other officers and employees of the Company have drawn to the detriment of the Company.

Accordingly, on 2 August 1754, Charles Robert Godeheu, a former friend of Dupleix since the latter was Director in Chandernagore, reached Pondicherry and replaced Dupleix as Governor of Pondicherry. Godeheu even came with an arrest warrant for Dupleix in case he did not comply with the wishes of the Company. He set free the English prisoners, called back Mainville from Trichinopoly against the advice of Dupleix, replaced Mainville with Maissin, imprisoned Papayapoullé, the revenue collector of the Company and asked Dupleix to submit details of his financial transactions. The numerous creditors of Dupleix were in for a shock when they knew that the Company would not re-imburse their debts with attractive interests.[33]

Dupleix submitted the accounts related to revenues and expenses, kept by Papaya. Dupleix argued that he had lent Muzaffar Jung and Salabet Jung 13 million francs out of his own pocket. As the nizam was unable to repay it, they had given Dupleix the right to collect the revenues of the province of Arcot in his own name. Papaya was in charge of collecting the revenues since 1751. But Godeheu did not want to have anything of it. Instead Papaya was imprisoned on 14 August 1754 as his vouchers showed that Dupleix had received Rs. 33 lakh as revenue from Bahur, Villianur and 81 villages in Karaikal alone. Dupleix claimed that this was not Company's money. Godeheu pretended that the amount belonged to the Company and not to Dupleix.[34] That sealed the fate of Dupleix. Besides, the widespread corruption in which Dupleix, Bussy and their subordinates indulged since so many years cast a long dark shadow on their reputation.

Dupleix also asked Ananda Ranga Poullé to produce his personal accounts as well as that of the Company's. But Poullé, who was so prompt since so many years to please Dupleix in every way, took his own time and produced it just a day before Dupleix's departure to France on 15 October 1754. This was a very unkind and ungrateful parting gesture of Ananda Ranga Poullé to a man who had made him what he was.[35]

At this critical juncture, Ananda Ranga Poullé forgot about all his astrological predictions regarding the glorious future of Dupleix and himself. They were all false. Instead, he asserted that Madame Dupleix was the cause of Dupleix's debacle. He quoted the Hindu scripture *Saptha Shastras* to affirm that sorrow would follow anyone who was guided by a woman. He further told Godeheu that during Le Noir's time religious freedom was respected and therefore the town prospered, houses were built inside and outside the town and the population increased. But during Dupleix's period there was not a house outside and the houses inside stood empty with only mud walls. The town was so impoverished that money and goods were scarce and people lived in fear. He admitted that Le Noir accepted presents, but not bribes, while Dumas made money by all means. But he denounced Dupleix for his ill-gotten wealth. He opined that during Le Noir's time the Company made profits, but when Dumas was governor the profits fell by half and during Dupleix's period trade suffered a lot.[36]

Papaya was kept in prison without food, so that his stools were bleeding. His son, Alankara Poullé and son-in-law too were imprisoned in the Fort dungeon. Papaya's houses were sealed.[37]

Godeheu left Pondicherry in February 1755. He was succeeded by Commandant Duval de Leyrit, who was none other than the brother of Duval d'Epresmesnil, the brother-in-law of Dupleix, who was earlier chief of Madras. Kandappa Mudali was the *dubash* of Duval de Leyrit.[38] Leyrit was as condescending and merciless as Hébert and Dupleix in the treatment they meted out to their Indian subordinates.

The barbarity to which Kandappa Mudali, Savariraya Pillai, *amaldar* (village tax collector) and a certain Periyanna Mudali were subjected to in the Fort dungeon where they were shut up like Nainiappa Poullé, in the 1750s has no parallel in the history of Pondicherry and French colonization in India. They were grossly ill-treated there and were taken by the French soldiers to the prison at Villianur in the morning of 4 September 1759. The soldiers beat them and pushed them with butt-ends of the musket, dragged them all along by the leg, and subjected them to all sorts of cruelties all along the road to Villianur in full view of those living in the streets. It seems that Papaya, who was released earlier, was behind the imprisonement and ill-treatment of the three. On seeing this atrocity, Ananda Ranga Poullé wrote:

'Never has such atrocity and injustice been displayed in this town for these 50 or 60 years, never have I ever seen anything like this'.

Kandappa Mudali was released in July 1760.[39]

On another occasion, Chinnadu Mudali Lazar, the brother of Pedro Canagarayenr was bed-ridden with legs and hands swollen. When there was a threat to Pondicherry from the English, there was a forced collection of money in the month of May 1760. Lazar was nevertheless brought to the Fort in a palanquin and asked to pay Rs. 20,000. When he told that he could afford only Rs. 10,000, he was shut up in the dungeon of the Fort like Nainiappa Poullé decades earlier and Kandappa Mudali. Ananda Ranga Poullé interceded on behalf of Lazar and told that Lazar's ancestors had served the Company since three generations as courtiers and therefore he deserved some respect and a better treatment, especially when he was willing to pay Rs. 10,000. But his words fell on deaf ears.[40]

When Dupleix left Pondicherry with his wife and daughter by the name of Chonchon on 15 October 1954, early in the morning, he probably never thought that he would never again see Pondicherry and India where he had spent nearly 35 years. Ananda Ranga Poullé, the old loyal servant of Dupleix was there on the seaside to send him off. But many of his friends and associates had abandoned him by then.

Ananda Ranga Poullé knew many things about the wars and the trade and the expenditures and financial transactions in which Dupleix, his wife and his subordinate officers were involved. Probably he knew that Dupleix would never return to Pondicherry, given the magnitude of the problems in which he was steeped. But the Company directors never thought that it was necessary to enquire from Ananda Ranga Poullé regarding the actions and financial transactions of Dupleix. Besides, Poullé never interceded in favour of Dupleix with Godeheu or any other French authority, with the intention of redeeming Dupleix. Neither did he ever think of going to France like his relative

Guruvappa in the 1920s to defend Dupleix. Neither did Dupleix approach him for that purpose.

Nevertheless Dupleix was not an altogether impoverished man when he left. The goods that he took with him to France comprised precious stones, silver cutlery, horses, cows, buffalos, camels, donkeys, brids, pigs, tables, several sacks of rice and wheat and his other possessions and objects were worth Rs. 11.15 lakh. Dupleix left the management of his *jagir* at Vazhudavur with the French officials Du Bausset and Delarche asking them to pay his creditors out of its revenues and send accounts of the payment to him in France. Vazhudavur was taken over by the English later. Earlier he had leased out his lands at Ozhukarai to the Reddi Christian cultivators directly for a lengthy period. We do not know what became of these lands after his departure.

In France, Dupleix possessed a two storey building at rue des Capucins in Paris. He also had a castle and lands near Domfront and a countryside villa at Villeneuve Saint Georges, where Jeanne resided.[41]

In October 1754, the French Company possessed Pondicherry, Karaikal, Mahé and Chandernagore, which were made up of 50,803 hectares, with a total population of 2,90,000. They also possessed some outposts called *loges* at Masulipatnam, Balasore, Jougdia, Cassimbazar, Dacca, Patna, Surat and Calicut which made up for hardly 100 hectares. They also had some places in the Carnatic like Senji and Thiagar. They also held as guarantee since ten months the four Circars of Chicacole, Rajamundry, Ellore and Mustapha Nagar.

The treaty signed by Godeheu with the English on 26 December 1754 confirmed all these possessions. Vazhudavur was taken back by the English. But the treaty laid limitations on the ambitions of the French in India, by accepting not to interfere in the rivalries of the Indian rulers and princes and indulge only in commercial operations. This contradicted the policy of Dupleix who freely interfered in the politics of the region by taking sides with the local princes and even provoking them. This seems to have laid unwittingly the first foundation stones of European colonialism in India, though it is not at all sure that Dupleix was aware of it or if he had ever worked for it.[42]

It has been calculated that the cost of Dupleix's interventions in the Carnatic and the Deccan amounted to 6,62,72,000 livres at least, of which 2,81,48,000 livres were paid by the princes and other Indian sources, 2,09,24,000 livres by the French Company and 72,00,000 livres out of Dupleix's own pocket, which were essentially made up of gifts by Indian donors and also debt incurred.[43]

It could be concluded therefore that Indian merchants and bankers financed the wars of Dupleix to a great extent, with a view to making profits. They were not in the least bit worried or were completely oblivious about the devastating consequences of their actions in favour of Dupleix. They too along with Dupleix have to be held responsible for the immense misery caused to the Tamil people by the incessant wars waged by Dupleix, by taking the side of one Indian prince against another, with the objective of generating revenue and amassing immense personal fortunes. Ananda Ranga Poullé had no doubt aided and abetted him in this respect in many ways as we have seen. All that ended in a terrible political and financial fiasco.

The Directors of the Company after assessing the financial aspect of the adventures of Dupleix in India thought that Dupleix had largely mismanaged his governorship of the French possessions in India since 1750 by interfering in the affairs and disputes of the Indian princes and indulging in incessant wars, which was not profitable to the Company shareholders ultimately. But Dupleix never saw the writing on the wall. He had to pay the price for it in France. He owed the Company 13 million francs, for which he was about to be imprisoned. His reputation was tarnished and he was completely discredited and derided.

His wife, Jeanne, not accustomed to the climate in France and who had lived like a 'Queen' in Pondicherry, died broken-hearted of rheumatism on 4 December 1756 trying hard to defend her husband's role in India. It was a desperate futile attempt by her that cost her life. She stood like a rock behind the man she loved. But she collapsed in the face of the mounting pressure upon her husband and the harsh Parisian climate. Nevertheless before she died she donated 10,000 pounds to the Brotherhood of Mathurins.

The very next year Dupleix married Mlle de Chastenay. On his part, Dupleix tried for seven long years to justify his actions in India. He declared that he sacrificed his youth, his fortune and his life to enrich France in Asia. But all his pleadings fell on deaf years. Dupleix's attempt to invoke nationalism and his love for the nation as responsible for all his actions in India had no takers. Nobody would believe him. Dupleix ran the risk of being sent to the dreaded Bastille prison. But before that could happen, he passed away in extreme misery and poverty on 11 November 1763 in his house in Paris. His *dubash* Ananda Ranga Poullé had died a couple of years before him on 12 Janaury 1761, just five days before the English captured and destroyed Pondicherry. His personal situation had degraded very much by then. Dupleix never knew that his *dubash* had passed away. He never even wrote to him. Neither did Ananda Ranga Poullé maintain any correspondence with him. Dupleix was behind the rise in power and wealth of Ananda Ranga Poullé. But the latter simply forgot him when his former boss was steeped in acute distress. In any case, most of Ananda Ranga Poullé's predictions and astrology had gone awfully wrong. Even his death which he said would occur when he would be 99, as written in his horoscope by the Brahmin astrologers went completely wrong.[44]

From the purely financial and material point of view, which was the view of the French East India Company, Dupleix had no doubt mislead the Company since 1750, by embroiling the French in the never-ending internecine quarels and conflicts of the Indian princes. As long as Dupleix scored victories, the Company seems to have turned a blind eye to his adventures. But once Dupleix started losing the wars one after one, the Company could no more tolerate the situation where the wars were impinging on the profits of the shareholders of the Company.

Until the death of Pedro Canagaraya Mudaliar, Dupleix did not indulge in any major conflicts for or against the Indian princes. Even the conquest of Madras in 1746 was not the work of Dupleix. But it was the work of La Bourdonnais. Dupleix would have wanted to retain Madras for the French indefinitely and thus deny the English a foothold in the trade of south India. The intention of Dupleix to attract the merchants of Madras to Pondicherry was also a failure. Finally he was forced to relinquish Madras to the English by the Company, which he did without challenging the decision that came from his superior authorities. In the meantime, he of course earned a name for himself by defending Pondicherry in 1748 when the English laid a prolonged siege of it. He made the English retreat. Naturally he was showered with praise for his valour and awards were bestowed upon him.

At that crucial time, Ananda Ranga Poullé took over as *diwan*. Thenceforth we could see a change in the attitude of Dupleix. During this period, he came under the spell of Ananda Ranga Poullé, which seems to have led him to wade into the local politics of the region. This entailed expenses. Naturally the profits of the Company diminished. At the same time, the local princes made use of him and his forces to capture power. Gradually the opinion developed that Dupleix was all powerful and he had the whole of south India under his feet. But the fact was that Dupleix was a king-maker, but not the king or *badshah*. He was still only a Company servant, answerable to the Company directors.

If Dupleix had won his wars, he would have of course been rewarded for his services, as that would have increased the profits of the Company. But Dupleix lost most of his wars. Above all, he was unable to dislodge the English from Fort St. David, near Cuddalore. All these losses gradually contributed to his undoing. Besides, a sort of nepotism had been practised by Dupleix. All his relatives and subordinate officers including Ananda Ranga Poullé and Papayapoullé amassed huge wealth, which never came into the accounts of the Company.

All such mismanagement of Company affairs in India by Dupleix seems to have exasperated the Company directors that they were forced to recall him to face trial for mismanagement and misappropriation of funds. From the purely material point of view, the Company directors were right in prosecuting Dupleix. He was certainly not a hero for them. He was rather a swindler and a cheat, who made use of the power conferred upon him by the Company for his own self-serving ends. Obviously there was nobody to defend Dupleix except himself and his devoted wife, because the crimes committed by Dupleix, not only financially but also otherwise were so conspicuous. Fortunately for him he died, before he could be imprisoned in the Bastille.

However, from the time, Ananda Ranga Poullé's diary was discovered,

Dupleix was gradually consecrated by the French writers and historians, as a hero of the French nation, who had contributed to establish colonialism in India. For those who consider colonialism as a service to humanity, Dupleix was of course one of the great heroes. But his role in the devastation of the Tamil countryside including Pondicherry economically and the incessant killings and depredations due to the wars in which he engaged seems to outweigh his role in the development of Pondicherry or Tamil Nadu. His predecessors fared much better and Pondicherry was more prosperous during their governorships. Dupleix had actually contributed to the downslide of Pondicherry and even Tamil Nadu and south India in every way due to his penchant to wage wars incessantly.

But if Dupleix must be consecrated as a hero for the wars he waged and for having showed the English the way to conquer India and subjugate it, then he is of course a hero for all English and French writers and historians as well as politicians and others, starting from Macaulay to Julien Vinson and Jouveau-Dubreuil. He was also a hero for the missionaries for his contribution to the spread of Christianity in south India and his actions in favour of the Jesuits. But for the Indians/Tamils who had suffered the consequences of Dupleix's actions and who had been devastated and subjugated in consequence of his actions, he is definitely not a hero, but the villain who laid the foundation stones for their slavery.

Now the question naturally arises if Dupleix was really the one who laid the foundations for colonialism in India or not. In the light of what we have seen above, it is not Dupleix who interfered first in local conflicts. When Dumas was governor of Pondicherry, he had sought the help of Chanda Sahib in his conflict with the raja of Tanjore, with the ultimate objective of retaining Karaikal, ceded to him by the latter in 1739, as a French settlement. Similarly when the Muslim nobility and others sought refuge in Pondicherry, Dumas gave them protection by not allowing the Marathas to enter Pondicherry. Thus Dumas was taking the side of one Indian prince against the other right from this period.

But unlike Dupleix, Dumas was acting in such a way only in order to protect his territories acquired legally. He did not wage any other type of war which exceeded the limits of his territories. This is where

Dupleix differed from him radically. Dupleix sent his troops to wage wars all over Tamil Nadu and south India. This was unprecedented. The English too following Dupleix were forced to take the side of one prince against the other, which ended finally in the defeat of Dupleix, his troops and his designs.

Besides, one has to note that Dupleix was not the originator of the Sepoy regiments in Pondicherry. It was actually François Martin who had recruited local men as sepoys in order to protect Pondicherry, as we have seen in the first chapter. It was followed by other French governors like Dumas. Dupleix only perfected the art of recruiting local fighting men as part of his army and created veritable regiments out of them, led by charismatic chiefs like Abdul Rehman alias Muzaffar Khan and Sheikh Hassan.[45]

NOTES

1. *ARP Diary*, VII, pp. 432, 433, 442; VIII, pp. 73, 81-3.
2. *ARP Diary*, VIII, pp. 82-3, 197.
3. De Closets d'Errey, *Précis Chronologique de l'Histoire de l'Inde Française*, Paris, 1934, p. 35; Martineau, *Dupleix et l'Inde Française*, I, pp. 80-1; G.B. Mallleson, *Dupleix*, London, 2001, pp. 59, 99, 107, 115.
4. *A Complete History of the War in India from the year 1749 to the Taking of Pondicherry in 1761*, pp. 6-13; De Closets d'Errey, ibid.; *ARP Diary*, VIII, p. 112.
5. Srinivasachari, *Ananda Ranga Pillai: The Pepys of French India*, New Delhi, 1991, pp. 259-60; Haudrère, op. cit., III, p. 991; *ARP Diary*, VIII, pp. 117, 315-17; Malleson, op. cit., 2001, p. 141.
6. *ARP Diary*, VIII, pp. 113, 114, 115; Law de Lauriston, *Mémoire sur quelques affaires de l'Empire Moghole*, p. xx fn; Le Treguilly, op. cit., p. 40; Orme, *History of Indostan*. Madras, 1913, I, pp. 237, 241, 305; Régnier, Un Manuscrit Français au XVIIIème siècle: recherche de la vérité sur l'état-civil, politique et religieux des Hindous par Jacques Maissin, Paris, 1975, p. 12; Chanda Sahib's tomb is found today in an extremely dilapidated state in the Muslim cemetery adjacent to the Nathar Vali dargah of Tiruchirapalli. It is so uncared and neglected that it might disappear sooner than later.
7. *ARP Diary*, VIII, pp. 162f, 184, 194, 200, 204, 214-17; Dodwell, *Calendar of the Madras Despatches*, 1920, p. xi; Castonnet des Fosses, op. cit., p. 362.
8. *ARP Diary*, VIII, p. xxiv; Sridharan, op. cit., pp. 53-4.
9. Gracias Dom Antonio, *Les Aventures d'un pseudo-Neveu de Madame Dupleix* 1933, pp. 1-11, 14, 45 and Introduction by De Closets d'Errey; Martineau,

DECLINE OF DUPLEIX 249

Dupleix et L'Inde Française, III, 379; Favier, *Les Européens et les Indes Orientales au XVIIIe siècle*, p. 85; Lettre de Benazet de Mathon, prêtre, Pondichéry, 16 Fév. 1753, p. 7, vol. 994, AME; Lettre du 14 Fév. 1754, Mathon aux Directeurs, F. 115-16, vol. 994, AME.
10. *ARP Diary*, VIII, pp. 136, 137.
11. *ARP Diary*, VIII, pp. 149, 243-4, 264; IX, p. 336.
12. Srinivasachari, op. cit., pp. 259-60; *ARP Diary*, VIII, pp. 129, 130f, 225, 232, 236, 237, 321, 322.
13. Régnier, op. cit., p. 14; Martineau, *La Politique de Dupleix d'après sa lettre à Saunders du 18 Juin 1752*, p. 88; De Closets d'Errey, op. cit., 1934, p. 35; Dodwell, op. cit., 1989, p. 70; Y.R. Gaebelé. créole et Grande Dame . . . , Paris, 1934, p. 257.
14. I/1/1 French in India, 1664-1810, pt. 1, p. 125, IOL.
15. Hamont, op. cit., p. 273; Régnier, op. cit., 24, 26, 28, 29; Cf. More, 'Origin, Ancestry and Identity of Hyder Ali', pp. 11-28; De Closets d'Errey, op. cit., 1934, p. 35.
16. Gaebelé, *Créole et Grande Dame, Johanna Begum, Marquise Dupleix*, p. 257; *ARP Diary*, VIII, p. 336; IX, p. 12; *A Complete History of the War in India from the Year 1749 to the Taking of Pondicherry in 1761*, pp. 13-15; Law de Lauriston, *Mémoire sur quelques affaires de l'Empire Moghole*, p. xx; col. C²204, ff. 70-2, A.N.
17. *ARP Diary*, VIII, pp. 337, 343.
18. Ibid., pp. 343, 348.
19. Cultru, op. cit., pp. 321, 322; Vincent, op. cit., p. 59.
20. Gaebelé, 'Enfance et Adolescence d'Anandarangapoullé', 1955, pp. 89, 90.
21. *ARP Diary*, VIII, 273, 282, 283, 433, 444; Col.C² 85, 235, A.N.; Cultru, op. cit., pp. 321-2, 323; Col.C² 85, 359, A.N.; Naf, 9165, ff. 95-121, BNF.
22. Sridharan, op. cit., p. 48.
23. Régnier, op. cit., p. 31; Dodwell, op. cit., 1989, pp. 72, 107; *Réponse de Dupleix à la lettre du sieur Godeheu*; Malleson, op. cit., 2001, 139-45, 146, 147, 152, 153; *ARP Diary*, VIII, p. xxii.
24. *ARP Diary*, VIII, 283, 399-400, 425.
25. *ARP Diary*, IX, p. 67.
26. Régnier, op. cit., pp. 31, 32; Lettre de Dupleix à Maissin, 4 Oct. 1753, Naf 9157, ff 318sqq, BNF; Adicéam, *Géographie de l'Irrigation dans le Tamilnad*, Pondichéry, s.d. p. 171; Dodwell, op. cit., 1989, p. 74; Hamont, op. cit., p. 276.
27. Cultru, op. cit., pp. 351, 359, 362.
28. Morellet, *Mémoire sur la situation actuelle de la Compagnie des Indes*, p. 124.
29. Martineau, *Dupleix, sa vie et son œuvre*, Paris, 1931, p. 145; Martineau, op. cit., 1929, pp. 8-11, 106; Naf.9159, f. 23, BNF; Vincent, op. cit.,

pp. 58-9; Marqui de Nazelle, op. cit., p. 130; Bionne, *Dupleix*, 1881, pp. 165, 289, 291.
30. Vigie, *Dupleix*, Paris, 1993, p. 402; *ARP Diary*, IX, pp. 248, 249, 251; X, p. 21.
31. Inde, P-75, f. 575, AOM; Sridharan, op. cit., pp. 41-2.
32. *ARP Diary*, IX, p. 6, X, p. 326; XI, p. 24; XII, 260.
33. *A Complete History of the War in India from the year 1749 to the taking of Pondicherry in 1761*, pp. 13-15; Law de Lauriston, op. cit., 1913, p. xx.
34. I/1/1, French in India, 1664-1810, pt. 1, pp. 101-8, IOL; Sridharan, op. cit., pp. 47-9.
35. Hamont, op. cit., pp. 293-4; Malleson, op. cit., 2001, p. 159; Naf, 9165, ff. 95-121, BNF; *ARP Diary*, IX, p. viii; Sridharan, op. cit., pp. 42-3.
36. Oubagarasamy, *Un Livre de Compte de Ananda Ranga Poullé*, p. xxxi; *ARP Diary*, IX, p. ix; Sridharan, ibid., pp. 46-7, 48.
37. *ARP Diary*, IX, pp. 52, 62-4, 112, 116, 159, 160; Oubagarasamy, ibid., p. xxxii.
38. *ARP Diary*, IX, pp. 8, 66, 240.
39. Correspondance du Conseil Supérieur de Pondichéry avec le Conseil de Chandernagore, III? P. IV; *ARP Diary*, IX, p. 240, X, p. 279; Régnier, op. cit., p. 33; Mémoire pour le sieur dupleix . . . , 1759, p. 110; Donneaud du plan, *Histoire de la Compagnie Française de l'Inde*, Paris, 1889, p. 546.
40. *ARP Diary*, X, 317-18; XI, pp. 403-4, 416; XII, p. 183.
41. *ARP Diary*, XII, pp. 87-8.
42. Ibid., X, pp. 174-5, 221, 224; Sridharan, op. cit., pp. 42, 43; Y.R. Gaebelé, *Créole et Grande Dame . . .* , Paris, 1934, pp. 276-89.
43. Law de Lauriston, *Etat Politique de l'Inde en 1777*, Paris, 1913, pp. 15-16; Clarins de la Rive, *Dupleix ou les Français aux Indes Orientales*, Lille, 1888, pp. 186-93.
44. Martineau, *Dupleix et l'Inde Française*, III, p. 26.
45. Vinson, *Catalogue des Manuscrits Tamouls*, 1867, p. 39; Guénin, *L'Epopée Coloniale de la France racontée par les Contemporains,* Paris, 1931, pp. 156-158; Gaudart, *Catalogue . . .* ,1931, p. 100; Nield-Basu, 'The Dubashes of Madras', *Modern Asian Studies*, 18, 1, 1984; *ARP Diary*, III, p. 103; G.B. Malleson. op. cit., p. 164; Y.R. Gaebelé. *Créole et Grande Dame . . .* , Paris, 1934, pp. 294-302.

CHAPTER 12

Conclusion

THE FRENCH GOVERNORS in Pondicherry since François Martin up to Dupleix never acquired any territory for France or the French Company through outright conquest. Instead the territories that they acquired were ceded by the Indian rulers and princes on certain conditions. In the course of the first half of the eighteenth century, they wanted to acquire territories in the coastal areas, especially for the purposes of trade and in order to augment their revenues. They or their bosses in France never had any grand plan to establish a French empire in India. They were more interested in making profits through trade than conquering territories.

Dupleix himself had never claimed in any of his letters or correspondence or reports either before 1754 or after that he was acting according to a grand plan that he had conceived to establish his power or the French power in India in any way. The 'grand plan' theory is a mythology fabricated by some French historians like Jouveau Dubrueil, which does not stand the test of enquiry and reason, as we have seen above. There have been also unsuccessful attempts by some French historians to portray Dupleix as a sort of vassal or feudatory of the Mughal emperor, which would imply that Dupleix was at the service of two masters, i.e. the French king and the Indian emperor at the same time.

But since Dumas' governorship, the French had taken to interfering in the quarrels of the Indian princes and rulers, taking the side of one against the other. Dupleix following Dumas made the interference of the French in Indian quarrels into a sort of tradition and policy. He stood to gain by this initially as some Indian rulers ceded territories to him and the French mostly on certain conditions as a sort of reward for taking their side and fighting their wars.

Dupleix never understood that the Indian rulers, right from Chanda Sahib to Salabet Jung were actually making use of the French troops and sepoys as well as Dupleix to assert their authority in the evolving political struggles in the Deccan, the Carnatic and Tamil Nadu. Dupleix thought that the Indian rulers whom he helped to win the wars and become kings and nawabs were subject to him, which they were not. They never took orders from Dupleix. They acted according to their own will and interests. They were friendly with Dupleix as it served their interests and as Dupleix served their interests.

However the constant interference of Dupleix in Indian affairs as well as his continued confrontation with the English, paved the way eventually to the ascendancy of the British in Indian affairs and politics, at the expense of the French of course. As a result it is simply a misplaced nationalistic zeal to conclude like many French and other historians that Dupleix was the founder of the French empire or a European empire in India or that Englishmen like Robert Clive followed the footsteps of Dupleix in founding the British Empire in India. Contrary to Dupleix who was always at the service of the Indian rulers until he was recalled, the English though they began like Dumas and Dupleix by taking the side of one Indian prince against another, very quickly realized, unlike the French, that they can strike it on their own in India due to the never-ending internecine quarrels between the Indian princes, their better organizational and warfare skills, aided by more sophisticated arms and ammunitions and their ever-increasing domination of the high seas.

Dupleix began by confronting the English in order to improve the trade prospects of the French in Pondicherry. In this he signally failed. Next, he interfered in the Indian political struggles to augment his trade and revenue prospects. Though he scored some significant victories in the beginning and obtained several concessions from the Indian rulers, yet very quickly under the influence of his advisers, ranging from his Tamil *dubashes* to his wife and the Superior Council members, he ended up mismanaging not just the political affairs but also the trade and commercial affairs of the Company. The French Company in Paris took serious note of the ominous developments and decided to recall Dupleix to put an end to the breakdown of the management of Company affairs in India.

The French Company would not pay the debts incurred by Dupleix due to the wars. Dupleix's defence of his record in India was never

CONCLUSION

adequate. Only his death put an end to his terrible ordeal to which he was subjected by the Company. His claim or rather the claims of some French historians like Jouveau Dubrueil and Julien Vinson that he worked solely for the glory of France and never for his personal gain was not tenable in the light of what we have seen about his total mismanagement of the Company affairs in India under his governorship, the nepotism that prevailed quite rampantly during his rule and the unscrupulous amassing of wealth not only by him and his wife but also by all his relatives, officers and subordinates, both Indian and French, at the expense of the interests of the French Company and the reputation of France to a great extent. Generally politicians who are in quest for power and prestige make use of illusory ideas like nationalism in order to legitimize their actions and behaviour. Dupleix was no exception to this rule.

The conquest of Madras by the French and the defence of Pondicherry against the English had earned Dupleix and the French a certain reputation. But the year 1749 saw the re-establishment of English power in south India. Dupleix, failing in his attempts to evict the English, sought to ally thenceforth with one Indian prince against the other.

Dupleix was not a general who led his armies to war. Instead he deputed others to wage his wars, while he stayed put in Pondicherry. Therefore he was insensible to the ravages and havoc caused by the wars to the Tamil people and countryside. The height of his insensitivity can be seen when, unable to subdue the Maratha king of Tanjore, he gave orders for the destruction of the eleventh century Chola dam in Tanjore which caused the death of thousands of people and cattle and destroyed the Tanjore Tamil countryside due to inundations. This insensitivity can also be seen when he gave orders for the destruction of the Shiva temple in Pondicherry, not caring the least for the feelings of the Tamils. He renewed this psychopathic insensitivity to local Indian feelings and sensibilities when the mighty Senji Hindu temples were dismantled and under his orders the marvellous pillars of those temples were dragged to Pondicherry from Senji in bullock carts to adorn his palace in Pondicherry.

On account of his erratic policies, Pondicherry, which was relatively prosperous during the governorships of Dumas and Le Noir, dwindled not only in population but also in prosperity during his rule. Merchants were hardly attracted towards it, unlike Madras. Naturally the people of Pondicherry suffered immensely due to the consequences of the incessant wars, waged by Dupleix and his policies in general. But Dupleix was insensitive even to the pathetic condition of the people of Pondicherry under his rule. On the whole, Dupleix's insensitivity to the sufferings and feelings of the Tamil people might stem from the frustrations and failures that he underwent in his life, both private and public, as pointed out by the French historian, Legoux de Flaix.

Neither Dupleix during his lifetime, nor any French official or missionary or even the Pope who was the official head of the missionaries, either during Dupleix's governorship or later, regretted or tendered the least apology for the destruction of the temples in Pondicherry and Senji which hurt the feelings of the Tamils very much. To heap insult upon injury, in the year 1870, the French erected a magnificent statue for Dupleix in Pondicherry standing victoriously on top of the sculpted temple pillars brought from Senji during Dupleix's governorship. Though in the late nineteenth century, the French scholar Julien Vinson expressed his regrets for the destruction of the Pondicherry Shiva temple, he regretted not because the destruction hurt the feelings of the Tamils, but because in his view precious temple inscriptions, which might have shed light on Pondicherry history was lost in the process. Julien Vinson even thought that the Indians would have been better off under the benevolent and generous French colonization rather than under the mercantile and monarchical British rule, if Dupleix had won his wars.

However Dupleix adopted a different attitude towards the Muslims. When the Shiva temple was destroyed in Pondicherry, Dupleix had given orders to destroy the mosque that stood near the fort. But the Sepoy chief Abdul Rahman threatened to rise in revolt along with other Muslims if that happened. Dupleix naturally beat a hasty retreat because he was dependent on the Muslim sepoys to wage his wars. He knew that it was with the help of these sepoys that he was able to defend Pondicherry against the English in 1748. The sepoys were involved in all his wars. The English too had their own sepoys, recruited among the Indians. Thus there was certain collaboration on the part of Indians with the European rulers at the military level in the process that led to the colonization of India. This collaboration was not of course on an equal footing, as the sepoys were always subordinate to the Europeans and were their paid servants. But it is a historical fact that the Indian sepoys too participated in the conquest of India by the Europeans.

Similarly the French colonizers collaborated with the merchants of Pondicherry and Tamil Nadu in order to trade and make profits. Their *dubashes* or *diwans* or intermediaries were mostly Indians. This had given rise to the idea that the Indians merchant and colonizers were in partnership with one another on an equal footing. Nothing is more erroneous than this view because these merchants and *dubashes* were always at the service of the French.

When the *dubashes* were not Christians, all sorts of pressure were brought upon them to convert to Christianity. Besides, the *dubashes* were absolutely at the mercy of the French governors and colonizers, especially when the latter's interests collided with those of the former. The tragic and shameful treatment meted out to *dubash* Nainiappa Pillai, as well as to *dubash* Papaya Pillai and Kandappa Mudali by the French governors because they failed to toe the line of the French, must remove all doubts with regard to the idea that the French colonizers and Indian merchants were in partnership with one another or held each other in mutual respect. Instead, the *dubashes* and the merchants were always submissive to the French colonizers. Even Ananda Ranga Poullé had to resort to the art of flattery in his dealings with Dupleix, most certainly fearing that he might be subjected to the same horrible treatment as endured by his uncle, Nainiappa earlier, if he did not do so.

Of course since François Martin's time, it was the habit of the French to borrow money from Indian merchants in order to carry on with their trade. Even Dupleix borrowed money from these merchants in order to wage his wars. Besides, *dubashes* like Ananda Ranga Poullé actively encouraged Dupleix to wage his wars. This would naturally imply that the Indian merchant class too participated in their own way in the colonization of India by the Europeans, not as equal partners with the French, but rather as subordinates.

Dupleix and his predecessors as well as other French colonizers and missionaries had a high regard for their own French culture, values and religion and even food habits. Much of the Christian values were actually the values of the French. They considered themselves as culturally superior to the 'pagan' Indians in every way. They generally thought that the Indians whether Hindus or Muslims, were only fit to be converted, in order to become civilized. The missionaries especially deployed their zeal in obtaining converts, with official patronage right from François Martin's time. Dupleix and his wife were great patrons of Christianity.

Right from the time of François Martin, Christianity was favoured by the French through various means. Governors like François Martin, Le Noir and Dumas did not go to the fullest extent to extirpate Hinduism or Islam from Pondicherry, as they were more intent upon trade and revenues. In fact, they were more tolerant towards the Indians and their culture and traditions. Naturally the population of Pondicherry increased during their governorships due to migration of merchants, weavers and workers from Tamil Nadu. Pondicherry and its people were relatively prosperous. But this was not the case during the second stint of Hébert as governor and especially during the governorship of Dupleix and his coterie.

François Martin was the principal founder of modern Pondicherry. Le Noir and Dumas developed it to an appreciable extent. But during Dupleix's period, this development seems to have slackened a lot as Dupleix was mostly engaged in completing the projects started by his predecessors, besides waging incessant wars. As far as the development of Pondicherry was concerned, the credit should go to François Martin, Le Noir and Dumas more than anybody else. Unfortunately these personalities are least remembered in Pondicherry today and in historical circles. Instead Dupleix seems to have stolen the show due to the misplaced zeal, view and propaganda unleashed by some later day French historians and governors like Julien Vinson and Jouveau Dubreuil that Dupleix strove for the glory of the French nation and the affirmation of European supremacy and had laid the foundation for the conquest of India, by the English. This is not entirely surprising because men who had fought numerous wars and caused immense destruction and misery and countless killings like Alexander, Djenghiz Khan and Napoleon are glorified and held in high esteem in their respective nations and the world over more than the others. Dupleix naturally belongs to this category of men, at a lower scale of course.

The French missionaries and colonizers in India were not some isolated individuals, operating independently in Pondicherry or India. They were part of organized European structures, systems and hierarchies, which they sought to implant in India. The French East India Company based in Paris, was a multi-national trade organization, in the sense that they operated in different countries of the eastern world. Similarly Christianity was a multinational religious organization, whose headquarters was located in Rome. The French colonizers and missionaries took orders from their authorities in Paris and Rome respectively. The former were involved in trade of goods, while the latter were in the spiritual business.

While in the former there was a certain give and take, the latter only wanted to give or rather market their ideas, values and beliefs among Indians, and not take anything from them. This naturally led to a lot of friction, especially when the colonizers took the side of the missionaries, as it was the case since François Martin's time as governor. Its ultimate manifestation was during Dupleix's governorship when under the influence of Jesuit missionaries he gave orders to destroy the Shiva temple in Pondicherry.

It is wrong to think that only goods can be marketed. Even ideas, values and beliefs or rather culture, disconnected from actual facts, needs to be marketed also. The marketing processes of goods and ideas are similar. Both aim to dominate the minds of the people through various means including coercion, persuasion, violence and force. It is quite obvious that in Pondicherry Dupleix sought to dominate trade also through force, coercion and violence, while the European missionaries with the help of the colonizers sought to impose Christianity on the local people by resorting to the same force, coercion and violence, though they also employed other techniques of marketing their beliefs and culture like persuasion, propaganda, preaching, etc.

The Tamils were living in a world of their own, with their caste system, priests, temples, shastras, astrologers, traditions and customs. Divided as they were on caste and religious lines, the question of nationalism of the European type never arose among them. They were largely oblivious to the fact that they were directly and indirectly being confronted with a new way of life i.e. the European way of life in their own lands.

European arrival and presence in India heralded the beginning of a cultural clash between the Europeans and Indians. It was for the Indians to gradually adopt and adapt to the European way of life and the colonial system that they put in place in the territories under their control, and not the other way round for obvious reasons. This was pointed out by none other than Dupleix himself when he remarked casually to Ananda Ranga Poullé, that he, a strict follower of Hindu traditions and customs, had taken to having his meagre food on a table, seated in a chair, like the Europeans, instead of the traditional habit of squatting on the floor to eat. This was the beginning of the Europeanization or rather modernization of the Indian/Tamil culture as abserved by Dupleix himself. Of course, Ananda Ranga Poullé was not in a position to take note of the implications of this crucial remark of Dupleix, in spite of all his erudition.

Therefore it is wrong to assume generally like Holden Furber that there was mutual respect and cooperation between the Indians and Europeans in the early phase of colonization. As far as the French in Pondicherry were concerned, we cannot even assume like P.J. Marshall that there was a sort of 'master-bania' relationship between the French and the Tamils/Indians. Instead, the relationship had all the trappings of a 'master-subordinate' relationship, where the subordinate eventhough he might be *dubash* was always at the mercy of the colonizers. Ananda Ranga Poullé was pleased to call himself the 'slave' of Dupleix. Of course, the element of force and violence was omnipresent in the European presence, trade and colonization of India as pointed out by Irfan Habib and as we have seen in the preceding pages.

In the year 1870, Joseph François Dupleix's gigantic life-size statue was erected at Place Dupleix (Dupleix Square) in front of the beach. It stood above Hindu sculpted pillars brought from Senji during Dupleix's period. But after the integration of Pondicherry with India in 1954, this statue was removed to the premsies of the French Consulate, as it was held that it hurt the feelings of the Hindus, as the statue stood above Hindu sculpted columns. Later Joseph François Dupleix's gigantic dark statue was shunted to one corner of Pondicherry in the southern end of the Pondicherry beach, adjacent to a public toilet and a private guest house that blocks the expansion of the beach towards the south.

The statue of the Indian nationalist Jawaharlal Nehru has taken the place of Dupleix's statue in Place Dupleix, though he had nothing to do with the history of that place historically speaking. In front of Nehru's statue, a gigantic statue of Mahatma Gandhi, the Father of the Indian nation had come up at the very place which served as port, where French colonizers and settlers right from François Martin and also of course Dupleix disembarked.

Nobody even knows that it was Dupleix who built the rampart and the wall on the beach to protect Pondicherry from the bombardments of the English.

There is not even a plaque to remind the curious visitor the contribution of Dupleix to the development of Pondicherry beach as we find it today. But his statue relegated to one corner stares helplessly at the passers by and the curious visitor who come in swarms today to enjoy the breeze of the beach and the beauty of the beach itself, that owes its existence to Dupleix.

The road named after him as Rue Dupleix (previously known as Vazhudavur Road) had acquired more nationalisitic nomenclature and today it is known as Jawaharlal Nehru Street. But Ananda Ranga Poullé, who was collaborator of Dupleix and who had encouraged and advised Dupleix in all his warlike adventures, was more fortunate. He did not face the axe of the nationalists due mainly to the Diary he produced. His name has been retained for the road on which the Governor's palace is located as Rue Ananda Ranga Pillai. This road was previously known as Rue du Magasin du Tabac (Tobacco Shops Road). There is even a library of the Pondicherry University named after him. Nobody remembers Dupleix's wife name in the Pondicherry of today or the role that she played in the history of Pondicherry by the side of Dupleix. Her memory has simply sunk into oblivion.

It is significant to note nevertheless that Ananda Ranga Poullé stands out as the typical example of Indian collaborators in the European colonial enterprise in India. He never for a moment thought in terms of the interests of Indians or Tamils during his tenure as *diwan* of Dupleix. He aided and abetted Dupleix in all his perilous and murderous adventures in the Tamil country and south India and also encouraged him to become the *badshah* of India. His role in the devastation of the Tamil countryside and the killings of numerous Tamilian people, as advisor to Dupleix, was as great as that of Dupleix himself. Dupleix was insensitive to the feelings and sufferings of the Tamils. But Ananda Ranga Poullé was no better. Without the collaboration of such charecters, Europeans would never have colonized India. Besides, men like Abdul Rehman and his brother Sheikh Hassan lent the military muscle to European colonial enterprise.

Abdul Rehman and Sheikh Hassan are of course forgotten by the people of Pondicherry and south India. But Ananda Ranga Poullé, the prime collaborator in the European colonial enterprise is celebrated even today in Pondicherry and south India, whereas his uncle Nainiappa Poullé, who was also diwan earlier for about ten years, sacrificed his life and wealth and his diwanship, for the sake of what he considered as purely Indian interests. He met with the most appalling and tragic death in the humid dungeon of Fort St. Louis, which stood in what is known as Bharati *Poonga* or Park today. Nainiappa Poullé has simply vanished from the memory of Pondicherrians and south Indians, though he had heroically resisted colonial and missionary enterprises in his own way in the early days of colonization. A small obscure road is named after him in a corner of southern Pondiccherry. That is what remains of him as memory today, whereas his nephew Ananda Ranga Poullé is hailed as one of the greats of Pondicherry and Tamil Nadu history, in spite of his collaborative role with the colonizers. Ananda Ranga Poullé reaped of course huge benefits for himself and his family and descendants due to this collaborative role, which laid the foundations of European colonialism in India. I do not think that any other *diwan* or *dubash* or intermediary of the European colonisers in India, had done more than Ananda Ranga Poullé, to hasten the subjugation and colonization of India by Europeans.

However, there was one positive aspect of Dupleix's presence in Pondicherry. Though he had caused many wars, killings and damages in the Tamil country and south India, yet he had made Pondicherry as the centre of his political action in south India during his governorship. He thus raised the status of Pondicherry at the national and international level from a relatively obcure French colony to the main theatre of action for the French in south India. As governor of Pondicherry, Dupleix of course was the king-maker. But he was never the king. He had no grand design to found a French colonial empire in India. But he etched Pondicherry thenceforth in the national map of India, Europe and France. This was to have a long lasting impact, both for the French and the Pondicherrians/Indians who would never want to part with this legacy of Dupleix which conferred a unique Franco-Indian identity for Pondicherry, embedded in history.

Bibliography

ARCHIVES AND LIBRARIES

Archives des Missions Etrangères, Paris
Archives du Ministères des Affaires Etrangères, Paris
Archives Nationales, Paris
Archives d'Outre-mer, Aix-en-Provence, France
Bibliothèque Arsenal, Paris
Bibliothèque Internationale de Documentation Contemporaine, Paris
Bibliothèque Municipale de Versailles, Versailles
Bibliothèque Nationale de France, Paris
British Library, St. Pancras, London
Centre d'études de l'Inde, Paris
Centre de Documentation Française, Nanterre, Nanterre
Ecole Française d'Extrême Orient, Paris and Pondicherry
Institut Français de Pondichéry, Pondicherry
Institut National de Langues et Civilisations Orientales, Paris
National Archives of India, Pondicherry
Romain Roland Library, Pondicherry
University of Pondicherry Library

PERIODICALS

Epigraphia Indica
Indian Antiquary
Le Semeur, Catholic monthly of Pondicherry
Neithal Kural (Tamil monthly)
Revue Historique de l'Etat de Pondichéry
Revue Historique de l'Inde Française

INTERVIEWS

Bouchet, Jacqueline, Dr. Editor of *Lettre du C.I.D.I.F.*, France, old resident of Pondicherry.
Bouchet, Roland, editor of *Lettre du C.I.D.I.F.*, Boulogne.
Antony, Cyril, editor of the Gazetteer of Pondicherry, hailing from Nagerkovil
Annoussamy, Justice David, former Madras Court Judge, hailing from Pondicherry.

Kessavaram, J. of Pondicherry, late ex-Attaché Commercial, French consulate, Calcutta.
Mannar Mannan, writer, poet and son of Tamil poet Barathidasan of Pondicherry
Mathurakavy, Veera, retired Tamil teacher and journalist.
Nallam, Dr. Chevalier. Prominent physician of Yanam, settled in Pondicherry
Sala, Georges, late French Administrator of Yanam.
Subbiah, Saraswati, late Pondicherry Communist party leader V. Subbiah's wife, social activist.
Perrier, Yves, late Franco-Indian official and administrator of French Pondicherry.

BOOKS

Adicéam, Emmanuel, *Géographie de l'Irrigation dans le Tamilnad,* Pondicherry, s.d.
Adigal, Ilango, *Cilapatikaram,* ed. V.V. Saminatha Iyer, Madras, 1924.
Aiyangar, Krishnaswami, *South India and her Muhammadan Invaders,* London, 1921.
Alalasundaram, R., *The Colonial World of Ananda Ranga Pillai, 1736-1761, The Only Native Account,* Pondicherry, 1998.
———, *Some Sketches from Ananda Ranga Pillai, 1736-1761,* Pondicherry, 2001.
Ames, Glenn, Joseph and Ronald S. Love (eds.), *Distant Lands and Diverse Cultures: The French Experience in Asia, 1600-1700,* Westport, 2003.
Antony, Cyril, *Gazetteer of Pondicherry,* 2 vols., Pondicherry, 1982.
Anquetil-Duperron, *Recherche Historique et Géographique sur l'Inde,* Paris, 1786-8, 3 vols.
———, *L'Inde en rapport avec l'Europe,* Paris, An. VII, 2 vols.
Arasaratnam, S., *Merchants, Companies and Commerce on the Coromandel Coast 1650-1800,* Delhi, 1986.
———, *Maritime Trade, Society and European Influence in Southern India, 1600-1800,* Hampshire, 1995.
Arasaratnam, S. and Aniruddha Ray, *Masulipatnam and Cambay: A History of Two Port-towns,* New Delhi, 1994.
Aravanan, Ka. Pa., *Anandarangar Natkurippu Aayvu,* Puduchery, 1992.
———, *Islamiyar Kalat Tamizh Makkal Varalaru,* Chennai, 2012.
———, *Tamizh Makkal Varalaru, Nayakar Kaalam,* Chennai, 2013.
Ayyar, Narayana C.V., *Origin and Early History of Saivism in South India.* Madras, 1936.
Bamboat, Zenobia, *Les Voyageurs Français dans l'Inde aux XVIIe et XVIIIe siècles,* Paris, 1933.
Bayly, Susan, *Saints, Goddesses and Kings: Muslims and Christians in South Indian Society, 1700-1900,* Cambridge, 1989.

Bernier, François, *Voyages de Bernier*, Amsterdam, 2 vols., 1699.
Bhandarkar, R.G., *Early History of the Dekkan Down to the Mohammedan Conquest*, Calcutta, 1957.
Biddulph, John, *Dupleix*, London, 1918.
Bionne, Henri, *Dupleix*, Paris, 1881.
Bonnassieux, Pierre, *Conseil de Commerce et Bureau de Commerce, 1700-1791, Inventaire Analytique des procès-verbaux*, Paris, 1900.
Boscawen, Edward, *Relation du Siège de Pondichéry*, levé par les Anglais le 17 Octobre 1748, Bruxelles, 1766.
Boudriot, Jean, *Compagnie des Indes, 1720-1770*, Paris, 1983.
Bourdat, Pierre, *Eighteenth Century Pondicherry*, Pondicherry, 1995.
———, *Les Grandes Pages du 'Journal' d'Ananda Ranga Pillai. Courtier de la Compagnie des Indes auprès des gouverneurs de Pondichéry (1736-1760)*, Paris, 2003.
Bourdonnais, A. Mahé de la (ed.), *Mémoire Historique de B.F. Mahé de la Bourdonnais, Gouverneur des Iles de France et Bourbon*, Paris, 1827, 1890 (rpt.).
Boxer, C.R., *Portuguese Conquest and Commerce in Southern Asia, 1500-1750*, London, 1985.
Braudel, Fernand, *Capitalism and Material Life, 1400-1800*, London, 1985.
Cambridge, R.O., *An Account of the War in India between the English and the French on the Coast of Coromandel for the Year 1750 to the Year 1760*, London, 1761.
Carré, Henri, *François Martin, Fondateur de l'Inde française, 1665-1706*, Abbaye S. Wandrille, 1946.
Castonnet des Fosses, *Le R.P. Charles de Montalembert*, Paris, 1886.
———, *L'Inde Française avant Dupleix*, Paris, 1887.
———, *L'Inde Française au XVIIIème siècle*, Paris, s.d.
———, *Dupleix, ses expéditions et ses projets*, Paris, 1888.
———, *La Rivalité de Dupleix et La Bourdonnais*, Paris, 1888.
———, *La Chute de Dupleix: ses causes et ses conséquences*, Anger, 1888.
———, *Dupleix. Ses Dernières Luttes dans l'Inde*, Paris, 1889.
Campbell, Thomas J., *The Jesuits 1534-1921*, vol. I, London, 1921.
Celestine, P., *Early Capuchin Missions in India: Pondicherry, Surat, Madras 1632-1834)*, Sahibabad, 1982.
Chagniot, Jean, *Les Temps Modernes de 1661 à 1789*, Vendôme, 1973.
Charpentier de Cossigny, *Lettre Critique sur l'Histoire des Indes Orientales de l'Abbé Guyon*, Genève, 1744.
Chassaigne, M., *Bussy en Inde*, Chartres, 1976.
Chaudhuri, K.N., *The Trading World of Asia and the English East India Company, 1660-1760*, Cambridge, 1978.
Clarins de la Rive, A., *Dupleix ou les Français aux Indes Orientales*, Lille, 1888.

Cobban, A., *A History of Modern France*, 4 vols. London, 1962.
Cohn, Bernard, *Colonialism and its Forms of Knowledge: The British in India*, Princeton, 1996.
Cojandé, Dairianadin, *Les Deux Premiers Modeliars de la Compagnie des Indes*, Pondicherry, 1975.
———, *Mémoire de Me. Pedro Canagarayamoudeliar*, Pondichéry, 1984.
Cole, Charles Woolsey, *Colbert and a Century of French Mercantalism*, 2 vols, New York, 1939.
Correia-Afonso, J., *Jesuit Letters and Indian History, 1542-1773*, Bombay, 1955.
Cotton, Julian James, *Inscriptions on Tombs or Monuments in Madras Presidency*, Madras, 1905.
Crepin, Pierre, *Mahé de la Bourdonnais, gouverneur-général des Iles de France et de Bourbon (1699-1753)*, Paris, 1922.
Cultru, Prosper, *Dupleix, ses plans politiques, sa disgrâce, Etude d'Histoire Coloniale*, Paris, 1901.
Dagliesh, W.H., *The Company of the Indies in the days of Dupleix, 1722-54*, Philadelphia, 1933.
———, *La Compagnie des Indes au temps de Dupleix*, Seaton, 1938.
Darwin, Charles, *On the Origin of Species*, Cambridge, 1966 (rpt.).
David, Georgette, *Pondichéry. Porte de l'Inde,* Paris, 1999.
———, *Pondichéry. Des Comptoirs Français à l'Inde d'aujourd'hui*, Paris, 2004.
De Barros, Joao, *Asia. Primeira Decada*, Lisboa, MCMXLX.
De Cossigny, Charpentier, *Replique de M. Cossigny à la réponse injurieuse de M. l'Abbé Guyon au sujet de la lettre critique sur l'Historie des Indes Orientales*, Francfort, 1744.
De Closets d'Errey, Henry (ed.), *Résumé des Lettres du Conseil Supérieur de Pondichéry à divers*, 2 vols., Paris, 1933.
De Closets d'Errey, Henri, *Résumé des Lettres du Conseil Supérieur de Pondichéry à divers, du 1 Aôut 1725 au 31 Décembre 1742 et du 8 Décembre 1749 au 14 Novembre 1760*, Paris, 1933.
———, *Précis Chronologique de l'Histoire de l'Inde Française (1664-1816)*, Paris, 1934.
———, *Résumé des Lettres du Conseil Provincial de Madras avec Mahé de La Bourdonnais. Dupleix, le Conseil Supérieur et divers*, Paris, 1936.
———, *Résumé des Actes de l'Etat Civil de Pondichéry, de 1761 à 1784*, Tome III, Paris, 1937.
———, *Histoire de l'Inde Française, 1664-1814. Institutions Religieuses et Artisanales de l'Inde, son folklore*, Paris, 1940.
De Place, Agnès. *Dictionnaire Généalogique et Armorial de l'Inde Française, 1560-1962*, Paris, 1997.
Dehaines, Chrétien, *Dupleix. Notes Biographiques et Historiques*, Lille, 1888.
Delacroix, S. (ed.), *Histoire Universelle des Missions Catholiques. Les Missions Modernes*, II, Paris, 1957.

BIBLIOGRAPHY

Deloche, Jean, *Senji (Gingee) A Fortified City in the Tamil Country*, Pondicherry, 2000.

———, *Le Papier Terrier de la Ville Blanche de Pondichéry, 1777*, Pondicherry, 2002.

———, *Origins of the Urban Development of Pondicherry according to Seventeenth Century Dutch Plans*, Pondicherry, 2004.

———, *Le Vieux Pondichéry 1673-1824, revisité d'après les plans anciens*. Pondicherry, 2005.

———, *Pondicherry: Past and Present*, Pondicherry, 2007.

———, *Old Mahé (1721-1817) According to the Eighteenth Century French Plans*, Pondicherry, 2013.

Dernis, Elie, *Recueil des titres, édits, déclarations, arrêts, règlements et autres pièces concernant la Compagnie des Indes Orientales établie au mois d'Août 1664*, 4 vols., Paris, 1755.

Deveze, M., *Histoire de la Colonisation Française en Amérique et aux Indes au XVIIIème siècle*, Paris, 1948.

Diagou, Gnanou, *Principe de Droit Hindou*, I, Pondicherry, 1929.

Diagou, Gnanou (ed.), *Arrêts du Conseil Supérieur de Pondichéry*, 6 vols. Pondicherry, 1935-41.

Dikshitar, V.R. Ramachandra, *The Cilappatikaram*, Tirunelveli, 1978 (1st pub. 1939).

Dodwell, H., *The Records of Fort St. George, French Correspondance, 1750 and 1751; the Siege of Madras, 1758-1759*, Madras, 1914.

———, *Report on the Madras Records*, Madras, 1916.

———, *A Calendar of Madras Records, 1740-1744*, Madras, 1917.

———, *Calendar of the Madras Despatches, 1744-1758*, Madras, 1920.

———, *Dupleix and Clive: The Beginning of Empire*, London, 1967, 1989 (rpt.).

Dodwell, H. and Frederick Price (eds.), *The Private Diary of Ananda Rangapillai – Dubash to Joseph François Dupleix, Governor of Pondicherry: A Record of Matters Political, Historical, Social and Personal from 1736 to 1761*, New Delhi, 1985.

Donneaud du Plan, *Histoire de la Compagnie Française de l'Inde*, Paris, 1889.

Druon, Henri, *Les Français dans l'Inde au XVIIe et XVIIIe siècles. Martin, Dumas, Dupleix, La Bourdonnais, Bussy, de Bellecombe, Suffren*, Paris, 1886.

Duarte, Adrian, *Les Premières Relations entre les Français et les Princes Indigènes dans l'Inde au XVIIe siècle (1666-1706)*, Paris, 1932.

Dubois, J.A., *Hindu Manners, Customs and Traditions*, Oxford, 1906.

Du Fresne de Francheville, *Histoire de la Compagnie des Indes avec les titres de ses concessions et privilèges, dressée sur les pièces authentiques*, Paris, 1746, 1788 (nouvelle édition).

Duperron, Anquetil, *L'Inde en rapport avec l'Europe*, Paris, 1798.

———, *Législation Orientale*, Tome I, Amsterdam, 1778.

———, *Observatons: Paulin de Saint Barthélémy. Voyage aux Indes Orientales*, T. III, Paris, 1808.
Duplais, Léonie, *L'Amiral Dupleix*, Paris, 1885.
Dupleix, Joseph François, *La Politique de Dupleix d'après sa lettre de Saunders du 18 Février 1752 et son mémoire du 16 Octobre 1753*, 1927, microfilm, BNF.
Dupleix, Marquis Joseph François, *Catalogue des Manuscrits concernant Joseph François Marquis*.
Dupleix, *Gouverneur-Général des Etablissements Français dans l'Inde, appartenant à M. Le Marquis de Nazelle*, Laon, 1903.
Dupuis, J., *Les Ghats Orientaux et la plaine du Coromandel*, Pondichéry, 1959.
Duquesne, *Journal d'un Voyage fait aux Indes Orientales*, Rouen, 1721.
Elliot, Sir Walter, *Coins of South India*, London, 1886.
Esquer, A., *Essai sur les Castes dans l'Inde*, Pondicherry, 1870.
Fabre des Essarts, Alfred, *Dupleix et l'Inde Française*, Paris, 1886.
Favier, René, *Les Européens et les Indes Orientales au XVIIIe siècle*, Paris, 1997.
Ferroli, D., *The Jesuits in Malabar*, Bangalore, 1951.
Filliozat, Jean, *Catalogue du Fonds Sanscrit*, Paris, 1941.
Forrest, Sir George, *The Life of Lord Clive*, Delhi, 1986.
Foster, Sir William, *History of the East India Company*, London, 1925, 1926.
Francis, W., *Madras District Gazetteers, South Arcot*, Madras, 1906.
Froideveaux, H. and A. Martineau, *Histoire des Colonies Françaises et de l'Expansion de la France dans le monde*. V, Inde, Paris, 1932.
Furber, Holden, *Rival Empires of Trade in the Orient, 1600-1800*, Minneapolis, 1976.
Gadjindrin, Baskara, *Historie de Podichéry de l'An 1000 à nos jours*, Pondicherry, 2004.
Gaebelé, Yvonne Robert, *Créole et Grande Dame, Johanna Begum, Marquise Dupleix*, Pondicherry, 1934.
———, *Marquise Dupleix, 1706-1756*, Pondicherry, 1956.
Gaebelé, Yvonne Robert, *Histoire de Pondichéry de l'An 1000 à nos jours*. Pondicherry, 1960.
Gaebelé, Yvonne Robert and K. Sadagobane, *Catalogue Général des Livres de la Bibliothèque Publique de Pondichéry*, Pondicherry, 1960.
Gallois-Montbrun, M.A., *Notice sur la Chronique en langue tamoule et sur la vie d'Ananda Ranga Pillai'*, Pondicherry, 1849.
Garstin, J.H., *Manual of South Arcot District*. Madras, 1878.
Gaudart, Edmond, *Procès-verbaux des délibérations du Conseil Supérieur de Pondichéry (1701-1741)*, Pondichéry, 1913-36, 6 vols.
Gaudart, Edmond, *Les Archives de Madras et l'Histoire de l'Inde Française. Première Partie. Période de François Martin. 1674-1707*, Pondicherry, 1936.
———, *Catalogue des Manuscrits des anciennes archives de l'Inde Française*, 8 vols. Pondicherry, 1927-42.

BIBLIOGRAPHY

———, *Exposition Coloniale Internationale*, Paris, 1931.
———, *Catalogue de Quelques Documents des Archives de Pondichéry*, Paris, 1931.
———, *Les Privilèges du Commerce Français dans l'Inde*, Pondicherry, 1935.
———, *La Criminalité dans les Etablissements Français de l'Inde*, Pondicherry, 1938.
Gaudart, Michel, *Généalogie des familles de l'Inde Française, XVIe-XXe siècles*, Eaubonne, 1976.
Gautier, Judith, *Dupleix*, Vincennes, 1912.
Gennes, Pierre de, *Mémoire pour le sieur de La Bourdonnais avec les pièces justificatives*, Paris, 1750.
Géringer et Chabrelie, *L'Inde Française, ou Collections de dessins représentant les divinités, temples, meubles, ornements, armes, ustensiles, cérémonies religieuses et scènes de la vie privée . . . des peuples hindous qui habitent les possessions françaises de l'Inde*, dessinée par Géringer et Chabrelie, 2 vols., Paris, 1827.
Gopalakrishnan, Orsay, M., *Ananda Ranga Pillai Natkurippu (1751-1752)*, Chidambaram, 2003.
Gordon, Stuart, *The Marathas, 1600-1818*, Cambridge, 1993.
Gracias, Ismail, J., Dom Antonio José de Noronha. Evêque d'Halicarnasse. *Les Aventures d'un pseudo-Neveu de Madame Dupleix (1720-1776)*, tr. From Portuguese with Introduction by De Closets d'Errey, Paris, 1933.
Guet, M.I., *Origines de l'Inde Française*, Paris, 1892.
Guérin, Eugène, *Dupleix*, d'après les documents inédits tirés des archives publiques et privées de France et d'Angleterre, Paris, 1908.
Guénin, G., *L'Epopée Coloniale de la France racontée par les Contemporains*, Paris, 1931.
Guyon, Abbé, *Histoire des Indes Orientales. Anciennes et modernes*, 3 vols., Paris, 1744.
Gupta, Ashin Das and M.N. Pearson (eds.), *India and the Indian Ocean, 1500-1800*, Calcutta, 1987.
Hamilton, A., *A New Account of the East Indies*, 2 vols., Edinburgh, 1727.
Hamont, Tibulle, *Un Essai d'Empire français dans l'Inde aux XVIIIème siècles. Dupleix d'après sa Correspondance inédite*, Paris, 1881.
Harris, J., *History of the French East India Company*, London, 1744.
Hatalkar, V.G., *The Relation between the French and the Marathas*, Bombay, 1958.
Haudrère, Philippe, *La Compagnie Française des Indes au XVIIIe siècle, 1719-1795*, 4 vols., Paris, 1989.
Haudrère, Philippe (ed.), *Les Français dans l'Océan Indien au XVIIIe siècle. Un Mémoire inédit de la Bourdonnais, 1733 et Journal du Voyage fait aux Indes sous les ordres de la Bourdonnais, 1746 par M. de Rostaing*, Paris, 2004.
Heras, J., *The Aravidu Dynasty of Vijayanagar*, I, Madras, 1927.
Herpin, E., *Mahé de la Bourdonnais et la Compagnie des Indes*, Saint-Brieuc, 1905.

Hultzsch, E. *South Indian Inscriptions,* Madras, I, 1890.
Hultzsch, E. and V. Venkayya, *South Indian Inscpritions,* II, Madras, 1916.
Hultzsch, Eugen (ed. & tr.), *South Indian Inscriptions,* III, Madras, 1899-1903.
Johnston, William (tr.), *Fra Paolina Da San Bartolomeo: A Voyage to the East Indies,* London, MDCCC.
Josselin, *Histoire de l'Inde Française, 1664-1814,* Pondicherry, 1940.
Jouveau-Dubreuil, G., *Ancient History of the Deccan,* tr. V.S. Swaminatha Dikshitar, Pondicherry, 1920
———, *Dupleix ou l'Inde Conquise,* Pondicherry, 1941.
Kaeppelin, Paul, *Les Origines de l'Inde Française, La Compagnie des Indes Orientales et François Martin, 1664-1719,* Paris, 1908.
Kalladan, K. (ed.), *Puduchery Marapum Maanpum,* Puducherry, 2002.
Kanakasabhai, V., *The Tamils eighteen Hundred Years Ago,* New Delhi, 1997.
Karashima, Noboru, *South Indian History and Society: Studies from Inscriptions A.D. 850-1800,* Delhi, 1984.
Kieffer, Jean Luc, *Anquetil-Duperron: l'Inde en France au XVIIIème siècle,* Paris, 1983.
Kormocar, Kalichorone, C., *Dupleix et Chandernagore,* Calcutta, 1963.
Krishnaswami, T.B., *South Arcot in Sacred Songs,* Omalur, 1937.
Kumar, Sampath and Carof André (tr. & ed.), *History of Pondicherry Mission: An Outline,* Pondicherry, 1999.
Kuppusamy, S. *Kalvettukalil Puthuvai Pakuthigal,* Puthuvai, 1974.
Kuppuswamy, S. Bahour (comp.), G. Vijayavenugopal (ed.), *Pondicherry Inscriptions,* I, Pondicherry and Paris, 2006.
———, *Putucceri Manilakkalvettukkal,* II, Pondicherry, 2010.
La Croze, M.V., *Histoire du Christianisme des Indes,* La Haye, 1758.
La Farelle, E., Lennel de (published by) *Mémoire et Correspondances du Chevalier et du Général de la Farelle,* Paris, 1896.
La Porte, Eugène, *Catalogue Général des Livres de la Bibliothèque Publique de Pondichéry,* Pondicherry, 1942.
Labernadie, M.V., *Le Vieux Pondichéry (1753-1815), Histoire d'une ville coloniale française,* Pondicherry, 1936.
Lafrenez, Jean, *Précis d'Histoire de la Mission de Pondichéry,* Pondichéry, 1953.
Lambropoulos, Vassili, *The Rise of Eurocentrism,* Princeton, 1996.
Laude, F.N., *Dupleix. Le Siège de Pondichéry en 1748. Extraits des mémoires inédits de Rangapoullé,* Pondichéry, 1870.
Launay, Adrien, *Histoire des Missions de l'Inde – Pondichéry, Maïssour, Coimbatore.* Paris, 1898.
Law de Lauriston, Jean, *Mémoire sur quelques affaires de l'Empire Moghole, 1756-1761,* Paris, 1913.
———, *Etat Politique de l'Inde en 1777,* Paris, 1913.
Le Goux de Flaix, *Essai dur l'Indostan,* 2 vols., Paris, 1817.

Le Fèvre, Claude Noël, *Eloge Historique de Dupleix*, Paris, 1818.

Le Gentil, *Voyage dans les mers de l'Inde fait par ordre du roi à l'occasion du passage de Vénus sur le disque du soleil le 6 Juin 1761 et le 3 du même mois 1769*, 2 vols., Paris, 1779-81.

Legoux de Flaix, *Essai sur l'Indoustan avec le tableau de son Commerce*, 2 vols., Paris, 1807.

Le Mascrier, Abbé Jean Baptiste, *Histoire de la Dernière Révolution des Indes Orientales*, 2 vols., Paris, 1757.

Le Treguilly Ph. and Morazé Monique (eds.), *L'Inde et la France. Deux siècles d'histoire commune (XVIIe – XVIIIe), Histoire, sources, bibliographie*, Paris, 1995.

Lehuraux, Alfred, *La Découverte de Dupleix-Fatheabad*, Pondichéry, 1944.

Logan, William, *Malabar Manual*, Madras, 1889.

Longchampt, E., *Dupleix et la politique coloniale sous Louis XV*, Reims, 1886.

Love, Henry Davison, *Vestiges of Old Madras. 1640-1800*, London, 1913.

Lucenay, L. Dupleix, *Conquérant des Indes Fabuleuses*, Paris, 1946.

Luillier, le sieur, *Nouveau Voyage aux Grandes Indes avec Instructions pour le Commerce*, Rotterdam, 1726.

Lyall, Sir Alfred, *British Dominion in India*, London, 1893.

Mac Pherson, David, *The History of European Commerce with India*, London, 1812.

Malleret, Louis, *Pierre Poivre (1719-1786)*, Paris, 1974.

Malleson, G.B., *Dupleix*, London, 1891, 2001 (re-edition).

———, *History of the French in India from the Founding of Pondicherry in 1674 to the Capture of that Place in 1761*, London, 1893.

Manet, Raghunath, *Les Bayadères, danseuses Sacrées du temple de Villenour*, Pondicherry, 1995.

Manickam, M., *Trade and Commerce in Pondicherry (1701-1793)*, Tellicherry, 2001.

Manning, Catherine, *The Intermediaries: South Indian Traders and their Relation with the French, 1720-1750*, Cambridge, 1988.

———, *Fortunes à Faire. The French in Asian Trade, 1719-1748*, Aldershot, 1996.

Manucci, Niccolao, *Storia Do Mogor or Mogul India – 1653-1708*, tr. William Irvine, 4 vols., London, 1907-8.

———, *A Pepys of Mogul India 1653-1708* (Abridged edn.), London, 1913.

Marcel de Fréville, *Une Année Coloniale au XVIIIème siècle. Dupleix aux Indes*, Paris, 1904.

Margry, Pierre, *Relations et Mémoires inédits pour servir à l'histoire de la France dans les Pays d'outre-mer, tiré des archives du Ministère des Colonies*, Paris, 1867.

Marquis de Nazelle, *Dupleix et la Défense de Pondichéry*, Paris, 1908.

Marshall, P. J., *East India Fortunes: The British in Bengal in the Eighteenth Century*, Oxford, 1976.
Martin, François, *Mémoire de François Martin, fondateur de Pondichéry (1665-1694)*, 3 vols., Paris, 1931-4.
Martineau, A., *Lettres et Conventions des Gouverneurs de Pondichéry avec les divers princes Indiens, 1666 à 1783*, Pondicherry, 1911.
———, *Inventaire des Anciennes Archives de l'Inde Française*, Pondichéry, 1914.
———, *Les Origines de Mahé de Malabar*, Paris, 1917.
———, *Correspondance du Conseil Supérieur de Pondichéry et de la Compagnie*, Pondicherry, 1920-34, 6 vols.
———, *Résumé des actes de l'état-civil de Pondichéry de 1676 à 1735*, I, Pondicherry, 1917; II, de 1736 à 1760, Pondicherry, 1919-20.
———, *La Politique de Dupleix d'après sa lettre à Saunders du 18 Juin 1752 et sa mémoire du 16 Octobre 1753*, Pondicherry, 1927.
———, *Dupleix et l'Inde Française*, 4 vols., Paris, 1920-8.
———, *Les Dernières Années de Dupleix, Ses Dettes et ses procès avec la Compagnie des Indes*, Paris, 1929.
———, *Dupleix, sa vie et son œuvre*, Paris, 1931.
———, *Bussy et l'Inde Française, 1720-1785*, Paris, 1935.
———, *Bussy in the Deccan*, Paris, 1941.
Marquis de Nazelle, *Dupleix et la Défense de Pondichéry*, Paris, 1908.
Mathew, K.S. and S.J. Stephen (eds.), *Indo-French Relations*, Delhi, 1996.
Mathew, K.S. (ed.), *Indian Ocean and Cultural Interaction A.D. 1400-1800*, Pondicherry, 1996.
———, (ed.), *French in India and Indian Nationalism 1700 A.D.-1963 A.D.*, 2 vols., Delhi, 1993.
Mentz, Soren, *The English Gentleman Merchant at Work: Madras and the City of London, 1600-1740*, Copenhagen, 2001.
Misoffe, Michel, *Dupleix et La Bourdonnais*, Paris, 1943.
More, J.B.P., *Freedom Movement in French India: The Mahé Revolt of 1948*, Tellicherry, 2001.
———, *L'Inde Face à Bharati. Le Poète Rebelle*, Tellicherry, 2003.
———, *Maridas Poullé of Pondicherry, 1725-1796: A Pioneer of Modern Indological Studies and the First Modern Exponent of Indian Philosophy, Religion and Literature*, Pondicherry, 2004.
———, *Muslim Identity, Print Culture and the Dravidian Factor in Tamilnadu*, Hyderabad, 2004.
———, *The Telugus of Yanam and Masulipatnam: From French Rule to Integration with India*, Pondicherry, 2007.
———, *Rise and Fall of the 'Dravidian' Justice Party 1916-1946*, Tellicherry, 2009.

BIBLIOGRAPHY

———, *Portuguese Interactions with Malabar an its Muslims in the 16th Century*, Pondicherry, 2013.
———, *From Arikamedu to the Foundation of Modern Pondicherry*, Chennai, 2014.
———, *Origin and Foundation of Madras*, Chennai, 2016.
More, J.B.P. (ed.), *La Civilisation Indienne et Les Fables Hindoues du Panchatantra de Maridas Poullé*, Pondicherry, 2004.
———, *Offerings to the Muslim Warriors of Malabar: Foundation Document of Colonialism and Clash of Civilisations*, Chennai, 2015.
More, Leena, *English East India Company and the Local Rulers in Kerala: A Case Study of Attingal and Travancore*, Tellicherry, 2003.
Moreel, Léon, *Dupleix, Marquis de Fortune et Conquérant de l'Inde*, Dunquerque, 1963.
Morellet, Abbé, *Mémoire sur la situation actuelle de la Compagnie des Indes*, Paris, 1769.
———, *Recueil des titres, édits, déclarations, arrêts, règlements, etc., concernant la Compagnie des Indies Orientales (1664-1788)*, 3 vols., Paris, 1765-89.
Nainar Husain, M. (ed.), *Tuzaki-Walajahi*, I, Madras, 1934.
Nayeem, M.A., *External Relations of the Bijapur Kingdom (1489-1686 A.D.)*. Hyderabad, 1974.
Neill, Stephen, *A History of Christianity in India: The Beginnings to A.D. 1707*. Cambridge, 1984.
Norbert, R.P. Capucin, *Mémoires Historiques sur les Missions des Indes Orientales*. 2 vols., Luques, 1744.
———, *Mémoires utiiles et nécessaire, tristes et conoslans sur les Missions des Indes Orientales, & c.*, Luques, 1742.
Oaten, E.F., *European Travellers in India*, London, 1909.
Olagnier, Paul, *Les Jésuites à Pondichéry et l'Affaire Naniapa (1705-1720)*, Paris, 1932.
———, *Le Grand Colonial Inconnu. Le Gouverneur Benoist Dumas*, Paris, 1936.
Orme, R.A., *History of the Military Transactions of the British Nation in Indostan*, London, 1765, 1803 (rpt.).
Orme, Robert, *History of Indostan*, 2 vols., Madras, 1913.
Oubagarasamy, Bernadotte (tr.), *Un Livre de Compte de Ananda Ranga Poullé, Courtier de la Compagnie des Indes (Introduction et Notices Biographiques par Edmond Gaudart)*, Paris, 1930.
Owen, Sidney James, *Dupleix and the Empire of India*, New York, 1887.
Pannikar, K.M., *Asia and Western Dominance: A Survey of the Vasco Da Gama Epoch in Asian History, 1498-1948*, London, 1959.
Pillai, Vaiyapuri S., *History of Tamil Language and Literature*, Madras, 1957.
Pattabiramin, P.Z., *Quatre Vieux Temples des environs de Pondichéry*, Paris, 1948.

BIBLIOGRAPHY

Paulin de Saint-Barthélemy, *Atlas pour servir au Voyage aux Indes Orientales*, Paris, 1808.
Paulin de Saint-Barthélemy, *Voyage aux Indes Orientales*, I, Paris, 1808.
Pillai, Tecika, *Anantarankapillai*, Madras, 1955.
Poullé, Narayana, *Histoire Détaillée des Rois du Carnatic*, tr. Gnanou Diagou, Pondichéry, 1939.
Price, Frederick and Henry Dodwell, *The Private Diary of Ananda Ranga Pillai*, 12 vols., Madras, 1904-28.
Raghavan, V., *Anandaranga Vijaya Campu of Srinivasakavi*, Tiruchirappalli, 1948.
Rajayyan, K., *Administration and Society in the Carnatic, 1701-1801*, Tirupati, 1966.
———, *The Rise and Fall of the Poligars of Tamilnadu*, Madras, 1974.
———, *History of Madurai (1736-1801)*, Madurai, 1974.
———, *History of Tamilnadu*, Madurai, 1982.
Ramasamy, A., *History of Pondicherry*, Delhi, 1987.
Ramaswami, N.S., *Political History of the Carnatic under the Nawabs*, Delhi, 1884.
Rangacharya, V., *A Topographical List of the Inscriptions of the Madras Presidency Collated till 1915*, 3 vols., Madras, 1919.
Ray, Aniruddha, *The Merchants and the State: The French in India, 1666-1739*, New Delhi, 2004.
Raynal (Abbé Guillaume), *Histoire Philosophique et Politique des Etablissements et du Commerce des Européens dans les deux Indes*, 6 vols., Amsterdam, 1770.
Regnier, Rita, A., *Un Manuscrit Français au XVIIIème siècle: recherche de la vérité sur l'état-civil, politique et religieux des Hindous par Jacques Maissin*, Paris, 1975.
Richards, John F., *The New Cambridge History of India: The Mughal Empire*, Cambridge, 1993.
Rodzig, N.T., *Une Page de l'Historie de l'Impérialisme Français au XVIIIe siècle: Dupleix dans l'Inde (1732-1754)*, Yaroslav, 1929.
Roubaud, Louis, *La Bourdonnais*, Paris, 1932.
Saint Barthélemy, Paulin de, *Voyage aux Indes Orientales*, 3 vols., Paris, 1808.
———, *Atlas pour server au voyage aux Indes Orientales*, Paris, 1808.
Said, W. Edward, *Culture Imperialism*, London, 1994.
Sarma, M.N. and M.V. Sastry (eds.), *History and Culture of the Andhras*, Hyderabad, 1995.
Sebastain, A., *Pathinettam Nootrandil Puduvaiyin Vazhkai Nilai*, Puducheri, 1991.
———, *Puduchery Mudal Governor François Martin Vazhkai Varalaru* (Tamil), Chennai, 2000.

Scholberg, Henry and Emmanuel Divien, *Bibliographie des Français dans l'Inde*, Pondichéry, 1973.
Sen, S.P., *The French in India: First Establishment and Struggle*, Calcutta, 1947.
Seth, M. Jacob, *Armenians in India*, Calcutta, 1992 (1st pub. 1937).
Sewell, Robert, *List of Antiquarian Remains in the Presidency of Madras*, vol. I, Madras, 1882.
Sewell, Robert (ed.), *A Sketch of the Dynasties of Southern India*, Madras, 1883.
Sherwani, A.K., *History of the Qutb Shahi Dynasty*, New Delhi, 1974.
Sicé, Constant, *Almanach de Pondichéry*, Pondichéry, 1834, 1838 (rpt.).
Silambu, Selvarasu, *Ananda Rangapillai* (Tamil), Puttu Dilli, 2008.
Sonnerat, *Voyage aux Indes Orientales et à la Chine*, I, Paris, MDCCLXXXII.
Sottas, Jules, *Histoire de la Compagnie Royale des Indes Orientales, 1664-1719*. Paris, 1905.
Sridharan, M.P., *Papers on French Colonial Rule in India*, Calicut, 1997.
Srinivasachari, C.S., *Ananda Ranga Pillai: The 'Pepys' of French India*, New Delhi, 1991.
———, *A History of Gingee and its Rulers*, Annamalainagar, 1943.
———, *Histoire de Gingi*, tr. into French by Edmond Gaudart, Paris, 1940.
Stephen, Jeyaseela, *Portuguese in the Tamil Coast: Historical Explorations in Commerce and Culture, 1507-1749*, Pondicherry, 1998.
———, *Trade and Globalisation*, New Delhi, 2003.
Stephen, Jeyaseela (ed.), *Literature, Caste and Society: The Masks and Veils*, Delhi, 2006.
Subrahmanyam, Sanjay, *The Political Economy of Commerce, Southern India, 1500-1650*, Delhi, 1990.
Subramanian, Lakshmi (ed.), *The French East Company and the Trade of the Indian Ocean: A Collection of Essays by Indrani Ray*, New Delhi, 1999.
Sundararajan, Saroja, *Glimpses of the History of Karaikkal*, Madras, 1985.
Tavernier, Jean Baptiste, *Travels in India*, ed. & tr. V. Ball, 2 vols., London, 1889.
Thomas, Sir Herbert, *Some Years of Travels into Diverse Ports of Africa and Asia the Great*, London, 1665.
Thompson, MacLean (ed.), *Dupleix from his Letters, 1742-1754*, London, 1933.
Thurston, Edgar and K. Rangachari, *Castes and Tribes of Southern India*, New Delhi, 1993 (rpt.), 1st pub. 1909.
Tibetts, G.R. (tr.), *Arab Navigation in the Indian Ocean before the Coming of the Portuguese*, London, 1981.
Vaissière, Pierre, *Dupleix*, Paris, 1933.
Valentino, Dr. Charles, *Notes sur l'Inde*, Paris, 1906.
Valmary (ed.), *Pondichéry en 1746*, Pondichéry, 1911.
Varadarajan, Mu., *A History of Tamil Literature*, tr. from Tamil by E.S. Viswanathan, New Delhi, 1988.

Venkatesan, Na., *Varalatril Villianur'*, Chennai, 1979.
Veyssière de Lacroze, M.V., *Histoire du Christianisme des Indes*, 2 vols., La Haye 1758.
Vigiè, Marc, *Dupleix*, Paris, 1993.
Vincent, Rose, *Le Temps d'un Royaume: Jeanne Dupleix (1706-1756)*, Paris, 1982.
———, *Pondichéry, 1674-1761: l'Echec d'un rêve d'empire*, Paris, 1993.
———, *L'Aventure des Français en Inde – XVIIe-XXe siècles*, Paris, 1995.
Vincent Rose, Kroell et al., *Pondichéry 1674-1761, L'Echec d'un rêve d'empire*, Paris, 1993.
Vinson, Julien, *Catalogue des Manuscrits Tamouls*, 1867.
———, *Les Français dans l'Inde, Dupleix et Labourdonnais: 1736-1748*, Paris, 1894.
Vissière, Isabelle and Jean-Louis (eds.), *Lettres Edifiantes et Curieuses des Jésuites de l'Inde au dix-huitième siècle*, S-Seine, 2000.
Voltaire, *Précis du Siècle de Louis XV et Fragments sur l'Inde*, Œuvres *Complètes*, Tomes XXVII and XXXVI, Paris, 1826-8.
Watson, I.B., *Foundation for Empire, English Private Traders in India, 1659-1760*. Delhi, 1980.
Weber, Henri, *La Compagnie française des Indes, 1604-1875*, Paris, 1904.
Weber, Jacques, *Les Etablissements Français en Inde au XIXéme siècle (1816-1914)*, 5 vols., Paris, 1988.
——— (ed.), *Compagnie et Comptoirs. L'Inde des Français, XVIIeXXe siècle*, Paris, 1991.
Wheeler, Talboys, *Madras in Olden Times*, 3 vols., Madras, 1862.
———, *Early Records of British India: A History of the English Settlements in India*, London, 1878.
Wilks, H., *Historical Sketches of South India*, 2 vols., Madras, 1869.
Will, Sir Foster, *Guide to the India Office Records, 1600-1858*, London, 1919.
Yule, Colonel Henry (tr & ed.), *The Book of Ser Marco Polo*, 2 vols., London, 1903.
———, *Cathay and the Way Thither*, vols. I & II, London, 1866.
Yule, Colonel Henry and A.C. Burnell, *Hobson-Jobson: A Glossary of Colloquial Anglo-Indian Words and Phrases and of Kindred Terms: Etymological, Historical, Geographical and Discursive*, London, 1903, 1994 (new edn.).
Zay, E., *Histoire Monétaire des Colonies Françaises*, Paris, 1892

ARTICLES

Annoussamy, David, 'Cultural Interactions in South India (1400-1800)', in K.S. Mathew (ed.), *Indian Ocean and Cultural Interaction (A.D. 1400-1800)*. Pondicherry, 1996, pp. 93-103.

Annoussamy, David, 'Le Journal d'Ananda Rangapoullai', La Lettre du C.I.D.I.F., 2005, pp. 151-62.
Appadorai, Arjun, 'Right and Left Hand Castes in South India', *Indian Economic and Social History Review*, 1974.
Arasaratnam, S. 'Indian Intermediaries in the Trade and Administration of the French East India Company in Coromandel, 1730-1760', in Les Relations Historiques et Culturelles entre la France et l'Inde, I, Sainte Clothilde, 1987.
Cojandé, Dairianadin, 'Lazaro de Motha, alias Tanappa Modéliar' (premier courtier de la Compagnie, mort en 1691), *Revue Historique de Pondichéry*, tome II, 1973, pp. 29-32.
Delaitre, 'Mémoire Historique de ce qui s'est passé dans l'Inde du 1er Décembre 1750 au 20 Février 1754, ed. A. Martineau, *RHIF*, 1910, tome 2, pp. 243-310.
Deloche, Jean, 'La Mémoire de Moracin sur Masulipatnam', *Bulletin d'Ecole Française d'Extrême Orient*, LXII, 1995, pp. 125-49.
Diagou, Gnanou, 'Sur quatre documents inédit découvert par Mme.Robert Gaebelé dans les Archives d'Ananda Ranga Pillay', *Revue Historique de l'Inde Française*, 1952, vol. 8.
―――, 'Compte-rendu de la pose d'une plaque commémorative sur la maison natale de Dupleix à Landrecies', *RHIF*, tome 8, 1952, pp. 257-62.
―――, 'Histoire de deux cloches de l'église des Capucins de Pondichéry', *RHIF*, 1952, tome 8, pp. 251-4.
Freville de, 'Une Armée Coloniale au XVIIIème siècle: Dupleix aux Indes', *Revue des Questions Historiques*, 1904, LXXVI, pp. 417-44.
Furber, Holden, 'Asia and the West as Partners before Empire and After', *The Journal of Asian Studies*, vol. XXVIII, no. 4, 1990, pp. 711-21.
Gaebelé, Robert, Yvonne, 'Ariancoupam, Terre d'Histoire et de Prière', *Revue Historique de l'Inde Française*, vol. 8, 1952, pp. 1-10.
―――, 'Du Nouveau sur la famille d'Ananda Ranga Poullé – Dubhash de Dupleix', *RHIF*, vol. 8, 1952, pp. 123-4.
―――, 'Enfance et Adolescence d'Anandarangapoullé', *Revue Historique de l'Etat de Pondichéry*, 9e vol., 1955, pp. 1-134.
Gallois-Montbrun, Joseph-Armand, 'Notice sur la chronique en langue tamile et sur la vie d'Ananda-Rangapillai', Pondichéry, 1849.
Gaudart, Edmond, 'Les Archives de Madras et l'Histoire de l'Inde Française', *Revue Historique de l'Inde Française*, tome VI, 1936.
Gravelle, Charles, 'Gingi', *RHIF*, 4ème vol., 2ème partie, 1920, pp. 1-55.
Gravelle, Charles, 'Pondichéry et ses Environs', *RHIF*, vol. 5, 1921-2, pp. 29-32.
Guet, Louis, Les Origines de l'Inde Française, Jeanne Begum (Madame Dupleix), Revue Maritime et Coloniale, Numéros d'Aôut, Septembre et Octobre 1892.

Habib, Irfan, 'Merchant Communities in Pre-colonial India', in J. Tracy (ed.), *The Rise of Merchant Empires: Long Distance Trade in the Early Modern World, 1350-1750*, Cambridge, 1991.

Haudrère, Philippe, 'The Compagnie des Indes Orientales', in Rose Vincent, ed., *The French in India: From Diamond Traders to Sanskrit Scholars*, Bombay, 1990.

Heras, H. Rev., 'The Marathas in Southern India', *Historical Miscellany, BISM*, Poona, 1928.

Jouveau-Dubreuil, G., 'Les Français à Pondichéry avant 1773'. *RHIF*, VIII, 1952, pp. 195-217.

———, 'Notes sur Pondichéry', *Revue d'Histoire des Colonies Françaises*, 1952.

———, 'Le Commerce des tissus de coton à Pondichéry aux xviie et xviiie siècles', *RHIF*, 8ᵉ vol., Pondicherry, 1952, pp. 224-33.

———, 'Le Port de Pondichéry', *Revue Historique de l'Etat de Pondichéry*, 9ème vol., 1955, pp. 254-7.

———, 'Un Miracle au Large de Pondichéry', *RHEP*, 9ème vol., pp. 304-8.

———, 'Les Indes Françaises: Pondichéry en 1935'. *RHEP*, 9ème vol., pp. 318-21.

Jouveau Dubreuil, 'Les Colonnes du Pier', *Revue Historique de l'Etat de Pondichéry*, vol. 9, 1955, pp. 250-3.

———, 'Histoire Ancienne et Moderne: Les Soldats Français à Gingi', ibid., pp. 271-5.

Kennedy, Brian, 'The Making of a Nawab: François Joseph Dupleix 1697-1763', *Bengal Past and Present*, Jan-Jun 1977, pp. 50-64.

———, 'Plan de Pondichéry en 1699', *RHEP*, 9ème vol., pp. 259-64.

Krishnamurthy, B. 'Puducherry to Pondicherry: A Study of the Intercultural Relations between India and France during the Seventeenth and Eighteenth Centuries', in K.S. Mathew (ed.), *Indian Ocean and Cultural Interaction (A.D. 1400-1800)*, Pondicherry, 1996, pp. 104-21.

Krishnamurthy, B., 'Colbertism and French East India Company's Trade with India during the Seventeenth and Eighteenth Centuries', in P. Malekandathil and T. Jamal Mohamed (eds.), *The Portuguese, Indian Ocean and European Bridgeheads*, Tellicherry, 2001.

Lernie-Bouchet, Jacqueline, 'Les Modéliars de la Region de Saint-Thomé. Caste: Savalla Velaja. Un Essai de généalogie', *La Lettre du CIDIF*, nos. 16-17, pp. 99-102.

Le Treguilly, Philippe, 'La présence Française en Inde: aléas politiques et militaires', in Le Treguilly and M. Morazé (eds.), *L'Inde et la France: Deux Siècles d'Histoire commune XVIIe –XVIIIe siècles*, Paris, 1995.

Lernie-Bouchet, Jacqueline, 'Les Modeliars de la Region de Saint-Thome, Caste: Savalla Velaja: Un Essai de Généalogie', *La Lettre du CIDIF*, nos. 16-17, pp. 99-102.

Marshall, P.J., 'Masters and Banians in the Eighteenth Century Calcutta', in

B.B. Kling and M.N. Pearson (eds.), *The Age of Partnership: Europeans in Asia before Dominion*, Honolulu, 1979, pp. 191-215.

Martin, F., 'l'Inde et les Nations Européennes', 15 Février 1700, no. 4, in Pierre Margry (ed.), *Relations et Mémoires inédits pour servir à l'histoire de la France dans les pays d'outre-mer, tiré des archives du Ministère des Colonies*, Paris, 1867, pp. 115-48.

Martineau, Alfred, 'Benoist Dumas', in *Revue d'Histoire des Colonies Françaises*, 1920, pp. 145-61.

Martineau, Alfred, 'Law et la Capitulation de Srirangam', *Revue d'Histoire des Colonies Françaises*, 1927, pp. 81-126.

Mathew, K.S., 'French Missionaries, Tamil Catholics and Social Changes in Pondicherry (1674-1793)', in Jeyaseela Stephen (ed.), *Literature, Caste and Society. The Masks and Veils*, Delhi, 2006.

More, J.B.P., 'The Marakkayar Muslims of Karikal, South India', *Journal of Islamic Studies*, 2, 1, Oxford, 1991.

———, 'Muslim Evolution and Conversions in Karikal, South India', *Islam and Christian-Muslim Relations*, 6, Birmingham University, 1995.

———, 'Bengal Navy and the First Anglo-Mughal Confrontation', in *The Visvabharati Quarterly*, New Series, vol. 10, no. 4, January-March 2002, pp. 49-60; and in Stephen Jeyaseela (ed.), *Trade and Globalisation*, New Delhi, 2003.

———, 'West European and Mughal Interaction during the Reign of Aurangzeb', in Pius Malekandathil and T. Jamal Mohammad (eds.), *The Portuguese, Indian Ocean and European Bridgeheads*, Tellicherry, 2001, pp. 570-1.

———, 'Some Maritime Aspects of the Indian Ocean Region (1600-1760)', in K.S. Mathew (ed.), *Indian Ocean and Cultural Interaction, A.D. 1400-1800*, Pondicherry, 1996, pp. 130-48.

———, 'Hindu-Christian Interaction in Pondicherry, 1700-1900', *Contributions to Indian Sociology*, vol. 32, no. 1, January-June 1998, pp. 97-121.

———, 'Hindu-Christian Interaction during French Rule in Pondicherry', in J.B.P. More (ed.), *Religion and Society in South India*, Tellicherry, 2006, pp. 71-105.

———, 'A Dravidian Muslim Sufi', in J.B.P. More, *Religion and Society in South India*, Tellicherry, 2006, pp. 127-36.

———, 'Religious Conversions in Pondicherry and the French (1703-1878)', in J. Stephen (ed.), *Literature, Caste and Society: The Masks and Veils*. Delhi, 2006, pp. 311-40.

———, 'Origin, Ancestry and Identity of Hyder Ali', in *Religion and Society in South India*, Tellicherry, 2006, pp. 11-28.

———, 'Cheikh Ibrahim, Chef Musulman de Dupleix à Pondichéry: Identité et Origine', *La Lettre du C.I.D.I.F.*, Paris/Boulogne, Novembre 2009.

———, 'Notice sur François Martin, le bâtisseur de Pondichéry et sur son

Enterrement à Fort Louis (Bharati Poonga)', *La Lettre du C.I.D.I.F.*, Décembre 2010, pp. 42-6.

Mouradian-Legaud, Anne, 'La Société à Pondichéry au XVIIIème siècle (1673-1771), in *Position des Thèses de l'Ecole de Chartres*, Paris, 1971, pp. 129-36.

Nield-Basu, S., 'The Dubashes of Madras', *Modern Asian Studies*, 18, 1, 1984.

Ray, Indrani, 'Dupleix Private Trade in Chandernagore', *Indian Historical Review*, I, 1974, pp. 279-94.

Richard, Francis, 'Les Missions Catholiques', in Le Treguilly and M. Morazé (eds.), *L'Inde et la France:Deux Siècles d'Histoire commune XVIIe–XVIIIe siècles*, Paris, 1995.

Sastri, K.A., Nilakanta, 'New Pages from Ananda Ranga Pillai Diary', *Journal of the University of Madras*, vol. XIV, no. 2.

Sridharan, M.P., 'Notes on Benoist Dumas', in *The Indian History Congress Proceedings*, Kurukshetra University, 1982.

Srinivasachari, C.S., 'The Maratha Occupation of Gingee and the Early Years of their Rule Therein', in *A Volume of Studies in Indology*, no. 75, Poona printed series, Poona.

―――, 'A Little Known Phase in the Career of Chanda Sahib, 1741-48', *Indian Historical Records Commission*, 1930.

―――, 'The First Indian Courtiers of the French East India Company', *Proceedings of the Indian Historical Records Commission*, vol. XVII, Baroda, 1939.

―――, 'The Later Representatives of a Great Family of Courtiers of Pondicherry', *Indian Historical Records Commission*, 1941.

Stephen, Jeyaseela, 'Socio-Economic Role of Pedro Kanagaraya Mudaliar in the French Colony of Pondicherry, 1711-1746', *Revue Historique de Pondichéry*, vol. XVIII, 1995, pp. 15-32.

―――, 'Urbanism and the Chequered Existence of the Indo-French town of Pondicherry, 1674-1795', Revue Historique de Pondichéry, vol. XIX, 1996, pp. 29-64.

―――, 'Maritime Trade in Pondicherry and the Role of the French in Globalisation, 1674-1693', in Stephen Jeyaseela (ed.), *Trade and Globalisation*, New Delhi, 2003.

Tillaivanam, Su, 'Puduvai Varalatril Sila Mukya Thedalakal', in K. Kalladan (ed.), *Puduchery Marapum Maanpum*, Puducherry, 2002, pp. 75-81.

Vincent, Rose, 'Zenith in Pondicherry', in Rose Vincent (ed.), *The French in India*, Bombay, 1990.

Vinson, Julien, 'Pondichéry Sauvé', *RHIF*, 4ème vol., 2ème partie, 1920.

―――, 'Sur les noms de Pondichéry et Karikal', *RHIF*, 4ème vol., 2ème partie, 1920.

Weber, Jacques, Review of Hallet, Anne-Sophie's 'Les Malabars Chrétiens dans

BIBLIOGRAPHY 281

La Mission du Carnate au XVIIIème siècle', Mémoire de Maîtrise, Université de Nantes, in *La Lettre du Cidif*, nos. 12-13, 1995, pp. 7-11.
———, 'La Mosaïque Pondichérienne', in Rose Vincent, ed., *Pondichéry. 1674-1761. L'échec d'un rêve d'empire*, Paris, 1993, pp. 147-57.
———, 'La Vie Quotidenne dans les Comptoirs', in Le Treguilly & M. Morazé, eds., *L'Inde et la France: Deux Siècles d'Histoire commune XVIIe –XVIIIe siècles*, Paris, 1995.

MISCELLANEOUS

A Complete History of the War in India from the Year 1749 to the Taking of Pondicherry in 1761, London, MDCCLXI.
'A Critical Study of Ananda Ranga Pillai' by N. Ranganathan, n.d., unpublished paper.
'A Note of Pondicherry' by N. Ranganathan? n.d. unpublished paper.
Almanach of Pondicherry, by Constant Sicé, 1839.
Annuaire des Etablissements Français dans l'Inde, 1938-1939, Pondicherry, 1939.
Correspondance du Conseil de Chandernagore avec divers, 1745-1757, Pondicherry, 1919.
Correspondance du Conseil Supérieur de Pondichéry avec le Conseil de Chandernagore, ed. A. Martineau and E. Gaudart, 3 vols., Pondicherry, 1915.
Correspondance du Conseil Supérieur de Pondichéry et de la Compagnie 1726-67, publié avec Introduction par Alfred Martineau, Pondicherry, 1920, 4 vols.
Country Correspondence, 1748
Exposition Coloniale Internationale de Paris, Paris, 1931.
Gobalakichenan, M., 'Ananda Rangapillai's Extended Diary', unpublished paper, n.d.
Hallet, Anne-Sophie., 'Les Malabars Chrétiens dans La Mission du Carnate au XVIIIème.
Siècle. *Mémoire de Maîtrise*, Université de Nantes, 1995.
Interview avec Frère Faucheux, in *Le Trait-D'Union*, Janvier, 1945; Novembre 1994, pp. 29-30.
Les Nations, les castes et les sectes de Pondichéry – Ms. 991F, Archives de Versailles.
Lettre de Godeheu à M. Dupleix, Paris, 1760.
Lettres Edifiantes et Curieuse écrites des Missionnaires Etrangères de la Société de Jésus, 25 vols., Paris, 1717-42.
Lettre Edifiantes et Curieuses, Mémoire de l'Inde, Tomes 10-15, Nouvelle Edition, Paris, M.DCC.LXXXI.
Lettres Edifiantes et Curieuse écrites des Missionnaires Etrangères de la Société de Jésus, Mémoires des Indes, vols. X to xv, Toulouse, 1810.
Lettre du Révérend Frère Faucheux à Mme. Robert Gaebelé que lui avait demandé

la situation exacte de la pagode de Vedapureeswarar, Yercaud, 20 Décembre 1952, *Revue Historique de L'Inde Française*. Vol. 9, 1955, pp. 322-3.

Mémoire pour M. de La Bourdonnais, Paris, 1748.

Mémoire sur les Etablissements de la Compagnie et sur son commerce dans les Indes Orientales: Dupleix des Gardes, Pondichéry, 8 Oct 1727 – A.N. Colonies C²20, pp. 30-65.

Mémoire pour la Compagnie des Indes contre le sieur Dupleix, Paris, 1763.

Mémoire pour le sieur Dupleix contre la Compagnie des Indes avec les pièces justificatives, Paris, 1759.

Missions Catholiques Françaises dans l'Inde: Mission de Pondichéry, Mission de Maduré *et Mission de Vizagapatam*. Pondichéry, 1943.

Mss. Fr. 6231. *Mémoire sur la Compagnie des Indes Orientales, 1642-1720.* BNF.

Mss. Fr. 12087 & 12088. Dupleix. Récit de guerres et plans, y compris Pondichéry, BNF.

Mss. Fr. 25286 – Christianisme – Copie de l'acte de donation faite d'une église aux Capucins.

Missionaires de Pondichéry, 28 Mai 1676.

Mss. Fr. 13071 – Christianisme – Extrait de l'Histoire de l'état présent du Christianisme au Malabar . . . de la persécution de Tanjaour.

Mss. Voyage des Indes Orientales depuis l'isle de France jusqu' à la rivière du Gange et le retour en France avec des remarques sur le commerce et une instruction pour faire ce voyage par M.le Chevalier***, officier des vaisseaux du roy, 1725 et 1726. Bibliothèque Arsenal, Paris.

Missions Catholiques Françaises dans l'Inde. Pondicherry, 1943.

Mss. Affaire des Indes. 897. Nottes Critiques sur l'histoire des Indes anciens et modernes par M.l'Abbé Guyon, BNF.

Mss. NAF. 8871. Correspondance de Père Coeurdoux sur la religion et la langue hindoue, BNF.

Mss. NAF. 9352. *Double du Registre de Baptêmes de la Chapelle de l'Eglise de St.Lazare de R.P. Capucins de Pondichéry depuis 1676 au 1718.* BNF.

Mss. NAF. 9354. Etat de l'Empire Mogol – 1716, BNF.

Mss. NA. 9357. Papiers de Dupleix, BNF.

Mss. NAF. 9359. Mémoires ou éclaircissements raisonnés sur les nouvelles concessions de Mazulipatnam, dépendances et autres provinces données dans le Dékan à la Compagnie des Indes, BNF

Mss. NAF. 9364. Sur Gouverneur de Pondichéry, Hébert et la vie de Dupleix et sa famille avant Pondichéry

Mss. *Puduceriyammanperil Virutham* (Strophes sur la déesse de Pondichéry), 341$^{2°}$ in Indien 578, BNF.

Mss. *Puduceritinasaridai anubandhanm* (Table des Histoires Quotidiennes de Pondichéry) – 158, in Indien 578, BNF.

Mss. *Puducheritalukka.* 442 (Acte Judiciare), in Indien 578, BNF.

BIBLIOGRAPHY

Pitoeff, Patrick. 'Yanaon, un Etablisssement de l'Inde Française entre 1817 et 1870', M.A. dissertation, University of Nanterre, 1980.
Pondichéry en 1746. La Compagnie de l'Inde, Pondichéry, 1911.
Procés-Verbaux des délibérations du Conseil Supérieur de Pondichéry, ed. E. Gaudart, A. Martineau, 3 vols. Pondicherry, 1912-13, 1914.
Procés-Verbaux des délibérations du Conseil Souverain de la Compagnie des Indes, I, Pondichéry, 1911; II, III, Pondicherry, 1913-14.
Ranganathan, Dr. *Ananda Ranga Pillai* (Tamil), Pondicherry, 1988, manuscript form, pp. 98
Rapport de Dupleix sur la famille de Chanda Sahib (1750) – Ms. 367F, Archives de Versailles.
Records of Fort St. George. Diary and Consultation Book, Madras, 1930-1; Letters from Fort St. George, 1931-32; Despatches to England, Madras, 1929-32.
Recueil des titres, édits, déclarations, arrêts, règlements, etc., conçernant la Compagnie des Indes Orientales (1664-1788). 13 vols., Paris, 1765-89.
Relation du Siège de Pondichéry, 1749, 6863, Archives d'Outre-mer, Aix.
Réponse du sieur Dupleix à la lettre du sieur Godeheu, Paris, 1763.
Review by J.B.P. More of M.P. Sridharan's *French Colonial Rule in India*, Calicut, 1997, in *Contribution to Indian Sociology* (n.s.), 31, 1, 2000, pp. 155-6.
Revue de l'Histoire des Colonies Française.
Revue Historique, 1952, Ariyankuppam.
Revue Historique de l'Etat de Pondichéry, vol. IX, pp. 233-7.
Revue Historique de Pondichéry, Commemoration volume of Me. Cojandé Dairianadin, no. XIV, 1981-6.
Revue Historique de Pondichéry, XVIII, 1995.
Sridharan, M.P., 'Relevant Data on Dupleix', International Seminar on Indo-French Relations and Indian Independence, 22-6 September 1997, Pondicherry University.

Index

Abbé Jean Baptiste le Mascrier 19
al-Mahri, Sulaiman 27, 33
Almanach of Pondicherry of 1839 38
Ananda Ranga Poullé's Diary 22
Ariyankuppam Church 146, 170, 173, 199
Ariyankuppam River 27, 38, 44, 48, 63, 76, 116, 130, 168, 173
Ariyankuppam village 44, 77, 99, 128, 170, 173

Bhonsle, Raghoji 125, 127, 128, 194

Capuchin Father Louis 35, 47, 48, 67, 101, 109, 110, 119
Capuchin missionaries 35-6, 40, 81-2, 91, 201
Carnatic tensions and conflicts 153-64; Dupleix feared an invasion of Pondicherry 154-5; Nawab Safdar Ali Khan 153; capture of Madras 156-64; Anglo-French war 154; situation in Karaikal 155
Carnatic wars, Dupleix trapped in 194-8; Trichinopoly, restoration of Hindu rule in 194-5
Carnatic/Deccani conflicts 213-25; Dupleix Fathiabad built at Vellimedupet site 215; Dupleix was theoretically in control of the Deccan 221; French in the Deccan 220-5; Mohammad Ali Khan joined Nazir Jung at Vazhudavur 213; Muzaffar Jung declared Chanda Sahib as the nawab of Arcot 215; Nazir Jung's troops were corrupted by Dupleix 214; part of the Deccan came under French control 221-2; wars, devastations and acquisitions 213-20
Castelnau, Bussy, lieutenant 143, 157, 167, 169, 173, 207, 208, 213, 220-5, 230-2, 239, 240
Cathedral of San Thomé 39
Cattel, Antoine 34, 36, 38
Chandernagore 19, 45, 68, 101, 119, 138-41, 155, 164, 176, 202, 240, 243
Chelingue 34
Cheras 26
Cholas 26
Christian brokers 41
Christian *diwans* 89
Cojandé Dairianadin (Cozhandai Dairianathan) 38, 39
Cojandé Savarirayen (Cozhandai Aavarirayen) 38-9
Cozhandaiappa 34-9, 41, 42, 44, 122

da Mota, Lazaro 36-44, 55, 56, 74, 75, 79; Company's *dubash* 74
Darwin, Charles 22
Darwinian principle of evolution 22-3
de Closets D'Errey, Henri 38-9, 208
de Courchant, Beauvollier 96, 98, 101
de la Farelle, Chevalier 23, 97
de la Prévostière, Pierre André, governor of Pondicherry 85, 88, 89, 96
de Molta, Anthonio 41
des Fosses, Castonnet 23
Diaz, Maria 41, 42, 44
Dulivier, governor of Pondicherry 74, 75, 79-82, 85, 115; nominated

Saveri as co-*Mudaliar* to assist Nainiappa 79; struck a conciliatory note with the Hindus 81
Dumas, Pierre Benoist, governor 83, 87, 96, 98, 104-5, 115-34, 141-2, 145, 146, 154, 155, 169, 189, 199, 216, 219, 231, 241, 247-8; cleanliness drive in Pondicherry 117; developments in Mahe 120-2; developments in Pondicherry 116-20; fortifications of Pondicherry 116; governorship 251; in Tiruvannamalai 127; Karaikal, acquisition of 122-5; Marathas, Muslim refugees and further acquisitions 125-30; Mudali, Pondicherrian Prakasa 124; pepper trade 120-1; Safdar Ali Khan, treaty with Marathas 128-9; traded not only in goods, but also in human beings 120
Duperron, Anquetil 33
Dupleix, Joseph François, decline of 228-48; Ananda Ranga Poullé 149-50; as governor 141-50; at Chandernagore 138-41; Canagarayen, Pedro, benefits from the French 146-7; Chanda Sahib's troops besieged Trichinopoly 228; destruction or partial demolition of the Chola dam by the French 237; *dubashes* 145-50; fall of 235-48; famine and epidemic, role in conversion of some Hindus to Christianity 202; Father Coeurdoux 199-200; French father Artaud, apostle of the Parayas 203; governorship, early phase 138-50; higher castes enjoyed certain privileges 144-5; Lazar Mudaliar 147-8; left hand castes and right hand castes, problems continued 145; made fortune through trade 141; Mahé de Villabague 148; missionaries considered Brahmins as principal obstacle to their mission 204; mounted another mission to capture Trichinopoly 234; Nellithope village was inhabited only by Christians 199; nominated as director of the French factory 138-9; Pondichery and Karaikal became vulnerable and were unprotected 230; promotion of Christianity 199-205; slave trade was quite prevalent 143-4; Tambi Reddipalayam 199
Dupleix, Joseph François: constant interference in Indian affairs 252; different attitude towards the Muslims 254-5; insensitivity to sufferings and feelings of Tamil people 254

Essai sur l'Indostan 25
Europe, Anglo-French rivalry 19
European ships 17
European traders 17; and Indian merchants, partnership of 15; 'master and bania' relationship 15; trading purposes to 16

Fathers of *Missions Etrangères* 42
Fort St. David or Devanampatnam 167-78, 189
French missionaries of the *Société des Missions Etrangères* 41

'Grand plan' theory 251
Guérin, Eugine 23
Guet, Louis 24-5
Guruvappa 44, 84-7, 91, 99, 100, 101, 107, 116, 138; awarded the title of *Chevalier de l'Ordre de Saint Michel* 86; conversion of 85-9; nominated as *diwan* or *Mudaliar* of the Company 86; nominated as the new *Mudaliar* 86-7

Hamont, Tibulle 22-3
Hébert, Chevalier 58, 74-9, 82-6, 89, 91, 100, 105, 149, 187, 188, 219, 241, 256; first person to envisage the education of girls 78
Herzen, Gabriel Monod 28
Hindu-Christian interaction 50-9: Bijapur sultans lost power to the invading Mughals 52; Capuchins and the missionaries of *missions etrangères* 50-1; caste obstacle 56; conversion of Hindus to Christianity 56; de Qerelay, Jean Jacques 51; de Tournon, Cardinal Maillard 50; Europeans mixing freely with the Parayas 58-9; François Martin prohibited Hindu processions 53; higher caste Chrsitians as *diwans* 56; Hindu 'idolatrous' priests and priestesses, father Tachard's views of 53-4; Jesuits adopted Hindu customs and habits 50-1; Mankulam tank 55; Nainiappa Poullé, business in Madras 51; paucity of conversions in Southern India, missionaries held European colonizers responsible 58; Persian-speaking Bijapur sultans 51; religious conversions in Pondicherry 55

Idayar caste 75
India: European arrival and presence in 258; European penetration into 17; French colonies 18; French missionaries and colonizers in 257
India, French colonies 18; Governor Dupleix 19, 20; Pondicherry 18; territorial acquisitions 19; Treaty of Versailles 19
Indian rulers, main functions of 18

Jones, William 33
Jouveau-Dubreuil 24, 27, 28, 67, 247

kadaikovil or *bazaar* temple 41
Kalatiswaran temple 76; *devadasis* 77
Khan, Nasir Mohammad 28-9
Khan, Nawab Daoud 90-1
Khan, Nawab Dost Ali 125-6
Khan, Sadatullah, Nawab of Arcot 87, 90-1, 110, 117, 118

Le Noir, Pierre Christophe, governor of Pondicherry 46, 47, 87, 96, 98-111, 115, 118, 131, 133, 139, 141, 142, 145, 241, 253-4, 256; Guruvappa, awarded *Chevalier de l'Ordre du Saint-Michel* 100; high caste conversions to Christianity 99; *Moonu Kaasukku Odiponavanga* 100; non-Pariah higher caste men 100; oriental studies and knowledge, interest in 101; trade 100-1; 'tribunal de chaudrie' established 102
Le Noir's governorship, favouritism towards 'higher caste' Hindus and Muslims 103-8; caste disputes between right-hand and left-hand castes 103; freedom to Hindus to practice their religion 105; reparations carried out at the Vedapuriswaran temple 103; set of rules concerning the catholic religion 106-7; severe punishments during French rule 105
Lodi, Sher Khan 18, 28-9, 33, 35, 51, 54, 91
Louis XIV 43, 49, 88, 197, 234; embroiled in the Spanish war of succession 88

Madras, capture of 156-64; Dupleix ordered troops to ravage the black town of Madras 159; Dupleix proceeded to nominate a council of Madras 159; Paradis' victory at Adyar 161; war between the

English and the French 156
Mahé 19, 21, 96-8, 108, 111, 120, 139, 143, 154, 155, 161, 168, 169-70, 173-4, 185, 191, 195, 207, 218, 220, 223, 233, 243; developments in 120-5; Iruvalinad Nambiars 97; Kurangod Nayar 97; political entity under the control of the French 97-8
Malabar coast 16, 34, 96-8, 107-8, 111, 121
Maratha Hindus 51, 125
Martin, François 19, 25, 33-41, 43-4, 51-6, 58-9, 62, 74, 77, 78, 83, 84, 89, 92, 101, 109, 111, 122, 131, 133, 142, 169, 180, 182, 187, 218-19, 248, 251, 255-7, 259; appointed Christians as his *dubashes* 64; Christian *dubashes* of 66; developments in Pondicherry 45-50; French Jesuit missionaries under his governorship 65; legacy of 64-8; Pondicherry and South India, turmoil and upheavals all around 68; rule in Pondicherry 66
Martineau, Alfred 23-4, 40
Masulipatnam, French factory 98
missionaries of the *Mission Etrangères* 42
Missions Etrangères 43
Mollandin, André 96
Montbrun, Armand Gallois 20, 88
Mouliapa, André 38, 39
Mudaliar 34, 38, 39, 40, 42, 77; to the Tamils 34
Mudaliar, Canagaraya or Canagarayen/ Pedro 38-40, 44, 82, 83, 85, 87, 89, 92, 100, 102, 105, 107, 118-19, 124, 126-31, 143-50, 156-8, 162, 173, 199-202, 245
Mudaliar, Dairianatha 44
Mudaliar, Lazar 36, 40, 43-4, 146, 147
Mudaliar, Tanappa 39, 42, 43, 44, 84
Murungapakkam 76

Nayakar, Muthu Krishnappa 27-8, 33; rule in Senji and Pondicherry 28
Norbert 36, 40
Notre Dame de la Conception or 'Our Lady of Conception' 43
Notre Dame des Anges 36, 37, 87, 140

Pandichery of the Tamils 27; godown (*Pandasalai* or *Pandikasalai*) 28
Pandichery/Puducheira 27
Pandyas 26
parayas 37
Pondicherry, caste and religion in 60-4; Brahmins 60; castes hierarchically ranked 61; *Ellaiamman* Kovil or border goddess temple 62; endogamous castes 60; *kitchi kadai* to the Tamils 64; Manakula Vinayagar temple 62; Mirapalli 63, 64; multi-layered caste system 62; 'Tamizhar' or Tamils 60; Vanniyars 60
Pondicherry, besieged by the Dutch 45; Bharati Poonga 48; *Boulevards* of Pondicherry 47; Capuchin father Louis 48; development and expansion 96-111; developments in 45-50; Dutch plan of 1694 47; Dutch town-planners 47; French at loggerheads with the sultan of Golconda 49; import-export activity 49-50; Martin, François 45-8; Ozhukarai or Oulgaret, village cluster of 49; negative impact on trade 88-9; Petit canal 48; *Sainte Thérèse* street and quarters 49; white town 46-7
Pondicherry, siege and its aftermath 167-78; Dupleix organized Pondicherry's defence against the English 168; Dupleix's orders to burn down all the villages neighbouring Pondicherry 168; English under Admiral Boscawen

besieged Pondicherry 172-3; Treaty of Aix la Chapelle 175
Portuguese traders 16-17
Pouchiammal 42
Poullé, Ananda Ranga (Pillai) 20, 22, 24, 25, 42, 43, 56, 60, 61, 80, 84, 85, 87-8, 102, 109, 111, 119, 124, 126, 127, 130-1, 139, 142-50, 157-61, 167-8, 170-4, 176-8, 181-91, 197, 200, 204-6, 216-20, 233-5, 240-6, 258-60
Poullé, Nainiappa 51, 74-7, 79, 80, 82-6, 89-92, 115, 149, 158, 176, 188, 205, 241-2, 255, 260; martyrdom 82-5; nominated as the *Mudaliar* or *dubash* 75-6
Poullé, Tiruvengadam 87, 91
pre-European traders with India 15-16
Presentation of the Blessed Virgin 42

Rue Dupleix/Vazhudavur Road 259

Sahib, Chanda 122-5
Saint Lazare Church 36-7
Samba 43
Senji Nayak Hindu temples, destruction of 206-8
Société des Missions Etrangères 91

St. Paul Church of the Jesuits 42, 43

Tamil country 26
Tamizhakam 26
Thaniappa Mudaliar of the Agambadi caste 39
Timothy, Lazarus 39

Varadaraja Perumal temple 76
Vedapuriswaran (Shiva) Temple 43, 52, 53, 54, 60, 62, 65, 75-7, 79-81, 84, 103, 105, 132, 146-7, 172, 176, 239; destruction of 180-92; fighting capabilities and morality of the Tamils 181; Hindus, contradictions in the stand with regard to temple 184; low castes and outcastes not even allowed to enter 181-2; desecrated by some miscreants 181; Poullé, Ananda Ranga, indifferent attitude towards destruction 184-92; role played by Madame Dupleix 183
Vijayanagar empire 26-7
Vinson, Julien 22-3

'White Man's Burden' 25

Yanam, factory at 98-9